★ TYLER BRIDGES ★
BAD BET ON THE BAYOU

Tyler Bridges is a reporter for *The Miami Herald*, where he was part of one team that won the 1999 Pulitzer Prize for investigative reporting, and another that won the 2001 Pulitzer Prize for breaking news. He covered the 1990s legalization of gambling in Louisiana as a reporter for *The Times-Picayune* of New Orleans and has won numerous awards for his work. He is the author of *The Rise of David Duke*.

D1374025

Books by Tyler Bridges

Bad Bet on the Bayou

The Rise of David Duke

BAD BET ON THE BAYOU

BAD BET
★ ★ ★ ON THE ★ ★ ★
BAYOU

The Rise of

Gambling in Louisiana

and the Fall of

Governor Edwin Edwards

★ TYLER BRIDGES ★

Farrar, Straus and Giroux

New York

♥ ♠ ♦ ♣

To my siblings—Steve, Mary Chris, Bev, Lorna, Hilary, and Alison—from their little bro

Farrar, Straus and Giroux
19 Union Square West, New York 10003

Grateful acknowledgment is made to the following for permission to reprint illustrations: to Ronnie Jones, Louisiana State Police Archives, for the photograph of Francis Grevemberg; to Robert Mann for the photograph of Edwin Edwards's stump speech; to Walt Handelsman for his cartoons; to The Times-Picayune for the photographs of Christopher Hemmeter (by Ellis Lucia), of Edwin Edwards with Christopher Hemmeter and Wendell Gauthier (by Matt Rose), of Max Chastain and of the riverboat Flamingo (both by Ted Jackson), of the site of the New Orleans casino and of Edwin Edwards (with Candy Edwards) discussing his indictment with the press (both by G. Andrew Boyd), and of video poker machines, Carlos Marcello, Edwin Edwards at the opening of the Harrah's casino, and Edward DeBartolo Jr.; to the FBI for the photograph of Frank Gagliano Jr., Anthony Carollo, Joe Gagliano, and Joseph Marcello Jr.; and to The Advocate (Baton Rouge, La.) for the photograph of Geoffrey Santini and Eddie Jordan Jr. (by Travis Spradling) and the photographs of Edwin and Stephen Edwards and of Edwards speaking to the press (both by Stephen Bill Feig).

Library of Congress Cataloging-in-Publication Data
Bridges, Tyler.
    Bad bet on the bayou : the rise of gambling in Louisiana and the fall of Governor Edwin
    Edwards / Tyler Bridges.— 1st ed.
       p.   cm.
    Includes index.
    ISBN 0-374-52854-3 (pbk.)
    1. Gambling—Louisiana.   2. Gambling industry—Corrupt practices—Louisiana.
3. Political corruption—Louisiana.   4. Edwards, Edwin W.   I. Title.

HV6721.L8 B75 2001
795'.09763—dc21   00-052765

Designed by Abby Kagan
Map designed by Jeffrey L. Ward
www.fsgbooks.com

1   3   5   7   9   10   8   6   4   2

Contents

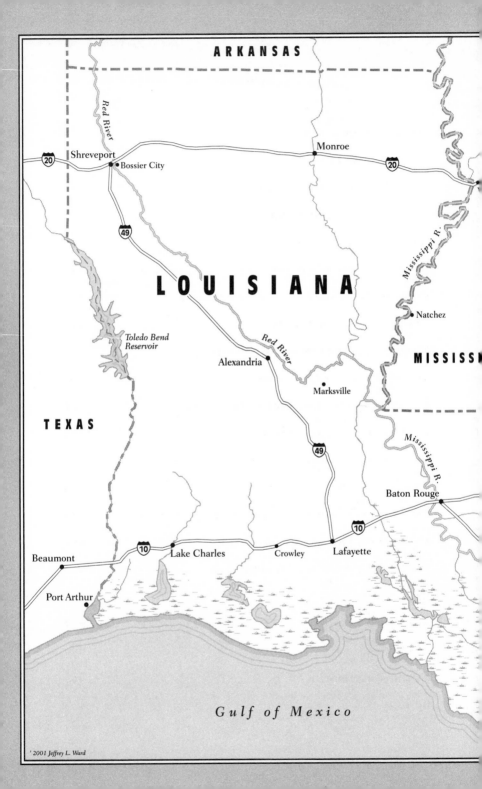

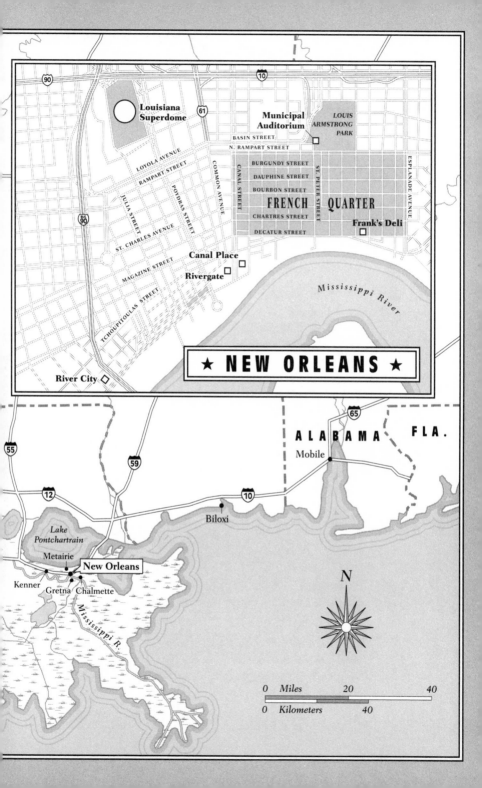

★ NEW ORLEANS ★

BAD BET ON THE BAYOU

Introduction

There are said to be several truths in Louisiana politics. One is that an honest politician is one who stays bought. Another is that politics is theater, and there is always demand for an encore.

Writing nearly forty years ago, *New Yorker* correspondent A. J. Liebling called Louisiana "the westernmost of the Arab states" and said the state's politics were "of an intensity and complexity that are matched, in my experience, only in the republic of Lebanon."

Liebling was writing about Louisiana while Earl Long, Huey's younger brother, was governor. Earl Long once offered this advice on Louisiana politics: "Don't write anything you can phone. Don't phone anything you can talk. Don't talk anything you can whisper. Don't whisper anything you can smile. Don't smile anything you can nod. Don't nod anything you can wink."

Huey Long, in one of his more immortal remarks, once said in a speech at Louisiana State University: "People say I steal. Well, all politicians steal. I steal. But a lot of what I stole has spilled over in no-toll bridges, hospitals . . . and to build this university."

Louisiana is our most exotic state. It is religious and roguish, a place populated by Cajuns, Creoles, Christian Conservatives, rednecks, African Americans, and the white working-class New Orleanians known as "Yats." While northern Louisiana is mostly Protestant and conservative, southern Louisiana, settled by French Catholics, is noted for its love of good food, good music, and good times. *Laissez les Bons Temps Rouler*— Let the Good Times Roll—is the unofficial motto. Louisiana is rich in outrageous stories and colorful characters. It is notably poor in the realm of political ethics. As Richard Leche, governor during the late 1930s, put it, "When I took the oath of office, I didn't take a vow of poverty." Leche's approach to governance landed him in jail, convicted of bribery charges.

Over the past thirty years, Louisiana has seen a parade of elected officials convicted of crimes. The list includes a governor, an attorney general, an elections commissioner, an agriculture commissioner, three successive insurance commissioners, a congressman, a federal judge, a State Senate president, six other state legislators, and a host of appointed officials, local sheriffs, city councilmen, and parish police jurors (who are the equivalent of county commissioners). Of the eight men and women elected to statewide office in 1991, three—Governor Edwin Edwards, elections commissioner Jerry Fowler, and insurance commissioner Jim Brown—were later convicted of crimes. The FBI said more people—sixty-six—were indicted on public-corruption charges in Louisiana in 1999 than in any other state. Public corruption was the Louisiana FBI's top priority, and would remain so for the foreseeable future.

One reason may be that throughout its history, Louisiana has been ripe for domination by political and economic elites. A succession of French and Spanish rulers plundered Louisiana. After they relinquished control to Americans, large plantation owners—growing primarily sugar and cotton—exploited slave and then sharecropping labor. Lumber barons, financial houses, and railroad interests gained power in the early 1900s, giving way, beginning in the 1920s, to those who controlled the leasing and production rights to oil and natural gas. No matter who held power after Louisiana became a state, following a model established by the French and Spanish colonial rulers, decision making was centralized, giving the governor and elected officials enormous influence. This created plenty of opportunities for bribes and public corruption.

One native summed it up this way. "We're just not genetically disposed to handle money," lamented political consultant James Carville, who was from Carville, Louisiana. "We ought to bring in the legislature from another state—maybe Wisconsin or Minnesota—to handle our money. In return, we'll handle the cooking and entertainment for them. They'll handle our fiscal oversight, and we'll handle their cultural matters."

In the 1990s, the potential for corruption would prove even more alluring in the Bayou State. From 1990 to 1992, Louisiana legalized a statewide lottery; a land casino in New Orleans that promised to be the world's largest gambling hall; fifteen floating casinos on lakes and rivers; and video poker machines in bars, restaurants, and highway truck stops throughout Louisiana. The owners of these cash businesses would turn to politicians to get an operating license, win a zoning variance, or have the competition stifled. Gambling and Louisiana would prove to be an incendiary mix.

In legalizing gambling, Louisiana was jumping on a bandwagon that swept the United States in the 1980s and 1990s. From 1974 to 2000, the number of states with casinos rose from one (Nevada) to eleven, states with lotteries went from fourteen to thirty-seven (plus the District of Columbia), states with Indian-run gambling increased from zero to twenty-seven, and states with state-regulated video poker or video lotteries went from zero to nine. In 1999, Americans lost $58.2 billion of what they bet, or more than what they spent altogether on movie tickets, recorded music, theme parks, spectator sports, and video games.

With the gambling explosion came political corruption. Two former West Virginia State Senate presidents were convicted of taking payoffs from gambling interests, seven Arizona legislators were caught taking money in exchange for voting for gambling, Missouri's House speaker of fifteen years resigned in the wake of a federal investigation into gambling-related dealings, the former House speaker in Florida went to prison in part for not paying taxes on income from Bally Entertainment, and one of Atlantic City's mayors since the advent of legalized gambling there went to prison on gambling-related charges.

But no state came close to matching Louisiana in this area.

Overseeing the legalization of gambling in Louisiana in the 1990s would be a unique individual, and he would certainly have a unique challenge. Some called him the "Last Great American Populist." Others knew him as the "Cajun King." Still others called him the "Silver Zipper." His name was Edwin Washington Edwards, and from 1992 to 1996, he would serve a fourth term as Louisiana's governor. He had first moved into the Governor's Mansion in 1972, and for the next twenty-four years, he flaunted his fondness for easy cash, pretty women, and high-stakes gambling as he dominated Louisiana's politics and used his razor-sharp mind and catlike reflexes to stay one step ahead of the law.

Bad Bet on the Bayou tells the story of what happened when Louisiana legalized gambling in the 1990s under Governor Edwards. It is the tale of what happened when the most corrupt industry came to our most corrupt state, under a governor who reveled in a catch-me-if-you-can philosophy.

But the seeds of what happened during the 1990s were sown much earlier. Louisiana is a pro-gambling state, so the only question throughout its checkered history has been whether the wagering was wide-open or undercover.

To a remarkable degree, the political and social history of Louisiana is intertwined with gambling. Two games of chance that were invented in Europe—craps and poker—were popularized in Louisiana during the nineteenth century before spreading throughout the rest of the country. Gambling flourished on riverboats operating out of New Orleans during the twenty-five years that preceded the Civil War.

The biggest gambling scandal in the country's history occurred in the Bayou State during the post–Civil War era. From the 1930s to the 1960s, numerous Louisiana politicians allowed the mob to operate slot machines and casinos, in exchange for payoffs. Two twentieth-century governors—Earl Long and Edwin Edwards—have been gambling addicts. Then, after nearly a hundred years of illegal gambling following the shutdown of the state lottery in 1892, Louisiana in the 1990s plunged headlong into legalized gambling. Today, gambling once again is the state's dominant political issue.

Indeed, gambling in Louisiana is older than the state itself. When the original French settlers in the eighteenth century were building a colony in the swamp—which today is the French Quarter—Jean-Baptiste Le Moyne, Sieur de Bienville, New Orleans's founder, had to intervene frequently to stop illegal games of chance. The French and the Spanish alternately owned and ruled Louisiana from 1699 to 1803. Throughout these 104 years of control, Louisiana residents enjoyed games of chance unencumbered by the moral concerns of the Puritans and Anglicans who settled the northeastern United States. By 1810, seven years after Thomas Jefferson bought most of modern-day Louisiana from Napoleon, New Orleans was a freewheeling port, and the city had more gambling halls than New York, Boston, Philadelphia, and Baltimore combined. In an 1820 letter to the *Baltimore Chronicle,* a recent visitor to the Crescent City wrote, "I was in New Orleans but a very short time. I saw but little and heard sufficient to convince me that gambling and sensual pleasures were practiced to such a degree to destroy domestic happiness and tranquility." Gambling was illegal but thrived behind closed doors. By 1823, New Orleans officials had decided to legalize gambling and make money off of it. Reasoning that "we should compel the devil to pay tribute to virtue," they set up six "gambling temples," each of which paid $5,000 a year to help underwrite the city's Charity Hospital and the College of Orleans. John Davis Sr., impresario of the Opera House, opened the first sumptuous casino in New Orleans in 1827. It was at the corner of Orleans and Bourbon Streets in the French Quarter.

By then, Bernard Xavier Philippe de Marigny de Mandeville, a New Orleanian, had introduced the game of craps to America. Marigny, born in 1785, was the son of a rich Creole planter. When his father died, Marigny, at sixteen, became so wild that his guardian shipped him to England with the hope that life among the British might improve his manners. Instead, Marigny spent most of his time gambling. His particular favorite was a new French game called "hazard." After returning home, Marigny taught it to his Creole friends. According to one account, when Yankees saw the Creoles playing hazard, they referred to the pastime as "Johnny Crapaud's" game, using a pejorative that built on the stereotype of the French as frog eaters. The game was soon called "crapaud's," which was later abbreviated to "craps."

Marigny, in the meantime, was steadily losing his fortune. Gambling debts forced him to subdivide his plantation in New Orleans's Faubourg Marigny neighborhood, just downriver from the French Quarter. After one particularly disastrous run of the dice, he had to sell the land on both sides of a newly opened street, which he sardonically named "Rue de Craps." It remained Craps Street for about fifty years until a church in the mid-nineteenth century was built in the neighborhood. It was then given the name it bears today, Burgundy Street.

Marigny's vices didn't end with gambling. He was a great lover, albeit not very discreet. Inevitably his wife would catch him in his latest infidelity and express her strong disapproval. According to local lore, he would stop her with a grand gesture and proclaim: "Madame, I wish to inform you that I possess in the highest degree every vice of a gentleman!" In the end, Marigny's vices left him almost penniless. When he died in 1868, he was eulogized as "the last great Creole gentleman."

Poker, too, came to the United States through New Orleans. It was derived from "poque," a Persian game popular in France and elsewhere in Europe. The earliest references to poque in the United States mention it being played with a twenty-card deck on riverboats operating out of New Orleans in the 1830s. Americans not only changed the name, but also expanded the deck to fifty-two cards and added such features as the jackpot, wild cards, bluffing, and the ante.

By the mid-1830s, an estimated six hundred to eight hundred gamblers regularly worked the steamboats that traveled the Mississippi River between New Orleans and St. Louis. Many steamboat captains considered it bad luck to leave port without a gambler on board.

The professional gamblers were known for their sharp dress and for the variety of ways in which they cheated. They were adept at palming cards and dealing from the bottom of the deck. They hid cards in their vests, under the table, up their sleeves, and in their belts. They used little mirrors to read their opponents' cards and had poker rings fitted with needlelike points to make tiny indentations in the backs of cards. They made most of their big killings with marked cards.

One of the era's noted gamblers was Colonel Charles Starr, a tall, handsome, imposing man who was celebrated as the river's biggest liar. To hear Starr tell it, he owned at least half of the plantations on the Mississippi River and gambled only because he was tired of counting his money. He embellished his boasts by hiring slaves to meet the steamboat at each landing, then barking out elaborate instructions to them about operations of the plantation he claimed to own nearby. Starr acquired a sizable fortune gambling, but he lost it playing faro. Reduced to cadging food, he entered a New Orleans restaurant where he had been a welcome guest during his prosperous days and ordered a seven-course meal. The manager, knowing Starr had fallen on hard times, demanded payment in advance. Without a word, the colonel left the establishment. In an hour, having pawned his overcoat for $5, he returned and ordered the best meal on the menu. When it was served, deliberately and very carefully he turned each dish upside down, then walked out. Late that night, as the story goes, Colonel Starr died.

The heyday of riverboat gambling came to an end with the Civil War. Many of the riverboat gamblers joined a Confederate company called the Wilson Rangers. "A finer-mounted troop of cavalry, we think, can hardly be found anywhere in the South than the Wilson Rangers," the newspaper *The True Delta* wrote proudly in October 1861. It was a sham, George Devol, a noted riverboat gambler, later disclosed in his autobiography. "When we were ordered out to drill (which was every day), we would mount our fine horses, gallop out back of the city, and the first orders we would receive from our commanding officer would be 'Dismount! Hitch horses! March! Hunt shade! Begin playing!'" Gathered in groups of four and six, the soldiers would play cards all day until the weather cooled. The order would then be given out: "Cease playing! Put up books! Prepare to mount! March! March!" When the cavalrymen returned to New Orleans, "the people would come out, cheer, wave handkerchiefs and present us with bouquets" because they thought the men had been drilling to protect them. When they were finally sent out to do battle with Union troops, they hightailed it back to New Orleans at the first sign of trouble, buried their uniforms, and tried to pass for civilians.

When the war ended in 1865, Louisiana, like the rest of the South, was destitute. So the state's lawmakers three years later were ripe for a scheme peddled by a man who had cut his teeth selling Alabama and Kentucky lottery tickets. His name was Charles Turner Howard, and he offered this proposal to Louisiana lawmakers: If they would authorize a state lottery to be operated by a single private company for twenty-five years, the company would pay the state $40,000 a year to be earmarked for New Orleans's Charity Hospital. The amount offered was not large, but with Howard paying lawmakers an estimated $300,000 in bribes, the Reconstruction legislature agreed to his plan. Howard, bankrolled by a New York gambling syndicate, created the private Louisiana State Lottery Company.

The lottery started slowly, selling tickets mostly in New Orleans. But with lotteries banned throughout most of the country, the Louisiana Lottery in time became a national craze, especially after Howard, in a clever marketing move, hired two respected former Confederate generals to oversee the monthly drawings. Their prestige and reputations for integrity dramatically boosted sales, and the monthly drawings became grand public ceremonies, conducted in New Orleans's Charles Theater before large audiences.

After Reconstruction ended in 1877, Howard switched allegiances, reportedly spending $250,000 to help elect a Confederate war hero, Francis Nicholls, as the Democratic governor. In 1879, a crusading New Orleans newspaper, *The Democrat,* whipped up anti-lottery fever, charging that Howard had won authorization of the lottery eleven years earlier by bribing the Republican-controlled Reconstruction legislature. *The Democrat* also chastised the lottery for reaping huge profits while making only small payouts to winners. The newspaper figured the odds of winning the lottery at 1 in 76,076.

With the end of Reconstruction and Republican rule, the Democratic-controlled legislature repealed the lottery, and Governor Nicholls signed the measure into law. Howard, realizing he had erred in backing Nicholls, appealed the legislature's action to the federal courts, arguing that lawmakers lacked the authority to break his twenty-five-year operating agreement with the state. A judge named Billings sided with the lottery, keeping it alive. Responded *The Democrat*, "The Lottery Company owns Billings, body and boots, by right of purchase."

Having narrowly survived, Howard now set out for revenge. One of his first targets was *The Democrat*. As a reward for the newspaper's support in restoring the Democratic Party to power, Governor Nicholls had designated *The Democrat* as the state printer. But with the state now bankrupt, the $100,000 it owed the newspaper was calculated in scrip at 40 to 50 cents on the dollar. Determined to bankrupt the newspaper's owners, Howard got a compliant federal judge to rule that their scrip was worthless. Overnight, *The Democrat* could not pay its debts. Banks foreclosed on the newspaper and forced out its owners. Howard then gained control of the paper, silencing his bitterest foe. Shortly afterward, the federal court reversed itself and gave *The Democrat*'s new pro-lottery owners the full value of the scrip.

Howard moved forcefully on other fronts to solidify the lottery's political support. He showered money on local charities and on popular public works projects, such as those that reinforced the levee system. He gained the support of newspapers large and small by purchasing ads in them. He curried favor with politicians by giving them approval over the hiring of lottery employees. Howard hired lawyers and courted powerful civic leaders. Those who opposed him, he sought to destroy. After the ultraexclusive Metairie Racing Club turned him down for membership, he was so enraged that he bought the racetrack and turned it into a graveyard. Today, Howard himself lies buried there in perpetual triumph. He died falling off a horse.

By 1889, the lottery had reached the peak of its prosperity and power. "New Orleans became a city rapt, glassy-eyed, in its long fever," a magazine wrote later. "All other business seemed to be conducted as a sort of sideline to traffic in the magic tickets. Washington, Boston, Cincinnati,

Denver and San Francisco had corps of hard-working agents, selling tickets that cost 25 cents to $40. New Orleans—and Louisiana—talked lottery, ate lottery, and died lottery. Children misappropriated their Sunday-school coins, and beggars implored passersby for 'one more nickel' to be able to buy a 25-cent ticket. . . . No fad, no sport, no popular craze ever captured the imagination of Americans to the extent of the lottery; from one end of the country to the other, thousands of players clutched the slips and sweated out the drawings. In fact, 90 percent of the tickets were sold outside of Louisiana." An astonishing 33 percent of all the mail arriving at the New Orleans post office was addressed to the lottery company. By 1890, the Louisiana Lottery was collecting an estimated $28 million a year (about $532 million in 2000 dollars) with profits of $8 million (or $152 million in 2000 dollars).

To capitalize on the popularity, John A. Morris, the lottery company's new president, announced in 1890 that he wanted to renew the twenty-five-year charter, due to expire on January 1, 1894. To get the extension, Morris needed a two-thirds vote of the legislature and then a majority vote in a statewide public referendum. To sweeten the pot, Morris initially offered to increase from $40,000 to $500,000 the amount that the lottery would pay the state every year. But a backlash was setting in. A group of opponents formed the Anti-Lottery League of Louisiana, and in April 1890 more than a thousand people attended the first public meeting. Critics likened the lottery to a giant octopus that had stretched its tentacles throughout the political fabric of Louisiana.

Virtually all of the state's newspapers at the time were pro-lottery. So the anti-lottery league established its own newspaper, *The New Delta*. Meanwhile, a majority of state lawmakers signed a pledge promising that under no circumstances would they support the lottery proposition, and if they did, that would be conclusive evidence they had accepted a bribe. Francis Nicholls was governor again, and he turned down Morris's proposition to pay the state $500,000 a year. Undeterred, Morris doubled the offer.

Morris had a tough battle on his hands. However, he had plenty of disposable cash available to buy support. As one magazine at the time put it, the lottery "has commanded the support of every purchasable man" in the legislature. "Those it can buy it buys; and those it cannot buy it seeks to destroy. It has no politics and knows no party. It numbers among its servants Democrats and Republicans." One by one, Morris bought the vote of lawmakers who had pledged to oppose extending the lottery's charter. On the day that the House voted, a violent storm raged outside. Just as Representative S. O. Shattuck, who had introduced the bill, gave his vote, lightning struck the Louisiana State Capitol Building and extinguished its electric lights. Lottery opponents took this as a favorable sign, even though the House passed the bill by the necessary two-thirds vote, and the Senate followed suit. A senator who had pledged to vote against the lottery buried his face in his hands in shame when he switched sides. When the senator died nearly a year later, a belt containing $18,000 was found on him. It was presumed to be the remaining part of a larger bribe from Morris.

Governor Nicholls, a Confederate war hero, had lost an arm on the battlefield at Winchester and a foot at Chancellorsville. In his veto message, he wrote, "At no time and under no circumstances will I permit one of my hands to aid in degrading what the other was lost in seeking to uphold . . . the honor of my native State." Nicholls said he had been offered a $100,000 bribe to sign the bill.

The House mustered the two-thirds majority necessary to override Nicholls's veto. But when a pro-lottery senator fell ill, his side was one vote short of overriding Nicholls in the Senate. To get around that, the Senate simply announced that the override vote wasn't necessary since the Senate had already passed the bill once by a two-thirds margin. Declaring the bill approved, the legislature sent it to the Louisiana secretary of state for certification. He refused to grant it, however, which forced Morris to appeal to the courts. On a 3–2 vote, the Louisiana Supreme Court sided with the lottery. The bill to extend the lottery had passed and would go on the 1892 ballot for public approval.

Having narrowly secured the chance to continue in Louisiana, the lottery now had to fight for survival on another front: in the summer of 1890, President Benjamin Harrison, responding to a national backlash, asked Congress to pass anti-lottery legislation, declaring that "the people of all the states are debauched and defrauded" by the Louisiana lottery. Congress agreed, unanimously passing an anti-lottery bill. The measure prohibited the mailing of lottery tickets and circulars, closed the mails to newspapers containing lottery advertisements, and authorized the postmaster general to prohibit lottery agents from using money-order systems. The bill grievously wounded the lottery, since its main form of advertising was in newspapers delivered nationwide by the postal service. Two months after the bill passed, business at the New Orleans post office had fallen by one-third.

Morris gamely carried on. But the octopus, with its tentacles lopped off, was dying a slow death. In February 1892, Morris announced that the Louisiana State Lottery Company would not accept rechartering even if the electorate approved it. Opponents didn't believe him and campaigned vigorously against the measure. Church leaders led the opposition. The Catholic archbishop forbade the blessing of lottery tickets in local Catholic churches and declined a lottery offer to help reduce the church debt in his archdiocese. In April 1892, the people overwhelmingly voted against extending the lottery's charter, 157,422 to 4,225. To boot, Louisianians elected the lottery's most vigorous opponent, state senator Murphy J. Foster, as their governor. Foster squelched attempts to revive the lottery.

The lottery held its final drawing in December 1893. Afterward, the company moved its base of operations to Honduras. A shadow of its former self, the lottery operated there for several years, using swift boats to ferry the winning numbers to the United States. Finally, the federal government won further restrictions on the lottery, and the corrupt company shut down for good in 1907.

The worst gambling scandal in United States history was over, but gambling in the succeeding decades would endure in Louisiana, at times wide open, and at other times strictly underground.

During the 1920s in New Orleans, gamblers could bet legally with the bookies at the Fair Grounds racetrack or illegally at one of the hundreds of parlors known as handbooks that took horse race bets. Illegal lottery shops operated on many street corners. Speakeasies and soft drink stands alike offered slot machines. New Orleans mayor Martin Behrman and his Old Regulars political machine tolerated the different

forms of gambling as long as the operators of these illegal activities contributed to the machine's coffers during election season. If they failed
to do so, the police raided them.

Betting on the horses was especially popular. A woman who arrived
on the day the racing season opened complained that she "found it difficult to get a room in a hotel because the city was full of racetrack
gamblers from far and near. Racetrack gambling seemed to be the principal topic of conversation throughout the city." Handbooks seemed to
be everywhere. An account of gambling in New Orleans during the
1920s reported that a typical handbook "consisted of a room furnished
with a blackboard, telephone, telegraph, ticker tape, chairs, slips of
paper and racing forms with the latest betting information. Wire services provided the names of horses scratched and where the odds
stood a half hour before each race. Customers bet either in person, via
telephone, or through runners working for the operation. Roughly 10
to 15 minutes before the start of the race, a final summary of the betting odds at the track came over the wire, and a new wave of betting
continued until an employee yelled post-time. Poolrooms in the city
paid anywhere from $15 a week to $20 a day for racing results."

To sidestep local anti-gambling laws, the slot machines were known
as "mint vending" machines. They furnished a mint candy each time
a coin was inserted and paid off in slugs that could be replayed or
redeemed for cash. Slot machine operators claimed that these machines
were not gambling devices, since they furnished something of value for
each coin placed in the slot.

New Orleans did not have any casinos, despite its bawdy ways. The
casinos instead were in Jefferson and St. Bernard Parishes. In the 1920s,
Jefferson Parish, located just upriver from New Orleans, featured the
Beverly Gardens, Tranchina's, the Club Forest, Jack Sheehan's Suburban Gardens, and the Original Southport. The casinos in St. Bernard,
just downriver from New Orleans, were clustered in the town of Arabi,
on Friscoville Avenue. The leading casinos in St. Bernard were the
Arabi Club, the Jai-Alai fronton, and the St. Bernard Club. In both Jefferson and St. Bernard, the local sheriffs allowed the casinos to operate
in exchange for payoffs.

Not everyone liked this arrangement. Businessmen frequently complained that gambling siphoned off money that would otherwise go for legitimate businesses. Ministers, too, frequently railed against gambling. When the outcry became loud enough, the police would raid a few lottery shops and handbooks. When the heat was off—days or weeks later—the gambling establishments would reopen.

The stakes changed in 1935. Huey Long was now a U.S. senator, but he still controlled the state's politics. In May he announced that political leaders from Jefferson and St. Bernard had just convinced him to refrain from enforcing anti-gambling laws. "Ninety-five percent of the people in this grand and glorious old city and its environs love to gamble," he told reporters in New Orleans. "If they have got to gamble, I am in favor of letting the majority rule. I'm getting tired of using my police to close up every little gambling hole in New Orleans. . . . You can't close gambling nowhere where the people want to gamble." On the following day, the Jefferson and St. Bernard casinos, which had been closed for nearly five months, began to reopen.

Long didn't disclose that he also had secretly cut a deal with a New York mobster, Frank Costello, to allow him to corner the slot machine business in south Louisiana. It was a convenient deal for both sides. Costello was seeking a new market because New York City's newly elected mayor, Fiorello LaGuardia, had launched a crackdown against corruption that shut down Costello's New York slot machine empire. In return for letting Costello come to Louisiana, Long charged Costello a fee per machine, and he used the money to grease his political machine.

Long and Costello had met during the 1932 Democratic Convention in Chicago. By 1935, Long owed Costello a favor. In one account, Costello had saved a drunken Long from a severe beating by one of Costello's henchmen. In another, Long had impregnated a teenager, and Costello had kept the girl's mother quiet. Whatever the real story, by the summer of 1935 the number of slot machines in New Orleans and its environs had expanded dramatically. The machines, known as "chiefs" because they were decorated with the bronze head of an Indian, sprouted in bars, pharmacies, grocery stores, and gas stations.

Long's assassination in September 1935 did not end the arrangement. His top assistant, Seymour Weiss, his brother Earl, and New Orleans mayor Robert Maestri met a month later at an Arkansas resort with Costello, his deputy, Dandy Phil Kastel, and fellow mobster Meyer Lansky. There, they agreed to expand the slot machine deal into casinos and horse race bookmaking.

In December 1945, a new era in Louisiana's gambling history began when the Beverly Country Club casino opened in Jefferson Parish. With Bugsy Siegel just getting started in Las Vegas, many people considered the Beverly the country's finest casino. It had crystal chandeliers and moiré silk walls, meals were served with monogrammed silver flatware, and long-stemmed roses decorated tables. Big-name entertainers like Rudy Vallee and Carmen Miranda performed at the club. The casino featured high-stakes blackjack, craps, and roulette tables, as well as dozens of slot machines. On opening night, wreaths of flowers from well-wishers filled the entrance hall. Costello owned the Beverly along with Kastel, Lansky, and a young underworld comer named Carlos Marcello.

Marcello, who oversaw the Beverly's operations, had been born to Sicilian parents in Tunis in 1910. He had come to the United States with his mother that year to join his father, who had already immigrated to an area across the Mississippi River from New Orleans known as the West Bank. At fourteen, Marcello left school. By the age of twenty, he had been sent to jail for the first time, convicted of assault and robbery. After getting a pardon in 1935 from Governor O. K. Allen, Huey Long's stand-in while he served in the Senate, Marcello opened a bar in the West Bank town of Gretna. A short while later, with his brother Vincent, Marcello set up the Jefferson Music Company to distribute jukeboxes and pinball machines. In time, they strong-armed the bars and restaurants in Gretna and Algiers into using their equipment.

At five feet two inches, Marcello was a short, bullnecked, barrel-chested man with big hands, a disproportionately large head, and an imperious manner. He was known as "the Little Big Man." Without a high school education, Marcello never developed his English beyond that of a semiliterate white New Orleans laborer, the kind of Louisianian known as "Yat." In Marcello's vocabulary, "where are you?" was "where y'at?" (hence "Yat"), "that" was "dat," "nothing" was "nuttin'," and an "oyster" was an "erster." While Marcello didn't sound intelligent, he had immense physical energy, held up under pressure, and had a keen ability to read people. By the early 1940s, Marcello had caught Costello's eye. They entered into a deal whereby Marcello placed Costello's slot machines in the West Bank bars and restaurants in exchange for a percentage of the profits. In 1945, Costello rewarded Marcello with a 12.5 percent share of the Beverly.

In 1948, Earl Long was elected governor, and illegal gambling spread everywhere except conservative north Louisiana. Earl collected tribute from Frank Costello and Phil Kastel, and distributed the money to the Long political machine, according to his biographers, Michael L. Kurtz and Morgan D. Peoples. The FBI reported that Costello, who by now was the boss of the nation's most powerful Mafia family, contributed $500,000 to Earl's 1948 gubernatorial campaign, a huge sum at the time. On trips to New Orleans, Earl stayed at the Roosevelt Hotel, on the same floor where Costello and Kastel had suites. The Roosevelt was owned by Seymour Weiss, Huey's bagman. Weiss also owned the 1-2-3 Club, directly across from the Roosevelt. The 1-2-3 Club for years dominated the racing handbook and wire service operations in New Orleans, and it was a favorite of Earl's. It was during this time that Costello ousted the Fair Grounds' owners. The FBI afterward pronounced the racetrack the most "crooked" one in the country, with at least one race each day being fixed. Earl Long was a frequent visitor and won big by betting on fixed races. "Outside of politics, Earl's biggest passion was gambling, particularly playing the horses, as his father and grandfather had done," noted his biographers. "During racing season, he made regular trips to the track, and when the track was closed, he placed bets with bookies all across the country. An inveterate devotee of the racing sheets, he perused them every morning, made his selections, then got on the telephone to place his bets. . . . Earl, according to the FBI, also devised the ingenious notion that during racing season, all handbook operations in Louisiana would cease, so the gamblers would have to place their bets in person at the track. This allowed the mob to collect from track betting during racing season and from the bookies when the track was closed."

The Beverly and the other Jefferson Parish casinos could not have operated without the approval of Frank Clancy, Jefferson's sheriff. First elected in 1928, he was better known as "King Clancy" and ruled the parish with an iron fist. A stocky, ruddy-faced man, Clancy had his own deal with Costello. "The condition I let them operate on was 'jobs,'" the sheriff explained once. "They had to give a job to anybody I sent to them. I practically ran an employment agency. But that's politics. You got to have jobs to give."

The Item, a scrappy New Orleans newspaper, detailed the wide-open nature of Jefferson gambling in a 1947 series of articles under the heading "Clancy's Kingdom." In one of the first articles, the two reporters described how they posed as New York businessmen wanting to open a casino. They wrote about visiting the Billionaire Club casino, across the street from the Jefferson Parish courthouse in Gretna. A parish deputy sheriff inside told them they couldn't do anything without Clancy's permission.

In another article, the reporters explained that local law enforcement officials picked up cash payments from establishments that had slot machines. In return, the owners got police protection. As one bartender told the reporters, "Clancy could close our slots in ten minutes if he wanted to. We couldn't afford it. So we vote for him come election time."

In yet another article, The Item reporters described how they had been hunting for Beauregard Miller to talk about the illegal gambling. Miller was Gretna's town marshal, a post he had held since 1925. The newspapermen reported that they finally found Miller in the Bank Club bar, which his brother-in-law owned. The bar had slot machines, a dice table, and a handbook. Housemen, wearing eyeshades, chanted results from racetracks in Florida, California, and the New Orleans Fair Grounds. "On the front row, seated in a comfortable chair removed from the maddening crowd, sat a large, blue-jowled man, with his hat pulled over his forehead," the newspaper reported. "He thoughtfully chewed a cigar as he read over a racing form. 'I'm Chief Miller,' he told the reporters. 'What can I do for you?'

"'Is gambling a violation of the law in Gretna, Chief?'" one of the reporters asked. "The chief thought about that one for a moment. 'Yes, gambling,' he said, 'would be against the law.'

"'Well, Chief, is there any gambling going on right now in Gretna?'

"Chief Miller fixed his eye on the ceiling, meanwhile slipping the racing form in his pocket. 'Well, I'll tell you,' he said finally, 'I've heard that there is.'"

But Louisiana's wide-open gambling years were about to end, thanks initially to the single-minded efforts of a tall, soft-spoken Tennessean. His name was Estes Kefauver, and he was a first-term U.S. senator who hid his ambition behind a folksy manner. Kefauver was holding hearings throughout the country for his Select Committee to Investigate Organized Crime in Interstate Commerce when he stopped in New Orleans for two days of testimony beginning on January 25, 1951. Kefauver's hearings captured the public's imagination. New Orleanians crouched around radios listening to the testimony and gathered before storefronts—as if it were the World Series—to watch the live broadcast on television.

Kefauver had the power of Congress to hold in contempt any witness who failed to show up. So on the morning of January 25, he had an impressive list of witnesses waiting to testify at the New Orleans federal courthouse, including Carlos Marcello, Frank Clancy, Beauregard Miller, and C. F. (Dutch) Rowley, the sheriff of St. Bernard Parish.

The first to testify was Marcello, the boss of the New Orleans Mafia. Kefauver and his investigators asked Marcello 166 questions. Each time, reading from a little slip of paper he held in his lap, Marcello recited the same answer: "I refuse to answer on the grounds that it might incriminate me." Kefauver warned Marcello that he faced a contempt-of-Congress charge for refusing to answer the questions.

On the second day, Sheriff Clancy testified. He answered a few basic questions. But when Kefauver asked if he had attempted to enforce Jefferson's anti-gambling laws, the sheriff replied, "I refuse to answer on the grounds that it might tend to incriminate me."

A disgusted Kefauver said, "If there is any citizen of a parish that testimony should not tend to incriminate, it should be the sheriff of the parish." After more than an hour of questions, Kefauver dismissed Clancy, advising him that he, too, faced a contempt-of-Congress charge.

Sheriff Rowley was among those who testified afterward, and he pleaded ignorance when asked whether illegal gamblers operated in his fiefdom. "I know they're around, but I don't see them," he told Kefauver. "I don't look for them at all." Rowley explained that no one in St. Bernard complained about gambling.

Kefauver had subpoenaed Rowley's tax and bank records. He asked: How could Rowley amass $26,500 in savings while earning only $335 per month as sheriff?

Rowley refused to answer on the grounds that his answer might be incriminating.

Beauregard Miller, Gretna's town marshal, was the final witness. Kefauver asked him to identify Gretna's casinos. Miller ticked them off: the Bank Club, the Billionaire Club, the Clover, the New Garden, and the Blue Light Inn. Kefauver asked him why he let the casinos operate.

"Well, the people over there want gambling," Miller replied. "It was going on when I went in [in 1925]. Nobody opposes it. When it was closed down for a while, everybody wanted it to open up again. If I closed it down, I believe I would be defeated."

"In other words, if you closed it down, you wouldn't be reelected?" Kefauver asked.

"That's right, sir."

Miller went on to say that the casinos close up "when the newspapers put the heat on. Plenty of people work in those places. Without gambling it would be a dead town. The main business is gambling."

Four days later, the first aftershocks of the Kefauver hearings were felt. Sheriff Clancy ordered the casinos in unincorporated Jefferson

Parish to shut down at 6:00 p.m. This didn't include casinos like the Billionaire Club that were in Gretna, but it did include the Beverly Country Club, Club Forest, O'Dwyer's, and Luke and Terry's. At Club Forest, at one minute before 6:00 p.m., the stickman at the roulette table announced, "This is the last roll." As the clock struck six, casino workers hid the slot machines under canvas covers and the roulette table under a damask tablecloth.

If the Kefauver hearings landed the initial blow against gambling in Louisiana, Francis Grevemberg followed with the decisive blow. Grevemberg was the superintendent of the Louisiana State Police, named to that position in 1952 by the new governor, Robert Kennon. He was an anti-Long candidate who succeeded Earl Long. Governors traditionally chose a trusted ally as the superintendent. But wanting to emphasize a new era, Kennon chose Grevemberg, a highly decorated World War II veteran who had no police experience. Kennon didn't even meet Grevemberg until the evening of the governor's inauguration.

A solidly built former boxer with black hair and thick eyebrows, Grevemberg was determined to be a different kind of superintendent. He soon got his chance. On his fifth day on the job, an Associated Press reporter provided him with extensive evidence of illegal gambling in St. Bernard, Jefferson, New Orleans, and Baton Rouge. "Colonel, what are you going to do?" the reporter asked. Without much hesitation, Grevemberg cited the state statute that prohibited gambling. "Effective immediately, illegal gambling in Louisiana will not be tolerated," Grevemberg said, adding that if local law enforcement officials wouldn't enforce the law, the State Police would enforce it for them. The Associated Press article reporting his comments made headlines throughout Louisiana.

The day after the article was published, five men visited Grevemberg at his office. The cocky little man who did most of the talking introduced himself as Governor Kennon's state campaign finance chairman. He demanded that Grevemberg call the Associated Press reporter and retract his anti-gambling policy. "You tell the governor that if that's what he wants me to do," Grevemberg replied, "I'll go back to New Orleans and tell the whole story. The headlines will be as big as the paper is long. I'd tell the whole story. I'd be forced to resign, and I'd tell everything." The finance chairman told Grevemberg that he must not have understood that the men accompanying him—here he introduced them—represented gambling interests, and that each had made large contributions to the Kennon campaign. Grevemberg wouldn't budge.

Soon after, he launched his first raids against gambling houses. At the College Inn in LaPlace, an upriver New Orleans suburb, Grevemberg and six troopers kicked in the door, shut down the place, and made numerous arrests. "Heil Hitler! Heil Kennon! Heil Grevemberg!" the gamblers hooted. Undeterred, Grevemberg followed up with five raids at gambling houses in Bossier Parish, in northern Louisiana.

To his disappointment, Grevemberg found that local district attorneys would rarely prosecute the gambling operators whom he and his troopers had arrested. So he simply raided the same places over and over again until the owners gave up and shut down. Grevemberg also smashed the slot machines his troopers seized, making sure that the news media were on hand to publicize the destruction.

Some gambling operators devised intricate systems to foil Grevemberg. The 1-2-3 Club had a big handbook operation on the third floor. New Orleans's police chief was quoted one day in *The Times-Picayune* as saying he couldn't do anything against the 1-2-3 Club because his men could never make it upstairs in time to catch anybody gambling. Grevemberg took this mission on as a personal challenge. Two nights later, he visited the club, wearing eyeglasses and a false mustache. While sipping a drink, he memorized the layout. The next day, Grevemberg found a State Police trooper who had once worked in a gambling joint and had him apply for a job at the club. The trooper was hired as a hustler at the Roosevelt to recruit gamblers.

A few nights later, two men wearing cowboy boots and cowboy hats arrived at the hotel in a new Cadillac. After tipping everyone lavishly, saying loudly that business at their north Louisiana dairy was booming, they announced that they wanted to gamble. Hustlers from a variety of casinos and handbook operations converged on them. The men agreed to accompany the State Police hustler since they, too, were troopers in disguise. The three men were admitted to the 1-2-3 Club and then invited to ascend to the second floor. As a buzzer opened the door to the third-floor gambling emporium, two groups of State Police troopers led by Grevemberg burst into the club. With the troopers in disguise holding open the second- and third-floor doors, Grevemberg's group raided the club before the gambling paraphernalia could be hidden.

At first, gamblers tried to buy off Grevemberg, offering him a total of $650,000 in bribes to allow certain casinos to continue operating unmolested. When that approach didn't work, Sheriff Frank Clancy of Jefferson Parish called Grevemberg with a friendly warning: "If you don't stop the raids in New Orleans, St. Bernard and Jefferson, I hate to tell you what's going to happen to you. The guys you're playing with are playing for all the marbles. You're gonna end up a dead woodpecker." One evening, while Grevemberg was away from his New Orleans home, two men climbed onto his roof with the apparent intention of kidnapping his twin three-year-old sons. A neighbor saw the men and scared them away. There were no further incidents. A state senator who owned slot machines confiscated by the State Police did take a swing at Grevemberg on the Senate floor once. Grevemberg blocked the punch and then walked away, to avoid harming the overweight senator.

By 1955, Grevemberg had stamped out most illegal gambling in Louisiana. The St. Bernard casinos had shut down—some of the owners moved to Nevada—as had the Jefferson Parish gambling houses. (The Beverly Country Club, which Sheriff Clancy had closed in 1951, never reopened as a casino.) Grevemberg had a more difficult time closing down the handbook operations in New Orleans, even though Mayor Chep Morrison claimed that he opposed illegal gambling. Most police officers were taking payoffs from handbook operators in return for protection. Morrison, not wanting to offend the handbook owners' friends, family members, and patrons, only rarely disciplined a policeman caught providing protection.

In 1956, Earl Long was elected governor again. One of the men he defeated was Grevemberg, who finished fourth in the Democratic primary. Grevemberg had bowed to the urgings of clergymen and other do-gooders, who pleaded with him to be a candidate. While Grevemberg's raids had caught the public's imagination, big-money contributors stayed away from his campaign, and he raised only $50,000 to Long's $1 million. Clearly, Louisiana wasn't ready for an honest governor.

Earl Long's return to power seemed to signal a return to gambling's wide-open days. But Grevemberg's crusade had succeeded in changing public opinion enough to force the wagering mostly underground—except in Beauregard Miller's Gretna. In that Jefferson Parish town, Carlos Marcello, the New Orleans mob boss, continued to hold sway. A reporter for *The Saturday Evening Post* wrote in a 1964 article that at the Billionaire Lounge, across the street from the police station, he was offered "a $20 prostitute, $10 worth of barbiturates and gambling in the form of a slot machine, three blackjack tables and a completely equipped horse-betting room behind a wide-open door at the rear of the lounge." The reporter also played blackjack, roulette, and keno at the New Garden Club, a few blocks away. He reported that relatives of Beauregard Miller owned it. The magazine told the story of a Jefferson Parish bar owner named Richardson who refused to install a mob-owned payoff jukebox. In other cities, the bar man might have been shot or maimed—but not in Jefferson. "Instead, sheriff's deputies proceeded to raid his bar every Friday and Saturday night for two months, never filing charges but arresting and searching Richardson's customers," the magazine reported. Aaron Kohn, director of a private New Orleans anti-crime organization, observed, "For the most part, the philosophy of our mob is: Why risk the penalties of the law when you can use the law to impose your penalties for you?"

When *Life* magazine came to Gretna in 1967, Marcello remained in charge, running backroom casinos, prostitution houses, strip joints, bars, and restaurants. The governor was now John McKeithen, and he, like many of his predecessors, thought it was smart politically to turn a blind eye to Marcello. "Look at Grevemberg," McKeithen told *Life*. "He cracked down on gambling. He was tough. He went around with a flashlight and an ax, busting up little honky-tonk places. Do you know where he placed when he ran for governor?"

Still, the wide-open gambling days appeared to be over. With the rise of oil prices in the 1970s, severance taxes provided nearly 50 percent of the state's revenues. The government had millions of extra dollars, Louisiana's economy hummed, and there was little clamor to disregard the anti-gambling laws. Edwin Edwards occupied the Governor's Mansion. He loved to take gambling junkets to Las Vegas, but saw no need to bring gambling to the Bayou State. And if Edwards didn't want gambling, Louisiana wouldn't have it. He wielded power more forcefully than anyone since Huey and Earl Long. "He's the strongest sonofabitchin' governor we ever had," said Carlos Marcello, in a conversation wiretapped by the FBI. "He fuck with women and play dice, but won't drink. How do you like dat?"

Gambling was dying out even in Gretna. And by 1981, Marcello's reign was coming to a close. His normally impeccable judgment of people had failed. His associate in a deal to obtain state insurance business through bribes and kickbacks turned out to be an FBI informant. Marcello and Charles Roemer II, a top state government official, were convicted and sent to jail. By the mid-1980s, Frank Costello, Frank Clancy, Dutch Rowley, and Chep Morrison were dead. The St. Bernard casinos had been shuttered for years. The Beverly Country Club, once the country's finest casino, had burned down in a fire.

Yet gambling, with its long and storied history intertwined with Louisiana's politics and culture, was not gone forever. In the 1980s, the Oil Bust would devastate Louisiana's economy. State officials would turn to legalized gambling as the economy's salvation. Gambling would reemerge in the 1990s, and more forcefully than ever before, under none other than Governor Edwards.

Vote for the Crook

ecember 31, 1991, New Year's Eve. The large crowd at the craps table at Caesars Palace in Las Vegas was whooping it up. "Come on, mister! Two! Two!" cried out an eye-catching woman wearing a red and black jacket over a glittering metallic blouse. Her blond hair was picture perfect, her lipstick apple-red. The sixty-four-year-old silver-haired man standing to her right at the head of the craps table smiled at his young girlfriend's exuberance. Of medium build, he glided through life at his own pace. He could be cold, but when he turned on his charm, which was more often than not, few people could resist him. An acute sense of humor usually accompanied his charm, but his funniest remarks came not through storytelling—although he could tell humorous stories—but with lightning-quick comments that played off what others said.

On this evening, he was dressed casually: a flannel shirt, blue jeans, cowboy boots, and a leather belt sporting his initials, EWE. But as Edwin Washington Edwards shuffled a pile of yellow chips in anticipation of a winning roll of the dice, it was clear that he was no casual gambler. Each chip was worth $1,000, and he was playing with a pile of twenty to thirty chips. Whenever it was time to bet, Edwards laid down his chips with confidence and aplomb, showing no more anxiety than if he were putting down a $5 after-dinner tip. "Hard eight for a thousand," he called out to a dealer as he tossed a yellow chip onto the green felt. "For Mom and the kids!"

For a brief spell, Edwards was the "shooter," rolling the dice for all bettors gathered around the table. After a few throws, he turned the dice over to his companion, Candy Picou, a twenty-seven-year-old nursing student. She was easily the most animated player at the table. "Come on, mister! Two! Two!" she yelled as players prepared to roll the dice. At one point, Edwards handed her a couple of the $1,000 yellow chips. She waved them excitedly in the air.

Of all the games at a casino, Edwards liked craps best. It was fast-paced, and it was exciting. So any delays in the game frustrated him. Repeatedly, when the dealers were sorting out payments between rolls of the dice, Edwards called out in a Cajun accent familiar to Louisiana voters: "Give him the dice! You got to roll to win! You got to roll to win! Come on, mister, roll the dice! What, are you giving him lessons down there?"

Edwards's luck that day was uneven. At times, he bet on winning numbers, which caused Picou to shout in delight. But there were other rolls when he came up empty. His pile of $1,000 chips dwindled. Roll after roll, Edwards cried out for the number he wanted, and when it didn't turn up, he banged his fist hard on the table. Gradually, his luck improved. His numbers began to hit, one after another. The table erupted in cheers, and Edwards raised his arms in triumph. His mood brightened, and he began bantering with a group of men at the other end of the table. "Ocho! Ocho!" they called out.

"Ocho?" Edwards asked. "What language is that?"

"Spanish," came the reply. "It means eight."

"Eight? We're looking for a five," Edwards retorted. "If you're going to use a foreign language, at least use the right number."

Edwards was on a roll, and the pile of chips grew bigger. In time, they were worth $40,000 or $50,000. Soon, Edwards had his fill of action and cashed in his chips. He and Candy were ringing in the New Year at Frank Sinatra's show that night at the Riviera Hotel.

In Baton Rouge two weeks later, on January 13, 1992, Edwin Edwards took the oath of office for the fourth time as governor of Louisiana. His return would bring together two combustible elements: Louisiana's inclination for political corruption and Edwards's passion for gambling and deal making.

Edwards always said his love for gambling came from his mother, who played nickel poker and nickel *bourre,* a Cajun card game. He had grown up poor during the Great Depression. Born in 1927, he was reared in an unpainted farmhouse in central Louisiana that Edwards's father had built out of cypress wood. Eight miles outside of Marksville, in Avoyelles Parish, in a community called Johnson, his home had neither electricity nor running water. At night, the future governor, the middle child of five, did his homework by lamplight. But his father insisted that he and his siblings finish their studies early because the family couldn't afford much kerosene oil after the sun went down.

Edwards's father, Clarence, had only a third-grade education. His mother, Agnes, had left school after the seventh grade. When Edwards was a boy, they owned ten acres of farmland. Clarence Edwards share-cropped an additional forty acres, raising chickens, ducks, geese, pigs, cows, and sheep. Agnes Edwards was a midwife who taught her children to speak Cajun French.

Edwards began his schooling in a one-room schoolhouse where one teacher taught grades one through four. It soon became clear that he was easily the smartest of the bunch, with a razor-sharp mind that amazed his elders. Edwards quickly realized that with an education, he would not have to spend his life working in the hot sun plowing the fields.

Edwards was born the year before Huey Long was elected governor. Long exercised power for only seven years, but he was so forceful that his influence continued to dominate Louisiana politics after his assassination in 1935. For years afterward, Louisiana essentially could be divided into two political camps. One consisted of the populists, who advocated free textbooks, free medical care, and better roads, and tended to be colorful, sophisticated practitioners of politics, as well as tolerant of gambling. The other camp was described as favoring "good government."

In contrast with the populists, the "good government" crowd favored clean politics, less government spending, and lower taxes for business. Edwards was a populist. As a boy growing up in poverty, he became convinced by the actions of Huey Long and President Franklin Roosevelt that government was a vehicle to improve the lives of its citizens. "I remember when government made it possible for electricity to be brought to my house," Edwards recalled years later, referring to the Rural Electrification Act of 1936. "I remember when government made it possible for a bus to pick me up and drive me eight miles into town. I remember when government made it possible for me to eat a free hot lunch at school. I remember when government made books available to me that I otherwise would not have been able to have."

Although baptized a Catholic, Edwards became fascinated with the Church of the Nazarene, a conservative Methodist offshoot, during his junior and senior years in high school. Nazarenes dressed conservatively—women did not cut their hair and wore no makeup—and believed that a person who had been saved would fall out of grace by not continuing to lead a proper life. Edwards's association with the Nazarenes began when he and two of his brothers began accepting rides from churchgoers as a way of traveling to Marksville. The boys would go to the movies and visit friends in town before going to church at night. In time, Edwards converted. At the age of sixteen, showing an early confidence in public speaking, he preached before Nazarene assemblies and taught Sunday school. In his senior year at Marksville High School, Edwards decided to attend Louisiana State University. His parents were so unworldly that they didn't know it was in Baton Rouge, only ninety miles away. After his undergraduate studies—and a stint training as a naval pilot during World War II—Edwards went on to get a law degree from LSU in 1949.

With the law degree in hand, he married Elaine Schwartzenburg, his high school sweetheart, converted back to Catholicism at Elaine's insistence, and sought a place to practice law. While visiting his sister in the town of Crowley–in southwest Louisiana, an area known as Acadiana—he looked in the telephone directory and saw listings for only fourteen lawyers. Crowley had a population of 18,000. Edwards knew that Marksville, with a population of 2,500, had twenty-five lawyers. In addition, the only French-speaking lawyer in Crowley was getting on in years. "I said, 'This must be a good place to practice law,'" Edwards remembered years later. With a laugh, he added, "I later learned that the phone company had made a mistake, and there were more than fourteen lawyers." After he and Elaine moved to Crowley, he established his office above a drugstore and began practicing law, handling a variety of cases, but primarily representing people injured or killed on the job.

In Crowley the smooth-talking, handsome young attorney quickly made friends and political contacts. In 1954, Edwards entered the political arena by winning election to the Crowley City Council. He ran on a citywide ticket that included two black city council candidates, a racial coalition not seen in Louisiana since Reconstruction. In succeeding years, Edwards climbed the political ladder by winning elections to the Louisiana State Senate and the U.S. House of Representatives. He quickly made his mark by being one of the few southern congressmen to support the 1966 extension to the Voting Rights Act. But living in Washington, D.C., and being one of 435 congressmen bored Edwards.

In 1971, he ran for governor, the job he had always wanted. There were twenty candidates, and few people gave Edwards a chance. However, as it became clear that he could count on a strong base of Cajuns and blacks, his chief rival for that bloc of voters, Congressman Gillis Long, sought to undermine his campaign. Long, a cousin of Huey and Earl, paid for a man named Warren (Puggy) Moity to join the race and attack Edwards on a television show every Sunday in Lafayette. Moity "started off by saying I was fooling around with college girls," recalled Edwards. "And that didn't seem to make much difference. Then he accused me of running around with married women. That didn't seem to make much difference. Then he started accusing me of running around with black girls. That didn't catch on. In the final days of the campaign, he put the homosexual tag on me. . . . He called me

Tweety Bird and said I was always traveling with three or four young boys. . . . In Baton Rouge, in particular—I don't know why—that seemed to strike a responsive chord."

Edwards decided to defuse the attacks with humor. At a candidates' forum in Baton Rouge, Edwards deliberately arrived late. All of the other candidates were already seated at the head table. Edwards shook hands with a couple of his opponents and then got to Moity. He bent over and kissed Moity on the cheek. The large crowd at first was stunned and then roared with laughter.

With strong support from Cajuns and African Americans, Edwards won a spot in the Democratic runoff and then narrowly defeated his opponent, a good-government state senator named J. Bennett Johnston. Edwards went on to be elected governor, easily defeating his Republican opponent.

Like Huey Long, Edwards was a Democrat and a populist who championed the poor and the underprivileged. And like Long, he proved a contradiction, for he moved easily among the moneyed set and cut deals to steer work to friends and favored businessmen, who provided the money that fueled his campaigns. *The Times-Picayune* would dub this "The Louisiana Way": You had to pay someone close to the political decision makers to do business in Louisiana.

In some instances, the deals seemed to benefit Edwards personally, such as the news in the mid-1970s that he and his wife received as much as $20,000 from South Korean lobbyist Tongsun Park. Reporters constantly wrote about the various deals, some of which—such as the one involving Park—prompted grand jury investigations. The resulting news stories hurt Edwards's reputation in the short term, but when no charges were brought against him and the damaging headlines disappeared, the governor recovered his popularity. Edwards helped his cause because, unlike most politicians under fire, he rarely got defensive. Instead, he dismissed complaints with a wink and a few one-liners. For example, when asked about accepting illegal campaign contributions in the 1970s, he said, "It was illegal for them to give, but not for me to receive."

Edwards never hid his love of gambling, and he cracked jokes when confronted with questions about his womanizing. Responding to a book's claim that he once made love with six women in a night, Edwards smiled and said, "No, it wasn't that way. He [the author] was gone when the last one came in."

Edwards's approach disarmed Louisianians, who favored a live-and-let-live ethos anyway. "I think people realize that public officials are human and that we have our faults, our inadequacies," he explained once, "and if we don't try to be hypocritical or sanctimonious about it, I think they'll forgive us for it."

Stanley Bardwell Jr., a United States Attorney, put it another way: "I have to give Edwards credit. He's brilliant, he plays the system like a violin. He has an uncanny knack of charging headlong to the brink and knowing exactly where to stop . . . and he doesn't even try to cover his trail, he's that cocky."

For most of the twentieth century, taxes on Louisiana's prodigious mineral wealth—oil and natural gas—filled the state treasury. This had three advantages for whoever occupied the Governor's Mansion. First, it minimized the taxes paid by voters. Second, the mineral taxes financed the social and public works doled out by Louisiana's governors to a grateful citizenry. Third, it created lots of opportunities for graft.

During Governor Edwards's first term, he oversaw the modernization of Louisiana's state constitution—it had not been rewritten since 1921—and cleaned up several scandals from his predecessor's administration. He also got the legislature in 1973 to link the state oil and gas severance tax to a percentage of the market price. When prices jumped, the state earned millions and millions of additional revenue, and Louisiana's oil-based economy flourished. Flush with good times, Louisianians chortled at their governor's jokes and antics. In 1975, he was reelected with token opposition. During his second term, he continued to amaze Louisianians with his ability to have an answer to every question, a solution to every crisis.

Louisiana's two-term law kept Edwards from running for reelection in 1979. Still extraordinarily popular, in 1983 he challenged the incumbent Republican governor, David Treen, a good-government conservative. During the campaign, Edwards showed that his political reflexes were as quick as ever. Treen, he said in a devastating comment, was "so slow it takes him an hour and a half to watch '60 Minutes.'" Edwards also cracked, "If we don't get Treen out of office soon, there won't be any money left to steal."

Edwards was so confident of victory in the 1983 governor's race that he said he couldn't lose unless he was caught "in bed with a dead girl or a live boy." He was right. Edwards returned to the Governor's Mansion with 63 percent of the vote. He was the first person to be elected governor of Louisiana three times. Although the challenger usually raises less money, Edwards outspent Treen by $10 million. Sighed a befuddled Treen: "It's difficult for me to understand his popularity. But how do you explain how 900 people drank Kool-Aid with [Peoples Temple founder] Jim Jones?"

Edwards, fifty-six, didn't even wait for his inauguration to mark a return to the heady days of his first two terms. Before taking office again, he filled two 747s with some six hundred supporters, at $10,000 a head, for a weeklong trip to France that paid off a $4 million campaign debt. "The debt," wrote *The Times-Picayune* of New Orleans, "vanished in a spray of champagne at the Hotel George V, smoked salmon at Maxim's and dice at Monte Carlo." Edwards won $15,000 at Monte Carlo's dice tables and then told a dealer: "Give me a wheelbarrow for my money."

But when Edwards moved back into the Governor's Mansion in early 1984, oil prices were dropping because of oversupply. The state's finances soon were a shambles. Edwards rammed a $730 million tax increase through the state legislature, but it did not plug the gap. He had to cut government programs, weakening his power base. Louisianians stopped laughing at his jokes about womanizing and gambling. The hayride was over. Or, as Louisiana novelist Walker Percy put it, "The *bon temps* have just *roulered* out."

Meanwhile, federal authorities were closing in. More than a dozen grand juries had investigated Edwards over the years, but he had always stayed one step ahead of the law. As United States Attorney Stanley Bardwell noted, Edwards always seemed to know exactly how far he could go without running afoul of the law. In one instance, however, his activities were so flagrant that a federal grand jury indicted him in 1985 on charges that four hospitals paid him $1.9 million, while Treen was governor. In exchange, federal prosecutors alleged, Edwards agreed to grant state government permits so the hospitals could begin operations when, as expected, he became governor again in 1984. Prosecutors charged that Edwards needed the bribe money to pay off $2 million in gambling debts from Nevada casinos. Edwards denied the charges with his typical twist. "What's wrong with making money?" he asked. "You don't get rich as governor, you know. When I left office [in 1980], I was only worth about half a million, now I'm worth maybe 3 to 5 [million]. But I did it as a private businessman, not as governor. So there's nothing illegal about it." Edwards accused Republicans of trying to use the courts to oust him from office, having failed to do so at the ballot box.

As governor, Edwards frequently went to Las Vegas, usually on the casinos' tab. He played poker and blackjack, but he loved craps the most. It is the fastest-paced game, usually creating so much excitement that onlookers typically crowd around the table, cheering on those who toss the dice and bet. "I do not collect stamps, I do not collect coins, racehorses," Edwards said once. "I do not own boats or do things other people like to do. I like to gamble."

In time, the Las Vegas casinos rewarded him by treating him, as one reporter described it,

> like an Oriental potentate in the gambling mecca, where he is granted up to $200,000 in casino credit at the stroke of his pen. . . . He is classified by his favorite hotel-casino—Caesars Palace—among the 0.25 percent [1 in 400] of its customers whose importance as gamblers makes the company unwilling to share credit information with other casinos. Caesars even waives its maximum bet limit when Edwards steps to the table. . . . He eats his meals on the casinos' tab in the Strip's poshest restaurants. He sunbathes on casino-owned yachts at Lake Tahoe. He glides around town in casino limousines, and he and his entourage stay at luxury suites in the most popular hotels. All for free.

What can Edwards get from the Vegas casinos? "Anything he wants," a former Caesars Palace employee said.

Because the odds favor the casinos, in time nearly all gamblers become losers, and that is what happened to Edwin Edwards. In sensational testimony during his 1985 trial, Edwards testified that he had lost between $10,000 and $50,000 in thirteen of the preceding fifteen years. A Caesars executive testified that he had flown to Baton Rouge to retrieve suitcases full of cash from the Governor's Mansion—$400,000 in one case, $380,000 in another. Edwards attempted to hide his losses, prosecutors said, by gambling under the aliases of "T. Wong," "T. Lee," "B. True," and "Ed Neff." When he took the stand to defend himself, Edwards said he had always gambled within his economic means and offered a whimsical explanation for his aliases.

"How did you get the alias 'T. Wong'?" his attorney asked.

"The Chinese are pretty good gamblers," Edwards replied, "and one day this beautifully fantastic elderly Chinese gentleman was at the same table with me. His name was Mr. Wong. He made a bad roll, and I decided to quit. As they brought me the marker, I said [to him], 'Look, you're responsible for the debts. I'm going to sign your name.' The poor man didn't know I could use aliases, and he almost hit the ceiling. But I explained it to him."

"What about the name Ed Neff?" asked his attorney.

"One time I was gambling," Edwards replied, "and I had a bad streak of luck and ran out of chips. The dealer asked if I wanted more chips, so I said, no, I'd had enough, and when they brought me the marker, I signed it 'E. Nuff.' Whoever picked it up on the computer thought it said Ed Neff."

Outside the courtroom, Edwards kept up a daily show. One day, he arrived at the federal courthouse in a mule-drawn buggy that ordinarily hauled tourists around the French Quarter. "It's indicative of the [slow] pace of the trial," he cracked. On other days, as United Press International reported, he "has walked backwards for the benefit of television cameramen who usually have to backpedal to get their shots, sat on the courthouse steps for a group photo of the cameramen he calls 'the dirtiest dozen,' attended 'media night' at a French Quarter pub where he read a bawdy poem and his defense attorney James Neal tended bar [and] sat on the [courthouse] steps with his wife to wave at passersby. . . ."

In the end, Edwards's battle with the federal prosecutors was no contest. Nearly the entire jury sided with him, voting 10–2 to acquit Edwards on some charges, 11–1 on others. The judge declared a mistrial. In a press conference afterward, a reporter shouted at Edwards, "What's your answer to those who will say, 'Edwin Edwards is guilty as hell, but the prosecution just wasn't smart enough to get him?'"

Edwards paused and then smiled. "They're half right," he replied. Everyone knew which half he meant, except for the hapless prosecutors, who decided to try Edwards a second time. This time he was acquitted. "Edwin Edwards will return to run the state again," promised his brother Marion.

Edwards had won in court and indeed did return to run Louisiana again. Even so, the sensational revelations and his focus on the trial—and not on the state's pressing needs—had damaged him politically. To make matters worse, with the Oil Bust, he was no longer facing a forgiving populace. "Everybody laughs when the oil companies foot the bill for the graft," Lothar Richane, an unemployed offshore-rig hand, said at the time. "But now that it's coming out of my pocket, ain't nobody laughing." The state's treasury had run dry, and Edwards no longer could throw money at problems.

In January 1986, Edwards outlined his plan to revive the state's economy. It called for Louisiana to legalize ten to fifteen gambling casinos in New Orleans, Jefferson Parish, and St. Bernard Parish. The casinos had to be attached to hotels that had at least five hundred rooms. Edwards's plan also called for the legalization of a state lottery and the legalization of gambling on cruise ships on the Mississippi River out of New Orleans.

Each component of Edwards's plan was rooted in the state's history. In the twenty-five years before the Civil War, illegal gambling flourished on boats out of New Orleans. The Louisiana Lottery had attracted players from across the country in the years after the Civil War, until its massive corruption prompted Congress to shut it down in the 1890s.

Similarly, during the 1950s and 1960s, illegal casinos had operated in Jefferson Parish and in St. Bernard Parish. New Orleans also had a long history of illegal gambling. Now Edwards was seeking to reincarnate the illicit history in a legal way.

In all, Edwards predicted, the casinos, the state lottery, and cruise ship gambling would create 100,000 jobs and produce $600 million a year in desperately needed tax revenues. There would be so much new revenue, he predicted, that the legislature would have money to raise salaries for state employees and teachers, land values in New Orleans would rise dramatically, and crime would drop 20 percent. If the legislature didn't approve his proposals, Edwards warned, he would have to make crippling budget cuts that would force state employee layoffs and eliminate much-needed programs.

But with Edwards weakened politically by the trial and the state's economic troubles, opponents mobilized against his gambling plan. They argued that Edwards's proposals would increase crime, were anti-family, and didn't address the state's basic economic problems. They also argued that Edwards, with his penchant for wagering in Las Vegas, could not be trusted to oversee gambling. In the end, the legislature shelved Edwards's plan.

By the time Edwards ran for reelection in 1987, the state's economy was in a deep recession. The unemployment rate had reached 14 percent, the nation's highest. Not surprisingly, voters blamed the governor. Polls showed that his disapproval rating ranged from 52 percent to 71 percent, or as one legislator put it, "higher than any candidate not in jail and some who are." Because of his problems, Edwards had trouble raising money. "Nosey feds are making fund-raising a real drag," said political commentator John Maginnis. "A $100,000 contribution to Edwards was once considered a good investment. Now it's an open invitation to the grand jury."

To win reelection, the governor would have to overcome four major challengers. In Louisiana's open primary system, the top two finishers would make the general election runoff, regardless of political party.

Each of the four challengers—congressmen Bob Livingston, Billy Tauzin, and Buddy Roemer, and Secretary of State Jim Brown—figured that Edwards still had enough strength, particularly among black voters, to win one of the two runoff spots. The battle then was for that second spot, with the thinking that whoever faced Edwards in the runoff would defeat him.

Charles E. (Buddy) Roemer III, a bantamweight at five feet seven inches and 145 pounds, began the race the longest of long shots, at 1 percent in the polls. A four-term congressman from Bossier City, in northern Louisiana, the Harvard-educated Roemer had been an Edwards insider, managing Edwards's campaign in north Louisiana in the 1971 governor's race. His father, too, was an insider. When Edwards was elected governor, he named Charles Roemer II as commissioner of administration, the state's second most powerful post. But Charles Roemer abused his position. In 1981, he was convicted of taking bribes from Mafia boss Carlos Marcello in exchange for the awarding of state insurance contracts. By then, Buddy Roemer was a Democratic member of Congress and was beginning to inveigh against Louisiana's political system, a system that his father had been part of.

By 1987, Roemer had set his sights on slaying the dragon, Edwin Edwards himself. "I want a governor who puts our pocketbook ahead of his," Roemer said repeatedly during the campaign. Roemer aired tough-talking, plainspoken television ads in which he pledged to clean up Louisiana's corrupt politics, improve education, fight crime, cut taxes, eliminate wasteful government spending, and crack down on polluters who had made the state the most befouled in the nation. "The choice is between Edwin Edwards, who's gone corrupt, and Buddy Roemer, who's trying to start a revolution," Roemer declared in one television ad.

The state's newspapers, desperately yearning for a good-government candidate, one after another endorsed him. Voters, also hungry for change, responded favorably. On the night of the primary, Roemer finished first with 33 percent. Edwards finished second with 28 percent, and at 1:10 a.m. that evening, he shocked his supporters by announcing that he would not contest the runoff. Suddenly, his political career seemed over. "I guess the big jury has spoken," said United States Attorney John Volz, who had been the lead federal prosecutor in the failed attempt to convict Edwards.

"He was blessed with many gifts," said John Hainkel, a longtime state lawmaker and Edwards critic, thinking it was time to write his epitaph. "He is extremely glib and able to communicate. But he had a tragic character flaw. . . . He thinks of politics as a way to make money for himself and his friends rather than public service. That flaw finally brought him to his knees."

Although down, Edwards wasn't ready to concede he was out forever. "If Buddy Roemer isn't successful, maybe I'll be back," he mused with uncanny prescience just two days after the election.

Surrounded by a group of young, idealistic aides, Roemer got off to a strong start as governor in 1988. He won teacher pay increases, a teacher evaluation program, tough environmental enforcement, and strict limits on campaign financing. To balance the state budget, Roemer sold government airplanes, cut wasteful programs, and borrowed $1 billion to be paid off over ten years. He had staved off Louisiana's bankruptcy, and now he moved to his biggest gambit yet—a restructuring of the state tax system that he said would put Louisiana on sound fiscal standing and encourage more investment. It was put before the voters in April 1989. They rejected it decisively. Louisianans, tolerant of only so much good government, were tiring of Roemer.

After being ousted from the Governor's Mansion, Edwin Edwards had bided his time, hoping that Roemer would stumble and give him an opening to win back the governorship. When his successor did stumble, Edwards plotted with populist legislators to ensure that Roemer suffered more defeats. In the meantime, Roemer's wife, Patti, tired of living a politician's life, left her husband. Heartbroken, Roemer retreated into his shell, canceling appointments while he sat by the mansion's pool and brooded. The Roemer Revolution was derailing.

By 1991, Roemer was running for reelection and attempting to get back on track. One of the ways he sought to change his fortunes was by supporting two gambling bills. Doing so would invite criticism because Roemer had fervently opposed gambling during the 1987 gubernatorial campaign, a stance that had played well with his conservative north Louisiana base. But the gambling supporters convinced Roemer that the measures would benefit Louisiana and his own political fortunes.

Nearly one hundred years after the corrupt, privately operated Louisiana Lottery had shut down, the state had already begun to allow legal gambling. In 1990, the legislature gave voters the chance to amend the state constitution to legalize a state-run lottery. Louisianians approved it overwhelmingly. Now a year later a group of lawmakers wanted to open the door to gambling even further, although not as widely as Edwards had sought with his 1986 proposal to legalize big casinos throughout metro New Orleans.

One of the 1991 bills would legalize gambling on riverboats all over the state. The other would authorize a new form of gambling known as video poker.

The riverboat measure had been offered in previous years with little success. But by 1991, supporters had a new weapon to buttress their argument. Whereas a decade earlier only Nevada and New Jersey had legalized gambling, now other states were joining the bandwagon. Of specific concern to Louisiana was that Iowa, Illinois, and Mississippi all had legalized riverboat gambling within the previous two years. "We are losing our competitive edge," said Louisiana state representative Francis Heitmeier, the main House sponsor. By proposing to have the state take a hefty 18.5 percent cut of a riverboat's winnings, Heitmeier had another argument for his bill. "These guys," he said, referring to his colleagues, "don't want to vote for taxes, so I am giving them an alternative."

The Heitmeier bill limited the amount of gambling space on each boat to 30,000 square feet—the size of a small Las Vegas casino. It also called for a limited number of boats—fifteen—with a seven-member board appointed by the governor to award the licenses. There was nothing magical about the number 15, it was simply the number pulled from thin air by Jimmy Smith Jr., a New Orleans lawyer who wrote the draft version of the bill and lobbied for the measure. Smith worked for a group of men who owned boats—the *Natchez,* the *Cotton*

Blossom, the *Delta Queen,* and the *John James Audubon*—that offered daily pleasure cruises to tourists from Mississippi River wharves in New Orleans. These men weren't particularly enamored with gambling, but they had seen how owners of similar vessels in Iowa had lost their business to the floating casinos that had been authorized there. So they figured that if riverboat gambling was going to come to Louisiana, they ought to try to ensure that they be the beneficiaries. The Heitmeier bill required each riverboat casino to take three-hour cruises throughout the day. This seemed to give the pleasure boat owners an advantage, since they knew the river.

At the suggestion of the boat operators, the riverboat bill contained two additional features that attracted little attention at the time. One feature gave the riverboat's captain the right to keep the boat at dock if he determined that conditions on the water posed a threat to the vessel's safety. Gambling would be allowed to continue during this time. The other feature gave gamblers forty-five minutes to board the vessel before it left the dock and another forty-five minutes to exit once it had arrived back at the dock. The argument for this rule was that it would give everyone enough time to board and exit the boat. But it was actually a way to give patrons up to ninety minutes to gamble at dock. The distinction would be important because some gamblers would not like going out on the water. Boats earned more when the vessel was dockside.

The Heitmeier bill contained an additional important feature: it mandated that the boats be designed to look like the nineteenth-century paddle wheelers that had cruised up and down the Mississippi. This was meant to evoke romantic images out of Mark Twain—men in satin vests, women in flowing dresses—and thus attract hordes of free-spending tourists to Louisiana. The group backing the bill hired a Louisiana State University economist who said the measure would bring two million new visitors to Louisiana, generating $376 million a year in economic activity and creating 33,000 permanent jobs throughout the state. In reality, most observers thought New Orleans would receive the lion's share. It was assumed that nearly everyone would want to operate from New Orleans, since the Crescent City already attracted millions of tourists a year and had a long history of embracing gambling. To attract the support of lawmakers outside New Orleans, however, the bill also allowed gambling on the Calcasieu River in Lake Charles, on the Red River in the Shreveport–Bossier City area, on the Mississippi River in Baton Rouge, and on Lake Pontchartrain, which abutted New Orleans and the metro area's surrounding parishes.

As Heitmeier pushed the riverboat bill through the legislature, he emphasized that the measure was a painless way to raise revenue while spurring economic development—at a time when the state was still suffering from the Oil Bust. Heitmeier downplayed gambling's negative side effects. One of the few public objections was raised by Warren de Brueys, who headed the Metropolitan Crime Commission, the New Orleans group that was created in the 1950s to combat mobster Carlos Marcello and gambling payoffs to the police. If the legislature legalized riverboat gambling, de Brueys warned, lawmakers would open the door to a land-based casino that would have a particularly harmful effect on the state. De Brueys's warnings fell on deaf ears. By early July 1991, the House and the Senate had approved different versions of riverboat gambling. If leaders of the two chambers could settle on a compromise measure, Louisiana again would become a gambling state.

Video poker in the meantime was following its own path through the legislature. Legalizing video poker was the brainchild of a group of men who owned pinball machines, which were popular in bars and restaurants. It was a profitable if somewhat shady business—some of the owners had been convicted of operating illegal pinball machines. But the business changed in the late 1980s when illegal video machines began to crowd out the pinball machines. The new machines offered poker on a video screen and allowed the player to request replacements for some or all of the five cards displayed on the screen, as the player sought to assemble a hand that beat a predetermined "house" hand. Some bar owners, however, had reprogrammed the machines so that with a flick of the switch they could pay off winners. This was illegal but highly profitable for the bar owners. They netted $500 to $1,500 a week per illegal video poker machine.

In reaction, the pinball machine owners sought the assistance of their champion in the legislature, Representative Charles Emile

(Peppi) Bruneau Jr. of New Orleans. Bruneau spoke in the "Yat" accent of New Orleans that made it seem as if he hailed from Brooklyn. As a hobby, he collected old jukeboxes and pinball machines, and became such an expert in the field that he could guess the value and manufacturer of almost any machine. On social, tax, and race issues, Bruneau was an ultraconservative. Although he opposed a land casino, he supported other forms of gambling. His love for gambling came from his father, Emile, who owned a bar and who was the state boxing commissioner throughout the 1960s and 1970s. Emile Bruneau also was identified as an associate of Carlos Marcello.

The pinball owners and Peppi Bruneau agreed that they would push to legalize the video poker machines, with the argument that the state could drive the illegal machines out of business and begin raising revenue from the legal machines by imposing a tax on their winnings. State laws didn't have enough teeth to permit authorities to crack down on the illegal machines, they argued. "These machines are a fact of life," Bruneau said. "They are there from Caddo Parish to Plaquemines Parish, and from the Delta to Cameron Parish, and all points 'twixt and 'tween." The Bruneau bill would allow bars and any other establishment with a liquor license to have up to three video poker machines apiece, with the State Police regulating the operation. Each play would cost the gambler $1. To win over Roemer and other legislators, Bruneau pitched the measure as a way to raise money for the state without raising taxes and as a form of economic development for struggling bars and restaurants.

Bruneau's video poker bill ran into more opposition than did the riverboat measure in the summer of 1991. It sailed through the House, but then stalled before the Senate. Leading the opposition was Findley Raymond, lobbyist for the Louisiana Coalition of Charitable Gaming Organizations, whose members—many of them churches—owned and operated bingo halls. In a letter to the editor, Raymond spelled out his opposition to the bill. Video poker, he wrote, "would lead to widespread proliferation of the new-age slot machines in every neighborhood bar, restaurant, motel, bowling alley and other places that serve alcohol. The machines are the most addictive gambling devices invented to date. They spawn compulsive gambling and gambling-related crime."

Raymond also said that rather than legalize video poker, the legislature ought to give authorities the means to crack down on the illegal machines and to levy tougher penalties against operators.

In the face of this opposition, the video poker bill remained stuck in a Senate committee. Even if they cleared that hurdle, the bill's supporters calculated, they were one vote shy of approval on the Senate floor. On June 24, as the Senate committee was considering the bill, Senator Gerry Hinton, a Republican from the New Orleans suburb of Slidell, spoke up. Hinton had been a video poker opponent up to then, but he was open to switching sides. "I've got a friend of mine," Hinton said, "a constituent of mine, named Fred Goodson. He's a God-fearing Baptist like me. He owns the biggest truck stop in the state, and it's in my district. He ought to have the same right to put in those machines, just like bars do."

Bruneau and other video poker supporters didn't quite understand what Hinton was trying to do with his amendment, and they didn't know Goodson. Nor did they understand what it might mean to allow truck stops to have video poker machines. But they did realize they needed Hinton's vote to get the measure out of the Senate committee, and he could provide the twentieth and final vote necessary for approval in the thirty-nine-member Senate. So they let Hinton add the truck stop amendment to the bill. Nobody paid much attention to the vote that day or in succeeding days. Yet it would turn out to have huge ramifications down the road, for both supporters and opponents of gambling in Louisiana.

July 8 was the final day of the 1991 legislative session. A number of measures hung in the balance, as usual, including the riverboat gambling and video poker bills. Each measure had passed both chambers, but in different versions. For the bills to become law, the House and Senate had to settle on a single, compromise measure. Governor Roemer, in the meantime, had said he would sign the riverboat gambling bill, arguing that it would provide economic development. He was noncommittal on the video poker bill.

The video poker bill came up first. With Hinton on board, the Senate the day before had approved the measure, 20–17. Now the House had to vote on the Senate bill, which contained the Hinton truck stop amendment. With little discussion, the House approved the bill, 60–36, and sent it to Roemer.

The Senate approved the riverboat gambling bill, 22–10, and the House, with four hours remaining in the session, took up the bill. Peppi Bruneau, already having gotten his video poker bill through the legislature, delivered an impassioned speech in favor of the riverboat measure. He spoke after a conservative Republican from Slidell, Ed Scogin, had voiced his opposition. "We don't want these boats," Representative Scogin said emphatically. During a stirring closing, Bruneau addressed this comment. "Mr. Scogin, if you don't want to go, don't go. My people want to go. Let my people go!" By a 61–40 vote, the House agreed to let Peppi's people go. This bill also went to Roemer.

Two days after the two gambling bills passed, the *Baton Rouge Morning Advocate* printed an editorial pointing out the irony of the legislature's approving forms of gambling that Governor Edwards, the high roller, had not proposed. "About all that's left to legalize is the big on-land casinos, which might be irresistible to the next Legislature. . . . Within a few years, it's conceivable that a huge portion of the state's economy will revolve around gambling and related industries. And what will life be like in America's newest gambling mecca?" The editorial then noted that the legislature had approved more lenient rules for the riverboat casinos than originally proposed:

> Action on that bill also suggests that, as time goes on, lawmakers might be more receptive, not only to more types of gambling, but to looser restrictions on the games already legalized. Things will snowball. A larger gambling industry will be able to exert more pressure for expansion on the Legislature and local governments, then use that growth to exert even more pressure for even more expansion. Gambling lobbyists will be as common as oil or chemical lobbyists at the State Capitol.
>
> For good or ill, Louisiana is about to enter the world of big-time gambling. Are we up to it?

Eight days later, on July 18, Roemer signed the riverboat gambling bill into law. "This follows what Mississippi, Illinois and Iowa have done," he said. "We are the tourist center of the Mississippi Valley, and we should have it. . . . The bill is tightly drawn. It is acceptable and tight."

Roemer had mixed feelings about whether to let the video poker measure become law. Uneasy about gambling to begin with, he didn't think video poker would create jobs. Aware of his concerns, Representative Bruneau and Senator Don Kelly, who had guided the video poker bill through the Senate, told him that the bill would provide badly needed tax revenue for the state and help small bars and restaurants. By now, Roemer was aware of Senator Hinton's truck stop amendment and wondered if it would pose a problem. Bruneau assured him that he would get the legislature to eliminate the truck stops the following year if they did cause problems. Meanwhile, State Police officials said they could closely regulate the new form of gambling by having all the machines tied to a central computer. Reflecting his own ambivalence, Roemer let the video poker bill become law without his signature on July 31.

By then Roemer was facing an increasingly difficult reelection battle as the October 1991 open primary approached. Edwin Edwards was campaigning to be governor again. He loved being the Cajun King, having the governor's enormous powers at his disposal, having crowds flock to him wherever he went. As governor, Edwards could help his core consistency: the poor, the elderly, and African Americans. He also could help his friends and, many said, fatten his own bank account. There was another reason he wanted to run for governor in 1991: beginning with his election to the Crowley City Council in 1954, he had won twenty-two elections in a row before the 1987 loss. He wanted to avenge Roemer's victory and end his political career as a winner.

Meanwhile, a third candidate loomed on the horizon. His name was David Duke, and he was in the unique position of being stronger politically after losing a United States Senate election the year before. A Republican, Duke had won an astounding 60 percent of the state's white vote against the three-term incumbent, Senator J. Bennett Johnston, who had parlayed his 1971 defeat to Edwards into a Senate seat the following year.

As a grand wizard of a Ku Klux Klan faction in the 1970s and neo-Nazi apologist, Duke carried terrible political baggage. That same baggage, however, won him enormous press coverage, and Duke was a master at manipulating the media. Standing a couple of inches above six feet, with a trim build, sandy hair, and surgically enhanced looks that strengthened his chin and narrowed his nose, Duke was particularly effective in his television appearances.

Also, Duke's core issues, opposition to affirmative action, minority set-asides, and quotas—the same issues he had pushed in the Klan—had become winning issues with voters. Louisiana in 1989–1991 was rife with frustrated whites who felt that government programs meant to aid black people were responsible for their stagnant incomes or joblessness. Duke's arguments struck home even with some college students, who rallied behind him as the anti-establishment candidate. Duke, many people commented, said publicly what many Louisianians felt privately. In February 1989, Duke had tapped into voter anger by narrowly winning a House seat from the New Orleans suburb of Metairie. In 1990, he had campaigned strongly but lost the Senate race. In 1991, at forty-one, he ran for governor.

Perhaps fittingly, as the state headed into the gambling era, each of the three candidates for governor was a big-time gambler. Edwin Edwards, of course, loved high-stakes craps at Las Vegas casinos. David Duke, *The Times-Picayune* had just reported, also was a high roller at craps; the Horseshoe regularly flew him to its Las Vegas casino, meeting him at the airport with a limousine. Roemer, for his part, was a high-stakes poker player. As a congressman in Washington, D.C., he played in a regular game with House Speaker Tip O'Neill, *Washington Post* reporter Bob Woodward, and Supreme Court Justice Antonin Scalia. Roemer was successful enough to have to report his poker winnings on his income tax returns.

During the campaign, Edwards retained his base of blacks and Cajuns, Duke showed surprising strength, and Roemer lost support. In the open primary, Edwards ran first with 33.8 percent. Duke followed with 31.7 percent, and Roemer finished out of the money with 26.5 percent.

Edwards and Duke would face off in a four-week runoff election. To win, Edwards had to gain the support of Roemer supporters, who saw him as a crook and who feared he would usher in uncontrolled gambling. Throughout the campaign, Edwards, as he had done beginning in 1986, had proclaimed that casino gambling would uplift the state's downtrodden economy. Instead of wide-open gambling, as he had advocated unsuccessfully before, he now called for a single, huge casino in New Orleans. It would create 25,000 jobs, he promised, and create millions of dollars in tax revenue for New Orleans and Louisiana. But the prospect of a New Orleans casino under Edwards's control horrified many of Roemer's good-government supporters, who believed this would inevitably lead to corruption, crime, and lax morals. So in the waning days of his election battle with Duke, Edwards made a key promise: If elected governor, he would not push for a New Orleans casino.

In the final two weeks of the campaign, Roemer's supporters reluctantly backed Edwards. Two bumper stickers that became popular during the runoff campaign summed up their feelings. "Vote for the Lizard, not the Wizard," read one. "Vote for the Crook. It's Important," read the other. On election day, November 16, 1991, with the race attracting front-page news coverage in *The New York Times* and elsewhere, Edwards trounced Duke, winning 61 percent to 39 percent. Edwin Washington Edwards had been elected governor a record fourth time, even though exit polls showed that six out of ten voters thought he was a crook. Still, Edwards had promised to run a clean, honest administration. And he had promised not to push for a New Orleans casino.

So as Edwards prepared to take office in January 1992, many Louisianians asked: Could he be believed?

Edwards Plays His Hand

n the heady days after Edwin Edwards's victory over David Duke, many Louisianians who had voted for him only to keep Duke out of office were willing to believe his promises that he had changed. But one prominent family opposed to a New Orleans casino was not taking any chances. Not only was Edwards a big-time gambler with strong ties to the gambling industry, but neighboring Mississippi had just approved dockside gambling, and Iowa and Illinois had legalized riverboat casinos along the Mississippi River. Within days of Edwards's election, members of the Brennan family, New Orleans's most prominent restaurateurs, began to organize against a possible casino-lobbying campaign. Attending the initial meeting were four Brennans: Ella, the family matriarch; Ralph, her nephew; Cindy, her niece; and Ti Martin, her daughter. Together, they owned Commander's Palace, Bacco, Palace Café, and Mr. B's, which was where they met.

The Brennans invited a fifth person to join them that day. His name was C. B. Forgotston, forty-six, one of Louisiana's top business lobbyists. Forgotston, a native of rural Tensas Parish in northeast Louisiana (population 6,154), spoke in a folksy manner and liked to wear cowboy boots. His monogrammed cuff links, swimming pool, and Jaguar sedan attested to his success on behalf of his clients. Forgotston, it seemed, had gone to Louisiana State University with half of the legislature while getting his undergraduate and law degrees, and he knew the legislative process inside out. He had been around the legislature since 1968, serving as chief counsel for the House Appropriations Committee, as a senior staff analyst for the 1973 convention that rewrote the state's constitution, and then as a business lobbyist.

In the 1950s, when Forgotston was growing up in the one-stoplight town of Newellton, slot machines were everywhere—in drug stores, the town café, the town general store. The American Legion owned them and used the money to buy uniforms for the high school band and football team, and to subsidize the local hospital. Gambling was so commonplace that Forgotston didn't realize it was illegal until State Police superintendent Francis Grevemberg carried out highly publicized raids in the early 1950s in which he and his troopers confiscated slot machines in Tensas Parish and elsewhere that they then destroyed.

In 1986, Forgotston had represented a group of French Quarter merchants who wanted to put a Monte Carlo–style casino in an unused building in the French Quarter. The casino would have a dress code, no slot machines, and a prohibition on gambling by locals. Edwards killed the proposal because he wanted the legislature to approve his more expansive gambling plan. Over the next several years, Forgotston learned more and more about gambling from his business clients. In time, he became convinced that a casino would hurt—not help—the city's economy.

After exchanging pleasantries at Mr. B's, the Brennans got down to business. "We want to hire you to lobby against the New Orleans casino," Ella Brennan told Forgotston; the others nodded in agreement. "I know the casino people say it will mean new jobs and lots more business for restaurants like ours. And maybe it will. But we think a casino will change the character of the city. I remember my earliest years in the restaurant business in the '50s. Jefferson Parish was like Las Vegas. We saw what gambling was all about. The gambling people will end up running the town."

Forgotston was surprised at what she had to say. "You mean, you're all opposed?" he asked.

"Yes," replied Ella Brennan emphatically.

"I had heard everybody in the business community was for it."

"No," said Ella Brennan. "We think it's very important to try to stop the casino. What do we have to do to kill it?"

Forgotston had been around a long time. He had seen Edwards's worst excesses. Now he was caught up in the excitement of Edwards's triumph over Duke, a victory in which the business community rallied behind their longtime foe. Forgotston was among those who desperately wanted to believe that Edwards had changed, that during this term Edwards would do right so he would be lauded in the history books, that Edwards would not push a casino in the face of opposition from New Orleans. What did the Brennans have to do to kill the casino? "Just stand up and say you're opposed to it," Forgotston advised. "The Brennans being opposed should be enough to kill it." Forgotston would later call that "the most naïve statement of my professional career."

A few weeks after the Brennans' meeting, Edwards spent New Year's in Las Vegas with his young girlfriend, Candy Picou, whom he had met in 1990 at Maggio's, a Baton Rouge restaurant. When a *Times-Picayune* reporter, who staked out Edwards in Las Vegas, described his gambling in detail—betting $1,000 per roll of the dice—outraged readers called talk-radio shows. They said the governor-to-be shouldn't be wagering heavily at the same time the state was about to decide whether it wanted casino gambling in New Orleans. But James Gill, a *Times-Picayune* columnist, dismissed such complaints. "There cannot in any case be many people in Louisiana in a position to argue that gambling is immoral," Gill wrote. "Churchmen who ran bingo games have not a leg to stand on. Lottery players are gamblers like any others except that they have no apparent understanding of odds. Go to the [New Orleans] Fair Grounds on a Friday afternoon, and you will find judges and other pillars of the community pondering [horse racing] exactas. If a gambling boat operating off the Mississippi Gulf Coast should founder, there would be a day of mourning across Louisiana." Edwards, too, dismissed the complaints and promised once again that he wouldn't push for a New Orleans casino.

During his first month as governor in January 1992, Edwards seemed to keep his promise. He let lawmakers and New Orleans mayor Sidney Barthelemy take the lead in pushing for casino gambling. Some state legislators favored two or three casinos in New Orleans. Barthelemy wanted a single land casino in New Orleans. He said it would be the city's salvation. But Edwards stepped into the casino debate on February 14 when he announced that Barthelemy could not expect New Orleans to receive a percentage of the casino's revenue. The state would get all the tax revenue, he said, which he predicted would be $250 million a year. New Orleans would get its own share—$75 million a year in city sales taxes and other local taxes from the casino, Edwards said, because the casino would create 25,000 jobs and draw three to ten million more tourists a year. Giving the city a share of the casino's revenue would kill any casino bill, Edwards said. He explained that his approach was necessary to placate rural legislators, who consistently found success at home by decrying New Orleans as a sin-filled, crime-ridden city that got more than its fair share of state funds. Some country legislators had made a career out of running as the defenders of rural interests against big, bad New Orleans. Country legislators could support the New Orleans casino only if they could tell their constituents that the state—and not the city—would get all the casino revenue.

To enhance the bill's popularity among rural legislators, the casino's supporters chose Raymond (La La) Lalonde to sponsor the bill in the House. Lalonde, a fifty-one-year-old Democrat, was a wise choice. He was fervently pro-gambling, representing the southwest Louisiana town of Sunset, which billed itself as the cockfighting capital of the world. The director of a government-funded vocational-technical trade school, Lalonde was a wily House veteran who knew how to get bills passed and who, with his down-home manner, was popular among colleagues. Lalonde sponsored the 1990 measure approved by the legislature that created a lottery with a popular vote of the people, and he co-sponsored the 1991 bill approved by the legislature that legalized fifteen riverboat casinos throughout Louisiana. Lalonde also chaired the criminal justice committee, where the pro-gambling speaker, John

Alario, would assign the casino bill. Alario would stack the committee with enough pro-casino votes to ensure that it would approve the casino bill and move it onto the House floor.

On March 30, Edwards gave the opening address to kick off the 1992 legislative session. He was still insisting that he would stay away from the casino issue. "I do not have a bill to create one," he told lawmakers. "I'm not pushing for one. I'm not arguing with anybody about it." But he added: "It is one thing the city of New Orleans should be given an opportunity to do in order to attract tourists, create jobs, stimulate the city and provide $250 million in revenue for the people of this state without them having to pay additional taxes. . . . You don't like casinos? That's fine. Many people in good faith are opposed. But think about the 25,000 people in the city who don't have jobs. I'm talking about maids, bartenders, waiters, waitresses, taxi drivers, parking lot attendants, hotel employees, restaurant employees, clerks in shops, everybody in the city with basic skills and little education who cannot be doctors or lawyers or engineers or work in a computer factory, but who are looking for something to do."

Following Edwards's speech, the casino push intensified. Three men—along with La La Lalonde—would play central roles. The key strategist in the House was Sherman Copelin Jr., a forty-eight-year-old African-American representative from New Orleans. Political insiders in Louisiana likened him to Willie Brown, the shrewd speaker of the California State Assembly. Like Brown, Copelin favored expensive suits and fast cars, the art of the deal, and using his political power to enhance his private business dealings. Copelin represented New Orleans's Ninth Ward, a downriver neighborhood that at one time had been a bastion of the white working class. But with integration and white flight, poor blacks moved into the shotgun homes that dominated the Ninth Ward. Copelin, the son of a funeral director, graduated from the city's elite black Catholic high school—St. Augustine—and attended Dillard University in New Orleans on a music scholarship. At Dillard, Copelin grew interested in politics, winning election as student body president. In 1968, he was hired as an aide to New Orleans Mayor Victor Schiro, becoming one of the few blacks who held more than a menial city job.

With his oversized ambition, Copelin set out to make his mark. In the 1970s, with another young African American, Don Hubbard, Copelin took over a political organization known as SOUL. Every election, two dozen or so candidates would pay thousands of dollars apiece to SOUL to be on its endorsed ballot, which was distributed by hundreds of workers in the primarily black, low-income Ninth Ward. And on election day, SOUL had the most efficient get-out-the-vote effort in the city, marrying its large cadre of precinct workers with computers and phone banks. Copelin and Hubbard formed marketing companies that received a cut of the proceeds.

One of the politicians who owed a debt to Copelin and Hubbard because of SOUL was Edwin Edwards. In return, he helped them win a contract managing security, janitorial, and other services at the Louisiana Superdome. In 1975, Copelin and Hubbard branched out and promoted the Ali-Spinks heavyweight championship boxing match in New Orleans.

Copelin, like Edwards, danced close to the line that separated legal from illegal activities. In grand jury testimony, Copelin admitted receiving at least $3,000 in payments from a health foundation that had received public contracts from Copelin while he was at City Hall. At least one payoff, as his critics would always remember, came in a Canal Street rest room. In a separate deal, a consulting company formed by Copelin received $40,000 indirectly from the health foundation. Copelin and Hubbard were granted immunity to testify against the health foundation's president, who went to jail. In 1984, Copelin was caught registering his new car in neighboring St. Tammany Parish to pay lower sales taxes. He was forced to pay a fine. Copelin blamed the negative publicity on the white-owned press.

In 1986, Copelin used his political know-how and business contacts to win a special election to the Louisiana House of Representatives. Several years later, the Reverend Jesse Jackson presided over his wedding to a beautiful twenty-something Creole woman; Copelin got her a cushy job in City Hall. Calling himself "a black political superstar," he infuriated whites with his brazen manner and willingness to use his political power to earn a fortune. Among his many business ventures was a company that he formed to provide drug counseling to the poor. It earned him millions of dollars by exploiting a loophole in federal Medicaid rules. Copelin moved to Eastover, a gated residential development in eastern New Orleans outside his legislative district, but claimed that he still lived in his mother's modest Ninth Ward home. One morning, tipped off that political enemies were watching his house in an effort to prove that he was never there and lived elsewhere, he emerged in his bathrobe to do gardening in the front yard. As a longtime ally of Edwards, Copelin became speaker pro tempore in the House, the chamber's second-ranking position, when Edwards returned to office in 1992. Copelin was a natural point man to ensure the casino bill's passage.

On the Senate side, the key strategist was Don Kelly, a fifty-one-year-old five-term senator from Natchitoches (*Nak-i-tesh*) in central Louisiana. At six feet one inch and 235 pounds, Kelly had been a running back in college, and he still exuded physical power. He reminded those who met him of John Wayne. Kelly combined his intimidating physical presence with a crafty political mind to hold enormous sway over the Senate. He was said to be able to get twenty votes—a majority—for practically any issue taken up by the thirty-nine-member Senate. A successful trial lawyer, he wore cowboy boots and didn't say a lot. But when he did speak, others listened.

An outside lobbyist quarterbacked the casino effort. His name was Billy Broadhurst, and he was smart, foxy, and well connected to Edwards and his political allies. Broadhurst, fifty-one, came from Crowley, the small town in southwest Louisiana where Edwards set up shop after graduating from law school. When Broadhurst was a young lawyer in the early 1960s, he and Edwards were friends and law partners. After Edwards was elected governor in 1971, Broadhurst followed him to Baton Rouge, where he became a trusted confidant and influential power broker. In 1979, Broadhurst's law firm received more legal contracts from the state than any other law firm in Louisiana. But Broadhurst's ambition outstripped the Bayou State. Like several other sharp and ambitious political animals in Louisiana, he gravitated to Washington, D.C. There he flourished as a lobbyist, hosting an annual seafood luncheon called "Billy's Crawfish Kitchen" that drew nearly the entire U.S. Senate. In 1987, Broadhurst had maneuvered himself into traveling the country with Gary Hart, the leading Democratic presidential candidate. They were an odd mix, the reform-minded senator from Colorado, the product of a strict religious upbringing, and the good old boy from Louisiana, who loved a good time and a good deal. Raymond Strother, a Louisiana native who was Hart's media strategist, later said Broadhurst fascinated Hart because Hart had never met anyone like him. For Broadhurst, the attraction was simpler. He liked being close to political power.

In May 1987, Broadhurst's bubble burst. *The Miami Herald* reported that Hart and Broadhurst, both of whom were married, had recently chartered a 110-foot yacht to the Bahamas island of Bimini with two young women. In a photograph that was splashed across newspapers nationwide, Hart was shown holding maracas and wearing a T-shirt with the memorable name of the yacht: *Monkey Business*. Broadhurst was seated behind a set of drums, while the two women—Donna Rice and Lynn Armandt—were holding microphones. Two nights before the *Herald* published its story in May, reporters from the newspaper witnessed Rice and Armandt spending the night with Hart and Broadhurst at their neighboring townhouses on Capitol Hill in Washington, D.C. The ensuing scandal wrecked Hart's political career. It also ended Broadhurst's days in Washington. Shortly afterward, he filed for bankruptcy, got divorced, and became a political pariah. He was rescued in 1991 by his old friend Edwards, who asked him to manage his longshot gubernatorial campaign. Broadhurst took on the job, but he worked in the background. He would not emerge from the shadows until after Edwards took office.

Broadhurst got involved in the casino battle in early 1992 when Daniel Robinowitz hired him as a lobbyist. Robinowitz, a Dallas-based developer, was trying to win the rights to control the New Orleans casino—but he could do so only if the legislature legalized it. "I asked around and kept coming up with Broadhurst's name," Robinowitz remembered later. "When I went to Baton Rouge with Broadhurst the first time, we went over to the Senate, and Billy knew everybody. We went to the House, and Billy knew everybody." Broadhurst would help draft the casino bill and lobby for its passage. He would keep the most accurate tick sheet on how legislators would vote, working behind the scenes in the offices of Representative Copelin and Sammy Nunez, the president of the Senate. Broadhurst started out at a salary of $10,000 a month.

The legislature went into session on March 30, and during the next six weeks, the fortunes of the casino bill waxed and waned on almost a daily basis. In late April, disagreements among New Orleans legislators over the shape of the casino bill spelled big trouble. But the pro-casino side gained strength a few days later when a developer from Hawaii named Christopher Hemmeter unveiled a stunning $1 billion project along the Mississippi River that included a huge casino. Two weeks later, on May 6, groups opposing the casino for various reasons gathered enough strength that La La Lalonde had to cancel a hearing in which his committee was supposed to approve it. Lalonde particularly blamed the riverboat gambling interests, which, he said, feared that the New Orleans land casino would overshadow their boats. The riverboat casinos, although legalized in 1991, would not begin operations for more than a year. With the measure foundering, only Edwin Edwards had the political skills and the power to save it.

On May 12, Edwards convened a breakfast meeting at the Governor's Mansion with Mayor Sidney Barthelemy and members of the New Orleans legislative delegation. Edwards told them that the casino bill would die if they did not rally behind a single measure. And he told them that while New Orleans would not get a share of the casino winnings, he would come up with state money to help defray the city's costs for police, fire, and traffic services. Barthelemy and the lawmakers fell into line behind Lalonde's bill. On May 18, Edwards met with riverboat lobbyists and would-be riverboat owners, who had been clamoring for him to clear a logjam that had stymied the effort to get the riverboat casinos up and going. Almost a year after the legislature had legalized the casinos, Edwards was keeping his appointees from even beginning to decide who would get the fifteen operating licenses. At the meeting, Edwards told the riverboat officials that he knew they were anxious to move forward. But he also said that their opposition to the land-casino bill concerned him. If they would declare their support for the New Orleans casino, he thought he could expedite the riverboat process. Anybody who opposed it, he added, might have trouble getting a license from his appointed board. The next day, before a Senate committee hearing, the riverboat interests endorsed the New Orleans casino.

With these deft moves, Edwards was now ready to predict that the casino would pass. "All these do-gooders who've been talking about how we ought to do something else [to help the economy] have failed in six years to come up with alternative solutions to the problem," he told reporters.

The Times-Picayune, in an eloquent editorial, sharply disagreed:

> Where others have parking lots, we boast the French Quarter and a vast 19th-century housing stock; where others make do with Big Macs, we enjoy food that has no equal; where others have forsaken their core, we inhabit a vibrant downtown by the world's greatest river. . . . We understand the desperation of the oil-bust years because we, too, have lived them. But New Orleans, while poor, is not resource-less. Our jobless rate is no worse than the rest of the country's; in fact, it's better. The city is filled with people who are devoted to it and lack only the leadership that will harness their energies. We may be wanting, but to embrace gambling for lack of alternatives is to admit to the most abject poverty of all. Saying no to casinos means saying yes to our city and its future.

The Lalonde bill sought to chart a new direction in the casino business. Nevada, New Jersey, and Mississippi relied on the marketplace to determine the number of casinos in those states. In sharp contrast, the Lalonde bill permitted but a single casino for New Orleans and specified that it be on the site of the Rivergate, a 1960s concrete structure that had served as New Orleans's convention center until a larger hall was built in the early 1980s. The Rivergate now sat unused on prime property—one block from the Mississippi River, one block from the French Quarter, and within walking distance of ten thousand hotel rooms. In exchange for the monopoly, the casino would have to pay an

18.5 percent tax to the state, more than twice the rate paid by casinos in Las Vegas and Atlantic City. The bill included a provision stipulating a $100 million minimum tax payment per year to the state. The Lalonde bill specified something else—the casino would have no hotels or full-service restaurants. It would be freestanding. This feature of the New Orleans casino, unique in the United States, came at the insistence of local hotel and restaurant owners and French Quarter merchants who said the casino could boost the city's economy only if gamblers had to leave it to go eat, sleep, and find entertainment. Otherwise, gamblers might not spend their cash anywhere else in New Orleans, and the casino would benefit only its owners.

The casino bill contained an additional feature, one that would become controversial. Louisiana's 1974 constitution required the legislature "to define and suppress" gambling. Given that, how could the legislature legalize a New Orleans casino? How could anyone argue that a casino wasn't "gambling" and thus not subject to being "suppressed"? A crafty pol came up with the solution: The bill would call the casino "gaming," not "gambling." By making this small change, supporters argued, the legislature didn't have to "suppress" the casino, a view eventually upheld by the Louisiana Supreme Court.

On May 20, the Senate voted on the casino bill. "Gambling is no longer the issue in this state," Senator Don Kelly told his colleagues. "We have horse racing, video poker, bingo on every street corner. . . . This will be an economic boost for the city of New Orleans. If this doesn't pass, I don't know what those folks down there will do." The Senate heeded Kelly, approving the casino, 23–16.

The battle now shifted to the House. There, the pro-casino forces faced a more difficult task. The House was less populist and not as friendly to Edwards. Nevertheless, Speaker John Alario, a stalwart Edwards ally, predicted on May 21 that the House would approve the casino. "I've done an informal count based on discussions I've had with members of the House," Alario said, "and I feel comfortable the votes will be there when it's necessary." Casino opponents weren't giving up, however. Several hundred religious activists and civic leaders rallied at the Rivergate against the casino. They waved brooms and CASINO signs, and used a portable generator to power their public-address system because Mayor Barthelemy denied them access to the Rivergate's electrical system. A few days later, C. B. Forgotston, the lead anti-casino lobbyist, delivered 1,500 letters and cards to members of the New Orleans legislative delegation from casino opponents. Meanwhile, constituents making their views known via the House fax machine were sending so many faxes that staffers had to replace the paper daily. A tally sheet on June 3 showed 44 legislators favored the casino, 44 opposed it, and 17 were undecided in the 105-member House. Passing the bill required at least fifty-three votes, a simple majority.

On June 4, the House voted. Representative Copelin and Speaker Alario figured that they had secured a winning margin, although Edwards thought they needed a couple more days to be sure. The debate that day was long and contentious, with each side warning of doom and gloom if the other triumphed. "This thing smells," said Representative Peppi Bruneau, a New Orleans Republican who had sponsored the video poker legislation but opposed the land casino. "There is smoke, and there is fire here, and I suspect something is burning, and it is the people of New Orleans. . . . This thing smells. It is rotten to the core. It reeks of corruption. A done deal, a done deal, all in the hands of one man, the ringmaster of *Circus Maximus*."

Another opponent, Representative Jim Donelon, a Republican from Metairie, said, "We don't have to flush the Queen City of the South down the toilet. . . . We can do better than being croupiers. We can do better than being blackjack dealers."

Countered Representative Lalonde: "This is one important step to help New Orleans be self-supporting and pull themselves up by their bootstraps." He added: "I don't know how you feel about taxes, but I can vote for this rather than taxes."

Tension was running high on the House floor. Throughout the debate, Edwards was phoning legislators at their desks, and Copelin was walking up and down the aisles to ensure that the pro-casino forces would have the necessary fifty-three votes. But their plan hit a snag. In a surprise move, Mayor Barthelemy passed out notes to members of the New Orleans delegation, asking them to vote against the bill. Barthelemy was a strong casino supporter, but he was upset that Edwards had taken control of the project and was allowing him to select only one of the nine members on the board that would choose the casino operator. Worse yet, the city would not get a direct share of the casino tax revenue. Copelin went ballistic when he saw the note and tried to reach Barthelemy to change his mind. However, Barthelemy had disappeared. Casino opponents began to think that Alario would have to put off the bill until another day. At 3:50 p.m., however, Alario called for a vote.

Representative Tim Stine had been following the debate from his wheelchair in the far left corner of the House chamber facing the speaker. The thirty-five-year-old Democrat from Lake Charles was a quadriplegic, having been paralyzed in a diving accident eleven years earlier. Stine didn't have use of his hands. He pushed the voting buttons on his desk with his balled-up fist. Stine opposed the casino bill and believed that it should be up to voters statewide to decide whether New Orleans got a huge casino. Now, a few minutes before the House vote, Stine approached several Democratic legislators with a plan to confuse Alario. It sought to take advantage of the routine the speaker always followed during a vote. The speaker always began by saying, "The clerk will open the machine, and members will proceed to vote." About five seconds later, he would ask, "Are you through voting?" He would wait another five seconds and ask the same question. Then he would say, "The clerk will close the machine and announce the vote." Stine proposed to the others that when the clerk opened the voting machines, they would initially hit the green "yes" button on their desks. Just as the speaker was asking the clerk to shut the voting machines, they would hit the red "no" button instead. Stine figured that Alario had several "soft" votes in reserve—members who didn't want to vote for the casino, but would if Alario absolutely needed them to put it over the top. During the vote, no one knew the exact count except the clerk and Alario, who had a clicker on the speaker's rostrum that kept a running tally. The huge board on the wall above the speaker lit up with green and red lights by the members' names as they voted, but it did not give an ongoing tally. Stine figured that if several anti-casino legislators voted yes initially, Alario would not signal to the soft votes that he needed them before he asked the clerk to shut the machine. "Let's get Alario's clicker above 53 so he will think he has it," Stine suggested to his colleagues. They readily agreed. Meanwhile, Republican lawmakers elsewhere in the chamber were planning the same strategy.

With debate on the casino bill completed, it was time to vote. The House chamber buzzed with nervous excitement and anticipation. Alario directed clerk Butch Speer to open the voting machine. After a ten-second pause, Alario called out: "Are you through voting?" He paused a few seconds and then asked, "Are you through voting?" Alario paused again and said, "The clerk will close the machine and announce the vote."

"Forty-three yeas and 58 nays," Speer intoned.

The House had defeated the bill that would give New Orleans the world's largest casino. Tim Stine, Peppi Bruneau, Jim Donelon, and the other opponents cheered and let out whoops of relief. Their strategy had worked. Alario's vote counter had peaked at 51 briefly, but had slid down to 43 as casino opponents switched to the no column, and as soft votes, willing to vote yes only if the bill would pass, refrained from pushing the green button. Hearing the vote outcome at home in New Orleans, anti-casino lobbyist C. B. Forgotston yelled with joy. But as he began to calm down, Forgotston thought to himself: "We're going to have another major battle. It's almost automatic to have a second vote on a bill that's been defeated."

Forgotston was right. The next day, Alario signaled that the casino supporters weren't giving up. "It's closer than 43 votes," he said. "We weren't that far off. . . . So we have to go back and scramble and try to get people to change their minds." Added Edwards to reporters, "I don't think it's over till it's over."

The day after the House defeat, Edwards convened a meeting at the Governor's Mansion with Alario, Copelin, Lalonde, and other casino allies.

"What happened?" Edwards asked.

"Republicans played games with the voting buttons," Alario replied. "So my soft votes didn't think they were needed. But I'm confident we can get the necessary 53 votes."

Keeping his cards close to his vest, Alario was concocting a plan to combat the legislators who had switched their votes to the no column at the last moment. He was thinking about shutting down the voting machine early during a second casino vote. It would be an extremely devious maneuver, something that hadn't been done for many years and was sure to provoke enormous controversy. Alario was willing to try it nevertheless. It was probably the only way the casino bill could pass.

While they had unexpectedly lost the first vote, the result contained some pluses for Edwards and Alario. After weeks of compiling tick sheets on where legislators stood, they now had an actual tally that told them which House members they had to pressure, cajole, or entice to their side. Edwards had an arsenal of weapons at his disposal. A governor in Louisiana exercises enormous power because he has far more control over patronage than do governors in other states. The governor in Louisiana also has enormous influence in determining which legislative districts get money for bridges, roads, sewers, and health clinics— projects of vital importance to lawmakers. The governor has particular influence with rural legislators because he has a legal slush fund known as rural development grants that he can dole out as rewards. For rural legislators, getting a new road or bridge was more important to their constituents than letting New Orleans get the casino.

The meeting at the Governor's Mansion with Edwards, Alario, and the other lawmakers took place on a Friday. Over the weekend, Edwin Edwards swung into action. He called House members who had voted against the casino but weren't solid no votes. On the morning of Monday, June 8, Edwards invited several wavering lawmakers to the Governor's Mansion for one-on-one meetings. Edwards played deal maker, a role at which he excelled. One representative got new roads to switch his vote, another got an addition to a hospital, a third got the promise of new jobs for his constituents. Edwards was turning the tide in his favor. Casino opponents could not match his firepower.

That afternoon, Edwards met at the Governor's Mansion with Mayor Barthelemy. Four days earlier, Barthelemy's unexpected opposition had helped sink the bill. Now Edwards told Barthelemy that he had the necessary 53 votes, even if Barthelemy continued his opposition.

The casino bill was not scheduled to come up in the legislature that day. But Alario as the speaker had the authority to have the House take up a measure whenever he wished. In midafternoon, the two main lobbyists against the casino, C. B. Forgotston and Tom Spradley, met with legislators in the rear of the chamber and heard rumblings that Alario might bring it up that day. When Spradley went to lobby Representative Francis Thompson, a rural Democrat, Thompson sneered at him, "Do you entertain any serious notion that Edwin Edwards won't prevail? You ain't got a snowball's chance in hell!"

Edwards, in fact, had telephoned Alario at the speaker's rostrum to say that he had nailed down the votes needed to put the casino bill over the top. "If we got it now, we better do it while it's hot, before they change their minds," Alario told Edwards. The governor readily agreed.

As rumors spread throughout the House chamber that the casino bill might come up, Alario took up a measure sought by the labor unions. This bill proposed to gut the state's right-to-work law, which allowed workers to refuse to join unions. Alario brought up the bill for a specific purpose, although few people realized it at the time. The issue of whether to keep the right-to-work law was so important for both unions and business groups that all legislators made sure they were there for the vote. For his part, Alario needed them there for what would come next.

Just before the right-to-work vote, Alario called Representative La La Lalonde, the casino bill's sponsor, up to the speaker's rostrum. "After this vote, we'll move to pull it from the calendar," Alario told him quietly. Lalonde nodded. As Lalonde returned to his seat, labor's attempt to scrap the right-to-work law was defeated. As was common following a vote on a controversial issue, lawmakers immediately afterward turned to colleagues to share a thought or two on the outcome. Supporters of the measure, meanwhile, hurried to the rear of the House chamber to celebrate with their business allies. It was in this distracted setting that Alario intoned, "Mr. Lalonde moves to call from the calendar House Bill 2010."

"Shoot, that's the gambling bill," Peppi Bruneau said to himself as he hustled back to his seat from the back of the chamber. Pro-casino forces were taking up the bill unexpectedly, out of order, so they needed a two-thirds vote to introduce the measure unless no one objected. There was a brief moment while Alario and Lalonde held their breath because they didn't have the 70 votes needed to bring up the bill. But Bruneau, an expert parliamentarian, and the other opponents were still enjoying the glow from Thursday's unexpected casino victory and were celebrating the defeat of labor's bill moments before. Alario's strategy worked: they were caught off guard. Alario quickly announced that no one had objected to the gambling bill. Bruneau waved his arms seconds later in objection. It was too late. Lalonde had already begun explaining the bill.

The debate and parliamentary maneuvers lasted ninety minutes. Throughout the chamber, the mood was serious, even somber. Lawmakers knew they were about to take a historic vote. Outside, the sky had turned black, and a heavy rain was falling, which darkened the interior of the House chamber. Spotlights in the ceiling fifty feet above the House floor created narrow cones of light. As lawmakers moved about, they passed back and forth from semidarkness to light. The gray half-tones contributed to the chamber's surrealistic ambience.

Just before the vote, Tim Stine checked with his colleagues to see whether they all should switch their vote again. "Tim," advised Representative Jimmy Dimos, who had preceded Alario as speaker of the House, "I don't think this is a good time to do that. It may have worked one time, but it won't work again." The Republican legislators elsewhere in the chamber had reached the same conclusion, deeming it too risky. Headstrong, Stine decided he would do it again nevertheless.

At about the same time, Alario was softly calling to Butch Speer, the clerk, who stood just in front of Alario one step down at the front of the House chamber. Speer turned around to face Alario, resting his elbows on the speaker's rostrum. "Butch," Alario told him, "as soon as it gets to 53, I want you to close the machine." Speer had been clerk since 1984 and had never shut down the machine early. But with word having spread of how Stine, his allies, and the Republicans had switched their votes, Speer understood exactly the meaning of Alario's command. Speer was a bit nervous. "John," he replied, "I can't shut off the machine before you start talking."

"OK," Alario said, "as soon as I say the first word, shut down the machine." Speer nodded his assent.

Lalonde, meanwhile, was finishing his closing speech on why the legislature should legalize the New Orleans casino. When he was done, Alario announced, "The clerk will open the machine and members will proceed to vote." Speer pushed a green button on his desk to open the voting machines. A bell sounded, signaling to the legislators that they could now vote. Speer, like Alario, had a vote counter in front of him, and he saw it hit 40 yes votes almost immediately. Two seconds later it rose to 56—three votes more than were needed for the bill to pass. A second later, the yes vote dropped to 54 as two legislators switched to the no column. Speer put his hand behind his back and frantically signaled to Alario that he should begin talking because the counter was about to drop below 53. "Are you . . . ," Alario began to say.

Speer pushed the red button on his desk that shut the voting machines. There wasn't a moment to spare. His counter had 53 votes for the casino—the bare minimum needed—and 42 against. Ten members hadn't had time to vote. It didn't matter. The machines were locked shut. The casino bill had passed.

Even before Alario could announce the vote, anti-casino legislators began screaming about the voting board shutting down early. "What's the vote?" several could be heard yelling above the din. "What happened?"

Alario then announced the vote. Opponents were dumbfounded. "You've got to be kidding me! " screamed Representative Mitch Landrieu, fanning his arms in disbelief. "You can't be serious, man!"

"They stole this vote, pure and simple!" shouted Representative David Vitter.

"This is a Huey Long vote!" yelled Representative Bruneau. Passions were running so high that he thought a fistfight would break out.

The outcome stunned Representative Stine, who was sitting in the far corner of the chamber. After initially hitting the green button on his desk, he had pushed the red one with his fist. But Alario's maneuver had blocked his switch. His green light remained on. This meant that Stine had inadvertently voted yes and helped approve a bill that had passed with no votes to spare. Furious, Stine decided to demand that Alario and Speer tell him what had happened. He turned his electric wheelchair to the right and scooted over to the center aisle. He made a quick left pivot, saw that no one was standing in the narrow aisle, and then zipped past his colleagues down a slight incline and didn't stop until he was in front of the speaker's rostrum. A horde of screaming and hollering legislators were gathering there. Some were angry at how Alario and Speer had resorted to trickery to pass the bill. Others who were recorded voting for the bill were yelling that they needed to be in the no column. A few others shouted that while they had voted no, they needed to vote for the bill. Representative Steve Windhorst, a Republican from suburban New Orleans, was standing in front of the speaker's rostrum bellowing, "Speer, I want a copy of the vote! Give me a copy of the vote!"

"Steve! No!" Speer shouted back. "Not until we're done changing members!"

Normally, the tally sheet showing how members voted was released immediately. But Alario and Speer were holding on to it. Trying to mollify at least some of the angry members, they were busy moving legislators from one column to another, all the while being careful that the yes column kept 53 votes, the bare minimum. When they found a legislator who wanted to go from yes to no, they had to find another one who had voted no or hadn't voted and would move to yes. For ten minutes, as members crowded around them, Speer carefully drew arrows rearranging names on the vote tally. In the end, the sheet looked like the diagram of a football play as they moved a dozen legislators from one column to another. Among those whose votes Speer switched was Stine, who ended up in the no column. The final count was 53–50 with two abstentions.

Standing in the back of the chamber, Tom Spradley shook his head and thought to himself: "The fucker's passed. Louisiana is corrupt, it always has been, and it always will be. We're Third World, and we deserve to be discriminated against by the rest of the country. Louisiana's heroes are pirates—Jean Lafitte, Huey Long, Edwin Edwards—and they always will be." Standing next to Spradley, C. B. Forgotston felt sick to his stomach. Said Representative Garey Forster, "Day one of the casino, and there's already a scandal."

George Brown, who had been a lobbyist for the beer industry and other interests since 1953, hadn't seen anything like it since the days of Earl Long. Brown flashed back to a memory of Earl Long ordering House leaders, "Shut the damn thing down," until he had corralled his votes.

On June 11, three days after the House vote, the Senate, as expected, approved Lalonde's bill. The vote was 21–18. The next day, in a scathing editorial, *The Times-Picayune* wrote, "June 11, 1992, will long be remembered in New Orleans. It is the date when a Machiavellian governor, abetted by the top legislative leadership, recklessly manipulated a legislative majority into approving casino gambling."

Edwards offered a rosier view a week later when he signed the casino bill into law. "With the stroke of a pen," Edwards said, "we've taken the largest step toward economic development and the creation of jobs undertaken in Louisiana in the last twenty-five years. I predict without fear of contradiction that in a few short years everyone will look back and say we were right, this was a step in the right direction, that it has not and will not change the character of the great city of New Orleans." He predicted that the world's largest casino would open in New Orleans in a year.

But first, rival groups would fight a fierce battle over the right to develop the casino. Governor Edwards would not be the one to settle that battle.

3

Seducing the Big Easy

By 1992, New Orleans was an impoverished, crime-ridden city with seemingly little hope for improvement in the near term. After the go-go days of the 1970s, when rising oil prices had produced a slew of skyscrapers and good-paying jobs, the Oil Bust of the 1980s had floored New Orleans. Texaco, Amoco, Shell, Mobil—one after the other, the giant oil companies had dramatically downsized their New Orleans operations. This had a ripple effect throughout the city. Purchasing power fell, and companies in other industries began laying off workers. College graduates abandoned New Orleans for greener pastures. A poor city became even poorer. From 1980 to 1990, the percentage of the city's population living in poverty rose to 31.6 percent from 26.4 percent, making it the nation's third-poorest city, behind Laredo and Detroit. More than 10 percent of the population lived in dilapidated housing projects scattered throughout the city, and one in six of all housing units was vacant. No one had done a major development in more than a decade. "The city is an economic basket case," Arnold Hirsch, a history professor at the University of New Orleans, said at the time. Crime, meanwhile, was spiraling out of control. The city in 1992 would have 285 murders, placing it

among the country's homicide capitals. "We're like a 60-year-old Southern dowager that's fallen on evil times," said Patrick Taylor, a prominent oil man. The dowager needed a wealthy suitor.

Developer Daniel Robinowitz watched the decline of New Orleans
with dismay and with visions of being that suitor. Tall and thin, with a
prominent nose, graying hair, and large, expressive eyes, Robinowitz was
a native New Orleanian who had moved to Dallas in the 1960s after
flunking out of the University of Alabama because he partied too much.
After selling neckties for a while, he got the real estate bug in Dallas.
Robinowitz was prone to mispronounce words, but with an ability to
schmooze and understand what it took to complete a deal, he soon displayed a knack for developing apartments and commercial buildings.
"Daniel Robinowitz: A success at 27," *The Dallas Morning News* trumpeted in a glowing 1965 article. But like many young developers, Robinowitz became overconfident and overextended himself financially in
pursuing new projects. A business slump in the early 1970s forced his
real estate company into bankruptcy. He tried to restart his career with
two projects back in New Orleans, but they flopped. Still, Robinowitz
nursed a dream of striking it rich again, somehow, some way.

In 1991, he became convinced that the opportunity was at hand.
Casinos were expanding beyond Las Vegas and Atlantic City to places
like Deadwood (South Dakota), Davenport (Iowa), Joliet (Illinois), and
Biloxi (Mississippi). Louisiana had joined the bandwagon in 1991. In
two separate measures, the legislature had legalized fifteen riverboat
casinos throughout the state, as well as video poker machines in local
bars and highway truck stops across Louisiana. Robinowitz now asked
himself: Why not go a step farther and create a New Orleans casino? It
would be a natural, he thought. The city had a long history with gambling, still had a well-deserved reputation as a sin city, and attracted
eight million tourists a year. Robinowitz figured he could build a huge
casino in New Orleans, fulfill his dreams of putting the declining city
back on its feet, and make himself rich beyond imagination.

Robinowitz had the perfect site in mind—a prime piece of property
a stone's throw from the French Quarter and the Mississippi River. The
city's onetime convention center—known as the Rivergate—occupied

the site, which took up a full city block. Robinowitz figured he could renovate the building and promote a downtown casino as a huge draw for tourists with fists full of cash. Thousands of hotel rooms were within walking distance. There would be plenty of fun, and plenty of profits to go around. And with a feel for the city's byzantine politics, Robinowitz knew which levers of power to pull to make it happen.

In the summer of 1991, he met with New Orleans's mayor, Sidney Barthelemy. Barthelemy, who had won reelection the year before, strongly favored casino gambling, but he told Robinowitz that he didn't want a casino on every corner. In fact, he wanted only a single, Monte Carlo–style casino. By that, Barthelemy meant that he didn't want the casino attached to a hotel and restaurants, as was done in Las Vegas and Atlantic City. Hotel and restaurant interests also told Robinowitz that they favored a Monte Carlo–style casino. These demands actually meshed well with Robinowitz's emerging plan to put a casino at the Rivergate. He would have loved a Las Vegas–style casino, but more important was having a single casino supported by the mayor and the restaurant and hotel interests. Besides, Robinowitz figured, a monopoly casino would be a gold mine. Not only that, before anyone realized his plans, Robinowitz could buy the surface parking lots on the upriver side of the Rivergate and control prime spots for multistory parking garages worth millions of dollars.

Meanwhile, on the downriver side of the Rivergate stood three connected buildings: the twenty-nine-story Westin Hotel, the thirty-two-story Canal Place office tower, and a three-story shopping center anchored by Brooks Brothers, Saks Fifth Avenue, and a movie theater. Built in 1979, the Canal Place building and the Westin had gone bankrupt, casualties of the Oil Bust. The insurance companies that took over ownership of the two buildings were trying to unload them. Robinowitz figured that he could get a good deal on the entire complex and have the hotel and the restaurants he needed just across Canal Street from the Rivergate. The final step would be to build a covered walkway over Canal Street to connect the Rivergate casino to the Canal Place hotel and restaurants. If the pieces fell into place as planned, Robinowitz stood to make a fortune.

Given his checkered past and lack of money, Robinowitz needed a big-name partner. He spoke with Dan Chandler, son of former Kentucky governor "Happy" Chandler, a Las Vegas casino glad-hander who knew just about everybody. Chandler steered him to Steve Wynn, who had created Las Vegas's splashiest and most profitable casino, the Mirage, visited by an average of 25,000 people per day. Robinowitz flew to Las Vegas. When he entered the atrium leading to the Mirage casino—filled with welcoming tropical plants and flowers—he thought: "This guy is a genius. This is the guy I want to be my partner." When he met with Wynn, who was the Mirage's chairman, Robinowitz sketched his Rivergate casino plan on a yellow pad of paper. The idea intrigued the casino mogul. "Let's go see it," he told Robinowitz. Shortly afterward, in August 1991, they met in New Orleans. Robinowitz showed Wynn several potential sites for the casino. Wynn shook his head. Robinowitz then showed him the Rivergate. Wynn liked the site, but he told Robinowitz he would demolish the Rivergate and the Canal Place complex to build the kind of "must see" attraction that Wynn was known for.

Robinowitz in the meantime had been quietly lining up political support for his plan. Mayor Barthelemy was already on board. Robinowitz had also won over a key New Orleans city councilman named Lambert Boissiere and the president of the State Senate, Sammy Nunez. Helping Robinowitz navigate the political shoals was Eddie Sapir, a boyhood friend who had used his street smarts to win election to the New Orleans City Council years before and was now a municipal judge and investor in Robinowitz's real estate deals. On September 6, Wynn's private jet flew Barthelemy, Boissiere, Nunez, Sapir, and Robinowitz to Las Vegas. There, Wynn wooed them in his own particular style—letting them watch him feed the Mirage's bottlenose dolphins, taking them on a tour of Shadow Creek Country Club, which Wynn had developed, hosting several fancy meals, and giving them a lesson in casino gambling's new era. It was all about entertainment, Wynn said, making the casino itself the attraction. A phone call from boxing promoter Don King interrupted Wynn's lesson. The call turned unpleasant. Wynn shouted at King, who was clearly shouting back, before slamming down the phone. It was a bravura performance and only enhanced the strong impression that Wynn made on his visitors. On the flight back to New Orleans, they agreed that Wynn had the vision to build a spectacular casino for the city.

For Robinowitz, all the pieces were falling into place. He told Wynn that he wanted a fifty-fifty partnership. The Mirage owner laughed and offered him 20 percent and a $1 million yearly development fee instead. Robinowitz accepted. A week later, however, Wynn told Robinowitz that he could not give him a share of the casino, but would pay him $20 million instead. Robinowitz reluctantly accepted. They agreed to sign a contract in about a week.

On the morning of October 2, several days after accepting Wynn's deal, Robinowitz was sitting in his office in Dallas when his friend Eddie Sapir called. Sapir was excited. A developer named Christopher Hemmeter was in New Orleans, and he wanted to do the casino deal. Hemmeter had a private jet and wanted to stop in Dallas on his way back to Los Angeles to discuss the deal with Robinowitz. Sapir started telling Robinowitz about Hemmeter—that he was so rich he was on the Forbes 400 list, that he had built amazing resorts in Hawaii, that he was the nicest, most charming person you could meet. Robinowitz told Sapir that he knew about Hemmeter, that he had attended a hotel industry meeting in New York several years earlier where it was announced that a Hemmeter resort had fetched the highest selling price ever for a hotel. Robinowitz—like other ambitious developers—had written down Hemmeter's name. Nevertheless, Robinowitz told Sapir, he already had a casino deal with Steve Wynn; they were about to sign the formal papers. He told Sapir to tell Hemmeter not to bother stopping in Dallas.

Sapir called back after lunch. "Danny, you just got to meet Chris," he said. "He's the most incredible guy." Robinowitz again demurred, reminding Sapir that not only did he have a deal with Wynn, but that he had sold the three politicians—Barthelemy, Nunez, and Boissiere—on Wynn.

At 3:30 p.m., Sapir called back a third time. He wouldn't take no for an answer. "You've got to meet him," Sapir implored. "He is very rich. He's in the latest issue of *Forbes* magazine, the list of the richest people in America. Even if you don't do this deal with him, you need to know this guy." Robinowitz finally relented. "Fine," he told Sapir, "if he wants to waste the gas, have him come to Dallas."

Chris Hemmeter's plane arrived at about 6:30 p.m., and Robinowitz met him at Love Field. Robinowitz was immediately impressed with Hemmeter's warm and gracious manner, and how when he spoke, his voice was soft and reassuring. Hemmeter displayed an almost Zen-like serenity and made Robinowitz feel as if he were the most important person in the world. Hemmeter told Robinowitz that he was looking for a partner who knew how to build a project, and that Robinowitz had made a name for himself with his impressive work. "Eddie told me about your deal with Steve Wynn," Hemmeter continued. "You have a handshake deal. Not a signed contract. If you do the deal with me, you'll be my partner. If you do it with Steve, you'll just be a pawn. I know Steve. He's a good friend. But you'll just be his servant."

Hemmeter paused and then stepped up his pitch, but his soft voice took the edge off his boasts. He told Robinowitz how his hotels in Hawaii had revolutionized the resort industry. He mentioned that when Jimmy Carter had been dissatisfied with the architect's plans for his presidential library, Hemmeter had offered his own proposal. "The president loved it and used it as the design," Hemmeter said. "President Reagan," he added, "stayed at my home in Hawaii." As a developer himself, Robinowitz realized exactly what Hemmeter was doing—appealing to his own greed. He thought to himself: "I'm the snake, and Chris is playing the flute." But falling under Hemmeter's spell, he didn't mind. "I have one question," Robinowitz said. "Do you have the ability to put $100 million in the bank? The project I have put together costs about $300 million and will require about one-third equity."

"Nobody keeps $100 million in cash," Hemmeter responded, "but I have the assets. I'd have to sell some securities and bonds. I'd need thirty to sixty days. But take a look at the most recent *Forbes* magazine. You'll see how much I'm worth." Hemmeter added: "I want a real partner, somebody who will be like a brother. You'll own 30 percent. I'll pay you $1 million a year. And I'll give you the first two years up front."

Robinowitz was hooked. "Steve Wynn be damned," he thought. "This guy is a godsend. I was about to sign a deal with a guy who had changed the deal at the last minute and who everyone said is a tough guy to do business with—or I can do a deal with the sweetest, kindest guy, the world's best developer."

After dinner, Hemmeter flew back to Los Angeles, but he returned two days later to sign a contract with Robinowitz. Robinowitz broke the news to a Wynn assistant several days later: an infuriated Wynn was now out. Hemmeter was in. And Robinowitz had little idea of what he had gotten himself into.

Christopher Hemmeter was born in 1939 and grew up in Los Altos, a town that would later be in the heart of California's Silicon Valley. His father, George, was a mechanical engineer and inventor. Among his inventions: a device to keep car wheels balanced and a prototype of the newspaper vending box. George Hemmeter's more successful inventions at times made the family quite wealthy. But for various reasons, he would lose the money, so Chris and his brother and sister growing up were frequently "flat broke," as Chris would say later. Hemmeter also described an upbringing that portended his success as an adult. As a ten-year-old, he sold Christmas cards door-to-door, earning $400 in one week, he claimed. He would say he was president of his class from sixth to twelfth grades. What's more, he would add, he graduated from Mountain View High School with an astounding twenty-one letters in athletics—an average of five per year. He made all-conference in three sports: baseball, basketball, and swimming, he said.

But much as he would overembellish his hotels, Hemmeter exaggerated his high school feats. Mountain View High yearbooks show that he was president of his class for only two of his high school years, not the four he claimed. He did play sports, but the yearbooks state that he made varsity for only three sports—swimming, basketball, and baseball—and then only in his senior year. Charlie Cooke, who coached at Mountain View High School and remembered Hemmeter years later, said his onetime pupil didn't earn any letters, much less make all-conference. "Twenty-one [letters] is ridiculous," Cooke said. "That's the first lie he ever told." This was echoed by Hemmeter's best friend in high school, Steve Flynn, who said in the early 1990s, "I can't see how he would have earned 21 letters. I don't think he was all-conference in any sport."

Hemmeter described his rise in business as a Horatio Alger rags-to-riches story. He said when he moved to Hawaii in 1962 after graduating from Cornell University, he was $700 in debt and couldn't afford lodging, so he slept under a boat on the beach. This fanciful story contrasts with news accounts, which show that his father, George, had retired to Hawaii in 1959 with a stash of money to race sailboats, collect royalties, and manage his investments.

Christopher Hemmeter started his career as an executive trainee for a Sheraton Hotel on Oahu. Later he said when he told his boss he was quitting and would one day own hotels like the Sheraton, the boss scoffed at him. In 1964, at age twenty-five, Hemmeter borrowed $10,000 and took over an ailing restaurant called Don the Beachcomber. In early versions of this story, he would admit to borrowing the money with his parents' help; later, he would say he got the money on his own. Whichever version is correct, Hemmeter did turn the restaurant around. The secret to his success, Hemmeter claimed, in a story he frequently told, was that he began serving thicker but smaller cuts of meat at Don the Beachcomber, leading customers to believe they were getting more for their money. Profits soared. He opened other restaurants and was on the way to earning his first million. He moved into real estate, developing a retail shopping complex on Waikiki called King's Alley. In 1976, he moved into the big leagues, demolishing a nineteen-year-old hotel to build the 1,234-room Hyatt Regency Waikiki. To build it, he used his charm to secure a $75 million loan, then the largest construction loan in Hawaiian history. Featuring a waterfall in the lobby, the hotel was smashingly popular with guests. Hemmeter's stock with investors soared. In 1980, he built the Hyatt Regency Maui, which, with its crashing waterfalls, grotto bar, and free-roaming peacocks, instantly became Hyatt's most profitable resort. He followed this six years later with an even bigger hotel, the Westin Maui. The press began calling him Hawaii's "golden boy."

In 1987, Hemmeter demolished another hotel to create his first mega-resort fantasyland, the Westin Kauai. To do so, he met countless times with local officials and residents, who had blocked other developers. They had been expecting the typical confrontational developer, but found to their delight that he agreed to address many of their concerns. In the process, he won them over, which helped later when he didn't fulfill all his promises. Hemmeter sealed public support for the Westin Kauai, for example, by agreeing to establish an outrigger canoe club for local residents. On 580 acres along Kalapaki Beach, the 850-room Westin Kauai featured Hawaii's largest swimming pool—patterned after the pool at Hearst Castle in San Simeon, California—two Jack Nicklaus–designed golf courses, a $2.5 million Oriental and Pacific art collection, a seaside wedding chapel, fourteen elevators—including one inside a 100-foot cliff—and a two-acre reflecting pool with eight life-size marble horses rising in the spray of a 60-foot geyser. Guests could traverse the grounds in Elizabethan-style coaches drawn by Clydesdales or use mahogany launches to explore the forty acres of man-made lagoons, where kangaroos, monkeys, wallabies, and exotic birds populated islands, also man-made, in the lagoons. "The men who built the Acropolis were trying to outdo the pharaohs," Hemmeter told *People* magazine. "There's no reason we can't be building the great structures of the 20th century." *Forbes* estimated his net worth at $225 million.

In 1988, Hemmeter outdid himself with his most lavish resort, the 1,243-room Hyatt Regency Waikoloa. Built for $360 million and carved out of centuries-old lava flow on the big island of Hawaii, the beachfront resort transported guests to their rooms by monorail or canoe. Guests could frolic with trained dolphins ($55 an hour), take jet-airplane tours ($900 an hour), or lounge around a huge swimming pool featuring jacuzzis and artificial waterfalls. "We're not in the hotel business," Hemmeter told an interviewer. "We build experiences, not buildings." *The New York Times,* in an adoring piece, said he built the most "mind-boggling" resorts in the world. Following the Waikoloa opening, Hemmeter said he had seventeen more mega-resorts on the drawing board around the world. These luxury resorts, Hemmeter maintained, were the wave of the future.

The mega-resort age proved to be short-lived, however. The huge complexes were simply too expensive. To begin with, the resorts required battalions of employees. Just manicuring the Westin Kauai's grounds cost $100,000 a month, and it cost another $200,000 to feed, breed, and stable the Clydesdales. Occupancy rates were not the 85 percent that Hemmeter predicted but closer to 50 percent, which forced down room rates. What's more, the touches that Hemmeter imported from elsewhere didn't take root. The exotic animals died or swam away at the Westin Kauai. At the Waikoloa, many of the dolphins perished from contact with humans, and the man-made beach kept washing away. Both the Westin Kauai and the Waikoloa had trouble earning enough money to meet debt payments, much less earn profits. Financing for Hemmeter's other projects dried up. Meanwhile, his proposal to spend $1.3 billion to redevelop Honolulu's waterfront was rejected in favor of a more modest proposal. Angry and bitter, Hemmeter left Hawaii and resettled in Bel Air, California, where he spent $16 million buying two adjacent houses that he planned to merge into one. By now, Hemmeter had concluded that he could build mega-projects only by attaching them to casinos. He tried to buy the Dunes casino in Las Vegas in 1991, but couldn't raise the money. He did open casinos in the onetime mining towns of Central City and Black Hawk just outside of Denver. By law, the casinos were limited in size, but Hemmeter's won notice as the most lavish. Still pursuing his dream to build big and remake his fortune, Hemmeter in October 1991 discovered Danny Robinowitz and joined forces to construct a huge casino in New Orleans.

Having dropped Steve Wynn in favor of Chris Hemmeter, Robinowitz now had to get his political allies to change their allegiance, too. He called Mayor Barthelemy, Councilman Boissiere, and Senator Nunez and told them about Hemmeter: how he was the world's greatest developer, how he was fabulously wealthy, how he shared Robinowitz's vision for a New Orleans casino. On October 9, a week after his initial meeting with Robinowitz in Dallas, Hemmeter and his wife, Patsy, had lunch with Barthelemy and Boissiere at Antoine's, one of the city's grand French Quarter restaurants. Barthelemy and Boissiere instantly liked Hemmeter's soft sell, the way he talked not about making money, but about helping the community. He was so different from other developers they had met. Barthelemy and Boissiere enthusiastically accepted Hemmeter as Robinowitz's partner.

That afternoon, Robinowitz arranged for Hemmeter to meet with Steve Rittvo, New Orleans's premier urban planner. They decided to meet at the top of the World Trade Center, a thirty-three-story office tower situated between the Rivergate and the Mississippi River. From the bird's-eye view, Rittvo was to describe the various riverfront properties, many of which, providentially, were for sale. When Rittvo got off the elevator, he was struck by the sight of an impeccably dressed, well-coiffed, well-tanned man looking out the window. It was Hemmeter, and he exuded confidence. When Robinowitz introduced the two, Hemmeter impressed Rittvo as the warmest and friendliest person he had ever met. Rittvo instantly felt as if he had known Hemmeter for years. Hemmeter also impressed Rittvo by showing that he knew a great deal about Rittvo and his design firm. As Rittvo described the different riverfront properties below, Hemmeter showed that he had already begun envisioning what he might do. Hemmeter suggested a magnificent redevelopment of Jax Brewery, which was now a three-story shopping and restaurant complex in the French Quarter. He talked about closing historic Canal Street to link it with Woldenberg Park on the river. Rittvo responded by questioning whether Hemmeter could win approval to make wholesale changes of the city's most sensitive property. "As we work together," Hemmeter replied with a tight smile, "let's not be constrained by what other people can't do." Rittvo was skeptical, but couldn't help being swept up by Hemmeter's enthusiasm. Back in his office, he told his staff, "Either this is the biggest scam or I was in the presence of one of the greatest urban developers in America."

Robinowitz and Hemmeter decided they needed to duplicate the Mirage trip, only this time visiting Hemmeter's Hawaiian resorts. On

October 19, Barthelemy, Boissiere, Nunez, Sapir, and mayoral assistant Wayne Collier secretly flew to Hawaii. At Hemmeter's insistence, they brought their wives. Hemmeter picked up all the costs and treated them like visiting royalty. In their hotel room each night, they found bottles of wine, fruit baskets, and floral bouquets. The group spent the first night at the Westin Kauai. Hemmeter gave them a tour in a Clydesdale-drawn carriage. They took a mahogany launch to one of the hotel's restaurants. Like the others, Boissiere, a funeral home owner serving his second term on the city council, knew nothing of the hotel's problems. He was simply overwhelmed by the sights. He felt thrilled that Hemmeter wanted to come to New Orleans and make it the Queen City of the South again. Boissiere felt sure that Hemmeter could pull it off. "This guy could be the savior of New Orleans," he thought to himself.

The group spent the next night at the Waikoloa. Riding in a carriage drawn by four white horses, they passed the seaside wedding chapel. With the sun setting over the Pacific Ocean, Barthelemy turned to his wife and murmured, "I'd like to get married to you again here."

On their third day, the group toured Honolulu. They visited Governor John Waihee, who roundly praised Hemmeter, and they saw an office building that Hemmeter had restored. That night, Hemmeter hosted them at a home he had built at Black Point overlooking the ocean. Of course, it wasn't any ordinary home. With 29,835 square feet of living space, it had cost $43 million and featured marble floors throughout, Italian tile ceilings, and an oceanfront balcony that stretched longer than a football field. One bathroom had two of what Hemmeter said were the world's oldest Tiffany lamps, costing $500,000 apiece. The master bedroom alone was 5,000 square feet—making it bigger than most homes— and had a sitting room, a breakfast area, an exercise room, a jacuzzi, and a steam bath. Patsy had a series of Imelda Marcos–like closets, each one as big as a conference room. Ironically, since leaving Hawaii in 1990, Hemmeter rarely stayed there.

A limousine ferried each of the New Orleans guests to the home. At the top of the stairway leading into the bronze-cast front door, a photographer snapped a picture of each visitor. (By the end of the night, each guest would have a framed copy of the photo.) During dinner, a string quartet played classical music. Afterward, Hemmeter said he had a surprise for everyone. He led them to the game room downstairs. As they entered, a Dixieland band began playing "When the Saints Go Marching In." With a whoop, the New Orleanians pulled out white handkerchiefs and second-lined around the room. It was the perfect final touch. Barthelemy turned to aide Wayne Collier and said, "Even though I'm mayor of New Orleans, I never envisioned I would be in a place like this with the person who has built so much beauty."

While the New Orleans contingent basked in Hemmeter's Hawaiian paradise—the resorts' problems were not yet known publicly—an important political development unfolded in Louisiana. In the gubernatorial primary, Governor Buddy Roemer finished third and out of the money behind Edwin Edwards and David Duke. This meant that Roemer, the good-government politician who opposed the land casino, would leave office in January. It also meant that Edwards would almost certainly defeat Duke and become the next governor. Suddenly, Robinowitz's casino dream had become very real.

By early 1992, Hemmeter's plans were taking shape. He had adopted Robinowitz's proposal to build a casino on the Rivergate site with parking garages on the two upriver lots. But this wasn't grand enough for Hemmeter. By February he was sketching a plan that extended downriver four blocks into the French Quarter. It called for the building of a riverboat casino complex stretching from Toulouse Street upriver to Iberville Street along the riverfront. Hemmeter would construct a half-block-wide bayou for a riverboat casino that would make short jaunts up and down the fake waterway on tracks. On both sides of the bayou, he would build fake plantation houses. The complex would be three stories high; on the first two floors, Hemmeter would provide parking and retail stores. When Hemmeter showed the plan to Steven Bingler, a New Orleans architect he had hired, Bingler was incredulous. "Why would you want to create a fake river and fake plantations right next to the real river and just down the river from real plantations?" Bingler asked. "Wouldn't it make more sense to do something compatible with the French Quarter?" Bingler added that Hemmeter could not possibly win approval to carry out his project. The developer eventually agreed and quietly dropped the plan, but unhappy that Bingler didn't share his vision, he fired the architect a couple of months later.

Hemmeter and Robinowitz by now were beginning to attract press attention. On February 24, the *New Orleans City Business,* a weekly newspaper, headlined a story on them: JUST WHAT ARE THESE GUYS UP TO? The story noted that they had optioned or purchased several riverfront properties. "We want to create the most incredible mixed-use riverfront development in the world," Robinowitz told the newspaper, deliberately downplaying their interest in a casino. "Gaming is not our primary interest. It simply provides the impetus and the financial ability to create a mixed-use development in which gaming is a part, but only a part, and probably not the biggest part." The newspaper quoted a Hawaii real estate expert comparing Hemmeter to the late Walt Disney and wrote that "Hemmeter could be sitting on as much as $500 million in cash."

Operating from a suite in the Windsor Court, the city's most elegant hotel, Hemmeter adopted a textbook strategy for seducing the disparate interest groups that control New Orleans politics. This was an especially delicate task in an insular city that traditionally resisted outsiders. Complicating his job, a poll showed that only 31 percent of New Orleanians favored a single casino, and several business groups came out against the idea. Influential opponents like the Brennan restaurant family were arguing that a casino would wreck New Orleans's unique culture.

With advice from Robinowitz, Hemmeter began by hiring well-connected lawyers, architects, and political advisers. The most prominent among them were Eddie Sapir and Billy Broadhurst, a longtime Edwin Edwards confidant and influential power broker. As he had done with Barthelemy and Boissiere, Hemmeter also courted powerful politicians and businessmen at intimate dinners at the toniest restaurants in town. The city's financial woes made the power brokers susceptible to Hemmeter's inducements. With little extra money available in recent years, they had had few opportunities to snare patronage jobs and government contracts.

If that wasn't reason enough, few could resist Hemmeter's charm. He was always brimming with a contagious enthusiasm and praising New Orleans at every turn. His wife, Patsy, who reminded some of Grace Kelly, reeked of poise and money with her flawless skin, finely tailored clothes, and perfectly coiffed blond hair done up in a bun. At the small gatherings, Hemmeter solicited the views of his guests, listened closely to their comments, and promised to be sensitive to their concerns. When he met with French Quarter residents, for example, he stressed his interest in preservation. (They were unaware of his fake bayou/plantation plan, which they would have denounced.) To expand his political base, Hemmeter also secretly flew Governor Edwards on his plane to Aspen for a weekend of skiing and fine dining. Edwards thought that Hemmeter was an astute businessman with plenty of personality. Showing their adaptability to Louisiana fashion, Hemmeter and Robinowitz also showered gifts on lawmakers, sending nearly $500 in baby clothes to powerful state representative Sherman Copelin after the birth of his son, picking up the hotel tab of city councilmen staying at Caesars Palace in Las Vegas, and buying $200 cashmere sweaters apiece for Mayor Barthelemy and the councilmen. In all, Hemmeter and Robinowitz spent $70,000 on hotel bills, the sweaters, fruit baskets, and the like, and contributed $155,000 to the Louisiana Democratic Party.

Hemmeter took particular care to woo Ron Forman, the president of the Audubon Institute, which operated the city's zoo and aquarium. Hemmeter needed Forman for two reasons. First, Uptown whites, who still held economic power even as New Orleans became a majority African-American city, adored Forman, for renovating the zoo and building the aquarium. Second, Forman's aquarium was next to the Rivergate, which would give him some influence over any casino development. Hemmeter's charm worked on Forman, who was soon escorting Hemmeter around town to meet with various groups that respected Forman. On March 11, Forman hosted a coming-out party for Hemmeter at the aquarium, attended by influential businessmen and politicians. Afterward, Hemmeter dined with Barthelemy; John Alario, speaker of the Louisiana House; and Sammy Nunez, president of the

State Senate. Hemmeter had clearly made deep inroads into Louisiana's political and social circles.

One person who resisted Hemmeter's charms was Peggy Wilson, a gadfly member of the New Orleans City Council and a leading casino opponent. Wilson spurned an invitation to dinner at the Windsor Court with other City Council members. Hemmeter didn't give up. He arranged to visit her two weeks later at City Hall. After introductions, Hemmeter started in on his soft sell. Wilson wasn't buying. She interrupted to ask who he was hiring. When he named them, she replied, "Those are all the political hacks, the people who get all the political jobs." Hemmeter tried to find common ground, telling her that he, like Wilson, was a Republican. Hemmeter added that he knew Wilson appreciated good architecture. Well, he wanted to transform the Rivergate into a signature building like the Sydney Opera House or the National Gallery of Art in Washington. "I want to do something unique for New Orleans," he said.

"Mr. Hemmeter, New Orleans already is unique," Wilson replied. She added, "Look, Mr. Hemmeter, I've heard all about you. Have you ever seen the musical,'The Music Man'? You remind me of that guy. You remind me of a flim-flam man." Hemmeter remained calm, but inside he was seething. When the meeting ended, he smiled and thanked Wilson for the visit. When he stopped in Councilman Boissiere's office later, he complained, "I've never been treated that way by a public official." Back in the car, Hemmeter cursed Wilson, telling Robinowitz that she was a "bitch."

By early April, three major developments had occurred that would influence events to come. First, the city had secured ownership of the Rivergate site in a complicated land swap with the Audubon Institute and the Port of New Orleans. This meant that if the state legislature legalized a single casino at the Rivergate, the city would decide which company would lease the property. Second, Mayor Barthelemy had decided that he alone would make that selection—even though hundreds of millions of dollars would be at stake. The third development was that the city decided it would send out a request for proposals to allow anyone to bid for the right to lease the Rivergate site. Barthelemy said he hoped for ten bidders. Hemmeter obviously would be one of them. Barthelemy said New Orleans had to move quickly. Three casino companies—Caesars, Hilton, and Circus Circus—were proposing to build a huge gambling complex in Chicago, complete with a theme park, retail shops, and perhaps even a sports arena. Urban casinos, Barthelemy said, were the wave of the future.

Sidney Barthelemy was serving his second term as mayor, having first been elected in 1986. After graduating from St. Augustine, the city's elite Catholic high school for African-American boys, Barthelemy had aspirations to attend the seminary. Instead, he became a social worker and got interested in politics. In 1978, he was elected to the Louisiana Senate, the first black elected to that chamber since Reconstruction. In 1982, he won election to the New Orleans City Council.

Barthelemy, with his light skin, was a Creole, the dominant ethnic group in the black community. In the complex New Orleans world of racial politics, this gave him a large advantage over a darker candidate. In the 1986 mayoral election, Barthelemy triumphed in part because he was darker than the white candidate (thus attracting black votes and enough crossover whites) and lighter than the darker candidate (who appealed almost exclusively to black voters).

Shortly after Barthelemy took office, the Oil Bust hit and he was forced to lay off hundreds of city workers and eliminate popular government programs. With an economic recovery nowhere in sight, he endorsed a Monte Carlo–style casino as New Orleans's economic salvation. Tall and easygoing, he came to be known as the "gentle giant" and managed to successfully navigate his first four years. In 1990, Barthelemy, forty-eight years old, won reelection as mayor of New Orleans, even though he was widely derided as ineffectual and indecisive.

When Edwin Edwards took office in January 1992, Barthelemy was still advocating a small, European-style casino for New Orleans. Without an attached hotel or restaurants, the casino would fit snugly among the city's existing tourist attractions, he said. Barthelemy also suggested limiting the casino's operation to nighttime hours and requiring some sort of dress code. Hemmeter, however, was moving far beyond Barthelemy's vision, although he had conceded he could not build his

French Quarter riverboat casino fantasyland. By mid-April, Hemmeter was planning a Rivergate casino project that would be far bigger than Barthelemy's small casino and far grander than the one that Robinowitz had originally envisioned. Hemmeter began hosting small parties where he gave a slide show of his plans. His goal was to lock up the support of influential businessmen and politicians before other casino companies could even devise their proposals.

Hemmeter's biggest obstacle was turning out to be *The Times-Picayune*, New Orleans's daily newspaper. On April 16, the newspaper disclosed the secret trip to Hawaii in October by Barthelemy, Nunez, Boissiere, Sapir, and Collier. Three days later, the paper described in detail how Hemmeter was courting the city's power brokers. The following month, the paper broke the news that Hemmeter's Hawaiian resorts were lavish flops, and that he was unable to secure financing for any of his other projects around the world. "Chris is an absolute classic, smooth, handsome promoter," one hotel analyst who had known Hemmeter for years told *The Times-Picayune*. "He is very glib, very polished, is superb with politicians and is a great schmoozer. But all the glitter does not turn into gold with him." Hemmeter fumed at the newspaper's coverage, the first negative press he had received in his career. He said the newspaper was biased against him, pointing to its editorials against gambling, and he explored the possibility of starting a competitor to put *The Times-Picayune* out of business.

While battling the newspaper, Hemmeter was putting the final touches on his plan. On April 28, he unveiled it publicly. The grand event occurred at Jax Brewery, the onetime brewery in the French Quarter that had been turned into a festival marketplace of shops and restaurants. Some twenty reporters, ten television cameramen, and two hundred powerful businessmen and politicians gathered there. The room buzzed with anticipation. Hemmeter began confidently, speaking without notes and looking resplendent in a gray suit, blue shirt, purple handkerchief, and gold cuff links. With his contagious enthusiasm, he quickly outlined his plan, using a pointer to describe the architectural drawings behind him on a row of easels. Hemmeter said he was planning a $1 billion development that would create 7,800 jobs and reconfigure the fabled New Orleans waterfront. The ambition behind the plan was breathtaking by any measure. At $1 billion, it would be the most expensive development ever undertaken in the city, and the project's 7,800 jobs would make Hemmeter the state's single largest private employer. The developer promised that his plan would attract nine million new tourists a year to New Orleans and produce $250 million a year in new taxes. That would be enough to eliminate the budget deficits of New Orleans and the state of Louisiana.

The project's crown jewel would be a huge $400 million casino that Hemmeter called the Grand Palais. It wouldn't be just any casino, Hemmeter assured the audience. It would feature a soaring 100-foot rotunda, classical columns, and two grand halls on the first floor that he promised would rival Versailles's Hall of Mirrors in size and splendor. It would be, Hemmeter rhapsodized, "one of the great interior spaces of the world," comparable to Sydney's Opera House. The Grand Palais would have 250,000 square feet of gambling space, making it the world's largest casino. By comparison, the largest casinos at the time were the Taj Mahal in Atlantic City and the Mirage in Las Vegas, each measuring about 125,000 square feet. Although much bigger, the Grand Palais would have no hotel or restaurants, Hemmeter said. He was following the plan devised by his partner, Daniel Robinowitz, to avoid antagonizing local interests by including lodging and places to eat that would compete with existing establishments.

Hemmeter was proposing to build far more than just the Grand Palais. His development also called for a family-style arcade he called the Petit Palais; a 2,500-seat replica of the New Orleans Opera House, which had burned down in 1919, to be known as the Palais de L'Opéra; a Museum for the History of Music in America; two huge parking garages; a nineteenth-century horse-drawn trolley; a ten-acre riverfront park featuring a dramatic fountain "comparable to some of the great fountains in Rome, Paris and London"; an artisans' colony; and two ten-story arches with flanking colonnades and monuments to Thomas Jefferson and Napoleon at the foot of Canal Street, symbolizing the Louisiana Purchase. With the ten-story arches, Hemmeter said, Canal Street would come to rival the Champs Elysées.

There was more. Four blocks upriver from the Rivergate, Hemmeter would construct what he called the Cotton Club Riverboat Terminal. Inspired by the world's largest cotton press, once located on the New Orleans riverfront, the terminal would house four riverboat casinos and two cruise ships.

Altogether, Hemmeter said, "the project will position New Orleans to once again reclaim the title of 'Paris of the Americas,' restoring an important part of the city's nineteenth-century grandeur and speeding its development as a world class, international tourist destination."

New Orleans city councilman Lambert Boissiere could hardly contain his excitement as he watched Hemmeter describe the development. "It looks like the Paris of America," Boissiere said to himself. "That's a helluva dream—make New Orleans the Paris of America. He's outdone himself this time."

When Hemmeter was finished, the politicians and businessmen in attendance gushed over the plan and rushed up to pump his hand and slip him their business cards. Hemmeter beamed and murmured his thanks.

The Times-Picayune devoted much of its front page the following day to Hemmeter's plan. HEMMETER SHOWS HIS HAND, the newspaper headlined the story. Among those reading the coverage that morning was Wendell Gauthier (*Goat-shay*), a forty-nine-year-old powerhouse trial lawyer with a folksy manner, a tendency to mispronounce words, and an ever-ready smile that made him look like the Flintstones' Barney Rubble. Legal and political opponents frequently made the mistake of thinking he was a country bumpkin. Gauthier grew up dirt-poor on a small farm in Iota, a close-knit community in Cajun country. As a boy, he milked the family's cows every day. Gauthier lived across the street from the schoolhouse, so when the cows got loose, they would wander onto school property, and Gauthier would be summoned to walk them home. At the University of Southwestern Louisiana, Gauthier and his wife cared for the school mascot, a bulldog, to help pay for room and board. After graduating, Gauthier came to New Orleans, where he put himself through law school at night while operating a driver's education school during the day. He continued to run the driver's ed school during his first several years as a lawyer because he needed the extra money.

His first real break came in 1973 when he was approached by a friend whose family had been burned in their home after a faulty underground natural gas line exploded. Gauthier won $1 million, a major verdict at the time. He graduated to bigger and bigger cases in which defective products had killed or maimed innocent people. Another break came in 1982 when a Pan Am jet crashed in the New Orleans suburb of Kenner, killing more than 150 people. Gauthier by now had branched out into political deal making, and his friend, the mayor, recommended him to victims' families. He ended up representing sixty-two claimants and won big awards for them. Gauthier—or "Goat" as he was known to friends—was not only cunning, but his aw-shucks, down-home manner made him a favorite with juries.

In time, Gauthier went national. He became involved in large class-action lawsuits like the 1980 MGM Grand Hotel fire that killed eighty-five people in Las Vegas (the case was settled for $208 million) and the Dupont Plaza fire in San Juan, Puerto Rico (a $230 million settlement). A strong organizer and leader who knew how to soothe volatile egos, he typically headed the committee of high-powered lawyers that mapped strategy and negotiated with the corporation being sued. Coming from virtually nothing, Gauthier by 1992 was one of the country's most successful trial lawyers, owned a small share of the New Orleans Saints football team, had influence with numerous local politicians and judges, lived in a mansion in the New Orleans suburb of Metairie, and drove a Rolls-Royce.

As he read of Hemmeter's grand plan on April 29, Gauthier shook his head and frowned. He thought the plan was ridiculous, particularly the proposal for the Palais de L'Opéra in a city that couldn't support the opera. "This guy's out of touch with the needs of this community," Gauthier said to himself. He noted with suspicion that Hemmeter had not explained how he would finance the $1 billion price tag. "Why should we give an exclusive license to an out-of-town person?" he wondered. A plan began to take shape in Gauthier's mind. He would gather together a team of Louisiana businessmen and trial lawyers, and they would offer a competing bid. None of them had casino experience, but they all had political clout with either Governor Edwards or Mayor Barthelemy. Gauthier's father, for example, had been friends with Edwards from the time Edwards got his political start in Crowley in the 1950s. Another member of the group, racehorse owner Louie Roussel III, was currently the single largest political donor in Louisiana. Roussel's father had been an even bigger one, contributing $625,000 to Edwards's 1987 gubernatorial campaign. Another member of the group, Michael St. Martin, a trial lawyer from Houma, was among the small group of people who had a standing offer to visit Edwards at the Governor's Mansion whenever they wished. Gauthier also included two African-American businessmen in the ten-member group, something that Hemmeter conspicuously lacked in a city with a majority African-American population.

The group met on the first Saturday in May 1992 in a mock courtroom at Gauthier's law office. Gauthier outlined a plan. They would call themselves Jazzville. They would renovate the Rivergate, which would make their proposal much less expensive than Hemmeter's. Renovating the building also meant that they could open the casino in a year, compared with three years for Hemmeter. Taxes could begin flowing earlier to the cash-starved government. Gauthier also proposed having several casino companies operate different sections of the renovated building. Hemmeter had a huge advantage, Gauthier conceded, but they were the local boys. "We can't let this go to someone else," Gauthier cried out. "Let's join the battle. We will win, we're Louisianians."

As John Cummings, a New Orleans trial lawyer who was also part of Jazzville, put it later: "The people in that room expressed the thought that New Orleans was a Third World country that had been invaded by the economic interests of outsiders. If we were to be denied, then the people who we grew up with would have to look us in the eye and give it to King Kamehameha."

On June 11, the state legislature ended months of debate by legalizing the New Orleans casino.

On June 24, Hemmeter raised the bar for his competitors. He announced that he had teamed up with Caesars World, a premier Las

Vegas casino operator known for its glitz. Caesars officials had been studying whether to bid on their own, but had concluded that Hemmeter had too much of a head start. So when Hemmeter approached the officials about joining forces, Caesars agreed to manage the casino for a share of the proceeds but not put up any money. Hemmeter would be the developer and would secure the financing. The choice of Caesars was significant because it was Governor Edwards's favorite place to gamble. And by teaming up with Caesars, Hemmeter brought aboard Hank Braden IV, an attorney and former state senator who was a political consultant for Caesars. Braden was so close to Barthelemy that until the news broke that he had signed up with Caesars, he frequently conducted his private business in the mayor's suite of offices. With Caesars, Hemmeter also brought aboard two men close to Edwards: Bob d'Hemecourt, a trusted friend and political adviser, and George Nattin, a Louisiana native and Caesars executive who had always taken care of Edwards's needs in Las Vegas. The Hemmeter/Caesars partnership instantly became the prohibitive favorite. "That's it, the winner is Hemmeter/Caesars," said Michael Gaughan, owner of two small Las Vegas casino-hotels, in a widely shared response.

News of the pairing with Caesars was not entirely positive for Hemmeter. *The Times-Picayune,* continuing its aggressive coverage, pointedly noted that just a month earlier, Hemmeter had made "an absolute guarantee" that he would not join forces with Las Vegas casino operators, whom he labeled tasteless and greedy. "To have a Las Vegas influence and a relationship between New Orleans and Las Vegas is not good for New Orleans," Hemmeter had said. The newspaper, in an editorial a day later, slammed him for breaking his "absolute guarantee."

A news story the next day provided further ammunition to casino critics. It reported that Hemmeter had quietly scaled back his $1 billion proposal (to $572 million) so that it consisted now of the Grand Palais, the two parking garages, the Petit Palais arcade, and the Jefferson and Napoleon arches. Critics labeled the original April 28 plan a bait-and-switch trick to sell the public on the benefits of casino gambling. Hemmeter scaled back his plan, they noted, two weeks after the state legislature in Baton Rouge had voted to legalize the New Orleans casino.

Even though Hemmeter and Caesars had the inside track, other casino companies couldn't resist bidding for the right to lease the Rivergate site from the city to develop the casino. Everyone saw a New Orleans casino as a "can't miss" proposition. In the final-round deadline of September 16, there were three bidders besides the Hemmeter/Caesars team. One bidder consisted of Jazzville and its operator, Showboat, a second-tier gambling company with casinos in Las Vegas and Atlantic City. As with Wendell Gauthier's original idea, Jazzville was proposing to renovate the Rivergate in stages to ultimately build a 250,000-square-foot casino. The project would cost $198 million and create 10,400 casino jobs, and Jazzville officials predicted the casino win—the revenue after paying winning gamblers—would be $950 million per year when fully operational. Jazzville officials did not explain how they would finance the project.

A second bidder was Casino Orleans. This was a joint venture of Carnival Cruise Lines, three Louisiana businessmen, and Casinos Austria, which operated in Europe. Casino Orleans proposed to demolish the Rivergate and build a casino topped by a park and a pyramid. The project would cost $225 million and be financed mostly with junk bonds. It would create a 218,000-square-foot casino and 4,102 casino jobs. Casino Orleans projected a casino win of $580 million per year.

A third bidder consisted of two industry heavyweights, Mirage and Harrah's. Each had bid separately in the initial round in June. But Louisiana politics had come to disgust officials from both companies, so neither was willing to invest the time and money to bid separately for the final round in September. They named their joint project Casino Royale, and it called for bulldozing the Rivergate and building an ornate round casino of 120,000 square feet. It would be the smallest casino of those proposed but the second most expensive, with a $400 million price tag. The two companies projected a casino win of $500 million to $600 million a year and the creation of 6,400 casino jobs. Each company would put up $100 million in financing and borrow the remaining $200 million.

The fourth bidder was Hemmeter/Caesars. They were proposing to demolish the Rivergate to build the Grand Palais. It would have 200,000 square feet of gambling space and create 5,250 casino jobs.

Hemmeter projected a casino-win figure of $680 million a year, down from $1.2 billion when he originally unveiled his plan on April 28. The project was now less expensive because Hemmeter had eliminated all of the extra buildings, monuments, and parks that had dazzled the public earlier. He had added one feature: a sound-and-light show and lagoon that he would build on a two-block stretch of Canal Street fronting the Grand Palais. This proposal alarmed preservationists, who decried tearing up one of the city's most historic streets.

With the final bids in, Mayor Barthelemy announced that he would choose the winner on November 5. During the six weeks leading up to that date, a team of consultants hired by the city analyzed the four bids. The bidders, meanwhile, argued their case through the media and at a public forum on October 14. On October 25, *The Times-Picayune* weighed in with its own independent analysis. The newspaper hired two University of Nevada gambling experts—Bill Thompson, a professor of public administration, and John Mills, a professor of accounting—to evaluate the four bids. Thompson and Mills analyzed the bidders' ability to finance the project, the accuracy of their revenue and expense projections, whether they could meet hiring promises, the experience of the management team, their plans for parking. Their verdict: the Mirage/Harrah's proposal came out on top, followed by Hemmeter/Caesars, Casino Orleans, and lastly, Jazzville.

The newspaper's consultants said each of the four bidders underestimated expenses and thus overstated profits. Thompson and Mills rated Mirage/Harrah's the highest because of their strong records, especially with Mirage operating the world's most profitable casino in Las Vegas. The consultants liked Hemmeter's casino design and partnership with Caesars, but they noted that he had never built a casino, and they questioned his ability to secure financing.

The final decision would rest with Barthelemy. He scheduled a press conference for 3:00 p.m. on November 5, 1992, at City Hall. The day before, he shared his selection with Ron Nabonne, his closest adviser, and asked him to draft a speech. Two hours before the announcement, Barthelemy disclosed his choice to Wayne Collier, his top casino adviser, and a small number of other aides, but he asked them to keep it secret. Promptly at 3:00 p.m., Barthelemy, visibly nervous, stepped before a microphone facing a large group of reporters and interested observers. His wife, aides, and members of the New Orleans City Council stood behind him. Barthelemy began by saying he was making "the most significant announcement in this city's history." Barthelemy recapped the bid process and reiterated the casino's promised benefits. Then he announced the winner: Hemmeter/Caesars.

Listening to Barthelemy's announcement on a live radio broadcast at their office, Hemmeter, Robinowitz, and their advisers let out a whoop and began hugging and high-fiving each other. Jazzville officials, gathered at Gauthier's office in Metairie, swore at Barthelemy. One Jazzville investor, car dealer Ronnie Lamarque, said Hemmeter was nothing more than a used-car dealer. At the Mirage in Las Vegas and at Harrah's headquarters in Memphis, company officials asked themselves why they had gone ahead when they believed Hemmeter/Caesars had it sewn up. Speaking to the reporters, however, Barthelemy insisted he had evaluated each of the bidders on the merits, and had chosen Hemmeter/Caesars because they offered the best proposal. "We have a team of a world-class developer and a world-class operator," Barthelemy said.

That evening Hemmeter hosted a party at the Aquarium of the Americas, across Canal Street from the Rivergate. The champagne flowed as politicians and businessmen mingled with the developer. They told him that with this casino deal, he was set for life.

At the Governor's Mansion, however, this was not a foregone conclusion. In Baton Rouge the next day, Governor Edwards called his chief legal adviser, Al Donovan, to ask a question. Edwards had been unhappy that Barthelemy insisted on selecting the casino's developer before the state gambling board, which the governor had just appointed, had awarded the license needed to operate the casino. Edwards felt as if the tail were wagging the dog. "Al," Edwards asked, "what happens if the casino board selects someone other than Hemmeter/Caesars?" Donovan didn't know the answer.

4

An August Surprise

As 1993 began, many people were coming to the realization that Christopher Hemmeter had won only a partial victory when New Orleans mayor Sidney Barthelemy had selected him two months earlier to develop the land casino. At the time of the selection, winning Barthelemy's nod had seemed all that mattered. Now many people were pointing out that a state board appointed by Governor Edwin Edwards would award the operating license. In theory, it was possible that the board could select someone other than Hemmeter and his management partner, Caesars World. There was a problem with this theory: at the beginning of 1993, Hemmeter was so powerful politically that it seemed as if he and Caesars would win the state operating license by default.

Hemmeter still faced challenges, however. Many New Orleanians remained upset with how pro-gambling lawmakers and Edwards had rammed the casino through the legislature without giving them a vote. Hemmeter's casino design rankled others. He was still planning to build the world's largest casino, the Grand Palais. But where Hemmeter had originally said the casino was only part of a larger development project to benefit New Orleans, it was now clearly *the* project, since he had sliced away virtually all of the other pieces and in the process reduced the original $1 billion price tag to $490 million.

Hemmeter's Grand Palais would still be capped by a classical-style rotunda a hundred feet high and would feature many grandiose theme park–like touches that dismayed traditional New Orleanians. But he had changed elements outside the casino. Hemmeter now proposed to tear up two blocks of historic Canal Street to build a lagoon with a sound-and-light show. "Fountains, choreographed to music, will appear to dance as jets of water are transformed through a spectrum of color," said a description of the proposal. "Huge water cannons will send a fan-shaped screen of mist 50 feet into the sky, 100 feet wide, upon which shimmering images will come alive, through a sophisticated projection technology. Imagine jazz musicians and dancers, 50 feet high, enter-taining the audience with the music and imagery of New Orleans." Hemmeter said the show would function as a high-tech billboard. "The enormous popularity [of the laser show] will draw thousands to the casino lawn," the proposal said, "including many who might not have come to the Grand Palais otherwise. Once in the area, they will naturally gravitate to the [casino] to explore further entertainment pos-sibilities inside."

Those who gravitated inside would stroll on "The Big Easy Boule-vard" or "The Marching Saints Boulevard" to get to the slot machines and blackjack tables. Or they could take a boat ride—similar to Dis-ney's Pirates of the Caribbean—through the casino's interior, which would take up a full city block. Along the way, they would see a mish-mash of amusement park scenes. The boat ride would start with a "shark attack," followed by "bayou country" with a "swamp, snakes and marshes." Next came a "great rainforest," and a jaunt by a "shanty town." A tour of "Gator Alley" led to an attack by "pirates," followed by a welcome to a "southern mansion," capped by a "Louis Armstrong jazz extravaganza." The boat ride would conclude, bizarrely, with a "Venice street scene."

To many New Orleanians, the problem wasn't so much that Hemme-ter wanted to build a casino. They noted, after all, that New Orleans had a long tradition of gambling, and they didn't mind the city's red-light reputation. What they objected to was Hemmeter's imported brand of sin. George Schmidt, a bandleader, summed up that view in an interview with National Public Radio. "It's his immorality, it ain't our immorality," Schmidt said. "Now he's trying to tell us what we are supposed to be, you see. And we don't want to be that way, I can assure you. This city is suddenly going to be turned into . . . a gambling theme park, and we don't fall for that kind . . . of Disneyland crap down here." In late February, nine neighborhood groups called on Hemmeter to redesign the Grand Palais to conform more with New Orleans style and asked him to scrap the sound-and-light show. That same day, a group of local architects also criticized Hemmeter's plan.

Ever politically sensitive, Hemmeter mobilized a counteroffensive. He helped form "The Committee for 25,000 Jobs," stocked with labor leaders and builders, to rally the public. The group promised that the casino would create 20,200 permanent jobs and 6,500 temporary construction jobs. Hemmeter also wooed mayoral appointees like Allison Randolph III, who served on the city board that had to approve Hemmeter's plans. While others asked why fake New Orleans scenes should be built inside the casino when tourists could visit the real sites outside, Randolph offered the preposterous theory that Hemmeter's plan would encourage visitors "to look at the real thing." Hemmeter got Barthelemy and City Council members to rush his proposal through the planning process. The elected officials were all too happy to comply. They had decided to balance the city's budget with an anticipated $15 million one-time payment from Hemmeter. They dismissed critics who said that using one-time money for annual budget needs violated Public Finance 101.

Under Hemmeter's spell, Barthelemy and the City Council acceded to his demand that they sign a lease giving him control of the Rivergate site, even if he didn't get the state license to operate the casino. Governor Edwards, among others, told Barthelemy that he was making a serious mistake, that while Hemmeter was certainly the front-runner, the lease should contain a provision making it null and void if Hemmeter didn't get the state license. "What have you got to lose?" Edwards asked the mayor. But Barthelemy didn't trust the governor and wanted to tie the city's fortunes to Hemmeter's. It would prove to be a fatal mistake.

Forbes magazine, meanwhile, was joining *The Times-Picayune* in offering a skeptical assessment. In March 1993, *Forbes* slammed the project in an article headlined FANTASYLAND. The magazine questioned the plan's financial assumptions and accused Hemmeter of overestimating revenue and underestimating costs. Why? "In business as in sex," *Forbes* explained, "it's an ancient ploy: Promise whatever it takes to land the deal, then forget the promise. Once the casino is built and people are employed, Hemmeter will have the leverage to threaten to close down if the tax rate isn't lowered, more expenses aren't made deductible, or if he's not allowed to open hotel, restaurant or retail operations in the casino." *Forbes* also questioned Hemmeter's claim of being worth $200 million, saying problems at his hotels in Hawaii had caused his fortune to dwindle.

Louisiana politicians leaped to his defense. Edwards dismissed the article as "fiction." Barthelemy said he was confident that Hemmeter could finance the casino, but he refused to ask the developer to detail his financial worth. To do so, said Donald Zuchelli, the mayor's lead casino consultant, would be "an invasion of privacy."

On March 21, *60 Minutes,* then the country's most-watched television show, took aim at the project, suggesting that Governor Edwards's gambling habits made Caesars and Hemmeter a shoo-in. A hidden *60 Minutes* camera captured an unusual pastime for a governor: Edwards throwing dice at the craps table at Caesars Lake Tahoe over the New Year's holiday. Of course, as the show reminded viewers, it wasn't an unusual activity for Edwards. He had paid off hundreds of thousands of dollars in gambling losses with briefcases full of cash as governor in the 1980s. Apparently, his luck had improved on his most recent junket. Edwards wouldn't confirm a newspaper report that he had won $400,000, but said, "It was one of those weekends where everything went right." Edwards allowed that it was unusual for him to be winning big at a casino that was bidding for the license from his casino board. "I can understand people being suspicious about that," he told interviewer Steve Kroft. "And I recognize that. But on the other hand, that has caused me to be all the more careful in handling that situation."

For credibility's sake, and stung in particular by the nationwide broadcast, Edwards needed at least one other bidder so Hemmeter and Caesars wouldn't win the license by default. He encouraged his friends in the Jazzville group—who were dismayed over not getting the casino lease from Barthelemy—to remain in the game. As *Times-Picayune* columnist James Gill noted, "These folks knew their way around long before the first Louisiana politician saw the inside of a Hemmeter airplane or resort." The ten Jazzville lawyers and businessmen, all from Louisiana, were skeptical of Edwards's entreaties. But three members particularly close to Edwards, trial lawyers Wendell Gauthier, Calvin Fayard, and Michael St. Martin, kept checking with Edwards to see if the fix was in for Hemmeter/Caesars. Each time, Edwards assured them that it was not. This gave Jazzville enough confidence to plunge forward. "I've dealt with him in political situations for years, and he has never said anything untrue to me on a major decision," St. Martin would say later. "Why would he tell us to go forward and then give us the shaft? He might do that to an outside gaming company. But he wouldn't do that to his friends." Along with encouraging Jazzville to stay in the game, Edwards was trying to line up a partner for them. He struck out with Steve Wynn, who told Edwards, "The word over here is that it's a done deal."

Edwards next turned to Harrah's casinos. The company's founder, Bill Harrah, got his start in California during the Great Depression, operating a bingo-style game in a building he took over from his father on the Venice pier. The bingo hall flourished, but the police continually harassed his illegal operation. In 1937, Harrah moved to Reno, which was thriving; Nevada had legalized gambling six years earlier. His initial operation was a bust, however, and shut down two months after opening. He opened another bingo club in Reno, this time closer to the heavily trafficked area where major casinos were operating. He hit paydirt, for Harrah knew how to run a successful gambling operation. One of his secrets: knowing how to cater to customers. Harrah was among the first casino owners to put down carpeting, treat his guests with lavish attention, feature women dealers, and bus in customers. In time, Harrah operated profitable casinos in Reno and Lake

Tahoe. A lover of beautiful women and fast cars, he would have six wives and amass a vintage-car collection that would become famous worldwide.

In 1978, seven years after taking his company public, Harrah died. To pay estate taxes, his heirs had to sell Harrah's casino company. The price was $300 million, and the buyer was Holiday Inn. Pushed by an ambitious lawyer who stood six foot six and wore his hair down to his collar, the company was looking to move beyond its ubiquitous motels. The Holiday Inn lawyer was Michael Rose, and he believed that casino gambling presented far more opportunities than opening more motels.

Unlike his conservative colleagues at Holiday Inn's corporate head-quarters in Memphis, Rose knew the casino business. His father had been a slots manager at the Desert Inn, in Las Vegas. During one college break, Rose worked as a front-desk clerk at the Castaways casino-hotel; during another summer, he interned at a Las Vegas accounting firm. A native of Akron, Ohio, he graduated from Harvard Law School in 1966 and ended up practicing law in Cincinnati. As a partner in a major firm there, he began doing legal work for Holiday Inn, and in 1976 took a senior management position with the hotel chain. Shortly afterward, he got the motel chain to buy Harrah's and move the casino company headquarters to unglamorous Memphis. With his Las Vegas background, Rose thought that getting into gambling made good business sense. Not everyone at Holiday Inn agreed. The company's president and two of its board members resigned in indignation.

Under Rose, Harrah's enjoyed spectacular growth. Its three Nevada casinos performed better than ever before, and Harrah's opened a gambling hall in Atlantic City that quickly became the Jersey Shore's most profitable casino. In time, Rose sold the Holiday Inns and renamed Harrah's parent company. The new name was Promus—Latin for "one who serves," to emphasize the company's mission to serve shareholders, franchisees, and guests. With a reputation for good service, but without the flashy frills of Mirage, Harrah's became especially popular with Middle America. By 1992, Promus owned six Harrah's casinos (the one that opened in Laughlin, Nevada, was the sixth) and 68,000 rooms at Embassy Suites, Hampton Inns, and Homewood Suites hotels. But the six Harrah's casinos dominated, accounting for 80 percent of Promus's $1.1 billion in annual revenue. Throughout the gambling industry, Rose and Harrah's were held in high esteem. "Harrah's is an industry leader in terms of regulatory compliance, management expertise, profitability, employee relations and attention to problems with compulsive and underage gamblers," *The Times-Picayune* reported. "It has sustained a first-class image developed over more than 50 years, succeeding with what by casino standards is an understated style. . . ."

When Governor Edwards began wooing Harrah's in early 1993, company officials already felt burned by the New Orleans process. They had competed in 1992 for the fight to be chosen by Mayor Sidney Barthelemy to develop the New Orleans casino. Since Harrah's operated casinos in all the major gambling markets at the time, New Orleans seemed like a natural fit for the company. Why let Steve Wynn, Hilton, Caesars, or someone else get the prize? For Memphis-based Harrah's, New Orleans was practically in its back yard. So Harrah's was among the initial ten bidders in June 1992 for the right to lease the Rivergate casino site. However, seeing Christopher Hemmeter's head start, company officials joined forces with Mirage for the final round of bidding. In November 1992, Barthelemy selected Hemmeter/Caesars. Michael Rose was disgusted. He was convinced that politics, not merit, had sealed Hemmeter's victory. Rose said good riddance to New Orleans and its corrupt politics. Harrah's would not bid for the state license.

Now, in early 1993, Edwards was asking company officials to reconsider. "Why don't you join forces with Gauthier's group?" he urged Colin Reed, Harrah's senior vice president. "That would then give you some political muscle down here that you don't have." Reed was doubtful.

In late April, a Harrah's executive named Tom Morgan met with Gauthier at his law office to ask for help with the company's bid to operate a riverboat in the New Orleans suburb of Kenner. Gauthier had the advantage of being close to the town's mayor. But he dashed Morgan's hopes, saying that someone else had the inside track for the Kenner boat. Gauthier commiserated briefly with Morgan, and then said, "We're still in the hunt for the New Orleans land casino. We don't want an out-of-town developer to win without a fight. You know, we still need a casino operator, however."

Gauthier noted that Jazzville had teamed with Showboat in applying for the city's lease in 1992, but had since parted ways. "Why not join us?" Gauthier asked Morgan. "We need a major operator, and you're a major operator." Gauthier outlined the Jazzville plan. It was far less grandiose—and much cheaper—than Hemmeter's proposal. It called for renovating, rather than demolishing, the Rivergate, and Jazzville proposed to undertake the renovation work in stages, opening one part of the casino at a time. This reduced the risks, Gauthier emphasized to Morgan. The plan intrigued Morgan, and he said he would check with his bosses. They, too, were intrigued, but after much debate decided that they would remain on the sidelines. Harrah's officials were still gun-shy.

Edwards called them again, promising that they would have a fair shot. Gauthier followed up to emphasize that he and his partners thought the governor was offering a straight-up shot. After another internal debate, Rose and his top officers decided to take the plunge. Why? Harrah's was aggressively trying to expand beyond Atlantic City and Nevada. New Orleans, everyone said, was an ideal casino town, with eight million tourists a year. Jazzville already had a proposal in hand, which would minimize Harrah's costs. Plus, the Jazzville partners had pull with Edwards. Could he turn his back on friends? The new partnership, known as Harrah's Jazz, was betting that he wouldn't.

Because Mayor Barthelemy and Governor Edwards distrusted each other, the casino selection was a convoluted two-step process. Barthelemy had the right to award the lease to the Rivergate site, and he had selected Hemmeter/Caesars in November 1992. Now it was up to a nine-member board appointed by Edwards to decide who had the operating license. The board was created by the controversial casino bill that the legislature had approved in June 1992. Critics said that Edwards would control the casino by putting his cronies on the casino board. Edwards dismissed that notion. What qualities was he looking for? "Business and professional men and women," he said. "No politicians, no ex-politicians and no newspeople." Edwards said he especially wanted applications from people who had "a good reputation, experience in business or accounting or law and who are willing to give full time to the job." A day later, he said, "I want this to be the most pristine board ever appointed in the state of Louisiana." In time, that statement would haunt Edwards.

In a move aimed at disarming critics, Edwards's first selection was Billy Nungesser, sixty-three, the chairman of the Louisiana Republican Party. Nungesser, who owned an offshore catering business, was no country-club Republican. With thick red hair, a "Yat" accent, and an inability to speak a few sentences without mispronouncing a word, the chain-smoking Nungesser was a longtime Edwards foe. Wary of the governor's intentions, Nungesser canvassed friends on whether to accept the job. They all told him to take it, that he could do some good. However, John Volz, the United States Attorney who unsuccessfully prosecuted Edwards in 1985–1986, told Nungesser: "Billy, you can take it. But you're window-dressing. He'll control the votes."

Nungesser took the job, figuring he could still make a difference. Edwards trumpeted Nungesser's appointment. "I picked him in fulfillment of a statement I made during the [1991 gubernatorial] campaign," Edwards said, "that if a commission was formed it would be comprised not of my friends or of people with whom I have any political association, but with high-level people whose integrity and reputation are above reproach and would be expected to do the best job possible for the state."

Three months later, Edwards announced six more appointees. They were: Charles Webb, a New Orleans accountant; Bert Rowley, a real estate agent in the New Orleans suburb of Chalmette; Jack Frank, a pediatrician in Crowley, the Acadiana town where Edwards got his political start; Louise Rachal, a former professor at Tulane University, in New Orleans; William Hanna, a Shreveport businessman; and Max Chastain, a twenty-two-year veteran of the FBI.

In the coming days, Edwards named the final two appointees: James Vilas, director of an obscure worker training board in Baton Rouge, and David Fergurson, a Baton Rouge attorney. Edwards said the appointees would be freethinkers who would choose the best casino operator possible for New Orleans and Louisiana. "I'm very happy to gleefully say to my many critics that once again they were wrong," Edwards told reporters.

But were they? Rowley was a former state legislator recommended to the board by Senate president Sammy Nunez, who had worked with Edwards to get the casino bill passed and who had gone on Christopher Hemmeter's secret trip to Hawaii. (Rowley also was the son of Dutch Rowley, the sheriff of St. Bernard Parish during the wide-open gambling days of the late 1940s and early 1950s.) Dr. Frank had been the family pediatrician for Edwards's four children and had gambled in Las Vegas with the governor. Rachal was Barthelemy's choice for the board—Edwards had agreed to let the mayor make one selection. Hanna was a former Shreveport mayor close to Edwards's pal Gus Mijalis. Webb was recommended by state representative Sherman Copelin, a pro-casino wheeler-dealer close to Edwards. Vilas had been recommended by Victor Bussie, the powerful president of Louisiana's AFL-CIO, a longtime ally of the governor's. Edwards's girlfriend, Candy Picou, who was a nursing student along with Vilas's girlfriend, also recommended him. Fergurson was close to state senator Cleo Fields of Baton Rouge, another Edwards ally. Chastain didn't have a political patron, although he had been recommended by Jefferson Parish sheriff Harry Lee, who knew Chastain slightly but was close to Edwards. Chastain didn't know Edwards, but after seeing a news report on the casino board, put forth his name because he wanted to leave the FBI.

Edwards's critics soon had ammunition to question his choices. *The Times-Picayune* disclosed that Hanna and Webb had declared bankruptcy in 1991 and 1990, respectively. Hanna had owed more than $1 million, Webb $90,000. "How pristine is the commission going to be if some of its membership has declared bankruptcy?" asked state senator Dennis Bagneris, a New Orleans Democrat and an Edwards ally. Ten days later, the newspaper reported that Fergurson, too, had filed for bankruptcy, only two months before his appointment. *The Times-Picayune* followed a week later with a report that the Federal Deposit Insurance Corporation was alleging that Dr. Frank had approved "a series of risky, ill-advised loans that helped bring about the collapse of a Crowley savings and loan." The newspaper added: "This means that four of the nine casino board nominees have troubled business records—despite Edwards' promise the commission would be the most 'pristine' board in state history." Shortly afterward, Webb, Hanna, and Fergurson withdrew their applications to serve on the board, and Rachal was dropped because she refused to turn over personal financial information to Senate investigators conducting background checks.

Edwards appointed four others to replace them: Sallie Page, a filing clerk making $13,000 a year in the streets department in Alexandria; Leroy Melton, a lawyer who established the paternity of children for the Louisiana Department of Health and Hospitals in New Orleans; Gerard Thomas, a semiretired trial lawyer in Natchitoches; and Joan Heisser, a real estate agent and onetime beauty salon owner in New Orleans. Each of the four owed his appointment to a political patron: Page by Senator Fields, Melton by Representative Copelin, Heisser by Mayor Barthelemy—they had dated in high school—and Thomas by Senator Don Kelly, a powerful Edwards ally who had co-sponsored the casino bill and who practiced law with Thomas's son in Natchitoches. Of the four, only Thomas had the background and experience to qualify for the important assignment.

Edwards defended the nine-member board. "There is an independent who is neither Republican nor Democrat nor Communist nor Socialist: an ex-FBI agent," he said, referring to Max Chastain. "There is the former head of the Republican Party. There is a retired doctor whose credentials and reputation in his hometown are without question. There is a Hispanic and three blacks. I do think you have a well-rounded group." Few people were reassured. "The casino board shapes up to be a joke, and it appears you need to be either bankrupt or devoid of relevant experience to get the nod from Edwards," wrote *Times-Picayune* columnist James Gill. "A word in his ear from a political crony appears about all that is necessary."

At Edwards's suggestion, the board chose Chastain as its chairman. This was another adroit move by Edwards to neutralize critics. "I'm going to use you because of *your* reputation and because of *my* reputation,"

Edwards had told Chastain privately when he offered him the position. "Without you, I don't have a board." The fifty-two-year-old Chastain, who had thick white hair and unblinking blue eyes, had impeccable credentials. He had graduated from the U.S. Naval Academy and had been a navy pilot afterward before joining the FBI. With him as chairman, the board gained instant credibility. But Chastain was unfit for the job. He had had an undistinguished FBI career and was assigned to menial tasks when he retired to join the casino board. Naïve and unschooled in Louisiana politics, he was unprepared for the rough-and-tumble world he would find himself thrust into. Out of his element, he would make foolish decisions that would undermine his credibility over time.

Adding to the problems, most of the other eight board members seemed more concerned with serving their political patrons than with serving the public. Chastain noted privately that Melton, for one, didn't seem to do anything without first checking with Representative Copelin, a political deal maker who had recommended Melton to Edwards. Jack Frank was very close to Billy Broadhurst, a key member of Hemmeter's team. Frank and Broadhurst both hailed from Crowley, and they had adjoining apartments in New Orleans. Frank, for example, in late April 1993 asked the board to give added weight in its selection process to a bidder that had access to the Rivergate site. Frank was clearly acting to favor Hemmeter, who alone had rights to the casino site. On April 29, the casino board defeated Frank's ploy, but on a narrow 5–4 vote.

Several days later, with the board scheduled to spend three days discussing a set of rules to govern the selection process, Frank offered a group of amendments that the board quickly approved. The amendments cut off debate, established a set of rules that the board had not publicly discussed, and created an early June 4 deadline to select the casino operator. All of this favored Hemmeter. Board member Billy Nungesser was outraged. "We have spent zero minutes on a discussion of the most important task we have," Nungesser complained to his colleagues. "And it's a disgrace. We all ought to turn in our salaries because we haven't earned a dime." Casino Magic, a Mississippi casino company, said it couldn't meet the June 4 deadline and would not bid. *The Times-Picayune* editorialized: "The blatant disregard of due process and the rights of other board members displayed by Dr. Frank and his allies lends further credence to the view of those who have maintained all along that 'the fix is on.'"

Led by a weak, ineffectual chairman, the politically driven casino board lacked the background and experience needed to make a decision that would be worth hundreds of millions of dollars to the winner and that would have major ramifications for New Orleans for years to come. And four of the nine members would face questions about their integrity. Even officials representing the two final bidders vying for the casino license thought the board was a joke. But it was the "pristine" board that Governor Edwards had selected and that the Louisiana Senate had confirmed.

On June 4, 1993, Hemmeter/Caesars and Harrah's Jazz were the only two entities to make bids for the license. The Hemmeter/Caesars partnership proposed a 200,000-square-foot casino that would be the world's largest. The cost was still $490 million, but Hemmeter once again had changed his design plans. He had scrapped the controversial sound-and-light show and proposed instead to build a $15 million cuckoo clock that every fifteen minutes would mark great moments in New Orleans's history with a water-and-light show. Hemmeter proposed that the casino itself have a mishmash of themes that had little to do with New Orleans. Borrowing a page from Steve Wynn's newly opened Treasure Island casino, a "Lost City Casino" would include a replica of a pirate ship with animated characters. Another part of the casino would have an ancient Roman motif. A third area for upscale gamblers would feature a "Monte Carlo Casino" with an entrance fee and a dress code. A fourth area would be a hundred-yard-long replica of a Hong Kong street. While constructing the Grand Palais on the Rivergate site, Hemmeter proposed, he would operate a temporary casino elsewhere in New Orleans as a way of generating tax revenue in the meantime. As a sweetener in its bid, Hemmeter/Caesars proposed to advance a $200 million tax payment to help the state with its budget crunch and to pay up to 25 percent of its revenue in taxes annually instead of the required 18.5 percent.

The Harrah's Jazz proposal was simpler. It called for renovating the Rivergate in stages to create a 120,000-square-foot casino with a jazz theme. With an up-front payment of $100 million, the Harrah's Jazz proposal would cost $327 million. "The crucial difference between the two sides is in concept," commented *Times-Picayune* columnist James Gill. "Hemmeter's would be a so-called 'destination casino,' an elaborate entertainment complex imposed on the city to attract visitors who would otherwise not visit. The Jazzville notion is not to interfere more than is necessary with the charms that already bring people here."

The board set July 23 as decision day. Now it got nasty. Each side alleged to the board that the other had submitted an illegal bid, and at a public meeting, officials from each side bad-mouthed the other. Wendell Gauthier of Harrah's Jazz predicted that Hemmeter's Grand Palais casino would be an overbuilt flop. Hemmeter retorted, "You can't come in here on the sly and put up a cheap joint with a paint brush," derisively referring to the Harrah's Jazz plan to renovate the Rivergate. Each bidder hired private detectives to tail the other side's top officials and sort through their trash. Then, on July 13, Hemmeter/Caesars suffered a blow. *The Times-Picayune* reported that Hemmeter's partner, Daniel Robinowitz, had secretly given a portion of his ownership shares to Billy Broadhurst and New Orleans municipal court judge Eddie Sapir. Board members lashed out at Hemmeter and Robinowitz for not having disclosed the ownership. "Why were we the last to find out about this?" Chastain asked angrily. "There's every indication that this stinks."

Temperatures were now running high. A single decision would shower millions of dollars on the winning side. On July 20, the casino board called time-out. Acting on the legal advice of Louisiana's attorney general, the board ruled that both bids were indeed technically illegal. While on the surface the decision didn't seem to favor either side, it especially upset Wendell Gauthier. He thought Harrah's Jazz lost the advantage of having a superior offer, and he feared the decision would cause his skittish partner, Harrah's, to pull the plug once and for all. "It remains to be seen whether we will rebid for the land-based casino in New Orleans," Philip Satre, president of Promus, Harrah's parent company, told reporters.

The casino board gave Harrah's Jazz an extra five days to decide whether to bid. Harrah's executives caucused in Memphis. After much discussion back and forth, they decided that they had invested so much in New Orleans and were close enough to the finish line that they ought to go forward. On August 2, Harrah's Jazz and Hemmeter/Caesars made a second bid. Each sweetened its earlier offer with a promise of more cash to the state. Hemmeter/Caesars offered to pay higher taxes, while Harrah's raised its one-time up-front payment to $125 million—an increase of $25 million—to the state treasury. The board set August 11 as the date it would award the coveted license.

Over the final week, enmity between the two sides hardened. But with so much money at stake, members of each group grew nervous that their side might not win the bid and thus would be left out entirely. During a break in a casino board meeting two days before the final vote, Daniel Robinowitz asked John Cummings, one of the Jazzville 10, if Harrah's Jazz was interested in joining forces with his group. Hemmeter/Caesars might be willing to give Harrah's Jazz a 20 percent share of the casino, Robinowitz said. Cummings told him that he would discuss it with his partners. When he did, the partners agreed that Harrah's Jazz would make a counteroffer of 50 percent, although they decided they would settle for 33 percent, since Hemmeter/Caesars was the clear favorite. Billy Broadhurst informed Hemmeter of the counteroffer. The developer adamantly opposed cutting in Harrah's Jazz. "Not even 1 percent," Hemmeter said. "Not a nickel."

"Chris," Broadhurst asked, "would you rather have 100 percent of nothing or 75 percent of the biggest casino in the world?"

"Nothing," Hemmeter replied. "I am not doing a deal with them."

Hemmeter—and practically everyone else—believed that he and Caesars would win. Meeting in Hemmeter's suite the night before the vote, his team agreed they would triumph on a 6–3 vote.

On August 11, decision day, *The Times-Picayune,* on its front page, handicapped the nine-member board as follows: Hemmeter/Caesars could count on four votes: Leroy Melton, Joan Heisser, Bert Rowley, and Jack Frank. Harrah's Jazz had two sure votes: Billy Nungesser and James Vilas. The newspaper could not guess where the three others stood. They were: Max Chastain, Sallie Page, and Gerard Thomas. "Thus, while Hemmeter needs only one of the three undecided votes to win the competition, Harrah's Jazz Co. would have to sweep all three," the newspaper reported. Most observers expected at least one of the three to go with Hemmeter/Caesars. Some even expected a 7–2 vote for Hemmeter/Caesars.

A secret meeting the night before threatened to change the result. The meeting took place at the Metairie apartment of Sallie Page, who had seen her salary more than quadruple by getting appointed to the casino board. Governor Edwards had named her to the board at the request of Cleo Fields, who had been in the State Senate at the time but was now a congressman. It was Fields who showed up at her apartment that night. Fields, who like Page was African American, had attended Southern University in Baton Rouge with her children. Page's husband, a former city councilman in Alexandria, had been an early political supporter of Fields. Accompanying Fields to Page's apartment was Hugh Sibley, a white lawyer close to Fields and to Calvin Fayard, a trial lawyer who was one of the Jazzville 10. This was no social call. No, Fields was there at the behest of the Jazzville partners to sway Page their way. Jazzville feared that Melton and Heisser, the two other African-American board members, had convinced her out of racial solidarity to join them in backing Hemmeter/Caesars.

Page, fifty-one, had made little mark on the casino selection process and clearly was out of her league. She rarely spoke at board meetings, perhaps feeling uncertain because of her background as a filing clerk. But in private conversation with other board members, she would note with pride that her seven children had gone to college, and that several of them had embarked on fine professional careers.

At the apartment, Fields played the race card. He reminded Page that Hemmeter and Caesars did not have any African Americans among their top officials. Jazzville, he pointed out, had two: Burnell Moliere, who owned a janitorial company based in a New Orleans suburb, and Duplain (Pete) Rhodes III, whose family had owned a funeral home in New Orleans for years. Fields hammered away at Jazzville's racial advantage. Shortly before he left, he asked Page to join him in kneeling and praying for guidance in the following day's decision.

Meanwhile, a group of Harrah's Jazz officials were anxiously eating dinner at Galatoire's, one of New Orleans's grand French Quarter restaurants. While drinking copious amounts of alcohol, they debated endlessly their chances of winning the following day. On one thing they all agreed: they could not win without Page. They had learned of the meeting at Page's apartment and kept up with the evening's developments through constant conversations on their cellular phones. Afterward, the group repaired to the bar at the Westin Hotel, where the Harrah's officials were staying. Around midnight, George Solomon, another one of the Jazzville partners, called Calvin Fayard.

"What's the status?" Solomon asked.

"Cleo's turned her back around," Fayard replied.

Solomon and the others celebrated with another round of drinks.

Not everyone in Jazzville knew about the meeting. When Louie Roussel III, a racehorse owner and the wealthiest of the ten partners, arrived at Canal Place on the morning of the vote, he told one of his colleagues that they would get only two votes. Roussel brought his father to the meeting, and that added a small subplot to the drama by unnerving the Hemmeter/Caesars officials. The senior Roussel, known as "Mr. Louie," was nearing ninety, but still carried a reputation as a man who knew how to pick winners. Mr. Louie had earned a fortune in oil and banking, and was particularly close to Governor Edwards. When Edwards ran for reelection in 1987, the elder Roussel contributed an astounding $625,000 to his campaign. When Bob d'Hemecourt, who was also close to Edwards but was representing Caesars in the casino battle, saw Mr. Louie pull up at Canal Place in his limousine, he got a sinking feeling. D'Hemecourt had been sure that Hemmeter/Caesars would prevail. When he saw Mr. Louie, however, he told a Caesars official that they were in trouble, that Mr. Louie didn't show up to be with losers. Suddenly nervous, d'Hemecourt decided not to watch the vote in person, but to listen to it on the radio at Hemmeter's office.

The vote would take place across the street from Hemmeter's office, in a conference room where the board regularly met, at the casino board's offices on the twenty-seventh floor of Canal Place, overlooking downtown New Orleans and the Mississippi River. The board's offices also looked down on the Rivergate site, across Canal Street from Canal Place.

The board members sat behind a crescent-shaped dais, Page at one end, Rowley at the other, with Chastain in the middle. The room contained one hundred seats that might or might not be filled during meetings, depending on the day's agenda. But on August 11, a hundred seats were nowhere near enough; people were jammed into every nook and cranny of the room and spilled over into the hallway.

When the board members entered through a side door, James Vilas paused as he was about to walk by Frank Donze, who was covering the vote for *The Times-Picayune.* "There's gonna be a surprise," Vilas said with a smile. Meanwhile, the room was abuzz with nervous chatter. Sitting in the front row was Christopher Hemmeter; his wife, Patsy; and Daniel Robinowitz. Separated from them by the middle aisle, but also in the front row, were Wendell Gauthier; his wife, Ann; Calvin Fayard; and the Harrah's executive, Tom Morgan. Sitting behind them were John Cummings, Mr. Louie, his son Louie III, and Ronnie Lamarque, another Jazzville partner. Lamarque was wearing his lucky sport coat.

The board spent more than half an hour addressing unrelated mundane issues, as people in the audience shifted uneasily. At about 11:30 a.m., Chastain announced that the board was ready to vote. The casino board had drawn lots to decide the vote's order. Sallie Page, one of the three who were labeled undecided, was first. "Harrah's," she said. Several members of Hemmeter's team frowned. Gauthier grinned. Next, Frank voted for Hemmeter/Caesars. Then came Nungesser for Harrah's Jazz. Melton voted for Hemmeter/Caesars. None of these last three votes was a surprise. The next one was: Thomas voted for Harrah's Jazz. Heisser knotted the score, 3–3, by voting for Hemmeter/Caesars. Vilas then put Harrah's up by one. Rowley tied it again by voting for Hemmeter/Caesars. The tally was 4–4, and now it was up to Max Chastain to cast the deciding vote. Hundreds of millions of dollars hung in the balance.

In the days leading up to the vote, Chastain had been unable to make up his mind. One moment he would be for Hemmeter/Caesars, the next he would be for Harrah's Jazz. He hadn't gotten much sleep the night before as he lay in bed mulling his decision. More than anything else, he hoped he wouldn't have to cast the tiebreaking vote.

So when it came down to four votes for each side, Chastain seemed to feel the pressure immediately. He sat bug-eyed, saying nothing. Billy Nungesser, who was sitting next to Chastain, kicked him under the table. Finally, Chastain started to speak. His voice quavering with nervousness, he began by thanking his colleagues for thoroughly reviewing the bids. "By this vote, you can see how closely this board considers that the proposers were," he said. Chastain stopped, leaned forward, and announced, "I vote for Harrah's."

Several people in the audience shrieked in joy. Wendell Gauthier yelled, "Wow!" and leaped to his feet, arms in the air. He turned to his right, took three quick steps, and reached to shake hands with Hemmeter. Gauthier grabbed the developer in a bear hug. Hemmeter, a smile frozen on his face, gave a halfhearted hug in return. Gauthier, tears welling in his eyes, then turned to embrace his wife and several Jazzville partners. Reporters converged on him and Hemmeter. "We'll open January 1, 1994," Gauthier cried out. "Everybody on the street said this was a done deal," he added a few minutes later. "And we got criticized by everybody saying, 'Why would you waste your time and your effort?' But the governor convinced me that this was a level playing field. He kept saying, 'I'm not going to get involved, it's a level playing field.' If not for that, we wouldn't have got involved."

Hemmeter, who still held the lease to the casino site, pledged to work out an agreement quickly with Harrah's Jazz officials. "I've always said from day one that we would never go to court," he said. Hemmeter then exited the meeting room, strode past a giant model of his proposed casino—alongside which he had planned to hold a press conference after the board selected him—and took an elevator to his suite in the Westin Hotel adjoining Canal Place. Daniel Robinowitz, who had had the original dream to bring a casino to the Rivergate, wandered out of Canal Place and ended up at the New Orleans Aquarium next door. There, he stood in front of a giant shark tank with a group of schoolkids and pondered how Harrah's Jazz had snatched the casino away from him. After a while, Robinowitz went to Hemmeter's suite. "I'm broke, I'm bankrupt, I'm busted, I'm ruined," a disconsolate Hemmeter told him.

BAD BET ON THE BAYOU

An angry Robinowitz replied, "Chris, we have to regroup, we got screwed. We got cheated. Let's get everyone together." But Hemmeter was too disappointed to agree to do anything.

Edwards got word of the vote during a meeting at the Governor's Mansion. His executive assistant, Sid Moreland, handed him a piece of paper that read, "Casino board, 5–4, Harrah's." Edwards, who favored Hemmeter/Caesars because of his admiration for Caesars, would later say the result shocked him.

As soon as Chastain announced his choice, the vote was relayed by telephone to Mayor Sidney Barthelemy's close associate, Ron Nabonne. By prearrangement, Nabonne called Barthelemy with the result. "Sidney, it's 5–4, Harrah's Jazz," Nabonne said. Barthelemy was dumbfounded. He had seen Hemmeter's casino as the crowning achievement of his administration and in a foolish move was balancing the coming year's budget on an up-front payment by Hemmeter that was suddenly in doubt. Upon hearing the news, the blood drained from Barthelemy's face. He asked: "What happened? What happened?" His jaw trembled, as it did when he was extremely upset. "These guys made a bad decision," Barthelemy told Nabonne. "It's going to hurt the city. They chose the wrong group."

As they mulled over the vote, Barthelemy and Nabonne agreed that Governor Edwards had decided to make sure that his friends in Jazzville weren't cut out and that he, not Barthelemy, played the decisive role after the mayor had taken the lead by giving the casino lease to Hemmeter. "The governor didn't want to be second fiddle to you," Nabonne told Barthelemy.

Hank Braden IV, another close Barthelemy associate, who was working for Caesars, told the mayor, "I don't know how this will come out, but the governor will force a merger between Hemmeter and Harrah's Jazz."

"It'll be a fucking mess," Barthelemy responded.

Harrah's Jazz officials at that moment shared none of these concerns. They were too busy celebrating. Right after the vote, Michael St. Martin, one of the Jazzville partners, called his son and told him to bring refreshments to an impromptu party that Harrah's Jazz officials had just organized under the Rivergate's canopy. A short time later, St. Martin's son pulled up, the back of his pickup truck filled with Dixie beer and champagne bottles. The Harrah's Jazz officials toasted the future casino site, the city, the state, the casino board, and everything else in sight, including tourists gawking at the commotion. That night, Harrah's Jazz took over Jaeger's Seafood Beer Garden, a downhome place that specialized in fried catfish, shrimp, and soft-shell crabs. Ronnie Lamarque took the stage with a local band to sing a few vintage numbers, among them "A Million to One." For most of his partners, that had seemed the odds starting out.

Meanwhile, Hemmeter that night convened his team in his Westin Hotel suite. Like Barthelemy and his advisers earlier in the day, they tried to figure out what had happened. By now, the group had received an anonymous phone call saying that James Vilas, who had repeatedly acted as Harrah's Jazz's shill in board meetings, had unduly influenced the vote. Although Daniel Robinowitz had no specific proof, he suspected that Edwards had compromised Vilas. "Tell the governor, you tell that fucking crook those bumper stickers were right," he said, referring to a pro-Edwards bumper sticker from the 1991 governor's race against David Duke: "Vote for the Crook. It's Important." Robinowitz said they should go to the United States Attorney. Others advised against this, noting that they still held a valuable asset, the casino lease, without which Harrah's Jazz could not operate at the Rivergate. "We've got the lease," Hemmeter said. "We've got to protect that asset."

Why did Harrah's Jazz triumph? Perhaps the real story will never be known. Sallie Page did tell a reporter on August 11 that Jazzville's having two African-American partners was a key factor in her decision. So Cleo Fields's visit clearly played a pivotal role. (Fields would get his reward later. When he ran for U.S. Congress the following year, in 1994, he got $33,000 in contributions of $1,000 apiece from Jazzville partners and their associates within a ten-day period. Gauthier also would later hire Fields as co-counsel to play to African-American jurors in a case where he was seeking millions of dollars in damages.) What about the second deciding vote, cast by Gerard Thomas? He called the

Harrah's Jazz proposal "more practical" in economic terms, and he said the company's offer of up-front money was a better deal than the annual higher tax payments offered by Hemmeter/Caesars. Thomas, as has been noted, was close to Senator Don Kelly, an Edwards ally. What about Chastain? He told reporters that he had spoken to Edwards the day before and that Edwards told him to vote his conscience. Chastain said that like Thomas, he found the Harrah's Jazz scaled-down approach more sensible.

For his part, Edwards would say later he thought that the hidden ownership of Billy Broadhurst and Eddie Sapir influenced Chastain to vote for Harrah's Jazz and that Fields's meeting with Page secured her vote. What about Edwards? What role did he play? Critics like Robinowitz said later that Edwards steered the board to Harrah's Jazz so his friends in Jazzville could claim a piece of the pie, since Hemmeter already had the lease. Edwards always denied influencing the board, and no evidence emerged to contradict him. There are reasons to believe Edwards. The entity that he most favored was Caesars, and the company got cut out when Harrah's Jazz got the nod. In addition, he told aides privately before the vote that he thought Hemmeter/Caesars had a better bid. Finally, he knew things could get messy if the board chose Harrah's Jazz, since Hemmeter held the lease.

On the other hand, a Harrah's Jazz victory could benefit Edwards in some ways. It's worth noting that by not intervening on behalf of Hemmeter/Caesars, Edwards helped Harrah's Jazz—because he created the political opening that the Jazzville investors could exploit with Sallie Page. Ultimately, a victory by Harrah's Jazz, while creating a potentially messy situation, would not be linked directly to him, as would a victory by Hemmeter/Caesars. The media, led by *The Times-Picayune*, had already cast suspicion on the casino by tying Hemmeter/Caesar's expected victory to Edwards. This had undoubtedly gotten the attention of the FBI, which remained very interested in Edwards's activities. So having the board vote for Harrah's Jazz actually gave Edwards some political cover.

On August 12, reporting the casino board's vote the day before, *The Times-Picayune* ran a giant front page headline asking the question that was now foremost on everyone's mind: NOW WHAT? Hemmeter/Caesars held the lease to the Rivergate, the designated casino site, and Harrah's Jazz owned the official state gambling license. Neither one could operate without the other. But they were by now bitter rivals and had vastly different ideas for the casino. Hemmeter/Caesars wanted to raze the Rivergate and replace it with a gaudy, "must see" hodgepodge of architectural styles that Hemmeter dubbed the Grand Palais and that, with 200,000 square feet of gambling space, would be the world's largest casino. Harrah's Jazz, befitting Harrah's middlebrow approach to gambling, simply wanted to retrofit the Rivergate and open a 120,000-square-foot casino.

Immediately after losing the vote on August 11, Hemmeter had pledged his cooperation, saying he would not go to court. Four days later, he changed his tune. Meeting alone with Edwards at the Governor's Mansion, he said he deserved 50 percent of the casino project and would settle for no less. Edwards responded by telling Hemmeter that he should settle for one-third, with Harrah's getting another third and the Jazzville partners receiving the final third. "I'm not doing that," Hemmeter told him.

"Listen," Edwards replied. "If you don't do that, this damn casino will never get off the ground, there might be a ten-year lawsuit, and you're going to lose $200 million or $300 million of revenue."

Hemmeter looked directly at Edwards and said, "That wouldn't make any difference to me, $200 million or $300 million." Edwards thought to himself: "This guy isn't playing with a full deck."

Along with Robinowitz, Hemmeter met with Harrah's Jazz officials the next day and reiterated that he wanted 50 percent of the project. They countered by offering him 10 percent. The two sides also locked horns over whose proposed casino to build. Robinowitz, angry over the outcome of the casino board vote, further poisoned relations between the two sides. With Colin Reed, a Harrah's vice president sitting by his side, Robinowitz left open a file folder that contained separate photos of Vilas and two women who were friends of Wendell Gauthier and who Robinowitz thought had influenced Vilas's vote. Robinowitz did not say anything to Reed, knowing that he couldn't help but see the photos. Reed didn't say anything to Robinowitz, but at the first opportunity he pulled Hemmeter aside and demanded that Robinowitz not attend any more negotiations.

On August 17, Edwards announced that the two sides had reached a stalemate and that the "thing may just blow up in our faces." To Edwards, this meant he had to step in and force a merger. "I have a responsibility as governor to make sure it's done right," he told reporters. "We certainly need the $125 million [up-front payment promised by Harrah's] that's available to us, while the city certainly needs the money available to it. The people of the city and the state need the jobs, and we need the tax revenue." Playing the forceful mediator was a role suited to Edwards, who, despite his many faults, excelled in closing a proposed deal.

On August 18—a week after the casino board vote—he brought the two sides to the Governor's Mansion, Harrah's Jazz in one room, Hemmeter in another. Edwards shuttled between the two rooms. Hemmeter continued to insist on no less than 50 percent, while Harrah's Jazz would offer him no more than 10 percent. Edwards tried to reason with each side, suggesting that Harrah's get one-third, Jazzville get one-third, and Hemmeter get one-third. When neither group would budge, he warned them that they could end up with nothing. Still no luck. Then he decided to bring the two sides together in the mansion's living room. After everyone was in place, Edwards said, "I've called this meeting to see if there is room for a potential compromise, to see if the two groups can join forces in order to proceed in getting the project built. I've talked with Mr. Hemmeter, and he has said he is willing to contribute his lease. What about Harrah's Jazz? What are you willing to contribute?"

Colin Reed answered. "Why should we compromise? We have the license to operate the casino. We won a long, hard-fought battle."

Hemmeter jumped in with a menacing comment. "Yeah, we know how you got the license."

"I don't think you want to go into that," Reed responded tartly. "There may be some issues you don't want on the table."

Edwards cut in. "Mr. Reed," he said, "you have the license, but how do you plan to operate the casino when Mr. Hemmeter has the lease on the only site for the casino?"

"Governor, the city can give us the lease," Reed said, showing no willingness to bend.

"We're prepared to pay for the lease for its term," Hemmeter rejoined. "We'll tie it up for five years."

Edwards was growing exasperated. "I'll ask one last time, do you think there's any room for compromise?"

Reed and Hemmeter began bickering again. "Governor, I don't think Hemmeter has the financial wherewithal actually to build the facility," Reed said.

"I've already got the financing, and I have all the cash I need to build the facility," Hemmeter replied.

Edwards had had enough. He paused until everyone was watching him and then looked at his watch. "Gentlemen," he said, "it's 15 minutes after five on August 18." He turned to Hemmeter on his left. "What time do you have on your watch?"

"Governor, that's about the same time that I have."

Edwards turned to Reed on his right. "What time do you have?"

"About 5:15, Governor, the same as you," Reed replied.

"The reason I asked, gentlemen, is because I want to make special note of the time because this is going to be a day that people remember, a day when the state of Louisiana and the city of New Orleans lost a great opportunity to bring in an industry that would create a new source of revenue as well as badly needed jobs. It is also a day where you two groups will look back on how you left many millions of dollars on the table."

Edwards then got up and walked out of the room. For a few seconds, no one was sure what to do. Then everyone realized he wasn't coming back. Both sides left the Governor's Mansion. The casino deal looked on the verge of collapsing.

The next day, Hemmeter asked the casino board for another vote. In a court filing, he argued that Vilas, Harrah's Jazz's chief ally on the board, should be recused from a second vote because he was biased against the developer. Harrah's Jazz fired back, accusing Jack Frank of prejudice against the group because of his close association with Hemmeter adviser Billy Broadhurst. On August 23—12 days after the casino board's vote—Edwards attended a *Monday Night Football* exhibition game at the Louisiana Superdome, where the New Orleans Saints played the Chicago Bears. Senate president Sammy Nunez and House Speaker John Alario sat with Edwards in the governor's suite. The stalemate frustrated all three, and they were looking for a way to keep the casino alive. After some discussion, they settled on a plan. It called either for the casino no longer to be site-specific at the Rivergate, which would take away Hemmeter's ace card, or for the state to take control of the casino, giving some company a 15 percent cut to be the operator. Either move would be risky. In each case, Edwards would have to get the legislature to rewrite the casino law. But the legislature had legalized the casino in 1992, the previous year, with no votes to spare. It was quite possible that, given another chance to vote on the casino, the legislature might simply repeal it. The plan did have the virtue of giving Edwards a club with which to threaten Hemmeter and Harrah's Jazz.

The next morning, Edwards called Gauthier with a strongly worded message: "Listen to me well. I'm only going to say this once. There are people out of work in this state who need jobs. Get this thing together." Edwards then hung up. The two sides met that day at the Sheraton Hotel in Metairie. They made some progress, but Edwards remained concerned. He told them that he planned to hold a press conference at 3:00 p.m. the next day to announce plans for a special legislative session in two weeks to consider a state takeover of the casino—if they didn't reach a power-sharing agreement among themselves.

With a sense of urgency, the two sides resumed their meeting the next day, August 25, exactly two weeks after the board vote. Working against the time deadline, they reached a tentative deal at 2:00 p.m.

and flew on Hemmeter's Hawker jet to Baton Rouge to present it to Edwards. It was a shotgun wedding along the lines that Edwards had outlined: Hemmeter would get one-third, Harrah's one-third, and Jazzville one-third. Harrah's would have the lead role, and Caesars would be out. The new partnership, as Hemmeter had sought, would demolish the Rivergate and build the world's largest casino in its place. Harrah's Jazz reluctantly acceded to this because both Edwards and Mayor Barthelemy insisted on a new building as a condition of the agreement. Both politicians said this would create needed construction jobs and give New Orleans a "must see" casino. It would take at least a year to build the casino. In the meantime, the new partnership would agree to Barthelemy's demand to open a temporary casino at the Municipal Auditorium in New Orleans. The temporary casino at the gussied-up auditorium could open as early as December 1. In a triumphant appearance before the media, Edwards held aloft the hands of Hemmeter, Gauthier, and Harrah's representative, Tom Morgan. The agreement, he proclaimed, "will eliminate years of lawsuits and further controversy, which would have seriously delayed implementation of these plans, costing us thousands of jobs and millions of dollars in revenues." He added, "Everybody involved is coming out a winner: the city, the state, the entities involved and all the people who will get jobs as a result of it. And I'm as pleased as I can be."

The next day, a New Orleans attorney opposed to the casino activated a lawsuit he had filed four months earlier. The suit, filed by attorney Tommy Tucker, sought to block the Rivergate's demolition, arguing that under an obscure 142-year law, the city did not hold title to the property. Tucker's action at the time got little notice.

Rollin' on the River

Throughout 1992 and into 1993, the politicians, the media, and the public focused on the maneuvering to get the New Orleans land casino under way—while treating the effort to bring riverboat gambling to Louisiana as an afterthought. There were several reasons for this. First, the legislature had authorized fifteen riverboat casinos in mid-1991 while Buddy Roemer was governor, and he was not a full-fledged gambling supporter. This caused Roemer to wait seven months after the legislature had approved the riverboat bill before appointing the seven-member board that would decide which companies got the coveted fifteen licenses. (The Riverboat Gaming Commission was separate from the casino board that in August 1993 would select Harrah's Jazz to operate the New Orleans casino.) Roemer made his riverboat board appointments in January 1992, three months after he was defeated for reelection and days before he was to turn the governor's office over to Edwin Edwards. Edwards, in turn, was obsessed with getting the New Orleans casino. It was his chief priority as he began his fourth term in office. However, the gambling-boat project was a secondary issue for him, so he, too, took his time in getting the riverboat gambling board going.

By May 1992, however, the riverboats had become important to Edwards. By then, he was trying to push the bill to legalize the land casino through a skittish legislature. The potential riverboat owners—expecting to operate in New Orleans—were creating a roadblock because they didn't want to have to compete against a huge land casino. On May 6, Representative La La Lalonde, sponsor of the New Orleans casino bill, canceled a hearing in which his committee was supposed to approve the land casino because riverboat interests had secured enough votes to kill the measure. On May 18, an unhappy Edwards called a meeting at the Governor's Mansion with the expected riverboat owners and their lobbyist, George Brown. After everyone had taken their seats, Brown told the governor that they were tired of the delays and wanted to get the riverboats open. Edwards said he did, too. But first he needed their help. It was difficult for him to find the time to help the riverboats, Edwards said, if the riverboat interests blocked his New Orleans casino in the legislature. The implication was clear: anybody who wanted a riverboat license from Edwards's gambling board had better play ball. They knew Edwards's board would decide which companies got licenses and where they operated—Louisiana was not a free-market system, as were Las Vegas and neighboring Mississippi. As a show of strength, Edwards had the leaders of the Senate visit the Governor's Mansion that day and voice their support for him.

By the end of the meeting, Brown and another riverboat lobbyist agreed that they would publicly endorse the New Orleans casino the following day. With their pledge, Edwards ended the meeting by telling a joke. It was a dirty fable about incest between a daddy and his daughters. The point was that if you wanted to get something from Daddy, you had to do whatever he asked for. Everybody knew that Edwards was the daddy here. With legislators friendly to the riverboats providing crucial votes, the legislature in June 1992 legalized the New Orleans casino.

A month later, Edwards's riverboat board met for the first time, as several boat companies were moving forward with plans to win a license. At this point, most observers didn't even expect fifteen companies to bid for the licenses. The biggest question was which boats would get selected to operate in New Orleans, considered the prime locale for such an operation because of its huge tourist base. As the riverboat operators began developing their plans, they had to meet several requirements under the 1991 law. The boats had to be designed to look like nineteenth-century paddle wheelers, in the hope that this would attract tourists. In addition, the boats could have no more than 30,000 square feet of gambling space, making them equivalent in size to a small Las Vegas casino.

By the beginning of 1993, interest in operating a floating casino in Louisiana had picked up, and companies foresaw profits in towns other than New Orleans. It now seemed certain that at least fifteen companies would seek a license. On March 12, Edwards's riverboat board handed out the first four licenses. The winners were:

1. A partnership of Hilton Hotel and New Orleans Paddlewheels Incorporated, which operated two pleasure boats on the Mississippi River. The gambling boat would dock on the river by the New Orleans Hilton, two blocks upriver from the French Quarter and across the street from the Rivergate land-casino site.

2. Players Lake Charles, which would be operated by Players International, a small casino company. The boat would operate on Lake Charles in the town of Lake Charles, near the Texas border in southwest Louisiana.

3. Red River Entertainment, which would be a partnership of a hotel developer named Sam Friedman and Harrah's Hotel Casinos. (Harrah's at this point had yet to win the land-casino license.) This boat would operate on the Red River out of Shreveport in northern Louisiana, near the Texas and Arkansas border. The boat would not have to make daily cruises because the legislature in 1993 would vote to allow Red River gambling boats to operate full-time at dock, since the river frequently was too shallow to be navigable. By being at dock full-time, the boat would essentially be a small land casino.

4. A partnership of Casino America, which operated the Isle of Capri casino in Biloxi, and Edward J. DeBartolo Sr., the world's largest developer of shopping malls and the principal owner of the Louisiana Downs racetrack in Bossier City. DeBartolo's son, Eddie Jr., was well known as the owner of the San Francisco 49ers football team. The Casino America/DeBartolo boat also would be on the Red River, but in Bossier City, across the river from Shreveport. Like the Harrah's boat, the Casino America/DeBartolo vessel would remain dockside.

Two weeks later, on March 26, the riverboat board awarded four more licenses. This time the winners were:

5. A partnership of New Orleans businessman Louie Roussel III and Showboat, a small company with casinos in Atlantic City and Las Vegas. Roussel was one of the ten Louisiana businessmen who comprised the Jazzville group and were soon to partner with Harrah's and bid for the New Orleans land-casino license. The Roussel/Showboat vessel was to dock on Lake Pontchartrain, in New Orleans.

6. Horseshoe Entertainment, which would operate a dockside casino on the Red River, in Bossier City. Horseshoe already operated a small casino in Las Vegas.

7. Louisiana Casino Cruises, which would operate on the Mississippi River in Baton Rouge, near the State Capitol. It was a partnership of three Louisiana businessmen and Carnival Hotels and Casinos, which was best known for its cruise ships.

8. Jazz Enterprises, which also would operate on the Mississippi River in Baton Rouge, about one mile downriver from the Louisiana Casino Cruises site. Jazz Enterprises was a partnership of Louisiana businessmen and a small casino company known as Argosy.

By now, it was becoming clear that applicants with ties to Governor Edwards were getting the licenses. Of the first four boats:

- Barron Hilton, part of a partnership that would have a boat on the Mississippi River in New Orleans, knew Edwards from the governor's gambling junkets to Hilton casinos in Nevada. Hilton also had hired Bob d'Hemecourt, one of Edwards's closest friends and advisers, as a consultant.

- Players, with plans for a boat on Lake Charles, had hired Ricky Shetler, the closest friend of Stephen Edwards, the governor's elder son. Edwards during his first term had appointed Shetler's father to the Louisiana Highway Safety Commission, a highly sought-after post because of the public contracts it awarded.

- The Harrah's boat in Shreveport included Sam Friedman, a Holiday Inn developer, among its investors. Friedman was close to Gus Mijalis, one of Edwards's best friends. Friedman and his wife had contributed $7,000 to Edwards's gubernatorial campaigns since 1987.

- Casino America, planning to operate in Bossier City, had partnered with Edward J. DeBartolo Sr. because the shopping-mall magnate was close to Edwards. DeBartolo usually visited Edwards at the Governor's Mansion when he came to Louisiana to discuss matters involving the Louisiana Downs racetrack or a shopping center that he owned in New Orleans. During those visits, Edwards and DeBartolo often told each other that they ought to go gambling in Las Vegas together, but they never arranged such a trip. To get a little extra juice with Edwards, Casino America had hired Billy Broadhurst, who had been one of the governor's closest political associates, dating to their days in the same law firm in Crowley. It was Broadhurst who introduced Casino

America officials to DeBartolo. In the 1991 governor's race, Casino America and DeBartolo each gave Edwards $5,000.

Of the next four companies that got licenses, all but Jazz Enterprises, a Baton Rouge entity, had close ties to Edwards. In the case of Jazz Enterprises, company officials won the backing of Baton Rouge public officials and arranged for a number of community residents to express their support for the boat. Of the others:

- Louie Roussel's father, Mr. Louie, had enormous influence with Edwards. In the 1987 governor's race, when there were no limits on campaign contributors, Mr. Louie and his companies gave Edwards $625,000. His son Louie was particularly close to Stephen Edwards. In at least one instance, Edwards would directly intervene with local officials on behalf of Louie Roussel. Members of the Orleans Levee Board in 1993 would be reluctant to award a lease for Roussel to dock the casino boat on their Lake Pontchartrain property until Edwards called Levee Board members. Roussel then got his lease.

- Horseshoe Entertainment, planning to operate dockside in Bossier City, had the support of two state senators, Greg Tarver and Sammy Nunez, who were close to Edwards. Tarver and Nunez each had gotten Edwards to name a friend to the seven-member riverboat board.

- Louisiana Casino Cruises, planning to operate in Baton Rouge, had as its lawyer Sheldon Beychok, who had been an Edwards campaign fund-raiser.

By the time the riverboat board selected the second group of boats in late March 1993, companies from across the country were scrambling to win the right to operate in Louisiana. Where Edwards and others initially thought no more than fifteen companies would want to operate in Louisiana, now thirty-six companies would bid for the final seven licenses. What made Louisiana a hot ticket suddenly was the success of the Mississippi casinos. The Splash, which had opened in October 1992 in the Delta town of Tunica, had been so overwhelmed by gamblers on one occasion that regulators had to briefly shut down the casino because casino employees couldn't keep track of all the money coming in. Casino Magic in Bay St. Louis on the Gulf Coast, meanwhile, was so popular with gamblers that the company in May 1993 announced a 3-for-1 split of its stock. Shares that had sold for $5 in October 1992 now fetched $69. "People said: 'If you can do that in Tunica or Bay St. Louis, man, what can you do in New Orleans?'" Ken Pickering, chairman of the Louisiana Riverboat Gaming Commission, remembered later. The situation for the final seven Louisiana riverboat licenses was reminiscent of the children's game musical chairs. When the music stopped, the riverboat board would make winners out of seven companies, while the other twenty-nine would go home losers.

With millions of dollars of potential profits beckoning, the stakes were high. So after the riverboat commission selected the second group of boats on March 26, a frenzied scramble ensued as outside gambling companies sought to link with Louisianians close to Edwards. The outside companies that did join forces with Edwards insiders then sought to romance the seven riverboat board members and their political patrons in the legislature, for Edwards had appointed members as a favor to his key legislative allies.

Ronnie Harris wanted a riverboat license, but he wasn't betting on political ties to be successful. Ever since the legislature had legalized riverboat gambling in 1991, Harris had wanted a vessel in the town of Gretna, where he was serving his third term as the mayor. Harris, thirty-nine, had the affable manner of a local boy who had done good, but one who also knew that his continued success required the continued favor of the local community. Harris remembered that his town (population 17,000), across the Mississippi River from New Orleans, had a long association with gambling. Gretna had been mobster Carlos Marcello's base. As late as the mid-1960s, Marcello's illegal casinos had operated there, protected by the town marshal, B. H. Miller Sr. Harris wanted to dock a floating casino on the river downtown, a stone's throw from where four illegal casinos had operated in the 1950s and 1960s. "Nobody in Gretna was against gaming," Harris remembered later. "I thought we'd revitalize downtown. A riverboat in Gretna was a natural fit."

As 1993 began, Harris had developed a bottom-up strategy for winning a riverboat license. He would develop a proposal with a safe location, strong public support, solid financing, a respected casino operator, and minority participation. Once he had all these elements in place, he figured that he would have a convincing proposal for the riverboat board.

Harris's thinking was similar to that of a local political and marketing consultant named Bernie Klein, who had an aggressive, impatient manner that often rubbed people the wrong way in a city where waitresses still asked their customers, "Whatcha havin' today, hon?" After the legislature legalized riverboat gambling, Klein, forty-seven, had decided that this was his chance to score big. He put together a riverboat bid. By early 1993, he had teamed with a company that operated four small casinos in Reno. Klein certainly stood to score big: the Reno casino offered him $26 million if they got a license, plus a hefty annual income. Klein and his casino partner decided they wanted to operate in Gretna and be the town's preferred entry. On April 5, the Gretna Board of Aldermen endorsed Klein's bid. The proposed boat would be called the *Gretna Belle.*

On April 28, Mayor Harris, by chance, attended a crawfish boil at the Governor's Mansion. While there, he made a point of going up to Governor Edwards and telling him that Gretna wanted a riverboat. Given Edwards's well-chronicled knowledge of gambling, Harris was expecting to discuss the merits of the Gretna proposal. Instead, Edwards told him simply, "You're going to have to see Alario." Harris was dumbstruck. As he wandered away, he wondered why he would have to get the support of Representative John Alario, who was from the neighboring West Bank town of Westwego and was speaker of the Louisiana House of Representatives. After all, it was the riverboat board that would choose which companies got the seven remaining licenses.

Even as he was mulling over this question, Harris saw a disturbing scene. A former governor of Nevada named Bob List was at the crawfish boil on behalf of a Nevada casino company named Boomtown. Harris learned that Boomtown had hooked up with a politically connected West Bank family, the Skrmettas, who owned a plot of land along a waterway known as the Harvey Canal that fed in to the Mississippi River. When someone pointed out List at the crawfish boil, Harris saw the former Nevada governor chatting with Louisiana politicians as if he were right at home in the Bayou State. Suddenly it looked to Harris that his bottom-up theory of winning a license could be a severe miscalculation. Harris began thinking that you couldn't get a boat without support from on top, meaning Governor Edwards and Speaker Alario.

By chance, Edwards spoke at a technical school in Gretna the following night. When Harris went up to Edwards later to discuss the *Gretna Belle*, Edwards repeated, "Go see Alario." That same day, Bernie Klein had met with Floyd Landry, the riverboat board member named by Edwards at Senator Sammy Nunez's behest. Nunez, a veteran lawmaker from the St. Bernard Parish town of Chalmette, was president of the State Senate. Landry was a retired furniture salesman who had served on the St. Bernard Parish police jury. "Look, you have a hell of a project," Landry told Klein. "But you gotta get the man to turn the key." He then pointed toward Baton Rouge. Klein assumed he was referring to Edwards. Landry then added, "I don't make any of the decisions. I get my marching orders from Sammy."

The next day, April 30, Boomtown presented its plan to operate a riverboat on the Harvey Canal to the riverboat commission. The proposal was not well received. Boomtown and the Skrmettas had little parking, their site was near a neighborhood that had expressed its opposition to the project, and the Harvey Canal was hardly the tourist draw envisioned under the original legislation. Instead, it was an industrial corridor for barges. Harris couldn't imagine the riverboat commission awarding them a license, but he had concluded that politics, not a proposal's merits, had become paramount.

On May 5, Harris met with Speaker Alario. The meeting started well, as Alario seemed impressed by the time and care that Harris and

Bernie Klein had devoted to the *Gretna Belle*. Harris reminded Alario of the long history of gambling in Gretna, saying the town was the perfect spot for a riverboat. "Our proposal is so good," Harris added, "even *The Times-Picayune* could support it." Harris saw Alario stiffen. The speaker hated the anti-gambling newspaper, and now he thought that Harris was threatening to get it to attack him if he didn't support the Gretna boat. Harris quickly realized his mistake, but it was too late. Alario abruptly ended the meeting and said a frosty goodbye to Gretna's mayor.

Nonetheless, Harris and Klein pressed on, still not convinced that the riverboat board could turn down their proposal. On May 21, they presented their plan to the seven-member commission. It was easily the most professional presentation the panel had seen. Harris and Klein showed a twelve-minute video featuring interviews with Gretna residents, a history of the town, and an explanation of where the boat would dock. Bernie Klein noted that the Jefferson Parish Council had endorsed the boat and that he had 1,500 signatures of support from local residents. To top it off, Klein and Harris had a busload of supporters at the meeting, and they whooped and hollered their support for the *Gretna Belle*. The presentation had the feel of a successful political rally. When they were done, commission member Sam Gilliam came over to Klein and said, "You've got my support." A second commission member, Floyd Landry, winked and gave Klein a thumbs-up. Klein and Harris were elated. They were going to beat the politicians after all.

Meanwhile, Bill Dow was getting increasingly worried that he would not get a boat. Many people thought that if anyone deserved a license, it was Dow. He had been among the small group of men who had conceived the idea of riverboat gambling in Louisiana and had helped get the bill through the legislature in 1991. Dow, fifty-seven, a native northeasterner and former naval officer with a distaste for politics, had spent his entire career in the maritime business. Few people knew the Mississippi River better. His company owned three pleasure boats that operated daily from the French Quarter: the *John James Audubon,* the *Cotton Blossom,* and the *Natchez,* a 1,600-passenger paddle wheeler. Dow wasn't especially fond of gambling. But with Iowa, Illinois, and

Mississippi already having legalized floating casinos, he figured that riverboat gambling was inevitably coming to Louisiana. He wanted to make sure that he didn't suffer the same fate as pleasure boat operators in Iowa, which shut down, unable to compete with the gambling boats.

As 1993 began, Dow was partnered with a respected Las Vegas casino owner named Michael Gaughan to operate a riverboat casino from the French Quarter. They were calling their proposed vessel the *New Orleans Casino Belle*. Dow would provide the maritime know-how, and Gaughan would provide the casino management. As an added benefit, Gaughan had developed a bit of a relationship with Governor Edwards in 1986 when Edwards had first proposed to legalize gambling in Louisiana. On one trip to Louisiana, Gaughan had spent the night at the Governor's Mansion. But by 1993, Gaughan also had a healthy cynicism about Edwards. He remembered that in 1986 the governor had promised him that he would have the inside track for one of the five casinos he wanted built. The news excited Gaughan, until he learned later that Edwards had made the same promise to seven of his Las Vegas casino industry friends.

In March 1993, it appeared that the Dow/Gaughan partnership was in line to get a license. On March 26, the day the riverboat commission was to hand out its second set of licenses, *The Times-Picayune* even forecast that the *New Orleans Casino Belle* would be chosen. But the proposed boat had run into problems, as preservationists said its French Quarter site would bring too much congestion to the historic neighborhood. Competitors pointed to the controversy in quietly convincing the riverboat board not to select the Dow/Gaughan partnership on March 26. A few days later, Gaughan pulled out, telling Dow, "I find I'm politically ineffective in Louisiana. You need a new partner." Later he would say privately, "The state motto of Louisiana is corruption before leadership. It's a good old boy network. You gotta deal with somebody down there or you can't get in."

The riverboat board still had seven more licenses to award. So Dow immediately scrambled to find a heavy-hitter partner. On May 4, Dow announced that he had two new partners. One was a New Orleans developer named Darryl Berger, who brought two things to the table:

he had influence with local politicians, and he owned badly needed French Quarter parking lots. The other partner was far more important: ITT Sheraton, which was under new management and looking to get into the gambling business. The Fortune 100 company had a $3 billion line of credit, and the Sheraton chain included more than four hundred owned, leased, managed, or franchised hotels, resorts, and inns in sixty-one countries. One of those hotels was in New Orleans, and Sheraton promised to expand it if the company got the riverboat license. With these assets, many people saw the proposed Lady Sheraton Riverboat Casino as a shoo-in for one of the remaining seven licenses. It now looked like Bill Dow would get his riverboat casino after all.

Two other bidders were expected to get boats in New Orleans. One was the President Riverboat Casino, which had been the first company to open a riverboat casino after the era of riverboat gambling began in Iowa in 1991. Along with a boat in Davenport, the President operated a dockside casino in Gulfport, Mississippi. Officials with the President were so certain of their chances in Louisiana that they already had begun construction on their boat, and it was more than halfway complete by June 1993. The President's riverboat was supposed to dock on the Mississippi River, about ten blocks upriver from the French Quarter.

Developer Christopher Hemmeter and his partner, Caesars World, were expected to get the other license in New Orleans. Hemmeter already had in hand the lease to the New Orleans land casino, and he was the overwhelming favorite to get the land-casino state operating license, to be awarded in August 1993. However, he and his partner, Daniel Robinowitz, also wanted to operate a riverboat on the Mississippi River, across the street from the proposed Rivergate land-casino site. They were calling their boat *Caesars on the River*. Hemmeter and Caesars were seen as a lock for a riverboat license if for no other reason than Caesars Palace was Governor Edwards's favorite Las Vegas casino. Billy Broadhurst and George Nattin, longtime Edwards friends who worked for the riverboat partnership, frequently visited the governor in Baton Rouge.

Real estate and Atlantic City casino mogul Donald Trump also entered the high-stakes bidding contest. Trump announced that he wanted to operate a boat in New Orleans, the *Trump Princess*. He hired Bob d'Hemecourt, Edwards's close friend, to make it happen.

Another license was expected to go to a boat in Kenner, a Jefferson Parish town of sixty thousand people. Two companies wanted to operate in Kenner. One was owned by Al Copeland, a local hero for having founded the Popeye's Fried Chicken chain. Copeland remained popular even after Popeye's went bankrupt following an ill-fated 1989 merger. After the bankruptcy, Copeland was looking for new ventures, and gambling had caught his eye. Copeland was proposing to operate a boat in Kenner on Lake Pontchartrain that he would call the *Casino Cajun Princess*. As he developed his plans, Copeland had visited Edwards twice at the Governor's Mansion, telling Edwards that while he had the money to finance the boat and had the best site, he was concerned that politics might keep him from winning. "I don't want to waste time and money by applying if I don't have a shot," Copeland said. Edwards assured him that merit, not politics, would determine the winners.

The other company interested in the Kenner site was owned by Robert Guidry, who also owned a West Bank tugboat business. Guidry was taking exactly the opposite approach from Copeland's by betting that politics mattered most. Unlike Copeland, Guidry was not known locally. But he was close to Andrew Martin, Edwards's executive assistant, who introduced him to the governor. Guidry was calling his boat the *Treasure Chest* and was proposing to operate on the Mississippi River in Kenner. Few people paid attention to him until he began boasting privately of his ties to Governor Edwards. After one riverboat commission meeting, Guidry predicted to a group of riverboat officials that he would get a license, saying that he played in Edwards's regular poker game at the Governor's Mansion and made sure he lost big.

The unpublicized poker games were held every Thursday, starting in the late afternoon in the mansion's third-floor playroom. With a break for dinner, the poker playing would last frequently past midnight. It was a high-stakes game that required $10,000 to get in, and it wasn't uncommon for players to win or lose $10,000 to $20,000 in an evening. Like Bobby Guidry, several of the players were involved with companies bidding for a riverboat-casino license. Among the others was Gus Mijalis, who was not only a longtime Edwards friend, but also a highly paid consultant to Capital Gaming, which wanted to operate on the Mississippi River in New Orleans.

Edwards hated being interrupted by aides during the game. Why? One answer could be later reports that he usually came away a winner. He obviously selected the right people to play with. Too impatient, he was usually not a good cardplayer.

The vote for the final seven riverboat licenses was set for June 18. The days leading up to the vote were frenzied as the thirty-six bidders jockeyed for political position. Rumors were flying about who was close to Edwards, who had met with him, and who was likely to win. Riverboat board members and their staff were bombarded by phone calls. "What else can I do?" the riverboat callers would ask. "Am I in good shape?"

About a week before the scheduled vote, Ken Pickering, the chairman of the riverboat panel, quietly paid a visit to the Governor's Mansion. Ironically, Pickering, a fifty-five-year-old New Orleans lawyer and financial consultant who retained his "Yat" accent, had been one of Governor Roemer's appointees to the commission. He had gotten to know Roemer in 1971 when they were part of a citizens' group that endorsed a long-shot candidate for governor named Edwin Edwards. In Edwards's second and third terms, Pickering served as his commissioner in the Office of Financial Institutions, a state agency that regulated state-chartered banks, savings and loan associations, and credit unions. He had returned to the private sector by the time Roemer named him to the riverboat commission in January 1992. Pickering wasn't sure he would keep his post when Edwards returned to power that month. Several weeks later, as Pickering was getting his shoes shined in the Capitol basement, Edwards and his entourage walked by. When Edwards saw Pickering, he stopped and asked, "Hey, you want to be chairman of the Riverboat Gaming Commission? I'd like you to do as good a job as you did while you were commissioner of banking."

"I'll do that," Pickering replied.

Before the riverboat board in March 1993 met on two occasions to make its selections, Pickering each time had shown a list of boats he favored to Edwards, and the governor had blessed them. Now about a week before the final vote on June 18, a Friday, Pickering visited the Governor's Mansion to show Edwards a list of the seven boats he favored. All of them were in the New Orleans area. "Fine with me," Edwards told him. "I don't have any problems." The seven boats were:

- The *Gretna Belle* (Bernie Klein's entry)

- The *Lady Sheraton* (the Bill Dow/ITT Sheraton entry)

- *Caesars on the River* (the Christopher Hemmeter/Caesars entry)

- The *President* (the casino's boat was more than halfway built)

- The *Casino Cajun Princess* (Al Copeland's entry)

- The *Treasure Chest* (Robert Guidry's entry)

- *Casino St. Charles* (which was proposing to operate in St. Charles Parish, thirty miles upriver from New Orleans)

On Monday, June 14, Pickering had brunch with Bernie Klein and Klein's mother-in-law, Phyllis Landrieu, an old friend. After some chit-chat, Landrieu couldn't contain herself and asked Pickering, "So what's the deal? Is Bernie going to get a license?"

Pickering laughed and replied, "Yeah, he will. This thing is over. I've got my list. The governor's approved it. But I'm getting a lot of pressure so don't tell anybody."

Klein was thrilled. He stood to make at least $26 million. But because of Mayor Harris's doubts, Klein decided to hopscotch around the state, paying a final visit on several of the other six riverboat commission members. (Serving on the board was a part-time job.) On Tuesday, he visited Geraldine Wimberley, a certified public accountant who lived in the Acadiana town of Opelousas. Like Ken Pickering, Wimberley had been a Roemer appointee whom Edwards had kept on the board. The governor knew her slightly. When Klein met with Wimberley to pitch the *Gretna Belle,* she was noncommittal.

On Wednesday, Klein visited two commissioners who lived in Shreveport. One was Gia Kosmitis, a lawyer who had done legal work for Edwards's 1991 gubernatorial campaign. Edwards had appointed her to the riverboat commission at the behest of his Shreveport friend, Gus Mijalis. When Klein visited her office, Kosmitis expressed her support for the *Gretna Belle,* saying it was one of the best proposals.

Klein next met with Sam Gilliam, the commission's vice chairman. Edwards had appointed Gilliam to the board at the request of state senator Greg Tarver, a close associate of the governor's. As a college student, Gilliam had helped integrate a Walgreen's lunch counter in Baton Rouge, but not before the police had turned attack dogs on him and the other students. He was now vice chancellor for student affairs at Southern University's Shreveport campus. During the meeting with Klein, Gilliam was warm and supportive of the *Gretna Belle.* He asked Klein if he knew whether Pickering supported the boat. Klein told Gilliam about the brunch two days earlier, where Pickering had told him the *Gretna Belle* was on his list. "Well, then, you've got my support," Gilliam told him.

An ecstatic Klein then drove to Baton Rouge to meet with one final board member, Louis James, on the next day, Thursday, June 16. James also had been a Roemer appointee whom Edwards had retained. His legislative sponsor was Congressman Cleo Fields, who had been an Edwards ally in the State Senate. James was an elderly doctor who treated poor people at a small Baton Rouge clinic. When Klein arrived at the doctor's office, he found a note saying that James was meeting with the governor and would be back later. When James returned and met with Klein, he praised the *Gretna Belle* and told Klein that he supported it.

Klein could hardly contain his excitement afterward when he called Ronnie Harris to report the positive news. As he began to describe the expressions of support, a shaken Harris interrupted him. He told Klein that Governor Edwards had called him the day before with devastating news: while Edwards supported Gretna's getting a boat, the riverboat commission did not favor Klein and would not select the *Gretna Belle* proposal on Friday. Harris had immediately protested, saying that he and Klein had taken all the proper steps to be selected. Edwards acknowledged this, but said it didn't matter. It was possible, he said, that one of the boats that would get a license on Friday would have a problem with their site and would want to move to Gretna.

Klein couldn't believe what Harris was telling him. "Ronnie, what the fuck is going on?" he asked.

"I don't know," replied Harris. "I guess it's good old Louisiana politics."

In a panic, Klein called Pickering and said he needed to meet with him immediately. The riverboat board chairman invited him over to his West Bank home. When Klein arrived, he related what Edwards had told Harris. Pickering laughed and shook his head. "That son of a bitch, Edwin Edwards," he said. "Was he on the speakerphone with Ronnie?"

"Yes, he was," Klein replied.

Pickering laughed again. "He probably had people in his office, and he was just telling Ronnie that to appease them. I've seen him do it a million times. Go home, get some sleep. You'll be the first one to get your license tomorrow."

Klein felt a tremendous sense of relief. He thanked Pickering, bade him goodbye, and then called Harris. Exultant, the mayor invited him over. Klein stopped to buy a bottle of champagne. At Harris's home, they sat on his front porch and toasted a prosperous future.

The next morning, June 18, was decision day. There were literally hundreds of millions of dollars at stake. By the time the meeting ended, owners of seven companies would win the lottery. Earlier in the week, the rumor mill had the seven winners as Hemmeter/Caesars, the President, the Bill Dow/ITT Sheraton boat, the Al Copeland boat in Kenner, the *Gretna Belle,* and one boat each in the towns of Alexandria and Monroe.

On the morning of the vote, *The Times-Picayune* reported two companies had come from nowhere and were now in the running. One was called Casino Carnival, and its principal owner was Norbert Simmons, a New Orleans investment banker in partnership with Bally Entertainment, a major casino company. The Casino Carnival didn't yet have a place to dock its boat, however. This normally would have deep-sixed the application. But Simmons had tended to his politics. He had given a small stake in the enterprise to Vernon Shorty, who owned a New Orleans drug rehabilitation company and was a business partner of state representative Sherman Copelin. Copelin, in turn, was a close associate of Governor Edwards and had earned a small fortune in business through his political connections. Copelin also was close to Simmons and had lobbied Pickering, Edwards, and others on his behalf. Copelin and Simmons lobbied the three black members of the Riverboat Gaming Commission—Sam Gilliam, Louis James, and Veronica Henry—by pointing out that Simmons was the only potential black riverboat owner.

The second company that suddenly had a chance was owned by Capital Gaming International. The company had little experience in gambling and had shaky financing, but it had partnered with a firm operated by Gus Mijalis and his nephew Sammy. Fat, balding, and fun-loving, Gus Mijalis was a Shreveport businessman who was one of Edwards's closest friends. Mijalis loved to tell stories and crack jokes. Even if his joke wasn't funny, Mijalis would laugh so hard that anyone listening couldn't help but join in. On the trip Edwards took to Paris and Monte Carlo with 617 campaign contributors and friends following his 1983 election back into office, *People* magazine described Mijalis gambling at a Monte Carlo casino. "Mijalis rolls the dice, sweats copiously, addresses the croupier as 'Señor . . . Monsieur . . . Sumbitch' and rocks the crystal chandeliers with cries of 'Am I good!?' and 'Boola-boola! Boola-boola!'"

Not only did Edwards and Mijalis gamble together, they also did business deals together, not always to Mijalis's benefit. Mijalis was tried along with Edwards in 1985 and 1986 for the sale of state hospital permits. Like Edwards, he was acquitted. Mijalis was involved in seafood wholesaling, insurance, and banking. Caught overextended by the Oil Bust, he had gone bankrupt in 1991, owing $26 million to a host of creditors. But when Capital Gaming came to Louisiana looking to open a riverboat casino, Mijalis's friendship with Edwards mattered far more than his business troubles. As a measure of his influence, Mijalis had gotten Edwards to name Shreveport lawyer Gia Kosmitis to the riverboat commission. So Capital Gaming cut an astonishing deal with Gus and Sammy Mijalis. In return for serving as "consultants," Capital Gaming would pay them $26 million in cash and loans over seven years. The Capital Gaming/Mijalis boat was to be called the *Crescent City Queen* and was to be docked on the Mississippi, about ten blocks upriver from the French Quarter.

The riverboat commission's meeting was held in House of Representatives Committee Room 3 in the basement of the State Capitol. Thirty minutes before the 9:00 a.m. meeting began, all of the eighty seats had been taken, and everyone else had to stand alongside the walls.

When Pat Fahey walked into the room, he saw a disturbing sign. Fahey had been a member of the small group that had conceived riverboat gambling in Louisiana and lobbied the bill through the state legislature in 1991. Now he was to become general manager of the President casino, if they got a license. When Fahey walked into the room that day, he spotted Gus Mijalis with a huge grin on his face. "What is he doing here?" Fahey asked himself. He pointed Mijalis out to Ed Ellers, who was the President's president. Ellers began to perspire visibly. Mijalis and Capital Gaming were probably competing for the same available slot as the President.

When Darryl Berger walked into the room, he immediately felt like a fish out of water. Berger, a New Orleans developer, was part of the Bill Dow/ITT Sheraton bid. He had good political connections in the New Orleans area, but not in Baton Rouge. That day, Berger saw a room full of men who had close connections to Edwards and the riverboat board. While he thought of himself as something of a political insider, Berger suddenly felt, as he remembered later, "like they knew everything about everything, and I knew nothing about nothing. There was an air of a complete moral vacuum in the room—evil and immorality. It was all of Edwards' friends—a rogue's gallery."

About twenty minutes before the meeting began, a riverboat lobbyist named C. J. Blache asked Louis James, the Baton Rouge doctor who served on the commission, to meet him in the hallway. Blache represented Jazz Enterprises, owner of a Baton Rouge boat that had gotten a license in March. Blache wanted to talk to James because he had been hearing rumors that the board might revoke Jazz Enterprises' license. Blache was talking to James when two of James's colleagues called him away. They were Floyd Landry, the retired furniture salesman from St. Bernard Parish whose political benefactor was Senate president Sammy Nunez, and Sam Gilliam, the vice chancellor of student affairs at Southern University's Shreveport campus. Gilliam's political benefactor was Shreveport senator Greg Tarver. Before Blache walked back into the committee room, he noticed that Gilliam was showing a piece of paper to Floyd Landry and Louis James. But Blache didn't attach any significance to this.

About five minutes before the meeting began, Pickering was standing at the committee room's dais when Gilliam approached him. Gilliam asked Pickering to join him and Landry in the hallway.

"Whatcha got?" Pickering asked. "We're fixing to start the meeting."

"We got this list," replied Gilliam. "It's been approved by the governor."

"What list?" asked a puzzled Pickering. Gilliam showed him a typewritten list of six boats. "No, that's not the boats we're going to do," Pickering said. "The governor's already approved my list."

"We've got the votes to defeat you," Gilliam said.

"You'll have to do precisely that," Pickering said. By now he was seething, not because he thought they would succeed in overruling him—Pickering was sure that he had the votes and Edwards on his side— but because Gilliam would dare challenge his authority as chairman.

What Pickering didn't know at this moment was that Edwards was now supporting another list, even though he had told Pickering he supported *his* list. The day before, on June 17, Edwards had met at the Governor's Mansion with three of his top legislative allies, Senate president Sammy Nunez, House Speaker John Alario, and Speaker Pro Tem Sherman Copelin. Each was supporting a riverboat bidder.

After that meeting, an Edwards aide had phoned commission member Louis James and asked him to meet the governor at the mansion.

James, a quiet doctor who rarely spoke at commission meetings, was taken aback by the call. Edwards had never phoned him before. Nevertheless, James went to the Governor's Mansion, leaving behind a note for Bernie Klein, who was supposed to meet with him at James's clinic. At the mansion, Edwards tried to get a feel for which boats James was supporting. Before James left, Edwards handed him a typewritten list of six boats. Four boats on this list were not on Pickering's list. They were the Boomtown/Skrmetta boat that was to operate on the Harvey Canal (backed by Speaker Alario), the Capital Gaming/Mijalis boat, the Norbert Simmons/Bally boat (backed by Representative Copelin), and a fourth boat that was to operate on the Bayou Bienvenue in St. Bernard Parish. This boat didn't have a casino partner, had a lousy location, and barely had financing. However, it had the strong support of Senate president Nunez and commission member Floyd Landry. Before they parted, Governor Edwards urged Louis James to share the typewritten list with Veronica Henry, a New Orleans lawyer whom he had just named to the commission. That evening, James shared the list with Sam Gilliam.

The next morning, after Gilliam showed Pickering the new list, the chairman's face was flushed in anger. Bill Dow, ITT Sheraton's partner, sitting three rows from the committee dais, took note of this. Dow was used to seeing Pickering with an affable look and a ready smile. But when Dow saw the red-faced Pickering, he thought, "I wonder what the hell this is all about."

Without giving the anxious audience any clues to his anger, Pickering began the meeting and started speaking from notes. He thanked all of the applicants and reviewed the expected benefits of riverboat gambling in Louisiana. Pickering then described the official criteria for selecting the license winners. The riverboat commission next took up housekeeping matters, and this dragged on for a while. Soon, more than an hour had passed since the meeting had begun. The men and women in the packed room shifted uneasily. Finally, after a vote on a technical issue, Pickering announced, "I believe that is all the items we needed to take along those lines today." He then said the commission would take up what everybody was waiting for: the awarding of the seven final licenses. Pickering said he wanted to introduce one boat at a time, have the commission staff give a report on the applicant, have the commissioners debate whether to award a license, and then vote. He paused and announced the first boat on his list to be approved. "If the staff would first give us a report on the *Gretna Belle*," he said.

Gretna mayor Ronnie Harris, sitting in the committee room's first row, felt a wave of exhilaration. "This is it!" he thought. "We are going to get the license!"

Before Pickering could say another word, Sam Gilliam broke in and began making a convoluted statement. "Mr. Chairman, the commission wishes to voice a concern and share with you and the group here our consideration or assessment of all the applicants that have come through as they related to the criteria that's embodied in the act or rule-making that has been promulgated by this commission and, of course, the information that is found in the form and the application." Gilliam rambled on until Pickering interrupted him. "I don't know that I know what you are asking," he said.

Gilliam resumed speaking. Normally eloquent and forceful, he spoke now in a halting voice, stumbling over his words and making vague comments about what "we" the commissioners were seeking in applicants. He didn't look up at the audience. Bernie Klein, sitting a few feet away, was confused, as was most of the audience. What was Gilliam trying to do?

Then Gilliam made it clear. He announced that he was offering a list of six boats as an alternative to Pickering's seven. Gilliam listed his boats:

- The St. Bernard Parish boat (backed by Senate president Sammy Nunez)

- The Capital Gaming boat (backed by Gus Mijalis)

- The Norbert Simmons/Bally boat (backed by Representative Sherman Copelin)

- The Boomtown boat (backed by Speaker John Alario)

- The *Treasure Chest* (owned by Robert Guidry, who played poker with Edwards)

- The St. Charles Parish boat (which, it would be learned later, had a deal to pay Stephen Edwards's father-in-law $2.5 million)

Members of the audience audibly gasped at what Gilliam was doing. Bernie Klein broke into a cold sweat and felt nauseated. Pat Fahey, who was to be general manager for the President riverboat, thought: "Here it comes. We're getting screwed."

At Gilliam's request, the commission voted first on the St. Bernard Parish boat. Pickering asked if there was any debate. There was none. The secretary then called the roll. "I vote for it," said Geraldine Wimberley. "For it," said Veronica Henry. "For it," said Louis James. "For it," said Floyd Landry. "For," said Gia Kosmitis. "For," said Sam Gilliam. Pickering then voted no. The boat was approved on a 6–1 vote.

Next was the Capital Gaming/Mijalis boat. Without any debate, it was approved 5–2, with Wimberley and Pickering voting no. Third was the Norbert Simmons/Bally boat. It was approved 6–1 (Pickering). Fourth was Boomtown, approved 5–2 (Wimberley and Pickering). Fifth was the *Treasure Chest*. This boat was also on Pickering's list, so it was approved 7–0. The St. Charles Parish boat was next. It, too, was on Pickering's list. The vote was 6–1, with Wimberley opposed.

Now there was a bit of commotion. People in the audience popped out of their seats to dash outside and call company executives or their stockbrokers. Inside the room, the seven commissioners sat silent, unsure what to do next. Gilliam's list contained only six boats, and there was one more license to award. After a long pause, Pickering looked around at the other commissioners. Nobody said anything. Pickering then decided he might as well return to his list. Saying he favored having another boat in New Orleans, he offered the President casino's boat. Floyd Landry seconded the motion. Pat Fahey, the President casino's general manager, suddenly perked up. Could they get a license after all? No, it turned out. The President lost on a 5–2 vote, with only Landry and Pickering offering support. Ed Ellers, the President's president, immediately jumped out of his seat and ran out into the hallway to frantically call his boss with the bad news. Within thirty minutes, President stock would plummet 12 points on the Nasdaq exchange.

Inside the room, there was another pause. The meeting was no longer following a script. Gilliam had no more boats on his list. Pickering wasn't sure what to do. He decided to offer another New Orleans boat, the Hemmeter/Caesars entry. Wimberley seconded the motion and cast the first vote in favor of it. Veronica Henry and Louis James followed suit. Then Landry, Kosmitis, and Gilliam voted against. It was 3–3. Pickering then broke the tie, voting to give Hemmeter/Caesars the final license. Moments later, with all seven licenses awarded, he adjourned the meeting.

Pandemonium broke out. Winners let out whoops of delight. Losers shook their heads in a daze. Reporters swarmed around Pickering to ask what had happened. He waved them off and stormed out of the Capitol. On the left side of the room, Al Copeland, the fried-chicken magnate, who had begun the meeting secure in the knowledge that he was on Pickering's list, was swearing loudly. "I've been fucked," he said more than once.

Bill Dow and Darryl Berger, who had partnered with ITT Sheraton, were shaking their heads as they left their seats. "Sorry, you got screwed," a friend told Dow. Berger remarked to a reporter, "I've been around politics for a while, but I have never seen anything like this." Later, he would tell ITT Sheraton executives and Dow, "We lost today to Sammy Nunez, Sherman Copelin, John Alario, and Gus Mijalis. How could we have had a shot?"

Pat Fahey, as he was leaving the room, happened upon Mijalis. "You motherfucker," Fahey said, his voice rising. He walked out as Mijalis protested his innocence.

Still in shock, Bernie Klein walked up to Sam Gilliam, who was getting up from his seat. Only two days before, Gilliam had assured Klein of his support for the *Gretna Belle*. Now he had orchestrated the board's move to select boats with close ties to Governor Edwards and his legislative leaders over more qualified boats. "What the hell happened?" Klein asked.

Gilliam wouldn't look up. "I can't tell you now," Gilliam replied, shaking his head. "Call me later."

A few minutes later, Klein was standing in the parking lot in front of the Capitol when a black Mercedes pulled up. It was Pickering with his wife. "Ken, what happened?" Klein asked.

Pickering shrugged his shoulders. "You tell me," he said.

Pickering then said he would make the short drive to the Governor's Mansion to find out. At the mansion, he told Sid Moreland, Edwards's executive assistant, "Boy, I've been screwed but good," before Moreland ushered Pickering into Edwards's office. Barely able to contain his anger, Pickering began to tell the governor what had happened. Edwards cut him off. "Yeah, I heard," he said.

"I can't believe what happened," Pickering said.

"I guess that's the way the cookie crumbles," Edwards said. He paused and then asked, "Do you want to have lunch?"

Pickering said no and then left.

An agitated Al Copeland showed up at the Governor's Mansion a few minutes later demanding to see Edwards. The governor refused to meet with him. That night, Copeland told an associate that he should have been playing poker with Edwards at the Governor's Mansion and losing heavily.

A week after the vote, Bernie Klein flew to Shreveport to meet with Kosmitis and Gilliam separately. Still in disbelief, Klein wanted a direct answer about what had happened. "I told those guys we shouldn't do it this way," Kosmitis told Klein. She wouldn't elaborate.

Klein met Gilliam at his office on the campus of Southern University in Shreveport. Gilliam lamented the events of June 18. "You got screwed," Gilliam said. He then added, "I had no choice."

"What do you mean you had no choice?" Klein asked.

"They threatened me," Gilliam replied.

"What do you mean?"

"They threatened my life," Gilliam explained. "I am in a politically appointed position. If I didn't go along, I would lose my job, and that is my livelihood."

Klein and Gilliam then took a walk outside. "This was out of my hands," Gilliam said. "I had to vote the way they wanted me to."

"Who is 'they'?"

"I can't tell you," Gilliam replied.

6

Edwards Wheels and Deals

W hen Edwin Edwards became governor again in January 1992, he immediately named a new superintendent for the Louisiana State Police. The man he replaced had won high marks for his honesty and professionalism, while Edwards's choice, Paul Fontenot, didn't have a college degree, had not overseen a large organization before, and was not particularly popular among the State Police rank-and-file. But Fontenot, given the rank of colonel, was very loyal, the qualification that mattered most to Edwards. Fontenot had developed his loyalty while serving as Edwards's bodyguard during his first three terms in office.

It was nothing new for a Louisiana governor to choose a political crony to head the State Police. From its earliest days, the agency had served the whims of whoever was occupying the Governor's Mansion. So a typical superintendent focused more on protecting the governor's political interests than on the public interest. One notable exception was Francis Grevemberg, named by Governor Robert Kennon as the State Police superintendent in 1952. For the next three years, Grevemberg bucked considerable political pressure by shutting down the illegal casinos, slot machines, and horse racing handbook parlors that had flourished under Kennon's predecessor, Earl Long. Most of Grevemberg's successors—Fontenot included—were political hacks.

The State Police's traditional duties included acting as the highway patrol, providing the governor's bodyguards, and conducting criminal investigations. The agency under Fontenot would take on new responsibilities, thanks to the Louisiana legislature. When the legislature legalized video poker and riverboat gambling in 1991 and the New Orleans land casino in 1992, lawmakers established a mishmash of regulatory-oversight boards. A nine-member board appointed by Edwards selected the New Orleans casino operator and regulated its operations, without State Police involvement. A separate seven-member board appointed by Edwards selected which riverboat companies had the right to operate in Louisiana. But the legislature had left it up to the State Police actually to license the boats. This meant that after the Riverboat Gaming Commission had awarded fifteen boats what became known as "certificates of preliminary approval"—awarding the final seven on June 18, 1993—the State Police had to award the operating licenses. The State Police played a second role with gambling: licensing video poker operators.

Although the legislature had given the State Police the responsibility of licensing riverboat and video poker operators, lawmakers didn't provide enough funds to carry out the additional work. So while state gambling regulators elsewhere received extensive training and coursework as they started out, Louisiana State Police troopers—many of whom had spent most of their careers handing out speeding tickets—had little money to learn the intricacies of the gambling business. Nor was anybody with expertise in gambling hired into a senior position within the State Police. The troopers assigned to the agency's new riverboat and video poker divisions had to learn on the fly as they dealt with established gambling companies that could hire the best lawyers, accountants, and consultants that money could buy. Adding to the mismatch, while the gambling companies could call on a platoon of experts to represent their interests, the new State Police riverboat division had only one full-time trooper to carry out its duties: devise the new casino rules, establish a process to determine which boats would be licensed, and create a procedure to decide which individual casino owners and executives had a suitable enough background to be licensed. Overwhelmed and underfinanced, the State Police let the Riverboat Gaming Commission take the lead and decide which boats should operate in Louisiana, and the State Police would then award the licenses. It was supposed to be the other way around.

Video poker presented an even greater problem for the State Police. While the agency would license only fifteen riverboats, the State Police by early 1992 was getting dozens of applications *a day* from would-be video poker operators. Applicants had to provide personal and business information and be found suitable, a process meant to keep out the bad characters frequently attracted to gambling and its loads of cash. Under the new law, video poker applicants would be licensed if they had not been convicted of a crime in the past ten years, if they had "good character, honesty and integrity," if they had not been involved in any criminal or illegal gambling activity, and if they had lived in Louisiana for the past two years.

There were three types of applicants. The first was companies that manufactured the machines. A second type was companies that would buy the machines from manufacturers, lease or sell the machines to bars and restaurants, and then manage the accounts if they leased the equipment. The third group of applicants was the bar and restaurant owners—who could have three machines apiece—as well as operators of highway truck stops, who could have up to fifty machines apiece in their establishments. To carry out background checks on the various applicants, the Louisiana State Police Video Gaming Division had only five troopers. The flood of applications inundated their office. "It was overwhelming, really, there was so much coming in," State Police lieutenant Riley Blackwelder, who headed the Video Gaming Division, recalled two years later.

As the backlog of applicants grew, the would-be video poker distributors and operators began calling Edwards to complain. He responded by pressuring the State Police to streamline the licensing process. In May 1992, he told Colonel Fontenot to award conditional licenses immediately and then carry out the background checks. Edwards said the lengthy licensing process was limiting profits for the would-be operators and costing the state badly needed tax revenue. Edwards said that the State Police could yank the licenses of anyone who was later found not to meet the standards.

However, Blackwelder and his direct boss, Captain Mark Oxley, who headed both the riverboat and video poker divisions, resisted Edwards's suggestion. They had solicited advice from officials in South Dakota and Montana, which already had video poker machines in operation, on how best to get the industry under way in Louisiana. Montana had awarded conditional licenses, but the officials there had warned Blackwelder and Oxley that it was a huge mistake. Once they gave a conditional license, they found, no matter what they uncovered later, they ran into political and legal barriers when they tried to revoke the license. Whatever you do, the Montana officials advised the Louisiana officials, don't grant conditional licenses. Oxley and Blackwelder cited this advice when they expressed opposition to Edwards's idea.

Edwards continued to insist. In September 1992, he asked Lieutenant Blackwelder and Colonel Fontenot to meet him at the Governor's Mansion. Blackwelder, forty-seven, who spoke in the southern twang of his native Pensacola, had been in the State Police for eleven years. Wanting to do his job properly and not used to meeting with the governor privately, he was nervous heading into the meeting. But Blackwelder was convinced that his position was correct: awarding conditional licenses courted disaster. He explained this to the governor and told him what the Montana officials had said. Edwards replied that he didn't care about Blackwelder's personal opinion, that he wanted the State Police to award the conditional licenses. Edwards then leaned forward, looked directly across his desk at the State Police lieutenant, and said, "If you have a problem with that and cannot do it, we'll get somebody who can."

"Yes, sir," Blackwelder said.

The State Police began awarding the conditional licenses for owners of bars and restaurants. But Blackwelder and Oxley defied Edwards by refusing to award conditional video poker licenses to operators of truck stops and to people whose companies sold or leased the machines. Because bar and restaurant owners accounted for most of the backlog, the majority of the complaints disappeared, and Edwards did not punish the two officials.

In the meantime, Oxley and Blackwelder had been encountering problems with Edwards on other fronts as well. In May 1992, the two State Police officials decided to deny a video poker license to Joe Palermo, a Lake Charles businessman. Palermo had a convicted bookmaker on his payroll, repeatedly refused to allow the State Police to inspect his existing business operations, and refused to provide information on his wife, whom he listed as an officer in the proposed truck stop. Before informing Palermo of their denial, Oxley and Blackwelder told Fontenot of their impending action. Palermo, they knew, had been close to Edwards, securing a plum patronage job during the governor's third term.

On May 20, Edwards asked Fontenot, Blackwelder, and Oxley to meet him at the Governor's Mansion to discuss the decision. When they arrived, Edwards asked to meet privately with Fontenot. When the State Police superintendent emerged a few minutes later, he advised Oxley and Blackwelder that the governor supported the decision to deny Palermo a license. Oxley and Blackwelder heaved a sigh of relief. Five days later, however, Fontenot told them that Edwards had changed his mind and wanted to find a way to license Palermo. Edwards said Palermo was willing to meet the State Police concerns to obtain a license. Palermo would remove his wife from the company, agree to an on-site inspection, and remove the convicted bookmaker from the payroll. Edwards's direct intervention bothered Blackwelder and Oxley because they thought it politicized a licensing process that should be independent and above reproach. Nonetheless, after Palermo took these steps, Oxley and Blackwelder licensed him on June 8. That did not end the story, however.

Six weeks later, a Lake Charles state representative tipped them off about an article involving Palermo in the local newspaper that contained disturbing news. Palermo, the *Lake Charles American Press* reported, had just admitted in court that during a 1986 trip to a Las Vegas casino, he had made a $10,000 cash payoff to Robert Graves, who was then serving as Edwards's secretary of transportation. Palermo had testified as a witness for the prosecution against Graves. After learning this information from the newspaper, the State Police carried out an investigation that determined Palermo had gone to Graves's hotel room and dropped a hundred $100 bills on his bed. Palermo called this a "token of appreciation" for Graves's having helped convince state officials to pay Palermo $85,000 more than they had been offering for land that the state bought from him. Palermo also had testified in court that he had helped Graves forge bogus land documents to conceal $40,000 in income. Palermo's testimony helped Graves get a twenty-one-month prison sentence for tax evasion.

With the new information, the State Police investigators wanted to revoke Palermo's video poker license. Under long-established gambling law, a license was a "privilege," not a "right." This meant that the State Police had the authority to cancel a license at any time if officials determined that the license holder had violated the suitability standards. To the State Police officials, it was an open-and-shut case. While Palermo had not been convicted of a crime, he was a co-conspirator in a fraud case, and that violated the standard of "good character, honesty and integrity."

On September 14, 1992, Captain Oxley ordered Lieutenant Black-welder to begin proceedings to yank Palermo's license. On October 16, the deputy State Police superintendent, Lieutenant Colonel Kenny Norris, signed off on the decision. Oxley was moving deliberately to make sure that, given Edwards's earlier action, he was taking all the necessary steps. The thirty-six-year-old Oxley, who had thick black hair and was ruggedly handsome, had been in the State Police for seventeen years and had learned a thing or two during this time about Louisiana politics.

By mid-December, Oxley was about to send the revocation notice to Palermo when he met with Fontenot. To Oxley's dismay, the superintendent expressed his opposition to the move, saying that it wasn't fair to Palermo to revoke a license that the State Police had just given him. Oxley responded by explaining that the investigators didn't learn about Palermo's crooked activities until six weeks afterward. "If we had known this information earlier, we wouldn't have given him the license," Oxley said. Fontenot finally agreed grudgingly, but insisted on notifying Edwards of their plans. Oxley then sent the revocation letter to Palermo.

Two weeks later, on January 4, 1993, Fontenot had stunning news for his underling. "I want you to send a letter of reinstatement to Palermo," Fontenot said. Oxley protested. Fontenot interrupted him and made it clear that this was an order. Having no choice but to obey, Oxley felt humiliated. Here he was trying to do the right thing, and Fontenot was undercutting him to protect an associate of the governor's.

In the meantime, Edwards had intervened with the State Police on behalf of another suspect friend trying to get a video poker license. The applicant was Joe Terrell, who had been a top administration official during the governor's first two terms. Terrell had been convicted of failing to file a 1976 state tax return, and he had an outstanding federal tax liability of $80,000 at the time of his 1992 video poker application. His tax problems prompted Illinois officials to deny him a riverboat license in that state. On July 14, 1992, Captain Oxley advised Colonel Fontenot that he was planning to deny a Louisiana video poker license to Terrell because of his tax problems. A month later, Edwards asked Oxley to meet with Terrell and Fontenot to try to find a way to get Terrell licensed. Following the meeting, Oxley refused to buckle, telling Fontenot that the additional information did not help Terrell and that he was still planning to deny Terrell a license. That was not the end of this story, either.

On July 23, Edwards asked Oxley and Fontenot to meet with him and Terrell at the Governor's Mansion. Oxley was upset because Edwards was intervening once again. At the mansion, Edwards told Oxley that had it been him, he would have given Terrell a license. "You're being too technical," Edwards said. He then turned to Terrell and said, "You created problems for yourself by making false tax declarations and misrepresentations. But I think you've shown that you should be licensed."

"Governor," Oxley responded, "this whole thing is extraordinary. I've got a muscle in my back that's as tight as my fist from stress over this case. I'm trying to do the right thing. I don't think Mr. Terrell deserves a license." Edwards backed off. A month later, Terrell withdrew his application. Later that year, he advised the State Police officials that he had paid his back taxes. Terrell reapplied for a license and got it in January 1993.

Six years later, it would be revealed that in 1991 Edwards had loaned Joe Terrell and a business partner $600,000 and that by the time of Terrell's 1992 video poker application, he still owed the governor more than $100,000. This meant that in 1992 Edwards wasn't just intervening with the State Police to help a friend, but to help someone who owed him money.

The Terrell case would not end Edwards's intervention on behalf of political associates in the video poker industry. In December 1993, the State Police notified the owner of A.-Ace Video Gaming Company that the agency would be revoking its license. A.-Ace's owner was Robert Guidry. He had won a spot in Edwards's circle thanks to his close friendship with Andrew Martin, the governor's executive assistant. Guidry also played his cards right with Edwards—literally. He applied for a riverboat license, and although he had no experience in gambling, he bragged to other riverboat applicants that Edwards's board would license him because he played, and lost heavily, during the weekly poker games at the Governor's Mansion. Guidry, in fact, did get one of the coveted licenses during the dramatic June 1993 meeting at which the riverboat board favored boats associated with Edwards and his political allies over such bidders as the Fortune 100 giant ITT Sheraton and the President Riverboat Casino company, which had been the first such company in the nation and which already had a boat half built for Louisiana. Along with getting the license from the Riverboat Gaming Commission, Guidry had received a video poker license from the State Police. His video poker company, A.-Ace, acted as a middleman, buying machines from manufacturers and then leasing them to bars and restaurants. It was a highly lucrative business. The 176 machines that A.-Ace leased to 66 bars and restaurants in the New Orleans area earned the company $40,000 a month.

One of Guidry's business partners at A.-Ace was Frank Caracci (*Ka-ra-cee*). FBI documents disclosed that Caracci was a mob associate with long-standing ties to organized crime boss Carlos Marcello. In 1970, Caracci was convicted of bribing an Internal Revenue Service agent, sentenced to one year in prison, and fined $10,000. Two years later, he was convicted of transporting pinball machines for illegal gambling, sentenced to two years probation, and fined $10,000. (The pinball industry had gotten its start in Louisiana under mobster Frank Costello.) Like Carlos Marcello, Caracci enjoyed good relationships with Louisiana politicians. After his two convictions, he applied for a pardon. The New Orleans police superintendent opposed the request, writing, "Caracci has been identified by federal, state and local authorities as an organized crime figure in the New Orleans area." But because of his political ties, Caracci in 1976 was granted a gubernatorial pardon that restored his Louisiana constitutional rights. The governor? Edwin Edwards.

After his 1972 conviction, Caracci continued his involvement with the pinball industry. And when video poker began to loom as a possibility, Caracci sought to be part of the action. In 1990, he traveled with the deputy police chief of New Orleans, Antoine Saacks, to Las Vegas to meet with officials of a Las Vegas video poker manufacturer. (Saacks was a swashbuckling and controversial police official who had become a millionaire from his outside business activities while on the police payroll.) Caracci and Saacks ended up signing a contract to serve as the Las Vegas manufacturer's Louisiana representative in case the state legalized video poker.

In 1991, when a group of pinball machine owners discussed how to get the state legislature to legalize video poker, Caracci attended one of the first meetings. Because of his organized-crime ties, a colleague told him that the group couldn't afford to have him there again.

In 1992, Caracci hooked up with Robert Guidry. With his experience in the pinball machine industry, Caracci was a valuable commodity for Guidry; he already had relationships with bar owners who might want A.-Ace's video poker machines. In fact, Caracci signed a sweet deal with Guidry: as a commission he and his two sons would receive a 25 percent share of A.-Ace's profits from any video poker machines that the trio placed in bars and restaurants. Because Caracci placed 90 percent of A.-Ace's 176 machines, that 25 percent commission translated into $466,000 in payments from Guidry in 1992–1993. The State Police said the amount was so large that the Caraccis were in effect part owners of the company, something that Guidry had failed to report to the agency. On December 16, 1993, the State Police revoked A.-Ace's video poker license, citing Frank Caracci's role with the company.

The ruling had enormous implications for Guidry. Not only did he stand to lose a video poker business that was earning him $40,000 a month, but he was awaiting word at the time whether the State Police would grant him a license for his riverboat casino, the *Treasure Chest*. The boat had won a preliminary certificate from the Riverboat Gaming Commission five months earlier, but could not operate without the State Police license as well. Losing the video poker license would undoubtedly disqualify Guidry from getting the riverboat license, worth at least $25 million. So Guidry immediately appealed the video poker ruling against A.-Ace, and a judge friendly to the gambling industry temporarily blocked the State Police action on January 6, 1994.

On the following day came the inevitable summons to the Governor's Mansion for Captain Oxley, Lieutenant Blackwelder, and three other State Police officials. The governor wanted to discuss how the State Police had handled Guidry's case. After the showdowns over Joe Palermo and Joe Terrell, Oxley blanched at the thought of meeting with Edwards again, and with good reason. At the mansion, the governor wasted little time in expressing his displeasure. He told the State Police officials that they had mishandled the case and trampled on Guidry's rights in the process. Showing extensive knowledge of the case, he attacked the State Police on point after point, acting as if they and not Guidry were the defendant. At one point, Edwards accused the investigators of using "Gestapo" tactics against the *Treasure Chest* owner.

As Oxley listened, he thought the governor was engaging in the highly inappropriate role of trying the case on the spot. Edwards, Oxley thought, was acting like the judge and the jury, and the verdict in Edwards's mind was clear. "I can't believe he's doing this," Oxley told himself, over and over.

Also in the room that day was Stephen Edwards, the governor's elder son. He was representing the *Treasure Chest* in its efforts to win a riverboat license from the State Police. At one point, Oxley said he felt uncomfortable outlining the legal arguments against Guidry with Stephen Edwards in the room. The governor dismissed that concern.

Edwards said several times that while he and Guidry were personal and political friends, he was simply acting in the state's best interests. Edwards also said the State Police officials shouldn't feel threatened by his comments. But that's exactly how Oxley and Lieutenant Blackwelder felt: Edwards was trying to intimidate them so they would license A.-Ace. Nonetheless, after the meeting ended, Blackwelder and Oxley told Colonel Fontenot that they would not back down.

Guidry was forced to continue his appeals through the courts and possibly lose his video poker license and not get a riverboat license. But his case ended up before another friendly judge. Helping his cause, Caracci's associates testified to the mobster's fine character. Among them was Harry Lee, the longtime sheriff of Jefferson Parish—the parish's most powerful elected official—and a close friend of Edwards's. Sheriff Lee testified that he had encouraged Guidry to go into business with Caracci, adding that he hadn't known of Caracci's criminal past or mob ties. "I would have no problem with that," Lee added. "I have a lot of friends convicted of felonies. . . . A lot of people are uptight about that. I'm not." The judge decided in favor of Guidry, ruling that the State Police did not have adequate grounds to revoke his license. A.-Ace, ruled the judge, was not acting as a front for Caracci, and Guidry had made a good-faith effort to comply with all gambling regulations.

There was one immediate repercussion. A few days after the judge's ruling, Lieutenant Riley Blackwelder, who had consistently locked horns with Edwards over Blackwelder's licensing decisions, was transferred from his position as head of the Video Gaming Division. Blackwelder was shifted to a low-prestige position—heading the State Police supply unit. It was announced officially that it was part of a normal rotation. A high-ranking friend within the State Police told him that the real reason was his defiance of Edwards, but that if he valued his career—and Blackwelder did—he ought not to say anything publicly. Blackwelder followed this advice and kept quiet.

Meanwhile, the State Police officials had been carrying out their other major duties with respect to gambling—the licensing of the riverboat casinos. However, their work was causing dismay among officials with the fifteen boats that had won preliminary certificates from the Riverboat Gaming Commission in 1993. The riverboat officials thought that winning a preliminary certificate from the commission settled the question of which boats would operate in Louisiana. Commission chairman Ken Pickering had even said so after the commission awarded the final seven certificates at the dramatic June 1993 meeting in the State Capitol. Afterward everyone realized that the State Police under the 1991 law had the final authority to hand out licenses. Was it possible that the agency's officials would give licenses to boats that the Riverboat Gaming Commission had not tapped? There was certainly good reason to license others. Officials with several of the boats chosen by the riverboat commission had either little gambling experience, shaky financing, a poor site, or a combination of the three. In theory, the State Police could disregard the commission selections and give licenses to more deserving boats, like ITT Sheraton's, the President casino's, or the *Gretna Belle*, Bernie Klein's boat.

However, Governor Edwards, having secretly arranged for the board to choose his slate of boats at the June 1993 meeting, wasn't about to let the State Police select someone else. In September of that year, he began pressuring them to hold licensing hearings for the boats chosen by the commission. Once again, Colonel Fontenot acceded to his wishes. In the end, the State Police held licensing hearings for sixteen boats. Only one of them—a Baton Rouge vessel—hadn't been tapped by the riverboat commission. And that boat didn't get a State Police license. The agency licensed only the fifteen chosen by the riverboat commission.

There would be one final controversy involving Edwards and the State Police. It would come in the December 1993 licensing of a boat owned by Christopher Hemmeter, who by now also owned a one-third share of the Harrah's Jazz casino, which had yet to open. In June 1993, on a separate gambling front, Hemmeter and his partner, Caesars World, had secured one of the coveted fifteen preliminary certificates from the Riverboat Gaming Commission. They were planning to operate on the Mississippi River in New Orleans. But first, Hemmeter had to get a State Police license.

He and his team thought that this would be a perfunctory step. After all, Hemmeter was so friendly, likable, and upbeat that he could charm virtually anyone. And wasn't he supposed to be worth more than $100 million? At the same time, Hemmeter had an impressive list of references, including Peter Ueberroth, Lee Iacocca, and former President Jimmy Carter. If those credentials weren't enough for the State Police, Hemmeter had Billy Broadhurst running political interference. Broadhurst had been a law partner of Edwards's in Crowley and, after having been active in each of his political campaigns since then, was part of his inner circle.

Before Hemmeter could get the license, however, he would run head-on into a 350-pound, $30,000-a-year midlevel employee of the state's Department of Revenue and Taxation, Roland Jones. Jones had no firsthand knowledge of Christopher Hemmeter's glamorous world. He had grown up poor in New Orleans, without ever knowing his father. His mother died when he was in tenth grade. He lived alone for his final three years of high school, working part-time at a grocery store and receiving $20 a month in Social Security benefits as the child of a deceased parent. Jones could have become a poverty statistic. But he was a hard worker, determined to carve out a nice life for himself. With good high school grades, he attended Southern University in New Orleans and graduated fourth in his class of 650 students, with a degree in accounting. Jones then took an auditor's job with the IRS. In 1990, he moved to the state Department of Revenue and Taxation and became a respected employee.

Jones's department was called on to scrutinize the financial backgrounds of the boat applicants. By chance, in June 1993, he was assigned to investigate Hemmeter's background. Jones thought that it would be a simple task. He had followed the land-casino story in the press and was quite certain that Hemmeter was one of the world's richest men. Jones's co-workers teased him, telling him he had gotten the easiest assignment. Nevertheless, Jones was resolved to examine Hemmeter's finances thoroughly.

Soon, Jones had on his desk a stack of tax returns, corporate balance sheets, and bank reports from Hemmeter and his various business enterprises. As Jones plowed through them one day, he was struck by something: Hemmeter's statement of net worth to financial institutions showed personal assets of more than $100 million. That didn't surprise Jones. What caught his attention was that the statement also showed liabilities for Hemmeter of more than $100 million. At best, Hemmeter's assets just covered his liabilities. Jones sucked in his breath and thought: "I have more cash than this guy has." He called his boss, Earl Millet, and told him what he had found. "This would not preclude Hemmeter from getting a license," Jones said, "but this indicates we have to look more closely at his finances." Millet told him to keep digging.

As he resumed his work, Jones discovered that for years Hemmeter had paid off one loan by taking out another. In other words, he was robbing Peter to pay Paul. As the implication of this revelation sank in, Jones concluded that Hemmeter had built a house of cards that would eventually fall. Jones passed along this view to Millet, who again told him to keep digging.

A short time later, Jones uncovered more disturbing news. Hemmeter's two small Colorado casinos had mostly lost money and would be in the black, according to Hemmeter's estimates, only by increasing revenues 151 percent while reducing expenses 33 percent. This didn't make sense to Jones. If the casino's revenues went up, so would expenses, he figured. Hemmeter was applying the same financial logic to the Louisiana riverboat, which he was predicting would be the state's most successful boat. The question of Hemmeter's numbers was important not only for how the New Orleans boat would do by itself, but because the fate of Hemmeter's Louisiana riverboat was directly tied to the success of the Colorado casinos. Hemmeter had been trumpeting to

Louisiana officials that Salomon Brothers had raised $140 million in bonds for him. However, as Jones dug through the financial statements, he realized that Hemmeter was intending to divert $42 million of the $140 million to his Colorado casinos. This meant that if the Colorado financial projections were off—and Jones was sure they were—Hemmeter would need to draw money from his Louisiana venture. But there was little extra cash for the Louisiana riverboat. Along with diverting $42 million to the Colorado casinos, Hemmeter was planning to spend another $28 million of the $140 million for purposes other than the Louisiana boat. To Jones, the margin of error for Hemmeter's Louisiana riverboat would be too thin.

Jones also discovered that Caesars, a highly respected gambling operator, was no longer Hemmeter's partner in the riverboat because of the fallout over the soured New Orleans land-casino deal. After Harrah's Jazz had won the state operating license, Hemmeter had joined forces with them, leaving Caesars out in the cold. Caesars officials responded by cutting their ties entirely with Hemmeter, which meant they would not operate his riverboat. Hemmeter, with characteristic confidence, nonetheless decided that he could operate the riverboat casino without an experienced gambling partner.

Hemmeter also would be operating the riverboat without Daniel Robinowitz, the developer who had originally brought him to Louisiana. The two had similarly had a falling-out after the state casino board's decision. Robinowitz thought that Harrah's Jazz had improperly influenced board members to win the nod and wanted Hemmeter to go to the United States Attorney's office. Hemmeter had refused and ordered Robinowitz not to contact authorities with his suspicions. Instead, Hemmeter had joined forces with Harrah's Jazz and cut Robinowitz out of the loop, even as Robinowitz remained his partner in the land casino and the riverboat. By late 1993, with Robinowitz sharply disagreeing with Hemmeter on his plans for the riverboat, the two were barely on speaking terms. Roland Jones thought that not having the help of Caesars, and to a lesser extent Robinowitz, would cause problems for Hemmeter.

To make matters worse for the developer, Jones discovered that the twenty-some entities controlled by Hemmeter had shown a loss on their federal income tax returns during 1992. At the same time, all of his operations were burdened by debt. Of the $42 million that Hemmeter was planning to divert to his Colorado casinos, $33 million was to pay off debt for that venture. To Jones, this was another example of Hemmeter using new loans to pay off old ones, not to grow his businesses. "This is bullshit," Jones told himself. When colleagues in the taxation department learned of Jones's qualms about Hemmeter's finances, they reminded him that he could be incurring the wrath of Governor Edwards. You might lose your job, they counseled.

Hemmeter's licensing hearing took place on December 14, 1993, at the State Police Training Academy Auditorium in Baton Rouge. As Hemmeter drove in a limousine to the hearing, he and his partners agreed that getting the license would be a snap. Indeed, Hemmeter cut a confident figure when he began his presentation with an overview of his plan. He predicted great success, saying the boat would open in December 1994 on the Mississippi River. The developer also presented a rosy picture of his Colorado casinos before concluding, "We also look forward, subject to your approval . . . to not only uphold our form of operation setting forth the ethical, moral and legal standards at the highest possible level, but to assist with the growth of the industry in a proper and exciting fashion for the future years and the prosperity of this state." Hemmeter was standing at a podium, facing a raised stage. He went to take his seat. Roland Jones was invited to give his presentation. He had briefed the State Police officials earlier in the day on what he would say.

Jones was sitting on the stage with four State Police officers. One of them was Lieutenant Joey Booth, who was chairing the hearing. The other three would vote on whether to license Hemmeter. They were Captain Mark Oxley, Sergeant Marcal Poullard, and Sergeant Brian Etland. They were no match for the smooth developer and his phalanx of lawyers and financial experts. Neither Oxley nor Poullard had a college degree. Etland had a law degree, but had just joined the riverboat division and had little experience in finance or gambling.

Jones gave a brief overview of his findings. Etland then asked whether Jones had studied the company's finances: "Do you have an opinion as to . . . whether it's adequate to handle the financing?"

"In my opinion," replied Jones, "the gaming interest, given the facts that I have, would have difficulty paying back the $140 million."

The hearing room suddenly grew very quiet. Hemmeter shifted uneasily in his chair.

"And on what reasons do you base that?" Etland asked.

Jones explained that the Colorado casinos had lost $11 million in 1992 and had not earned any money until the last quarter when the casinos showed a $1 million profit. "When you take into consideration that the Colorado casinos up to this point have not shown a profit," Jones said, "and it is anticipated that the tax return for this coming year will also not reflect a profit, the revenue estimates for the subsequent years seem to me to be excessive."

The three State Police troopers asked Jones more questions. He continued to express his doubts about the venture, noting that Hemmeter was planning to use only half of the $140 million from Salomon Brothers for the Louisiana riverboat. Jones added that all of Hemmeter's companies had shown a tax loss the previous year. Referring to the two Colorado casinos and the Louisiana riverboat, Jones added that "if either one of those three casinos are not profitable, there's a possibility that [Hemmeter's company] could not repay its debt."

Sergeant Poullard announced that the State Police had no more questions for Jones. Lieutenant Booth then invited Hemmeter back to the podium. The developer moved quickly from his seat in the audience. He was seething at Jones's testimony, and he wanted to set the record straight. Nobody had ever challenged him in public like this before, and to have it come from some unknown government bureaucrat?

First, Hemmeter and his attorneys answered several questions by running through the developer's complex financial scheme. The three State Police officials seemed confused by the references to "warrants," "bond issuances," and "high yield investors." None of the three could match the financial expertise of Hemmeter and his attorneys. After several minutes of the financial discussion, Hemmeter asked to address the board. He started slowly, addressing specific issues raised by Jones. Yes, the Colorado casinos had lost money, but that was expected during the opening phase, he said. The casinos were now beginning to make money, Hemmeter added. He went on to say that, yes, his various companies had not shown a profit last year, but that was because they had taken advantage of federal tax write-offs that caused the companies to show losses. "To suggest that we would be incapable of repaying these bonds," Hemmeter said, "is to suggest that the most sophisticated financial institutions in the United States of America are collectively incorrect in their assessment."

Hemmeter had hit his stride. He was impassioned, he was indignant, he was compelling. He noted that in 1988 he had been listed among the Forbes 400 list of the nation's richest individuals. "And there were only three of us under the age of 50 who had accomplished it ourselves," he said. "I also might mention one last point: That I have always paid every bill that I have ever owed. Nobody with the Hemmeter organization or any company I have ever been involved with has come to us and said, 'You haven't met your obligations.'"

It was a bravura performance, one that left Sergeant Poullard, Sergeant Etland, and Captain Oxley spinning. Roland Jones, the state financial expert, had said that Hemmeter was financially unsuitable, that his business empire rested on a house of cards. But could they trust the word of a midlevel government employee they didn't know over Christopher Hemmeter, held by many to be a wealthy visionary who was promising to build the most spectacular riverboat operation in Louisiana?

Without allowing Jones to respond publicly, Lieutenant Booth announced that the licensing hearing would take a break and that the State Police officials would meet privately to decide Hemmeter's fate.

Throughout the morning hearing, Lieutenant Colonel Kenny Norris, the deputy State Police superintendent, had watched the proceedings from a seat just below the stage. Norris had no formal role in deciding whether Hemmeter would be licensed, and indeed had not uttered a word during the proceedings. Norris had decided to be there just in case anything unexpected happened, given the stakes and the possible political implications. He was glad he was there because he found Jones's testimony profoundly troubling. Norris thought that if he had a vote, he would not grant Hemmeter a license.

Norris was planning to join his State Police colleagues during the executive session. But first Norris, a forty-nine-year-old good old boy who had been in the State Police for twenty-three years, wanted to call his wife to ask her to make pork chops, rice, and gravy for dinner. As he headed toward the phone, Billy Broadhurst stopped him. Broadhurst, a confidant of Governor Edwards's, was part of the Hemmeter team and in fact stood to receive a $600,000 bonus if the boat was licensed. "I don't really see this as a big problem," Broadhurst told Norris. "Salomon Brothers wouldn't lend any money if there was a problem."

"I don't necessarily agree with that," replied Norris. "They lend money all the time and lose it. It looks to me like y'all got a problem." Norris excused himself and went to call his wife.

A few minutes later, as Norris walked toward the executive hearing room, he bumped into Wiley McCormick, who had been the State Police superintendent during Edwards's third term. McCormick was now a private business consultant, and he was at the Hemmeter hearing because he was representing another riverboat applicant and wanted to see how a hearing was conducted. Upon seeing Norris, McCormick said, "You guys have to make a tough decision today."

"Yeah," responded Norris, "somebody may not get a license today."

"I just saw Broadhurst on the phone in the hallway," added McCormick. "You're probably going to get a call from the governor." Norris laughed at the idea. McCormick loved to joke around, so Norris knew he wasn't serious. Besides, in all his years in the State Police, Edwards had called him only once before. There was no way the governor would be calling him.

Norris walked into the executive session room and sat down. Inside, Roland Jones, Lieutenant Booth, Sergeant Poullard, Sergeant Etland, Captain Oxley, and a few others were seated around a table. Poullard, Etland, and Oxley would decide whether to license Hemmeter. The State Police officials were asking Jones additional questions about Hemmeter's finances. After a few minutes, Norris joined in, saying he couldn't understand why Hemmeter would borrow funds for the New Orleans project and use some of that money to pay off debt in Colorado. "Where's the cushion for Louisiana?" Norris asked. "It looks like he's not financially solid."

It was about that time that a secretary poked her head through the doorway. "Colonel Norris, the governor wants you on the telephone," she said.

Norris looked up. "You got to be kidding," he said, thinking this was another joke. "I'm busy right now."

"No," she said. "It's really the governor."

The room suddenly went quiet. Norris sat up straight and then paused. As the others looked back and forth at each other, Norris pushed back his chair, stood up, and walked out of the room. Nobody said anything for several moments. They didn't have to. They all knew why the governor was calling.

Norris was nervous as he picked up the phone. After a brief greeting, Edwards said he didn't think Jones had provided accurate information at the hearing. He added, "Take it for what it's worth, State Police shouldn't worry about financial suitability. Y'all should concentrate on criminal suitability."

In fact, Norris knew that the 1991 video poker law specifically called for the State Police to examine an applicant's financial suitability.

"I kind of disagree, Governor," responded Norris. "I think the financial suitability is part of it, and I think Hemmeter's got a little bit of a problem."

"I don't think State Police should be worried about the financial suitability part," Edwards reiterated. He went on for several more minutes, being careful not to tell Norris specifically that the State Police should license Hemmeter. He didn't have to. Norris understood the message.

Norris walked back into the executive session room and sat down. There was a moment of silence. The others were waiting to hear what the governor had said. "We need to go ahead and make a decision," Norris said. "I'll tell you what the governor said later."

Poullard, Etland, and Oxley began debating the licensing matter. They would decide the licensing matter; Jones would not vote. Oxley asked Jones if Hemmeter had ever defaulted on a loan. Jones said he had not. The answer seemed to satisfy the three troopers. They then agreed that Hemmeter was financially solid and deserved a license. The officials would say later that Jones, in the private session, began to waffle from his public statements that Hemmeter would have a hard time paying back his loans. Jones would say that he did not backtrack. The officials would also say later that Edwards's phone call had not influenced their thinking, noting that Norris did not disclose the governor's comments until after they had reached their decision. The State Police officials would admit, however, that they knew without being told why Edwards had called.

Back in the public session, Lieutenant Booth announced the unanimous decision in favor of Hemmeter. "Welcome to Louisiana and riverboat gaming here in our state," Captain Oxley said to him. The tanned developer smiled broadly, shook hands with his lawyers, and thanked the hearing board.

As Roland Jones walked out of the hearing, he was upset, but kept his thoughts to himself. He had done his job, and he had done it well. But once Edwards had made the phone call, he knew how the State Police officials would rule. Jones shook his head and reminded himself that he couldn't help it if they had voted the wrong way. Besides, he was sure that future events would vindicate him.

7

Operation Hardcrust

O ne summer day in 1991, a short, bearded former Atlantic City casino executive visited a friend at an amusement park on Pier 84 in Manhattan. The former casino executive was Steven Bolson, and he wanted to convince his friend, Christopher Tanfield, to join him in a new venture. Tanfield, a heavyset thirty-two-year-old, until recently had been a concert promoter who booked vintage acts such as Frank Sinatra, Frankie Valli, and the Coasters. Bolson and Tanfield had gotten to know each other when Bolson was the chief marketing executive at the Taj Mahal casino, and Tanfield had tried to interest him in several entertainment acts. One was called "Celebrity Boxing with Little Richard." Bolson didn't bite at the proposal, but the two, both New Jersey natives, became friends nevertheless.

Bolson, forty-five, had a 1968 undergraduate degree from Tulane University, in New Orleans, and a law degree from Rutgers University. He began his professional career as a deputy New Jersey attorney general and then switched over to the gambling industry. In 1979, he became corporate counsel at Bally's Park Place Casino Hotel in Atlantic City. He changed direction in 1989 by becoming marketing director for the Taj Mahal. But in June 1991, Taj Mahal owner Donald Trump fired him in a management shake-up. Bolson next went to work for an Atlantic City law firm, but he continued to look for a new opportunity with a gambling company. Bolson began discussing several possible new ventures with Tanfield, who by now was running the Victory Park amusement park on Pier 84. The prospect that excited Bolson most stemmed from Louisiana's legalization of video poker at bars, restaurants, and highway truck stops. Video poker was a surefire moneymaker, he told Tanfield, as they sat that summer day in the air-conditioned trailer that served as Victory Park's office. Bolson told Tanfield that he knew Louisiana from his days at Tulane. Plus, he had a politically connected fraternity brother in New Orleans who would give him entrée to the state's movers and shakers. In Louisiana who you knew usually mattered more than what you knew. As a twelve-year casino executive, Bolson said he could provide the gambling know-how and the Louisiana political connections. Tanfield, in turn, had contacts in the investment community. Bolson proposed to his friend that he raise start-up capital and act as the chief salesman. Tanfield responded that he liked the idea, and they made plans to explore the venture further.

Tanfield had a partner in Victory Park named Eugene (Noogie) Gilpin, who happened to be in the trailer when Bolson and Tanfield discussed the possible Louisiana enterprise. A day or two later, Gilpin told Tanfield that he had overheard the conversation and could offer some assistance. A short time later, Gilpin secured a thousand-machine order from a Louisiana video poker company.

These events marked the beginning of a new threat to Louisiana's burgeoning gambling industry: Tanfield and Gilpin were associated with the Gambino crime family, which would attempt through the video poker venture to reestablish the Mafia in New Orleans.

The Gambino mob was headed by John Gotti. In 1990, the FBI described Gambino as having more than three hundred inducted members and another three thousand associates who worked for them. Law enforcement experts estimated that the family grossed $300 million a year from illegal gambling, loan-sharking, narcotics trafficking, and extortion from unions and businessmen in the garment, construction, waterfront, trucking, and garbage collection industries. The Gambino mob also exacted tribute from Atlantic City casino suppliers. By the summer of 1991, however, John Gotti was in jail, charged with arranging the 1986 murder of his predecessor.

Nevertheless, the Gambino family continued to conduct business, including a promising new venture in Louisiana. By October 1991, Noogie Gilpin had introduced Christopher Tanfield to John Gammarano, a soldier in the Gambino family and one of its biggest moneymakers. Tanfield pitched the Louisiana proposal to Gammarano, saying that video poker was a sure gold mine, but that he and Bolson needed investors. Gammarano liked the idea enough to fly with them to New Orleans to get the lay of the land there. Accompanying them was Joseph (Jo Jo) Corozzo, a onetime driver for Gotti who served as an acting capo (captain) in the Gambino family. When they arrived at their French Quarter hotel, Gammarano and Corozzo told Tanfield to sit tight, that they had to meet with associates—who were members of the Marcello family. Under organized-crime protocol, the Gambino family could not do business in New Orleans unless they included the local mob. In this case, it was the Marcello family.

Carlos Marcello, the patriarch, had come to New Orleans as an infant in 1910, emigrating with his mother from Sicily. After dropping out of school at fourteen, he started his criminal career by robbing banks. Following a stint at the Louisiana State Penitentiary, Marcello owned a bar, sold drugs, and became involved in illegal gambling enterprises with New York mobster Frank Costello. Shrewd and tireless, Marcello became so adept at getting Costello's slot machines into New Orleans area bars—and collecting hefty payouts each week—that Costello gave him a 12.5 percent share of the Beverly Country Club, which, when it opened in Metairie in 1945, was considered the country's most sumptuous casino. The boss of the New Orleans crime family at the time was Silvestro "Silver Dollar Sam" Carollo, but in 1947 the federal government deported him to Sicily. Marcello then took over, even though Carollo's son, Anthony, asserted that he rightfully deserved to be the new boss.

Standing only five feet two inches with thick shoulders and meaty hands, Marcello became known as "the Little Big Man." Over the next twenty years, he ruled the New Orleans underworld, received protection from local authorities, and developed political ties with such governors as Earl Long, Jimmie Davis, and John McKeithen. An astute business-man, Marcello made large profits from drug trafficking, prostitution, motels, loan-sharking, and illegal gambling. But Anthony Carollo, a New Orleans restaurant owner, continued to nurse the conviction that he should rule the roost and quietly agitated against Marcello. It took mob leaders from the Gambino and Colombo families in New York to settle the dispute in 1966 in favor of Marcello. Afterward, they marked the return to harmony by holding a luncheon at La Stella restaurant in Queens. Police crashed the gathering, arresting Carlo Gambino, Joseph Colombo, Carlos Marcello, his brother Joseph Marcello Jr., Anthony Carollo, Frank Gagliano Sr. (another New Orleanian), and several oth-ers. The arrests made headlines nationwide, but Carlos Marcello stayed out of jail and resumed his activities in Louisiana.

Many conspiracy buffs concluded that he was behind President Kennedy's assassination, in retribution for Attorney General Robert Kennedy's decision to deport him to Guatemala in 1961, upon discov-ering that Marcello had obtained a fake Guatemalan birth certificate to help prevent a possible deportation to Italy. Marcello returned from Guatemala to the United States a few months later and managed to stay one step ahead of the law until 1981, after he unwittingly took an FBI informant as a partner in a deal to obtain Louisiana insurance con-tracts through bribes and kickbacks. Marcello and Charles Roemer II—Governor Edwin Edwards's top aide and the father of future governor Buddy Roemer—were convicted and sent to jail. When Marcello was released in 1989 at seventy-nine, he was frail and affected with demen-tia. Control of New Orleans's mob family had passed to Anthony Ca-rollo and Frank Gagliano Sr. Like Carollo, Gagliano was the son of a onetime mobster. The Feds had deported his father, Giuseppe, to Italy in the 1950s.

Carollo and Gagliano lacked Marcello's intelligence and cunning, and under their stewardship the New Orleans mob shriveled. When the

Louisiana legislature in 1991 legalized video poker, Carollo, Gagliano, and a few cohorts were doing little more than operating illegal slot machines in a handful of New Orleans area bars. Nonetheless, Carollo and Gagliano, who were each nearly seventy, still dreamed of becoming rich big shots. So they jumped at the chance when John Gammarano and Jo Jo Corozzo—the two Gambino family higher-ups—came to New Orleans in October 1991 with the proposition that they enter the video poker business together.

They couldn't simply form a company and get under way, however. Under the new video poker law, Louisiana residents had to own a majority of each company, and the owners had to pass a background check by the Louisiana State Police. Either or both of these requirements would keep Tanfield, Bolson, Gammarano, Corozzo, Carollo, or Gagliano from legally being the owners. The six men were not to be deterred by mere laws, not with video poker's enormous profit potential at stake. At the suggestion of Carollo and Gagliano, they installed a New Orleanian named Aaron Mintz to head the video poker operation. Mintz's name was well known in New Orleans because his family had owned a furniture store there for nearly seventy years. The Carollos and the Gaglianos had bought furniture from Mintz's store for years, and Mintz and his family frequented the restaurants owned by Anthony Carollo and Frank Gagliano Sr.

At five feet six inches and 135 pounds, the elfin Mintz was a long-time leader in the Jewish community and had served on numerous local boards, including the Anti-Defamation League of New Orleans, the New Orleans Chamber of Commerce, and Junior Achievement of Louisiana. He had raised money for the United Negro College Fund and was a prominent member of the Zulu Social Aid and Pleasure Club, the nearly all-black Mardi Gras krewe that paraded in blackface and straw skirts. Within Zulu, Mintz had the honorary title of "Witch Doctor."

But Mintz, seventy, had serious credibility problems. In 1967, while chairman of the Vieux Carré Commission, which was responsible for preservation of the French Quarter, he and a friend were arrested and charged with receiving or offering to receive a $2,000 bribe to get the commission to approve the remodeling of a Bourbon

Street apartment building. Mintz pleaded no contest and received a two-year suspended sentence. However, thanks to Mintz's political connections, Louisiana's then-governor, John McKeithen, granted him a full pardon that expunged the plea from his record.

Mintz's name also was notorious because in 1984 his wife was found shot to death in their bedroom while he was at home. Mintz claimed that she had shot herself as he watched television downstairs. The police said Mintz staged the suicide, and they arrested him on second-degree murder charges. After a sensational trial, he was acquitted.

Adding to his problems, Mintz's furniture store had gone under in 1989, and in 1990 he had filed for personal bankruptcy. Nonetheless, Carollo and Gagliano trusted Mintz and thought that he remained a respected member of the New Orleans business community. Plus, Mintz had ties to Governor Edwards.

With Mintz in place, the mob leaders were ready to begin making decisions. On October 31, 1991, with the annual Halloween revelry convulsing Bourbon Street, they met two blocks away to fine-tune their plans over a formal dinner at La Louisiane, a restaurant owned by Carlos's brother Joseph Marcello Jr.

At first during the meal, Gammarano, Corozzo, Carollo, Gagliano, Joseph Marcello, and two others sat at one table talking business. They exiled Mintz and Christopher Tanfield to another table until they worked out the deal: Mintz would be the paper owner of the video poker company, since he was a Louisianian and didn't have an organized-crime background. Tanfield and Steven Bolson would have small stakes in the enterprise and would run it. The Gambino family and the Marcello family would each get 40 percent of the profits, with Tanfield and Bolson splitting the other 20 percent. Carollo and the Gaglianos also would have the important role of using their contacts to get New Orleans area bar owners to buy or lease the video poker machines. Joe Gagliano, one of Frank's sons, would drum up business, using the pseudonym Joe Stein. Ten days after the La Louisiane dinner, Tanfield moved to New Orleans and set up shop.

***

In the meantime, Bolson and Tanfield had been trying to land a deal with a video poker manufacturer. This was no simple task, since they had scant credentials, and only a handful of companies made the machines. By the fall of 1991, the situation looked bleak because International Gaming Technology, the industry leader, and most of the other manufacturers had made deals with other companies starting up in Louisiana. Bolson and Tanfield did have one promising lead, having courted Bally Gaming International. The company had a well-known name, but a series of mistakes had reduced its share of the video poker market nationwide to 20 percent. Yet, with the State Police estimating that twenty thousand video poker machines would be on-line through-out the state by the summer of 1992, Louisiana held more promise than anywhere else.

Bally Gaming was born from Bally Manufacturing's recent decision to split itself in two. Bally Manufacturing was headed by Arthur Gold-berg, a fitness buff who had assumed control in 1990. At the time, Bally was $1.5 billion in debt and on its way to losing $280 million on $1.4 billion in revenues. Goldberg stopped repaying the money Bally had bor-rowed to acquire casinos, slashed spending, and began divesting surplus divisions. One of those was the gambling equipment–manufacturing division, which became Bally Gaming International, with Bally Manu-facturing as its largest shareholder.

While their competitors were gobbling up the market in Louisiana, Bally Gaming executives fiddled at their Las Vegas headquarters. The indecision resulted in part from management disarray. It resulted also from Bally officials' uncertainty over whether they could get licensed in Louisiana. In 1971, Bally had been indicted on charges of operating an illegal gambling business with members of the Marcello family. The company had been acquitted, but the incident still tarnished Bally's reputation.

Bolson and Tanfield pursued Bally Gaming in 1991, and offered a deal: If Bally would make their company its distributor in the Bayou State, they could secure orders to sell some seven thousand machines. In December 1991, after months of indecision, Bally formed a partner-ship with the two New Jersey men. Bally had few other options.

Under Louisiana's new video poker law, out-of-state gambling machine manufacturers like Bally could not act as direct wholesalers. Instead, they had to sell their equipment to a distribution company owned by a Louisianian. This company would, in turn, sell or lease the machines to bars, restaurants, and highway truck stops. Similarly, a Louisianian had to own the company—known as the "route operator"— that would manage the video poker accounts. Under the deal proposed by Tanfield and Bolson, they would first create a company called Worldwide Gaming to buy Bally machines and to act as the distributor. Tanfield and Bolson would form a second company, Louisiana Route Operators (LRO), to manage the accounts once the machines were up and running. After the state took its 22.5 percent cut of the winnings, LRO would split the remainder with the establishment that leased the equipment. LRO would then pay Worldwide its share of the profits, and Worldwide, in turn, would pay Bally. Any money that Worldwide or LRO had left over would be profit for Tanfield, Bolson, and the secret mob owners.

With company officials still not sure if they could get licensed, a Bally executive in January 1992 made a reconnaissance trip to Louisiana. The executive, Tom Niemann, wrote in a memo afterward that he thought the trip had strengthened Bally's position there. Niemann described meeting with Bolson's politically connected fraternity brother from Tulane, a New Orleans advertising and public relations executive named Richard Sackett. Sackett held a prized patronage appointment to the Orleans Levee Board, courtesy of Governor Edwards. Niemann wrote, "Sackett is active in the political scene, friend of the governor's (who isn't?) and serves on state boards and commissions."

Niemann then flew to Shreveport to meet with Gus Mijalis, a seafood wholesaler who was one of Edwards's closest friends. Niemann knew that Edwards was expected to exert influence over the State Police in determining which companies and individuals got licensed. Niemann wrote in his memo, "Gus Marjolis [sic] indicated that a meeting with the governor may be good for everyone and he would pursue on our behalf."

In February, Niemann returned to Louisiana with another Bally executive, named Mike Wright. As Wright undertook the trip, he had grave reservations about Bolson, Tanfield, and Mintz. Recording his thoughts after an initial dinner with Bolson and Tanfield, Wright wrote, "They do not know the route business . . . and when I asked them some general questions about the business, they clearly showed their lack of knowledge. . . . I went to bed that night with nothing but uneasiness in regard to their ability to represent us."

On the following day, February 4, 1992, Wright drove with Bolson, Tanfield, and Mintz to Baton Rouge to meet with two local power brokers. The meeting buoyed Wright, as he recorded later: "I was amazed that Steve and Chris, being from the east coast, could gain inroads into the Louisiana scene so quickly. Either there is more to this than meets the eye, or they have done one fine job."

The highlight was an early evening fund-raiser for state senator Cleo Fields. For the video poker operators, the attraction was Governor Edwards, who was at the event to show his support for Fields, a political ally. Mintz was on a first-name basis with Edwards, having given money to his political campaigns since his first run for governor in 1971.

After a short speech, Edwards stepped down from the podium and started to walk through the crowd. He had stopped at a table laden with food, and had grabbed a big turkey leg dripping gravy, when Mintz maneuvered his new business associates to the governor's side. He introduced them to Edwards and described their business plans. Edwards nodded. One of the Bally executives asked, "Governor, how do we stand? Will our machines be licensed?"

Edwards then shook the big turkey leg at the men and said, "If Aaron Mintz is part of your business, Bally will be one of the first three or four companies licensed in Louisiana." Edwards turned away to bite into the turkey leg. Wright, Mintz, and the others walked away, exultant. As Wright wrote later, "If everything we were told and saw on this day is true, Bally has hit a home run in Louisiana."

Everyone involved in the Louisiana venture pressed ahead to get it under way. Tanfield and Bolson passed a background investigation performed by Bally security officials. In late February 1992, Worldwide Gaming and LRO applied to the State Police for their operating licenses. State representative Sebastian (Buster) Guzzardo, who served on the House committee that regulated video poker, arranged for Tanfield and Bolson to meet with State Police officials. In March, Tanfield and Bolson traveled twice to Bally's Las Vegas headquarters to arrange a deal in which Worldwide would be Bally's exclusive video poker distributor in Louisiana.

The plans hit a snag almost immediately. *The Village Voice,* a New York City weekly, reported in early March that the administration of Mayor David Dinkins had leased the city-owned Pier 84 to an amusement park company whose two principals owed the city $180,000 in back taxes. The article identified one of the men as Noogie Gilpin, describing him as a Genovese crime family associate with a 1985 felony conviction for running an illegal gambling operation. The article also identified Gilpin's partner in the company as Christopher Tanfield. Law enforcement agencies, the article added, tied Tanfield to the Genovese family. (Gilpin and Tanfield also had ties to members of the Gambino family and set up the Louisiana venture with them.)

The *Village Voice* article prompted Tanfield to huddle with Anthony Carollo and the Gaglianos. They agreed that Tanfield would notify the State Police that he was resigning from Worldwide Gaming and Louisiana Route Operators and relinquishing his 5 percent share in each company. They also agreed that the resignation would be a sham: Tanfield would continue to run the companies with Bolson, but for official purposes he would become a "consultant." In a letter to the State Police, Tanfield did not explain why he was "resigning," and indeed State Police officials took no special notice. The two companies were among hundreds seeking an operating license, and the State Police, overwhelmed by the volume of applicants, didn't have time to do adequate background investigations. Worldwide, LRO, Bolson, and Mintz secured their licenses in April and May. (There is no evidence that Edwards intervened on their behalf.)

Tanfield also did not explain to Bally why he was resigning. But two months later, Bally officials learned of the *Village Voice* article. A company executive did another background investigation of Tanfield, concluding this time that he was an "inappropriate association." Still, Bally didn't seek Tanfield's removal from Worldwide Gaming and LRO, rationalizing that he was just a consultant. Later, the failure to remove Tanfield would haunt Bally. However, in May 1992, Bally was deeply committed to its flawed Louisiana partners, to the point that company officials had begun advancing money to Worldwide Gaming and LRO. The first disbursement from Bally was $110,000, and it was crucial for the initial operation because the companies' principal partners—Tanfield, Bolson, and Mintz—were not putting up any of their own money. Nor were the hidden mob partners, whose role was to collect most of the expected profits. In truth, the Louisiana venture could survive only with Bally's financing its operations. By June, Bally had advanced $3.5 million to cover operating costs for the year. Bally also would establish a $20 million credit line for Worldwide to buy its machines, using the machines themselves as collateral. Bally officials would later admit that this was easily the company's riskiest financing arrangement.

Meanwhile, John Gammarano, the Gambino mob soldier invited into the venture by Tanfield, was trying to monitor the video poker enterprise. He tapped a New York lawyer named Paul Morabito to assist him. On June 22, 1992, Morabito visited New Orleans on a fact-finding trip. By now, Worldwide and LRO had established an office in Metairie and were eagerly awaiting July 1, which would be when the Louisiana State Police would allow the video poker machines to go on-line at bars and restaurants statewide. On previous trips to New Orleans, Morabito had asked Tanfield for specifics on the companies' finances, their business plan, and their various legal agreements. Tanfield had always brushed him off. Now, finally, Tanfield began providing some of the information that Morabito sought. But as Morabito examined the finances, he grew concerned. The companies owed Bally $3.5 million and were projecting an operating loss in 1992 of $300,000. And as Morabito scanned the ledgers, he found a key problem: exorbitant expenses.

Bolson, Tanfield, and Mintz were using Bally's money to feather their own nests. They were paying themselves $100,000 a year in salaries and then hitting up the companies for practically all of their living expenses. Mintz, for example, billed Worldwide $210 to pay his membership dues in the Mardi Gras Zulu parade, $1,125 for New Orleans Saints season tickets, and $1,338 to lease a car from Alamo. Mintz was so bent on sucking funds from the company that he was seen taking rolls of toilet paper from its Metairie office as well as rolling five-gallon jugs of bottled water to his car.

Bolson was even more voracious. Among other things, he had Worldwide pay for his family to visit relatives in Philadelphia, for his son to travel to New Orleans for Thanksgiving, for his daughter to get braces, and for his own psychotherapy treatment. According to Bally officials, Bolson also embezzled about $40,000 in company funds to remodel his Uptown New Orleans home, and then falsified company records to try to hide the expense. Later, he billed Worldwide $1,111 to pay for his move to a French Quarter apartment.

The greediness reflected a larger problem: Bolson and Tanfield were miscast as managers. To be fair, Bally made their job difficult because the company had failed to keep pace with its competitors technologically. Bally's machines were outmoded, lacking the push-button screens that had become popular with gamblers. However, Bolson and Tanfield exacerbated their technological disadvantage through a series of missteps and miscalculations. They misled Bally about the number of orders they had secured and then vastly overestimated their ability to sell the machines. They told Bally they had firm orders for 4,310 machines, pending orders for 600 more, and thought they could sell an additional 3,000. Bally responded by manufacturing 4,300 machines for Louisiana. Bolson and Tanfield sold only 1,800 of them.

Having spent a year as a casino marketing executive after a career in law, Bolson fancied himself a budding executive. However, he understood little about business finance, alienated employees with his arrogance, and never fully learned the video poker business, which was more akin to distributing pool tables and vending machines than running a casino. The key was not selling the machines, but placing as many of them as possible in bars, restaurants, and highway truck stops. Selling a machine provided a one-time $2,000 profit, while the video poker machines produced a steady stream of income—as much as $1,000 per week, per machine.

Tanfield was no better as a company executive. A slick talker who dressed like an extra in a mob movie—black shirt, white tie, gold necklace—he excelled at scheming. But he proved unable to handle the more basic tasks of a company executive, such as managing employees, ensuring that bills were paid on time, and hiring talented workers.

"I sat Chris down," Frank Gagliano Sr., the Marcello family underboss, once complained. "I said, 'Chris, I want a fuckin' weekly report of what you're doin'.' He looked at me. [He said], 'Okay, I'll do it.' [But] I ain't got but one fuckin' report written."

In July 1992, Paul Morabito advised John Gammarano to walk away from the Louisiana venture. In a conversation that month with Joe Gagliano, one of Frank Gagliano's sons, Morabito said, "My impression is that the business isn't being run as a business. Here we are six months down the road, and basically they're running it like a very loose type of situation. There is no real internal control as far as the budget is concerned. They want to have their cake and eat it, too." Privately, Morabito expressed amazement that Bally would continue funding such a slipshod operation.

As bad as the financial situation was getting, another development would prove even more devastating for Bolson, Tanfield, Mintz, and the Gambino and Marcello family members. They didn't know it was coming.

Even after Carlos Marcello's decline, FBI agents kept track of the new bosses, Anthony Carollo and Frank Gagliano Sr. In time, they discovered that Carollo, Gagliano, and their underlings would meet frequently at Frank's Deli, a French Quarter sandwich shop owned by Gagliano. To entice passersby, Frank's displayed thin loaves of Italian bread in the store window along with bottles of Italian wine and olive oil. But Frank's got far less traffic than the Central Grocery two doors down on Decatur Street, which claimed to have invented the muffuletta, a

ABOVE: *Mobster Carlos Marcello, right, waits to testify before the Kefauver Commission in New Orleans on January 25, 1951*
BELOW: *As superintendent of the Louisiana State Police in the early 1950s, Francis Grevemberg took dead aim at Louisiana's illegal slot machines and casinos*

In 1983, at the height of his popularity and political influence, Edwin Edwards gives a stump speech in Lake Providence as he campaigns to win back the Governor's Mansion

Times-Picayune *Pulitzer Prize–winning cartoonist*
Walt Handelsman on gambling

Smooth, charming, and debonair, developer Christopher Hemmeter wowed New Orleans politicians in 1992–93 with promises to build the world's largest casino

Governor Edwin Edwards played deal-maker in August 1993 in order to prevent squabbling between the competing interests from derailing the New Orleans casino. Left to right: Christopher Hemmeter, Edwin Edwards, and attorney Wendell Gauthier, who headed a group of Louisiana investors

Governor Edwin Edwards celebrates the Harrah's casino's opening on May 1, 1995, as Harrah's executive Ron Lenczycki looks on

Casino Board chairman Max Chastain played a pivotal role in deciding which company was to be awarded the New Orleans casino license, but later felt the strain as events spun unexpectedly out of control

The site of the New Orleans casino on December 3, 1995

While the pleasure boat Natchez *operated daily, owners of the riverboat* Flamingo *kept their vessel at dock, claiming that the Mississippi River was unsafe for cruising. Other riverboat casinos also failed to cruise*

Video poker machines sprouted in bars, restaurants, and highway truck stops throughout Louisiana

Outside Frank's Deli in New Orleans, an FBI surveillance camera captures, left to right, Frank Gagliano Jr., Anthony Carollo, Joe Gagliano, and Joseph Marcello Jr.

Former governor Edwin Edwards discusses his indictment with reporters on November 7, 1997. His wife, Candy, observes from behind

Edward DeBartolo Jr. owned the nation's most successful professional football team—the San Francisco 49ers—in the 1980s and 1990s, but he was out of his league trying to open a riverboat casino in Louisiana

Lead FBI agent Geoffrey Santini, left, and United States Attorney Eddie Jordan Jr. outside the courtroom during the trial. Assistant United States Attorney Peter Strasser is behind them

ABOVE: *Edwin Edwards and his son Stephen during the trial*
BELOW: *Former governor Edwin Edwards: "The Chinese have a saying . . ."*

round New Orleans sandwich with Italian cold cuts stuffed between thick pieces of bread. Tourists accounted for most of Frank's business, and that was one of the attractions for Carollo and Gagliano. Who would pay attention to a few old men sitting around one of Frank's dozen tables? By late 1991, Rick McHenry was paying attention. McHenry was a thirty-seven-year-old FBI agent with a low-key manner who was quickly becoming an organized-crime specialist. McHenry had been transferred to New Orleans in 1990 after spending six years investigating mob infiltration of labor unions in New York City, an assignment he almost didn't survive. During one raid in Greenwich Village, the night after Genovese family associates murdered a police detective, McHenry burst into a social club along with a group of agents. A mobster whipped out a Saturday night special and pointed it at him. McHenry lunged for the gun and pinned it and the man up against a wall without a shot going off.

In New Orleans, McHenry was assigned to the organized-crime squad and soon began tracking Carollo and Gagliano. From his New York work, McHenry knew that to break up the remnants of the Marcello family, he had to get microphones inside their regular meeting place. That was how the FBI had put Gambino boss John Gotti behind bars. So after learning that Carollo, Gagliano, and the others frequently met at Frank's Deli, McHenry set his sights on getting a judge's permission to bug the place.

By March 1992, the FBI had won approval to tap the telephone of a social club in Metairie, home of an illegal sports betting ring that involved two of Frank Gagliano's sons, Jack and Frank Jr. After the bookmakers moved their operations to a French Quarter apartment, the FBI got permission to bug the phones there, too. From the telephone taps, McHenry and another agent, Tom Metz, were surprised to learn that Carollo and the Gaglianos had become involved in a video poker business in Louisiana, but that they were trying to hide their presence. This excited the FBI agents because it showed that Carollo and the Gaglianos were trying to revive the Marcello family through an old standby: illegal gambling. Planting a bug inside Frank's Deli became even more urgent.

To get the lay of the place, McHenry and other agents ate lunch at the deli several times. They found the bread stale. So when it came time for the FBI and the United States Attorney's office to give the case a code name, they decided to call it Operation Hardcrust.

On June 22, 1992, with judicial permission, the FBI began tapping the deli's phones. That day, FBI agents listening in heard New York lawyer Paul Morabito call the deli to arrange for him and his traveling companions—whom he referred to only cryptically—to meet Carollo and the Gaglianos at the Meridien Hotel on Canal Street in New Orleans. The FBI dispatched agents to observe the get-together. They were able to identify the New Orleanians, but not the others.

Two months later, Morabito returned to New Orleans with Gammarano and Corozzo. Once again, they arranged over the telephone to meet with their New Orleans associates. This time, the FBI agents surreptitiously took photographs to identify the out-of-towners. Rick McHenry sent the photographs to the FBI's New York office. It didn't take long for an agent from New York to call his New Orleans colleague with excitement spilling from his voice. "Jesus Christ," the agent told McHenry, "you've got Corozzo and Gammarano down there. They're part of John Gotti's gang. We've been targeting those guys for a long time."

With compelling evidence of mob activity, the FBI got a judge's permission to approve the final step: secretly capturing the discussions inside Frank's Deli. On the night of September 8, 1992, FBI agents quietly broke into the deli and placed tiny microphones under two of the dozen tables at Frank's, including those where Carollo, Gagliano, and their associates usually conducted business. A week later, the FBI agents broke in again to place a mike under a third table and to put a tiny camera inside an audio speaker just above and to the left of the door connecting the kitchen to the dining room and deli counter. From then on, the camera would provide continuous live video to agents watching in the FBI's office—much like a closed-circuit television broadcast.

Listening in on the conversations at Frank's, FBI agents learned that the lavish expenses at Worldwide and LRO enraged Carollo and the Gaglianos. "We got to pay big salaries, rent fucking cars, this is bullshit," said Joe Gagliano, just past noon on September 10, sitting at one of the bugged tables.

A week later, a microphone recorded additional grumbling. "They got too much expenses," groused Frank Gagliano Sr.

"We don't hear nothin' but bullshit," added Anthony Carollo.

"They ain't makin' no money," chimed in Joseph Marcello.

"I ain't got a nickel yet," complained Frank Sr.

And this is how they passed the time: lamenting the shortcomings of Bolson and Tanfield and expressing their frustration with a venture that was supposed to revive their fortunes, but instead was threatening to go down the tubes. On September 23, John Gammarano, Christopher Tanfield's patron, came down from New York once again to try to soothe the anger of his Louisiana partners over the failings of Worldwide and LRO. "Chris is a great, great mover, good talker, but when it comes to businessman, it stops," Gammarano said in a meeting at Frank's Deli.

"Yeah, he's no businessman," agreed Frank Gagliano Sr.

Turning to Gagliano's sons, Gammarano then said, "When your father runs a business, he runs a business. He counts the nickels and quarters. If you don't do that in business, that's a mistake. Now he [Tanfield] is not that kind of guy. I'm not knockin' him. I'll put him anytime to go out and put a deal together. After that, you gotta have somebody that's got a business mind to run a business. Mistakes, it just keeps adding up."

In their frustration, the New Orleans mobsters began quarreling. Carollo and Frank Gagliano Sr. said they ought to sell their expected share of the businesses' profits. Given their age, they didn't want to keep waiting. After all, they could be dead before the profits began rolling in. Gagliano's sons favored holding tight. "We shouldn't get out of this business," Joe Gagliano told Carollo as they ate dinner at Frank's on September 24.

"If we grab a quick buck—" Carollo began to say.

"There's no quick buck," interrupted Joe Gagliano. A few minutes later, he added, "This business has not reached its potential. That's number one."

"Ain't no way," agreed Carollo.

"Number two, Bally loaned all this money and is not going to let this company go kaput."

Neither Joe Gagliano nor any of the others knew what to do, however. Frank Gagliano Sr. did have something in mind for Tanfield. "Listen, can I put him under the pressure?" he asked. "Let me handle Chris. He's full of shit. . . . These guys we gotta wise their minds up."

No one agreed with him, so a few minutes later Carollo was again moaning, "Too much expenses, that's the problem."

Referring to Tanfield, Frank Sr. then said, "He's Noogie's man. . . . We ain't got no man."

"The thing is we ain't got somebody in the office that we can trust," agreed Carollo.

"We don't want these New Yorkers," added Frank Sr.

The FBI agents couldn't help but laugh at the mob's predicament and ineptitude. Agent Rick Richard began referring to them as "The Gang That Couldn't Shoot Straight." Rick McHenry likened them to the characters in the '50s television series *The Honeymooners* because they were constantly coming up with harebrained schemes to make money.

Despite the problems at Worldwide and LRO, Bally kept advancing the companies more and more money. This prompted the FBI agents to conclude that Bally officials knew they were in league with the mob. There was precedent for this, they knew. Bally Manufacturing had done business with the Marcello family, which had resulted in the 1971 indictment for operating an illegal gambling business.

It was Bally Manufacturing that Tanfield and Bolson had originally approached in late 1991 about a deal in Louisiana. Soon they were shifted to Bally Gaming International after Bally Manufacturing had spun it off as a separate, publicly traded entity that manufactured video poker machines. Bally Manufacturing still owned a share of Bally Gaming, and there was strong overlap between the two companies through 1992. They shared a president and an executive vice president, and Bart Jacka was the director of corporate compliance for both companies, responsible for keeping undesirables out.

The president and chief executive officer of Bally Manufacturing, Arthur Goldberg, also prompted FBI suspicions. Before taking over the gambling company in 1990, he had run his family's trucking company in New Jersey. Agent Rick Richard learned from the FBI's Newark office that Goldberg's trucking company had put him in contact with the mob through its control of the Teamsters union. In the mid-1980s, Goldberg also was on the list of people authorized to visit Salvatore Joseph Profaci, a captain in the Colombo family, at the federal prison in Sandstone, Minnesota, Richard learned. In addition, in the mid-1980s, Goldberg's name was mentioned in a wiretapped conversation of two mob associates, James Gow and Anthony (Fat Tony) Salerno, at a New York social club, and in another wiretapped conversation between two mob associates in 1985. Adding it all up, Richard concluded that Goldberg was at least an associate of organized crime. Richard put his conclusions in writing when he asserted in a court filing that the FBI's Newark office had identified Goldberg as a Colombo mob associate. Richard was undercut somewhat in 1995 when a federal prosecutor in New Orleans called the term "technically incorrect." Still, Paul Coffey, who headed the Organized Crime and Racketeering Section of the Justice Department's Criminal Division, backed up Richard when he wrote in an April 19, 1995, letter to Goldberg's attorney, Michael Chertoff, that "if called upon to do so, the Government will successfully defend the premise of the assertion in question."

Goldberg vigorously denied allegations of mob ties, and New Jersey casino regulators gave him a clean bill of health in 1996. In addition, several former FBI agents who headed the Newark office said later they had investigated the mob allegations involving Goldberg and had found them untrue.

Bally Gaming officials would say later they hadn't known that their Louisiana partners were mobbed up, even though they worked on a daily basis with Worldwide Gaming and LRO. At a minimum, they exercised poor judgment by turning a blind eye to strong clues of criminal involvement in their business. Bally officials allowed Tanfield to continue playing an integral role in Worldwide and LRO even after learning in May 1992 that *The Village Voice* identified him as having connections to the Genovese crime family. In September, while the regulars at Frank's Deli were moaning about the problems at Worldwide and LRO, Bally corporate records show that midlevel company officials were raising concerns about their Louisiana partners.

In October, at the direction of another Bally executive, Bart Jacka asked a Louisiana private investigator to undertake background checks of fifteen people with business ties to either Worldwide Gaming or LRO. The list included Joe Gagliano, whom company officials now knew was working for Worldwide under the pseudonym Joe Stein, as well as Francis Pecora and Felix (Pete) Riggio III, both of whom had criminal records. In November 1992, armed with what the private detective found, Bally told Bolson that Worldwide and LRO had to cut loose Christopher Tanfield, Joe Gagliano, and Francis Pecora because of their suspected mob ties. When Tanfield and Gagliano got the news, they complained bitterly to Bolson, since both had played a key role with the companies. But Bolson had to obey the order.

Bally executives hoped that banishing Tanfield and Gagliano from Worldwide and LRO would end an unhappy episode. There was more bad news to come. Worldwide's accountant, in retaliation for being fired by Bolson, was turning over records showing that Bolson had embezzled $40,000 of company funds to remodel his Uptown New Orleans home. Among those given the records were Carollo and the Gaglianos. They were furious, but decided to follow protocol and asked Gammarano and Gilpin to come to New Orleans to help resolve the matter. On the evening of November 17, Bolson was summoned to the back room of a pharmacy in the New Orleans suburb of Kenner. Awaiting him were Gammarano, Gilpin, Carollo, Frank Gagliano Sr., and Joseph Marcello. Bolson was terrified when he walked into the room. Confronted with the evidence, he broke down crying. "Don't hurt me," Bolson pleaded. "Don't kill me. I'm sorry I took the money."

There was a long pause. Then Gammarano said, "Don't worry. Nobody is going to hurt you, and nobody is going to kill you. Don't worry about it. You're the only guy we have in there, so just relax." The meeting then broke up. Fortunately for Bolson, the Marcello family traditionally shunned violence.

A short time later, Bolson expressed his remorse in a telephone conversation with a Bally executive named Gary Simpson. "I done wrong here," Bolson said. "I'm ashamed of what I did. I fucked up and did wrong. It was not an organized crime thing. It was my own fucking problem because I don't have any money, mortgages up the rear and because I'm just squeezed."

Bally's president, Alan Maiss, was an industry veteran, having spent twenty years with companies that distributed slot machines and operated the routes. Once again turning a blind eye to wrongdoing, neither Maiss nor his bosses insisted on Bolson's ouster in November 1992, even though Bolson had admitted to embezzlement, and Worldwide and LRO were floundering under his management. Instead, Maiss asked a midlevel sales manager named Jerry Flynn to go to Louisiana and return with recommendations on how to get the enterprise back on track. Flynn had worked for Bally for the past year, after having worked for several other gambling companies. When Flynn called Bart Jacka and Gary Simpson for their thoughts, they advised him to make sure that Chris Tanfield and Joe Gagliano, because of their organized-crime ties, had no association with Worldwide and LRO. The news about mob involvement in the enterprise unsettled Flynn, so it was with some trepidation that he headed to New Orleans.

Flynn was shocked at what he found: Bolson regularly wrote checks to pay employees' salaries without the bank's having sufficient funds, and Worldwide had too many employees, except in the crucial sales and marketing department. There it had none. Flynn also found that practically no one at Worldwide had experience in the video poker business, and no company financial statements existed. Flynn discovered, too, that Worldwide had spent all but $300,000 of the $3.5 million advanced by Bally. He reported his findings to Alan Maiss.

In January 1993, Flynn returned to New Orleans, accompanied this time by Maiss. By now, the situation was getting desperate for Worldwide and Bally. In one meeting, Maiss asked whether Worldwide could collect a $30,000 debt owed by a St. Bernard Parish resident named Faye Vaughn. Maiss noted that New Orleans deputy police chief Antoine Saacks had told him the night before that "if anyone tried to collect this note that they would end up in the bottom of the Mississippi River." Someone else added that Vaughn's father was a big shot in organized crime and shouldn't be confronted to pay the debt. Maiss then suggested that Pete Riggio, a route operator who did business with Worldwide, could help collect the $30,000, since he had organized-crime ties.

Afterward, at the New Orleans International Airport, as they were walking to their gate, Maiss told Flynn that LRO was costing Bally so much money that he favored selling its routes to Riggio. "I don't necessarily like selling the route to Pete because of his organized-crime connection," Maiss told his colleague, "but I have information that the word on the street is that the O.C. [organized crime] people think Bally is OK and that they would take care of us. But because of the O.C. connection, it's the best way for Bally to get its money back from LRO."

Maiss's cavalier statements about Faye Vaughn and her organized-crime connections had already alarmed Flynn. He found Maiss's comments about Riggio even more distressing. "Alan," Flynn responded, "we are a public company so we have a moral and ethical if not a legal issue in knowingly selling the route to Riggio. We should sell LRO to someone else."

On the plane, Maiss again argued in favor of selling LRO to Riggio. "Alan, I still disagree," Flynn replied.

Back in Las Vegas, Flynn didn't discuss his concerns with his Bally colleagues. "I was afraid for my job at Bally, and physically afraid of the people involved in that," he explained later.

On January 8, 1993, the day after Maiss and Flynn returned to Las Vegas, Joe Gagliano and John Gammarano's lawyer, Paul Morabito, were in New Orleans, still cursing a crooked business deal gone bad. They laid most of the blame on Tanfield. "The party that admitted to it [the embezzlement of company funds] was the one with the beard [Bolson]," said Gagliano at Frank's Deli. "The other guy [Tanfield], he sat pat and didn't say nothin'. But he was the one that was the mastermind that taught the other asshole how to do it."

"I didn't like him [Tanfield], you know," responded Morabito. "I told everybody I don't like this kid. But Noogie thought he was the greatest thing to come along since 7Up. I had my battles with Noogie. I walked out [of the deal] down there. I said, 'Fuck you guys. I don't wanna have anything more to do with it.' That was way back in June when I saw the handwriting on the wall. I said, 'I'm wastin' my fuckin' time here. I didn't spend all this time and effort in here for two fucks to fuck up.'"

"Well, let me tell you," Gagliano said, "they fucked up. How stupid can somebody be, Paul? They musta think that people here fell off a fuckin' turnip truck."

"Yeah, banana boat," replied Morabito.

"You think there will be any kind of repercussion [with] our two lovely people?" asked Gagliano. "I hope so."

"I don't ask those type of questions," responded Morabito.

In March 1993, the FBI agents had gathered enough evidence to end the covert part of their investigation. They revealed the existence of Operation Hardcrust by issuing subpoenas of the mob figures. "OK, here it starts," noted *The Times-Picayune*. "Louisiana, a-quiver with the new-age gambling ga-gas, doesn't even have a casino on the ground or in the water yet—only a state lottery and a growing plague of video poker—and already the first federal investigation of possible gambling- and organized crime–related conniving is under way."

Two months later, Bally Gaming fired Alan Maiss, its president, and severed its relationship with Worldwide Gaming and Louisiana Route Operators. Cut off from their sugar daddy, the companies filed for bankruptcy. In September, the Louisiana State Police suspended the companies' licenses to operate in the Bayou State, citing mob ties. By then, Steven Bolson and Aaron Mintz had been ousted, with Bolson agreeing to help federal prosecutors by wearing a wire.

For the next eighteen months, the FBI gathered more evidence, and prosecutors developed their case. On May 31, 1994, the FBI arrested seventeen people associated with Worldwide and LRO, and charged them with illegally conducting a gambling business. Among the seventeen were three men associated with the Gambino family (John Gammarano, Jo Jo Corozzo, and Eugene [Noogie] Gilpin), four members of the Marcello family (Anthony Carollo, Frank Gagliano Sr.,

Joe Gagliano, and Joseph Marcello Jr.), and Aaron Mintz. Tanfield, Bolson, and Maiss had already been arrested by then. Bolson pleaded guilty to conducting an illegal gambling business, and Maiss pleaded guilty to not reporting that he was doing business with an illegal enterprise. For the seventeen who entered not-guilty pleas, a trial was scheduled for October 1995.

About a month before the trial began, the defendants' lawyers met in New Orleans to plot strategy. Christopher Tanfield's Pensacola-based lawyer, Tom Santurri, was on the speakerphone, listening in. After a while, the New Orleans lawyers apparently forgot that Santurri was on the line. They began openly discussing a strategy in which they would plead guilty in exchange for a light sentence and pin all of the blame on Tanfield. It was a fatal mistake. After getting off the line, a startled Santurri called his client and explained to him what his erstwhile colleagues were planning. That weekend, they cut a deal with federal prosecutors. Tanfield would plead guilty, get a light sentence, and take the witness stand against his brethren.

When the others learned that Tanfield would now testify against them, Gammarano, Corozzo, Gilpin, Carollo, Mintz, Frank Gagliano Sr., Joe Gagliano, and Pete Riggio pleaded guilty to lesser charges—while stipulating that they were not part of the mob. Carollo was sentenced to 44 months in prison and ordered to pay $500,000 in restitution to Bally. Frank Gagliano Sr. got 38 months, plus $250,000 in restitution. Joseph Marcello Jr. got 33 months and $250,000 in restitution. John Gammarano also got 44 months and $500,000 in restitution, while Corozzo got 36 months and was ordered to pay $250,000. Noogie Gilpin got 41 months and was ordered to pay $100,000. Aaron Mintz got 18 months and was ordered to pay $15,000 in restitution. Bolson and Tanfield, who cooperated with federal authorities, were sentenced to 21 and 18 months, respectively, in prison. Some minor figures in the case—Sebastian (Buster) Salvatore and two brothers, Anthony and Victor Tusa Sr.—decided to go to trial; all three were found guilty. In all, twenty-one people were convicted or pleaded guilty.

Afterward, the United States Attorney for New Orleans, Eddie Jordan Jr., in something of an overstatement, said the federal government's prosecutions had prevented the Marcello family from regaining its previous clout. "I consider this to be a crushing blow against organized crime," proclaimed Jordan. Federal authorities also crowed that they had kept the Gambinos from establishing a presence in New Orleans.

Yet not everyone got what they deserved. Alan Maiss got a slap on the wrist. He was sentenced to 12 months on probation and fined $5,000, although he was barred from doing business in the gambling industry.

Bally also escaped indictment. During the trial of Salvatore and the Tusas, federal prosecutors portrayed Bally not as a complicit partner, but as an unwitting victim. The company lost some $20 million in the venture, with the depreciated value of the machines it got back from Worldwide accounting for most of the loss. Joe Whitmore and Walter Wolfe, two Louisiana State Police investigators who assisted the FBI, were among those who thought that Bally executives had known too much to characterize the company as a victim. The investigators concluded that to strengthen their case, the federal prosecutors needed to show that the mobsters had victimized someone. (The prosecutors also said FBI agent Rick Richard's characterization of Bally Manufacturing executive Arthur Goldberg as an associate of the Colombo mob was "technically incorrect.")

The federal probe did net one elected official. State representative Buster Guzzardo, a seventy-three-year-old Democrat from Independence, a town two hours north of New Orleans, pleaded guilty in 1996 to providing illegal assistance to Worldwide and LRO. Guzzardo had arranged for Tanfield and Bolson to meet with a State Police official in 1992 while they were trying to get licensed and had asked the state fire marshal in 1993 to reinspect a Worldwide-affiliated video poker parlor in Baton Rouge that code violations had shut down. A few days after the phone call, the marshal allowed the poker parlor to reopen. For his help, Guzzardo came cheap. Worldwide gave him a $378 fax machine and $1,200 in cash, and paid his daughter's moving expenses from Colorado to Baton Rouge. As part of his plea bargain, Guzzardo was sentenced to three months at the nearest prison medical facility and was forced to resign his House seat.

Facing potential licensing problems in other states, Bally Gaming International could not survive the financial disaster and the negative publicity. In October 1995, Alliance Gaming Corporation, a much smaller company, swallowed Bally Gaming. Meanwhile, Bally Manufacturing got a new name: Bally Entertainment.

After serving time in prison, Bolson returned to New Jersey to run his father-in-law's check-cashing business, the Gaglianos resumed serving muffulettas to tourists at Frank's Deli, and Christopher Tanfield entered the federal witness-protection program, a wary man.

A Wet Hen and a Whitewash

While Governor Edwin Edwards was wheeling and dealing to secure riverboat and video poker licenses for friends and political supporters, officials with Harrah's Jazz were attempting to open the New Orleans land casino. With a license in hand after the casino board's 5–4 vote on August 11, 1993, Harrah's officials thought they would have smooth sailing to open the casino on January 1, 1994. But officials from the Memphis-based company would soon find themselves buffeted by the crosscurrents of Louisiana politics.

The problems for Harrah's began almost immediately after getting the license. Under Edwards's prodding, the three groups wanting to build and operate the New Orleans casino had joined in a shotgun wedding at the Governor's Mansion on August 25, 1993. Like many shotgun weddings, it was an uneasy relationship from the beginning.

The shotgun wedding was necessary because developer Christopher Hemmeter had the casino site lease (awarded to him by New Orleans mayor Sidney Barthelemy in November 1992), while the partnership of Harrah's and Jazzville had the casino operating license (given to them by the state casino board on August 11, 1993). Bitter rivals, neither could open the casino without the other. So at Edwards's insistence, Harrah's and the ten Jazzville lawyers and businessmen joined forces with Hemmeter, with each taking a one-third interest in the casino. Harrah's officials, however, would be in charge, since they alone could finance the project, while Hemmeter was nearly broke and the Jazzville 10 were short of cash. The new partnership would be known as Harrah's Jazz Company.

At the insistence of Edwards and Barthelemy, on August 25 the new partnership had agreed to Hemmeter's plan to demolish the building on the casino site, New Orleans's onetime convention center known as the Rivergate. Because of Louisiana's weak economy, Edwards and Barthelemy wanted to create the eight hundred jobs needed to raze the Rivergate and construct the huge casino. Barthelemy also wanted what he called a "must see" casino; a retrofitted Rivergate would produce something less, he argued. The construction work would take nine months to two years, so Harrah's Jazz would operate a temporary casino in the meantime. This was allowed under Louisiana's 1992 casino law as a way of accelerating profits for the casino operator and tax payments to the city and state. In an ill-advised move, both governmental entities were balancing their budgets with anticipated casino revenue.

Under the Harrah's Jazz plan, the temporary casino would be in New Orleans's Municipal Auditorium, a rectangular hall that for sixty-three years had been the scene of Mardi Gras balls, high school graduation ceremonies, circuses, concerts, and boxing matches. Al Jolson, Elvis Presley, James Brown, Bruce Springsteen, the Bolshoi Ballet, and the Flying Wallendas were only a few of those who had performed in the auditorium over the years. Just about every New Orleanian had attended an event there at one time or another.

It was Mayor Barthelemy who had insisted that the temporary casino operate in the Municipal Auditorium. He had three reasons: First, the city owned the aging structure. Distrustful of Edwards and state legislators, Barthelemy thought having the temporary casino on New Orleans property would strengthen the city's hands in any possible fights with the state and the casino operator. Second, the plan called for Harrah's to renovate the auditorium and then return the refurbished building to the city when the Rivergate casino opened. Harrah's thus would pay for repairs that the city couldn't afford. Third, the Municipal Auditorium was located in a neighborhood that Barthelemy had been trying to revitalize. The auditorium adjoined Louis Armstrong Park, into which few ventured at night, and the Treme (Trem-ay) neighborhood, populated mostly by poor African Americans. Although the temporary casino might be open for less than two years, Barthelemy thought that it could produce enough spillover to benefit Treme, which was filled with New Orleans's distinctive shotgun-design homes, but which in Treme had seen better days.

The Municipal Auditorium was located on Basin Street, two blocks from the French Quarter and fifteen blocks from the site of the permanent casino. It was a quick walk into the French Quarter from the auditorium or Armstrong Park, but it meant crossing North Rampart Street, which was lined with vacant buildings and tawdry bars. And in a city where short distances could mean the difference between safety and danger, the auditorium stood two blocks from a housing project where gunfire sometimes echoed at night. Back in June 1993, when it still looked as if the state board would choose Hemmeter to operate the New Orleans casino, Barthelemy had gotten the developer to agree to put the temporary casino in the Municipal Auditorium. Barthelemy had sway over Hemmeter, since he had chosen him to lease the Rivergate casino site.

However, the thought of putting the temporary casino in the Municipal Auditorium horrified Daniel Robinowitz, Hemmeter's development partner. Robinowitz had made a name for himself in Dallas before returning to his native New Orleans to devise the original vision for a huge casino at the Rivergate. It was also Robinowitz who had agreed in October 1991 to let Hemmeter be his partner and who had developed the game plan that Hemmeter executed to win over Barthelemy. But in the summer of 1993, before Harrah's and Jazzville would win the state operating license, Robinowitz questioned Hemmeter's plan to put the temporary casino in the Municipal Auditorium. One evening, Robinowitz drove Hemmeter by the auditorium and Armstrong Park. When they drove into the park, it was dark and deserted but for homeless people. "Let's get out and walk to Rampart Street," Robinowitz suggested.

"I'm not getting out of the car," Hemmeter replied.

"You just made my point," Robinowitz said.

He parked the car on North Rampart Street and said, "Chris, Steve Wynn said the two most important elements for a successful casino are walk-in foot traffic and hotel rooms. They put bodies in the casino. Chris, do you see anything like that here?"

"Well, the French Quarter is right here," Hemmeter said.

"There's no one out here," Robinowitz replied.

He then drove Hemmeter to the Rivergate site, which was on the far side of the French Quarter, in an area filled with high-rise tourist hotels. "See, there are people here," Robinowitz said.

The next day, referring to the auditorium, he told Hemmeter's lawyer, "That building is poison. It will make us die."

The proposed site also dismayed Gregory Meredith, a Salomon Brothers investment banker who was arranging the financing for Hemmeter. When Meredith visited the Municipal Auditorium in the summer of 1993, Hemmeter tried to sell him on the building's possibilities. Meredith thought it was the worst site imaginable. He said to himself: "Is anybody really going to get in their car and come here?"

Michael Rose, the chief executive officer of Promus, Harrah's parent company, shared these concerns. So, after having agreed to the Municipal Auditorium in the August 25, 1993, deal brokered by Edwards, Rose then tried to reopen the issue, and he made a special trip to New Orleans to plead his case with Barthelemy and Jim Singleton, an influential city councilman. Rose said Harrah's wanted to operate the temporary facility at a site proposed by Robinowitz—across Canal Street from the Rivergate, on a vacant lot next to the Westin Hotel and Canal Place. For the temporary building, Rose proposed constructing a simple structure that would be one-fourth the size of the permanent Rivergate casino. Not only did he dislike the Municipal Auditorium, but he also said having the temporary casino away from the Rivergate would confuse customers once the permanent casino opened.

City officials reacted swiftly to the Harrah's proposal. "It seems to me that they are going back on things they agreed to with the governor," said Barthelemy. Lambert Boissiere, a key New Orleans city councilman, was harsher. "They can pack up their bags and go home," he said defiantly. "If we can't have it the right way, we'd just as soon not have it. The governor and the rest of them can put that in their pipe and smoke it." Ron Nabonne, an outside advisor to Barthelemy, warned that the construction of the temporary casino at Canal Place would occur at the same time as the expansion of the nearby Aquarium of the Americas and the construction of the Rivergate casino across the street. "Logistically, it would be a nightmare," Nabonne said. Business leaders backed Barthelemy. Hemmeter's new partners dispatched him to win the mayor over privately. This time, the developer's renowned salesmanship didn't work. Barthelemy and the others would not budge. In a decisive meeting at the Governor's Mansion, Edwards backed the city. So on October 13, 1993, Harrah's officials announced they had backed down: the Harrah's Jazz partnership would accept Hemmeter's plan. They would demolish the Rivergate and replace it with the world's largest casino, although the building would not be as ornate as Hemmeter's. They would also operate a temporary casino in the Municipal Auditorium. Harrah's Memphis-based executives were not happy, but the company's number-crunchers said they could make money even at the Municipal Auditorium—and then lots more at the permanent casino.

In choosing to accept what was essentially Hemmeter's plan, the casino project became much more costly than what Harrah's and its Jazzville 10 partners had originally intended. Their bid before the state casino board had called for a $357 million project in which they would renovate the Rivergate and open the casino there in stages. The plan that Harrah's definitively accepted on October 13 was almost twice as expensive at $670 million. But Harrah's two partners—Christopher Hemmeter and the Jazzville 10—had little money. This meant that as costs rose, Harrah's would be the one to have to dig into its pockets. Making the Municipal Auditorium casino-ready, for example, would cost Harrah's $38 million. The city would then benefit from that investment because after Harrah's moved to the Rivergate casino, the city would take over the refurbished building and rent it out again for Mardi Gras balls and concerts. And Harrah's, instead of having the best site to attract gamblers to the temporary casino, agreed to put it inside a building located in a crime-filled area that was not within walking distance of the city's major tourist hotels. It was a decision that Harrah's would come to regret.

The six weeks that it took Harrah's, Jazzville, and Hemmeter to negotiate the final plan also postponed the scheduled opening of the temporary casino, from January 1, 1994, to February 15, Fat Tuesday, the final day of the Mardi Gras season and a local holiday. Soon, another delay was announced that pushed back the temporary casino's opening another six weeks to March 31, 1994. The opening of the Rivergate casino also was postponed, to March 5, 1995.

Finally, the $670 million project appeared to be on track. Then another problem cropped up, thanks to the efforts of a single man. His name was Thomas Tucker. Partial to bow ties, the opera, and preserving old buildings, Tucker, a fifty-year-old contracts lawyer, had devised a complex scheme several years earlier to allow the Orpheum Theater, where the New Orleans Symphony performed, to escape the wrecking ball. Now he wanted to save the Rivergate, which to the untrained eye was nothing more than a huge concrete building taking up an entire city block. But Tucker loved the uniquely designed roof, which provided the longest unsupported span of any concrete building in the world. Also he was appalled at the immensity of the casino project and how it threatened to overwhelm the city's most historic areas. Just downriver from the Rivergate site was the French Quarter. Just upriver was an area known as the Warehouse District, which was filled with nineteenth-century buildings that had been recently renovated—or soon would be—into hotels, condos, apartments, restaurants, coffee shops, and art galleries.

Tucker had already impeded the casino project during the first part of 1993 when Christopher Hemmeter, who had the casino lease, was pushing his proposal through the various city boards and commissions that had to give their approval. Hemmeter's plan not only included razing the Rivergate to build an extravagant casino, but also demolishing a row of five two- and three-story buildings from the 1850s to construct a nine-story parking garage. The proposal distressed Tucker, who was well placed to do something about it. He chaired an obscure city board known as the Historic District Landmarks Commission to which Hemmeter would have to present his plan. When he did, Tucker raised objections. Mayor Barthelemy, who had reappointed Tucker to the board, was furious, and he told his appointee, "I'll just tell him [Hemmeter] to bypass you."

What Barthelemy meant was that if the historic commission rejected Hemmeter's plan, Hemmeter and Barthelemy would get the New Orleans City Council, which was solidly behind the proposal, to overturn the decision. Tucker also knew this. So rather than rebuff Hemmeter's plan, he simply sat on it, the one thing Hemmeter and Barthelemy didn't want. Tucker and his allies on the board devised a long list of policy questions for Hemmeter to address and scheduled several public meetings to consider them. "Thomas Tucker and his commission have turned out to be heroes so far in the battle to protect New Orleans," wrote *Times-Picayune* columnist Iris Kelso, a casino opponent. Finally, after three months of delay, the City Council simply removed the historic commission from having any say over the project. However, Tucker won a partial victory when, because of the community opposition he had generated, Hemmeter dropped plans to demolish the 1850s buildings by agreeing to downsize his parking garage. For Tucker the victory only whetted his appetite for more battle.

Tucker was the rare kind of lawyer who enjoyed poring over hundreds of pages of forgotten court cases and technical legal documents. Therefore, when he got word that title of the city-owned Rivergate might be in question, he researched old documents exhaustively. Tucker made an astonishing discovery: a long-forgotten 1851 agreement indicated that the city didn't own the Rivergate land. The compact was between the city of New Orleans and a group of landowners at what was now the Rivergate site. The agreement was prompted by the Mississippi River's having changed course in 1820, which created land where the Rivergate now stood. In 1851, Tucker discovered, as part of a deal to create city streets, city officials agreed that New Orleans and the property owners jointly would get back title to the land if the streets ceased to be thoroughfares. When the Rivergate was developed in the 1960s and the streets were blocked, it appeared that the land should have reverted to the original owners. But no one at the time remembered the 1851 agreement. Tucker in 1993, however, uncovered it. He found two brothers—Harry and Henry McCall—who were descendants of a family that had signed the 1851 compact.

In April 1993, Tucker filed suit on their behalf, claiming title to the Rivergate property. He had the McCalls sue each other to avoid tipping off city officials or Harrah's Jazz interests that they were named in a lawsuit. Tucker didn't activate the lawsuit until August 26, 1993, the day after Governor Edwards got Harrah's, Jazzville, and Hemmeter to form the Harrah's Jazz Company and agree to raze the Rivergate. When the city and Harrah's officials learned about the lawsuit, they found that Tucker had created a potential legal barrier: How could they demolish the Rivergate if the city might not have legal title to the property?

Executives with First American Title Insurance Company were among those asking the question. Harrah's officials had turned to the company to provide $700 million worth of title insurance. But company officials wouldn't risk providing the insurance until Tucker's lawsuit was settled. This, in turn, kept Harrah's from beginning to raise the $670 million needed to finance the temporary and permanent casinos, because having title insurance was a prerequisite to getting financing. With this turn of events, Tucker almost singlehandedly stopped the casino in its tracks. "Tucker could be Jack the Ripper and not have caused more problems," said Donald Zuchelli, a casino adviser to Mayor Barthelemy.

To defeat Tucker, Harrah's hired a battery of New Orleans lawyers, and they challenged him on every legal front possible. Finally, after six months had passed, they got a judge to dismiss Tucker's lawsuit on a technicality. By then, Harrah's had had to endure more delays. Harrah's officials now forecast opening the temporary casino on August 1, 1994, with the permanent casino opening eleven months later, on July 1, 1995.

On March 2, 1994, Harrah's officials happily announced that they would undertake a two-week road show from May 1 to May 15 to get investors to buy $425 million in high-yield junk bonds that would finance what had now become a $720 million project. (Bank loans and equity from the partners would make up the $295 million difference.)

Before Harrah's officials could begin the trip, another problem cropped up. This time, Louisiana's attorney general, Richard Ieyoub (*I-yube*), was responsible. Ieyoub had been a little-known district attorney for Calcasieu (*Cal-ka-shoo*) Parish until Edwin Edwards and his political allies backed him for attorney general in 1991. With their support, he won the race and became the state's chief lawyer.

But by 1994, Ieyoub's political antennae were twitching. Polls showed that gambling, which had never been overwhelmingly popular, enjoyed only a narrow margin of support. Edwards, meanwhile, had lost public support following revelations that his children had tried to get into the riverboat-casino business. So Ieyoub was looking for a way to distance himself from Edwards and gambling. He found that way in April 1994. The issue was whether the Harrah's Jazz proposal selected by the casino board's 5–4 vote in August 1993 had changed so substantially since then that the board would have to rebid the license.

Harrah's and its Jazzville partner had won the license with a $357 million plan that called for renovating the Rivergate and opening the casino there in stages. After the shotgun wedding, the board had ended up with a more ambitious $670 million plan that called for demolishing the Rivergate, replacing it with a new building, and putting a temporary casino in the Municipal Auditorium. To a layperson, the changes seemed substantial enough to force the casino board to rebid the project and delay the casino once again.

Casino board members, who acted less as regulators and more as boosters, were happy to move forward without a rebid. Still, they asked Ieyoub to rule on the matter. His chief legal counsel on gambling issues, Jenifer Schaye, advised him that the law favored a rebid. But Ieyoub was mindful of the political implications. Governor Edwards and Billy Broadhurst, Edwards's political associate who was part of Harrah's Jazz, said a rebid was unnecessary. The Jazzville 10, whose large campaign contributions had helped elect Ieyoub, also pressured him not to call for a rebid. Unsure about how to decide, Ieyoub turned to his chief political consultant, Raymond Strother, for advice. In a final meeting in Ieyoub's office, Strother told him that calling for a rebid would distinguish him from Edwards and establish him in voters' minds as his own man.

On April 22, 1994, Ieyoub announced his decision. The changes, he said, are "so fundamentally different from the original" that they "cannot be considered minor, technical or insubstantial." The news hit Harrah's hard. Ron Lenczycki (*Len-zick-e*), president of Harrah's Casino New Orleans, said his company would postpone a job fair scheduled for the next weekend. "I can't have a job fair with the uncertainty that I don't know when we're going to start," he said. Following Ieyoub's ruling, the stock of Harrah's parent company, Promus, dropped $1.625 (5 percent) to close at $32. "Wall Street is very, very, very concerned about the process," said Christopher Hemmeter. "The bank group is very, very, very concerned about the process."

Edwards was furious. Aides said they had never seen him so angry. The governor had been counting on a one-time payment of $125 million from Harrah's—the company had already agreed to it—as a way to finance higher salaries for teachers. And now that money was in doubt because Ieyoub's decision postponed the date when that money would be available. If Edwards couldn't deliver the pay raises, teachers would undoubtedly believe that the governor had reneged on his promise. Privately, Edwards chewed out the attorney general. Publicly, he questioned Ieyoub's intellectual abilities and told reporters, "The delay caused by the opinion will seriously jeopardize the process and the hope that we could anticipate large amounts of revenue during the fiscal year [starting July 1]. In the meantime, we will continue to lose millions of dollars to Mississippi [casinos], and thousands of jobs are put on hold."

Times-Picayune columnist James Gill offered his usual tart assessment: "The governor was reduced to a condition reminiscent of a wet hen when Ieyoub decreed that another delay was necessary before Louisiana could enter the promised land of easy money." Speaking of the entire project, Gill added, "When the state finds itself back on square one at this late stage, you have to wonder how many ways we'll find to screw up when we actually start to build or maybe even operate the casino."

No one knew how long Ieyoub's decision might delay the project. It was clear, however, that if anyone else offered a bid, awarding the license could take months. With that in mind, Edwards and the pro-Harrah's gambling board discouraged other bidders, even as casino heavyweights Caesars World, Donald Trump, Bally Manufacturing, Hilton, MGM, and Mirage expressed interest.

The casino board set May 13 as the new deadline for bids. On that day, with dozens of T-shirt–clad employees cheering them on, Harrah's executives wheeled thirty boxed copies of their six-inch-thick proposal into the casino board's offices. There was one other bidder, however, an unknown company called Gold Shares. The company's bid consisted of a single manila envelope, and it was delivered by a man nobody recognized. This strange twist set casino board officials and Harrah's executives scrambling to find out more about the man. He was Willard Belton, a forty-five-year-old former city councilman from Lake Charles who had resigned from office in 1986 when he pleaded guilty to insurance fraud. Belton had formed Gold Shares in December 1993, and the company had no experience in the gambling industry. Further, Belton had failed to include in the envelope the $1 million check required of each bidder. Belton, who was African American, told a casino board official that he hadn't done so because Gold Shares was a minority-owned company.

Four days later, on May 17, the casino board put the New Orleans project back on track by disqualifying Gold Shares. By then, however, Ieyoub's decision had caused another costly delay. Harrah's officials announced yet another starting date for the temporary casino: December 1994. This would be nearly a year after the initial projected opening. Would there be more problems? On June 10, *The Times-Picayune* reported optimistically, "After more than a year of false starts, Louisiana's casino approval process finally appears to be on track, and regulators are confident gambling can begin in a temporary casino at the Municipal Auditorium by December."

It was not to be. Once again someone would create a roadblock to the star-crossed project. This time, it was the man who had just been elected to replace Sidney Barthelemy as New Orleans's mayor. His name was Marc Morial, and he had become mayor in April 1994 after Barthelemy was forced by the city's charter to retire after two terms. Not that Barthelemy could have won reelection. Problems with the casino and various scandals in his administration—most notably his attempt to use his office to award his son a scholarship at Tulane University—had won him scorn by the time he left office. Morial, in contrast, was very popular. His father, who went by the nickname "Dutch," had been elected in 1978 as the city's first African-American mayor. Marc Morial began his political career by winning election to the State Senate. He then ran for mayor. A fresh, young, energetic candidate at age thirty-six, he won easily.

His first major act was to threaten to derail the casino unless the state and Harrah's gave the city $32 million to cover the increased costs to New Orleans from the casino operation. Morial said that having the casino would force the city to pave surrounding streets and install new lighting and traffic signals, as well as hire more policemen and firefighters once it opened. He tabulated the total at $32 million, with $10 million of that being a one-time infrastructure expense. Without the money, Morial warned, on July 11, 1994, he would have the City Council void Harrah's lease with the city. This would throw the whole project into chaos.

Morial's threat infuriated Edwards. Following the constant delays, the project had finally seemed to be moving forward until Morial stepped in. Edwards argued that the city would receive up to $60 million a year in lease payments from the casino and sales tax payments from the increased economic activity. Morial maintained that the money was needed for New Orleans's chronically underfinanced budget. The state could afford to cover the city's costs, he said, and pointed out that the 1992 casino law called for the state to do so. Edwards replied that Morial was inflating his figures, and that the state could provide no more than $6 million. Morial said he needed more, and the City Council backed him up. "Now we'll find out how . . . badly this state wants this casino," said Jim Singleton, a city councilman. *The Times-Picayune* applauded Morial's threat: "Such municipal single-mindedness, unseen when the city needed it a long time ago, is both refreshing and reassuring as the opening of land-based gambling looms."

Engaging in brinkmanship, Edwards charged that if Morial didn't change his mind, "then there will be no casino." On July 12, the City

Council took the extraordinary step of declaring that a state of "public calamity" existed in New Orleans, a declaration that allowed the council to override its normal rules and schedule a vote for the next day on Morial's proposal to amend or cancel the casino lease. The casino "looks like it is down the drain after two years of work," observed state senator Dennis Bagneris of New Orleans.

Harrah's executives in Memphis watched these events unfold with increasing frustration. Louisiana's confounding politics once again were threatening to kill the casino. How could Morial expect Harrah's to pony up extra money to defray some of the city's costs when Harrah's had already signed a lease with the city? Morial so infuriated Harrah's officials that they asked themselves a more fundamental question: Was the casino worth it? Should they just bite the bullet and pull out of New Orleans?

Michael Rose, the chief executive officer of Promus, Harrah's parent company, was inclined to yank the plug. But two of his top deputies, Phil Satre and Colin Reed, argued that Harrah's should stay. They noted that Harrah's had already invested millions of dollars in the project and had put the company's prestige on the line. Besides, they argued, if they could resolve this problem and open the casino, it promised to be a big success. After much debate, Rose gave in. But he said Harrah's would not provide the additional money that Morial was demanding.

With the clock running out, on July 14, Morial blinked, with an assist from Harrah's two partners. Morial accepted a $22 million payment, which was $10 million lower than the amount he said the city needed. Of the $22 million, $6 million would come from the state and $4 million would come from Christopher Hemmeter and the Jazzville group; Hemmeter and Jazzville would sell bonds to be paid off over thirty years for the additional $12 million. "It was a day of historic negotiations for New Orleans, the day all sides pulled back from the brink of canceling a casino for New Orleans and worked out a better deal for the city," wrote *Times-Picayune* columnist Iris Kelso.

One day later, Harrah's executives announced yet another delay in the opening date for the temporary and permanent casinos. The

Municipal Auditorium casino would not open until March 1995, while the Rivergate casino would not begin operations until March 1996. What's more, financial problems at several of Mississippi's casinos had scared off potential investors. As a result, Harrah's executives said, interest rates during the various delays had risen on the $425 million in junk bonds that the company was planning to sell. This—and other additional costs—would increase the project's overall cost from $720 million to $780 million. Harrah's would have to spend more than twice what company officials had originally envisioned. By now, however, they had gone too far down the path of the New Orleans casino to turn back.

Not all the news for Harrah's was bad during the summer of 1994. Yes, having the Rivergate casino in a historically sensitive area of New Orleans made it vulnerable to Tommy Tucker's legal challenge. And not having broad public support for the project made it vulnerable to challenges by ambitious politicians like Richard Ieyoub and Marc Morial. But Harrah's could still count on Governor Edwards and his pliant casino board. Harrah's would need that support as it moved through the next stage of the process: getting the board to certify the top nineteen owners and executives in the Harrah's Jazz partnership as suitable to be involved with the casino.

This type of scrutiny was typical in casino states, and it was necessary because of the unsavory characters attracted to the gambling industry. Therefore, as in other casino states, investigators for the Louisiana casino board asked for detailed financial and personal information from the nineteen people, who included Christopher Hemmeter, Daniel Robinowitz, Billy Broadhurst, Eddie Sapir, Phil Satre, Colin Reed, and the nine Jazzville partners (they had bought out the tenth). Unlike other states, however, Louisiana's casino regulators, not wanting further problems for the New Orleans casino, did not give their investigators enough time to carry out their work. Nor did they give their investigators the authority to obtain law enforcement intelligence reports and to undertake criminal background checks. Harrah's officials, in particular, pressured board members and staff to speed up the suitability investigations. Despite the handicaps, the board's investigators, led by a retired Drug Enforcement Administration agent named

Dixie Boyles, discovered that two of the nineteen people had gambling problems, another was alleged to have engaged in cocaine trafficking, a fourth was believed to have had improper business dealings with an insurance company, a fifth had dubious ties to Governor Edwards, a sixth had been caught making improper gifts at least once to New Orleans politicians, and a seventh had pleaded guilty to not paying his taxes. However, the board, for the most part, wasn't interested in pursuing these allegations. Its attitude was summed up by the only question that one board member, Leroy Melton, a consistent yes-man for the casino project, asked of one of the Harrah's executives during a closed-door suitability hearing: Would the man speak at Melton's high school alma mater?

On July 14, the same day that the problem with Morial was resolved, the casino board voted on the nineteen. Six of the casino board members (Sallie Page, Joan Heisser, Gerard Thomas, Bert Rowley, Jack Frank, and Melton) found all nineteen suitable. A seventh board member, James Vilas, voted against Robinowitz and abstained on Sapir. An eighth board member, Billy Nungesser, found that only ten of the nineteen were suitable. The board's chairman, Max Chastain, was even tougher, finding that only nine of the nineteen were suitable. Among those that Chastain did not vote for were Hemmeter and Colin Reed, a top Harrah's executive.

Minutes after the vote, Chastain was handed a note telling him that Reed and Hemmeter had just telephoned, and each man very much wanted to talk to him. In an unusual move, Chastain left the meeting while it was in progress. When he returned a few minutes later, a shaken Chastain scribbled a note and passed it to Nungesser, sitting to his right. "I won't be here Monday," it read. Nungesser leaned over and asked him why. "Because," Chastain whispered, "Colin Reed told me I had destroyed his reputation by voting against him. Hemmeter said the same thing." Chastain was sure that Reed and Hemmeter would use their clout with Edwards to get him fired. Nungesser, who delighted in tweaking Edwards and the Harrah's officials, patted Chastain on the back and wrote: "Fuck them. Tell them to call Billy. I voted against them, too."

Nungesser may have lost that battle, but he would soon undertake another one that would pose a grave threat to the casino. It involved events surrounding the August 11, 1993, vote by the casino board in favor of Harrah's and Jazzville. Nungesser was a former chairman of the Louisiana Republican Party, and he was the one board member who seemed to put the public's interests first. He had provided one of the five votes for Harrah's and Jazzville over Christopher Hemmeter and his operating partner, Caesars World. But as an independent operator, Nungesser had been troubled when Hemmeter and Caesars a week later alleged that Jazzville had improperly influenced one of his colleagues, James Vilas. Hemmeter and Caesars, however, dropped the allegation when Hemmeter joined forces with Harrah's and Jazzville a week after that.

Nonetheless, Nungesser kept thinking about the allegation, and during the investigation of the nineteen key Harrah's Jazz executives and owners, he told his colleagues that they ought to subpoena Caesars officials to determine whether they had evidence of Jazzville improperly influencing Vilas. The other board members told Nungesser to drop the issue. He wouldn't, however, and he had an ally in Dixie Boyles, the board's chief investigator. Boyles, fifty-eight, had worked for the Drug Enforcement Administration for twenty-five years before retiring in 1990. He loved to fish in Louisiana's swamps and bayous, but he grew restless during his retirement. When friends in the FBI told him about the new casino board, he applied for a job and was hired. He liked the idea of helping keep the casino free of corruption. As Boyles investigated the charges involving Vilas and Jazzville, he decided that they warranted a serious examination. But the board on July 14 approved all nineteen key executives and owners without giving Boyles the green light.

Still, Nungesser persisted. He plotted with Boyles and Jenifer Schaye, the board's attorney, on how to win approval to initiate the investigation. Schaye, forty-seven, had an unusual background. She had been a nun with School Sisters of Notre Dame for twenty-three years before deciding in 1987 that she wanted to do something else. Schaye's religious order had sent her to law school, so she already had practical legal experience. When she left the order, she was hired by the attorney general's office. She soon proved to be a no-nonsense defender of the public good while learning how to navigate Louisiana's often treacherous political waters. In time, she became head of Attorney General Ieyoub's gaming division. In that position, she frequently butted heads with gambling interests. So when she and Boyles suspected possible wrongdoing by Vilas and Jazzville executives, she didn't hesitate. The two of them recommended to Nungesser that he raise the issue during a board meeting. "You shame them into doing it, where they can't say no," Schaye told Nungesser. He readily agreed. Nungesser outlined to the board why they had a legal and ethical responsibility to investigate the matter. His colleagues dismissed the notion, Vilas in particular expressing his opposition. Nungesser then asked Boyles to say whether he thought they should undertake an investigation. "Yes, I think we have to," Boyles replied, and then expressed his concerns. Wilmore Whitmore, the board's appointed president, spoke up in favor of Boyles. With his colleagues now on the defensive, Nungesser made a quick motion to have the board approve the investigation. The motion passed.

Boyles got to work and soon discovered that Hemmeter and Caesars had conducted their own investigation, after receiving an anonymous phone tip, and had uncovered evidence of links between Vilas and Wendell Gauthier, Jazzville's chairman and a nationally known trial lawyer. Hemmeter and Caesars turned over the documents to the board. The documents showed that Gauthier, who was married, was close to a young woman named Leslie Overton. The *Los Angeles Times* would later describe Overton as Gauthier's "girlfriend," while *Forbes* magazine would call her "his ladyfriend." The documents obtained by Boyles showed that Overton had rented Apartment 110 in a renovated warehouse known as the Henderson, three blocks from where the Rivergate casino would be built. However, the documents showed that the person who made the rent payments for Overton's apartment was Hayden Berry. He worked as a gofer for Calvin Fayard, a Denham Springs trial lawyer and Jazzville partner.

Donald (Chick) Foret, a New Orleans lawyer and private investigator hired by Hemmeter and Caesars, saw Vilas once with Overton, the documents further demonstrated. Foret showed separate photographs of Vilas and Overton to two security guards at the Henderson. A videotape obtained by Boyles recorded the guards saying they had seen Vilas and Overton together at the apartment building one evening, sharing a jacuzzi and a bottle of champagne. A law partner of Foret's, Gary Pendergast, testified in a deposition that while watching the Henderson, he had seen a man whom he believed to be Hayden Berry leaving Apartment 110 after packing a number of suitcases and throwing away two bags of garbage. Pendergast testified that he retrieved the garbage bags and found that they contained women's underwear and makeup. He also found a plane ticket in the name of Michelle Gauthier, one of Wendell Gauthier's daughters, for a trip in April or May 1993 between New Orleans and Puerto Rico.

To Boyles and Schaye, all of the information seemed to confirm troubling ties between Gauthier and Vilas, who under the casino law were not allowed to have dealings with each other outside of board meetings. Boyles and Schaye decided that Boyles had to talk with Leslie Overton. George Solomon, another member of Jazzville, had gotten her a job in Dallas at a magazine that his brother owned. When Boyles and another investigator interviewed her in Dallas, Overton acknowledged that she knew Gauthier and that she had met Vilas twice. On one occasion, she said, she had met him at a New Orleans bar while she was with Gauthier. On the other occasion, Vilas had given her a ride home after they bumped into each other one evening at a French Quarter bar.

Boyles and Schaye agreed that the tie between Gauthier and Vilas was strong enough that now they had to subpoena Gauthier, Hayden Berry, and Calvin Fayard of Jazzville. They didn't make this decision lightly because they knew that Gauthier, in particular, was a formidable legal force and had enormous political power. But the time had come to get his story. On the afternoon of October 7, 1994, Wilmore Whitmore, the casino board president, approved the request to subpoena Gauthier. Before Boyles and Schaye issued the subpoena, they went next door to the Westin Hotel bar to have a drink. A few minutes later, Gauthier walked up. Apparently, a mole on the board had tipped him off about the subpoena. "Should I go home and tell my wife about my girlfriend?" he asked Boyles and Schaye.

"I don't care who you fuck," Schaye replied. "I care who you pay to fuck."

The board's investigators then served Gauthier the subpoena. That night he called Whitmore and angrily demanded that he withdraw it. Whitmore refused. Gauthier called again the next day with the same demand. He added that he had documents, stolen from the board by a former employee, that would embarrass Whitmore if they became public. Despite the threat, Whitmore again refused.

Gauthier was scheduled to be deposed on October 17. On October 11, the casino board held its next regularly scheduled meeting. Board members had learned of the subpoenas. Max Chastain, who had kept his job despite his votes against Reed and Hemmeter, had been told of the exchange between Schaye and Gauthier from his son, who worked at the Westin Hotel. A waitress who overheard the conversation had told Chastain's son. A former FBI agent, Chastain was incensed that others would overhear them serving a subpoena.

During the board meeting, Chastain sharply criticized Schaye. Bert Rowley, another board member, added that he didn't understand the fuss over Gauthier, Overton, and Vilas, that it was nothing more than a few guys playing around. Gerard Thomas, a third board member, said he thought that Boyles and Schaye were wasting their time. In an unprecedented move, Chastain then dismissed Schaye, Boyles, Whitmore, and other staffers from the room so the board could meet alone. Nungesser, who would have objected to this move, was absent that day, ill at home. When the board members emerged forty-five minutes later, they directed Schaye and Boyles to terminate the investigation. The board further directed the investigators to return all documents to the people who had provided them, to cancel the Gauthier, Berry, and Fayard subpoenas, and to destroy copies of all records.

The orders shocked Schaye, Boyles, and Whitmore. Boyles thought it was a whitewash. Schaye said to herself, "We must have come upon it. Holy shit, we were right." Whitmore privately told Boyles to disobey the orders and protect the documents. When Nungesser got word at home, he raged to anyone who would listen that his colleagues were "crooks" and "rotten bastards."

Two FBI agents were waiting the next morning at the board's offices when members and staff arrived. Tipped off about the previous afternoon's events, the agents were there to seize the documents that the board wanted to destroy. Attorney General Richard Ieyoub, meanwhile, announced that Schaye, who worked for him, would not halt the investigation. Chastain issued a defensive press release that said that "there was no basis for concern that an illegal act had occurred, nor was there justification for further inquiry." Nevertheless, the actions by the FBI and Ieyoub prompted two Wall Street analysts to downgrade their recommendations for Promus's stock. "It raises more uncertainties, and the market doesn't need more uncertainties about doing business in Louisiana," said Dennis Forst, a gambling stock analyst with Hancock Institutional Equity Services.

Although fallout from the shutdown hurt Harrah's in the short term, the United States Attorney, L. J. Hymel, who took charge, didn't aggressively pursue the investigation. Hymel never explained why, but observers noted that he was close to Edwards. Ieyoub also dropped the matter, apparently having gotten all the political mileage out of it he thought possible. So in the end, the board's decision to shut down the investigation prevented its investigators from getting the full story on Overton, Vilas, and Gauthier, and whether their relationship had tainted the board's 5–4 vote in 1993 to award Harrah's Jazz the gambling license.

Tower of Babel

No longer troubled by an investigation into how it had won the license, Harrah's Jazz now had momentum to move forward with building the world's largest casino in New Orleans. On November 16, 1994, company officials announced that they had arranged financing for the project at last. A syndicate of banks led by Bankers Trust would lend $175 million, investors had purchased $435 million in junk bonds, and the three partners would put up $170 million themselves. Profits from the Municipal Auditorium temporary casino would provide the additional $35 million, since higher interest rates on the bonds had now raised the cost to $815 million. This was more than double the $357 million cost for Harrah's and Jazzville when the casino board had selected their bid back in August 1993.

On November 18, 1994, exactly twenty-nine months after Governor Edwin Edwards had signed the casino bill into law, work began on transforming the Municipal Auditorium into the temporary casino. At a ceremony marking the occasion, jesters in brightly colored satin costumes waved huge wands, and officials with Harrah's Jazz joked about the many barriers they had overcome to get to that point. "The Guinness Book of World Records called me this morning," said Wendell

Gauthier, Jazzville's chairman. "We made it. We're the project that has overcome more hurdles and more difficulties than any other project in the history of the world." The casino was scheduled to open on April 22, 1995. Demolition of the Rivergate would begin in January 1995, and the permanent casino on the site would begin operations in May 1996.

Besides snuffing out the investigation, the casino board was doing little to win the public's trust. Unschooled in policy making, chairman Max Chastain lacked the savvy to oversee a board whose members cared little about the public interest. Chastain's only experience running a meeting had come during his son's Little League career years before. Board meetings frequently spun out of control as members, engaging in petty squabbles, bickered endlessly on behalf of their political patrons. Unsure of himself, Chastain would call Governor Edwards's chief legal counsel, Al Donovan, so often for advice on minor matters that Donovan grew exasperated. So did Edwards. He called his friend Harry Lee, Jefferson Parish sheriff, to complain about Lee's having recommended Chastain's appointment. "Where did you get this guy?" Edwards complained.

"Governor," Lee replied, "you were looking for someone with a clean record, and he had one."

Edwards ended up concluding that Chastain was in way over his head, that he was a minnow in a tank full of sharks.

Despite his impeccable credentials—U.S. Naval Academy, FBI—Chastain made several blunders that called his integrity into question. He met with an attorney for a slot machine manufacturer that was seeking a license from the board, even though board rules prohibited this. He recommended to Harrah's officials that they consider selecting a particular company to provide furniture—another no-no. In a transgression that landed him on *The Times-Picayune*'s front page, he invited seven Harrah's Jazz officials to accompany him and others on a fact-finding tour of casinos and racetracks in the Far East. The nonprofit group that arranged the trip would let Chastain travel for free, thanks to payments from the Harrah's officials and others he invited on the trip. "The guy's playing with fire," a critic said. "He's getting too close to the people he's regulating." Two days after the news report, Chastain canceled the trip.

Other casino board members came under fire for their financial dealings. Board members were paid $60,000 a year, with Chastain as chairman getting $75,000, to do work that was considered full-time. In addition, the four board members who lived outside of New Orleans were reimbursed up to $1,200 a month for housing while attending the board's meetings in New Orleans. Newspapers reported that James Vilas, who lived in Baton Rouge, was getting reimbursed $1,100 a month to rent a French Quarter condominium from his mother. Vilas's mother, it was reported, borrowed $70,000 to buy the condo from a company that later won a $2.9 million casino contract. A second board member, Sallie Page, who lived in Alexandria, was getting reimbursed $729 a month to rent a three-bedroom apartment in Metairie that she shared with her daughter and son-in-law. A third board member, Gerard Thomas of Natchitoches, was getting reimbursed $80 a night for staying at a Metairie condo that he co-owned. The living arrangements of Vilas, Page, and Thomas violated state ethics rules, according to the Commission on Ethics for Public Employees.

There would be one final flap involving the casino board. Harrah's wanted to buy slot machines and computer software from a well-known company, Bally Gaming International, but Wilmore Whitmore, the casino board's appointed president, refused to approve the deal. Bally had done business with Worldwide Gaming of Louisiana, which authorities said was controlled by the Gambino and Marcello crime families. Bally's president, Alan Maiss, had pleaded guilty to a felony charge of knowing he was doing business with an alleged mob associate not licensed to distribute or operate video poker machines in Louisiana. Whitmore, in his report to the board, said Bally did not act aggressively or decisively enough when it discovered that Worldwide Gaming officials might have links to organized crime. In a state with a tough regulatory board, Whitmore's decision would have been the final word. But Bally, led by Sam LeBlanc III, a politically prominent New Orleans attorney, teamed with Harrah's officials to pressure the board to overturn Whitmore's decision. LeBlanc argued that Bally would lose a lucrative contract, while Harrah's officials argued that having to forsake Bally for another slot machine company would delay the casino's opening by months. Acting at Harrah's behest, Edwards also weighed in, telling Chastain that Bally's computer software was first-rate.

On February 1, 1995, the board overruled Whitmore and awarded Bally the license. The board's decision, opined *The Times-Picayune*, "reinforced the notion that Louisiana's gambling regulators are more concerned with protecting the powerful casino interests than the integrity of the industry in our state." Columnist James Gill wrote sarcastically that for a time, "the state casino board was derelict in its duty, which, of course, is to lick the boots of Harrah's executives whenever an opportunity arises." With the Bally decision, the board "showed who is master in the dog-eat-dog world of Louisiana gambling." Five days later, Gill added, "Last week in this column, members of the state casino board were described as boot-licking curs, and, naturally, a few people have demanded an apology. They are right. This column therefore begs forgiveness of all dog lovers."

Harrah's had succeeded in preventing a long delay, but the Bally episode forced the company to postpone the temporary casino opening a few days, to May 1. At long last, however, there would be no more delays. Nearly three years after it was legalized by the legislature, New Orleans finally would get its casino.

Harrah's organized a gaudy show to mark the occasion. Some five thousand politicians, prominent businessmen, community leaders, and other VIPs were invited to an open-air party immediately preceding the casino's opening. It was held in Congo Square, where slaves had once been sold, next to the Municipal Auditorium. On this evening, men wore tuxedos, while women were dressed in ball gowns. There was champagne, barbecued shrimp, beef tenderloin, and sweet potato pie. Harrah's handed out company paperweights to a special few to mark the occasion. Casino board members, who had the responsibility of regulating the company, were spotted carrying the paperweights as if they were hard-won trophies.

The most important dignitaries sat in chairs on a temporary stage under one of Congo Square's towering live oaks: Governor Edwards, New Orleans mayor Marc Morial, Harrah's executives, developer

Christopher Hemmeter, and the Jazzville partners, the last of whom were resplendent in matching white dinner jackets and black slacks.

As a festive crowd looked on, soul music favorite Irma Thomas sang a few numbers. Then it was time for the speeches. With the crowd buzzing in anticipation to begin gambling, the remarks were kept mercifully short. "Are you ready for Harrah's Casino New Orleans?" yelled Ron Lenczycki, the casino's president.

"Yeah!" the crowd roared back.

"Is this exciting or what?" shouted Wendell Gauthier.

"Let's celebrate," said Morial. "Let the games begin."

As usual, Governor Edwards was the star of the show. "I have never been to a casino before—," he said, pausing as the crowd began to laugh. Then he delivered the punch line "—for the purpose of making a speech." The audience hooted and hollered. Turning serious, he acknowledged how the casino debate had polarized the community. "Some will look at it as an abomination," he said. "I view it as economic development. I supported it because of the jobs it will create and the tourists it will bring. . . . I want to say to all who had objections and criticisms that I hope as the years unfold and you see how it stimulates this area, I hope you will agree with me that there are more pluses than minuses."

Edwards, Morial, and Lenczycki then dropped three large wooden coins into a fake ten-foot slot machine on the stage, and pulled the oversized handle. Three court jesters appeared in the window, which triggered fireworks, balloons, confetti cannons, and multicolored smoke bombs. The Municipal Auditorium's doors swung open at 6:40 p.m., and the VIPs streamed in.

The sixty-four-year-old building was unrecognizable to previous visitors. Bright Mardi Gras colors adorned the carpet. Carnival-themed masks and hand-painted murals covered the walls and stairwells. Huge jesters' heads, equipped with sophisticated surveillance cameras, hung above the main floor. Rows of brightly colored lights hung like necklaces from the rafters. Row after row of slot machines and video poker machines lined the walls. Blackjack tables and craps tables occupied the middle of the auditorium. Upstairs, there were high-roller tables and slot machines. In all, there was 76,000 square feet of gambling space. It was called the temporary casino, but its size made it bigger than Harrah's casinos in Las Vegas and Atlantic City, and it was grander than any Louisiana riverboat casino.

For two hours the VIPs had the casino to themselves. That's how things worked in Louisiana: the political insiders were always favored over average citizens. Mayor Morial and New Orleans city councilmen Troy Carter and Jim Singleton played blackjack. State senators Greg Tarver and Don Kelly played craps. Revius Orticke, who had been the first African American to serve on the Louisiana Supreme Court, played the slot machines, as did state senator Jon Johnson and former New Orleans mayor Sidney Barthelemy, who had a key role in making the casino a reality. "It's wonderful to see your dreams come true," Barthelemy told a reporter.

Edwards, however, didn't gamble that night. In 1992, he had promised that he would not gamble inside a Louisiana casino while governor. Wearing a dark suit and a red rose in his lapel, Edwards did stroll through the Municipal Auditorium. As he did, dealers, pit bosses, and slot machine attendants applauded. Edwards waved in response. Then at 8:45 p.m., the casino was opened to the thousands of ordinary folks waiting restlessly outside. "The poor people will spend money here," Herman (Shaky) Moreau said, shortly before he went in. "The poor people expect to make a fortune." By 9:00 p.m., the casino was jammed to its capacity of 10,500, and at 10:30 p.m., 500 people were still waiting to enter. After months of frustrating delays, Harrah's officials were ecstatic at the opening. So were investors. Promus's stock the next day rose 2⅛ points to close at 40⅞, a fifty-two-week high.

But a week after the opening, trouble struck once again. A storm that was projected to hit New Orleans only once every hundred years dumped eighteen inches of rain in three hours, flooding much of the city. Five feet of water collected in the Municipal Auditorium's basement, which housed much of the casino's electrical system. On May 19 at 1:00 a.m., Harrah's closed the temporary casino. The shutdown lasted for only three days, but it provided yet another reason to wonder if that casino might be hexed.

On June 12, Harrah's released the first month's financial figures. The casino win—how much Harrah's collected after paying winners— was a measly $11.3 million in May. This was only one-third of the $33 million that Harrah's was projecting for the temporary casino on a monthly basis. Showing the difficulty that Harrah's faced in matching its projections, the temporary casino and the five floating casinos in metro New Orleans *combined* took in $33.7 million in May.

Harrah's had forecast that tourists would account for 60 percent of the gamblers. In May, they accounted for only 44 percent. "The location at Basin Street, based upon our experience thus far, has proved to be more challenging than expected in getting tourists" to visit the casino, said Ron Lenczycki, president of Harrah's New Orleans. He predicted, however, that the market would pick up. "I still feel very, very confident," he said. But Joe Buckley, a gambling stock analyst at Bear, Stearns & Company, said there were "some serious questions about the New Orleans gaming market—how big it is, how deep it will be. But it's still early. In all fairness, you have to give them time to develop the tourism industry."

Up until this point, Wall Street, gambling stock analysts, and Louisiana politicians had few doubts about the project's viability. Practically the only dissenting voice was that of Tommy Tucker, who had already proved to be a considerable nemesis of Harrah's with his lawsuit over the Rivergate's title. Tucker loved to pore over complicated financial documents, and in April 1994, he had done his own analysis of the casino's numbers after reading projections devised by KPMG Peat Marwick, the nationwide accounting and consulting firm hired by the state casino board to review Harrah's financial projections. Peat Marwick said optimistically that Harrah's would be profitable enough to meet its financial obligations to the state and its creditors. In his analysis, Tucker made the astonishing discovery that Harrah's own numbers showed that a $720 million casino produced no additional gamblers or revenue compared to the $357 million casino that Harrah's and Jazzville had been planning when they won the casino license in August 1993. "I do not have a crystal ball," Tucker wrote in a letter to the casino board. "I do not pretend to know more about casinos or finance than others. But I have examined many cash flow spread sheets in my professional life. What is clear from this one [the Peat Marwick study] is that everything Harrah's projects must come true or the project will tub."

Casino board members dismissed Tucker's analysis, which conflicted with all of the other rosy reports. They refused his request to discuss it before the board.

Worse-than-expected results from two New Orleans riverboat casinos, as well as Harrah's poor first month, prompted others to start echoing Tucker's concerns. On June 18, 1995, *The Times-Picayune* published a special report on gambling in metro New Orleans with the headline A HOUSE OF CARDS? The subhead read: "Harrah's Future is Anyone's to Guess."

Nap Overton, a gambling analyst with Morgan Keegan & Company, was among those who remained bullish. "I think they'll do at least $20 million a month for the first year, and that is a very bad-case scenario," Overton said. But another analyst, Jason Ader of Smith Barney, reduced his estimate of casino win the first year to $12.5 million a month. "I'd feel a lot more comfortable with Promus if they had never gotten involved in New Orleans," Ader said.

On July 11, Harrah's released the June numbers. Casino win was up in June, but only to $13.2 million. Analysts remained concerned, but still foresaw better days ahead for Harrah's. "I look at [June] as a completely acceptable number," said Jim Murren, an analyst with C. J. Lawrence/Deutschebank Securities. "The trend is moving in the right direction."

Harrah's "can absorb the summer months," added Tom Ryan, an analyst with BT Securities. "What will be critical is their fall, winter, and spring." By October, Ryan predicted, the temporary casino would be doing $20 million a month.

On August 9, Harrah's released the July numbers: casino win had risen to only $14.8 million, still far below the projected $33 million. Dave Wolfe, an analyst with Oppenheimer & Company, called the result "disappointing." Ron Lenczycki, the casino president, said Harrah's wasn't disappointed, given New Orleans's humid summer weather. "We felt pretty good considering that July—next to August—is probably one of the softest months in the [New Orleans tourism] marketplace." Harrah's, however, did reduce work hours for 600 of its 3,000 employees. A few days later, Harrah's went even further by laying off 461 workers and shutting down 14,000 of the casino's 76,000 square feet of gambling space.

There were more ominous numbers. The company reported that losses for Harrah's Jazz in the first two months of operation were $38.4 million, which was higher than analysts had predicted. In a filing with the Securities and Exchange Commission, Harrah's reported that the temporary casino, which was supposed to produce $35 million to help cover the Rivergate casino's $815 million price tag, would not provide any extra cash.

A study for the New Orleans Metropolitan Convention and Visitors Bureau pointed out the problem. While Harrah's was expecting tourists to account for 60 percent of the gamblers, only 56 percent of visitors to the city knew about casinos in New Orleans, and only 24 percent expressed interest in gambling. C. B. Forgotston, the state's leading gambling critic, explained it this way: "Every city has its own unique attraction," he said. "The unique thing about New Orleans is the French Quarter, our food and our people. You don't see any of those in a casino. For tourists to come to New Orleans to gamble would be like a New Orleanian going to San Francisco to eat Cajun food."

On September 8, Harrah's released the August numbers: casino win was only $13.1 million. Harrah's Ron Lenczycki once again predicted better days ahead as the weather cooled. "Labor Day was very good," he said. But Times-Picayune columnist James Gill was ready to render a verdict: "They have a major flop on their hands with the temporary casino, which was supposed to take in $403 million in the year it will take to construct an eyesore where the Rivergate once stood. So far it cannot do even half the business the financial wizards at Harrah's forecast. . . . Anyone who invested in the junk bonds that were sold to finance casino construction also has reason to conclude that there are lies, damned lies and Harrah's numbers."

On October 6, Harrah's released the September numbers: casino win was only $12 million. Now, armed with five months of results, the

Wall Street analysts were ready to agree with Tommy Tucker and James Gill. Jim Murren of C. J. Lawrence/Deutschebank Securities called the numbers "horrible," and said, "There's no spin doctor in the world who can put a positive spin on $12 million." Added Dave Wolfe of Oppenheimer & Company, "It's got to be pretty disconcerting to investors and even [Harrah's] at this point. One has to question what the market really is in New Orleans and what it takes to get it closer to what people thought it would be. I think we are all kind of shaking our heads right now."

The results were disconcerting to Harrah's officials. They had begun promoting New Orleans in Houston and in their Las Vegas and Atlantic City casinos. They had tried to have shuttle buses take tourists to and from hotels and to the Municipal Auditorium. But the city's cab drivers, who had strong political pull, blocked the plan. Harrah's then began paying cab drivers to deliver customers. Hotel concierges, however, steered away tourists, telling them that the casino neighborhood was crime-filled. The situation that fall for Harrah's was getting desperate.

Wilmore Whitmore then landed a hard blow. Whitmore by now had stepped down as the casino board's president, but he was keeping tabs on the project's progress. A former bank president, Whitmore was particularly keen on the casino's numbers. On November 6, he told the Associated Press, in a news story published on *The Times-Picayune*'s front page, that Harrah's Jazz could not meet its debts after the permanent casino opened. Whitmore called on the board to hire an independent financial consultant to monitor the company's finances and devise a debt-restructuring plan to allow Harrah's Jazz to keep operating and avoid bankruptcy. "Look seriously at this and quit dreaming," Whitmore told the AP. "Once a trend has been set, you can't blame it all on the location of the temporary casino or the May 8 flood. There must be something peculiar about this market that Harrah's and everybody else overestimated. We must work out a plan."

Whitmore was basing much of his thinking on a Merrill Lynch analysis that had been issued on October 6 but that had not received any publicity. The report, prepared by junk bond analyst Richard

Byrne, concluded that the gambling market in New Orleans was so weak that the permanent casino would not earn enough even to make an $81 million interest payment on its junk bonds. Byrne said the permanent casino would collect $472 million during its first year, well short of the $618 million that Harrah's had projected. The lower revenue, coupled with the high 18.5 percent state tax on the casino win as well as a management fee due Harrah's Entertainment, would squeeze the permanent casino, Byrne said. Harrah's Entertainment could defer the $25 million management fee it was scheduled to receive, but the company would still have to make additional expenditures to cover shortfalls from the Harrah's Jazz New Orleans casino. "Recent results suggest that the gaming potential of the New Orleans market is limited," Byrne wrote. He added that junk bonds for Harrah's New Orleans casino were overvalued.

The casino board had been given copies of the Merrill Lynch report, but only one member was taking it seriously. That member was Fred Cassibry (*Cass-i-bree*), a retired federal judge named to the board by Governor Edwards to replace Billy Nungesser at the beginning of 1995. At first, it seemed that in replacing Nungesser, whose term had expired, Edwards had eliminated the board's only independent voice. But Cassibry turned out to be a crusty, no-nonsense critic of Harrah's and his colleagues' pro-casino attitudes. For example, Cassibry had strongly backed Whitmore when Whitmore in early 1995 wanted to deny Bally Gaming a license to sell slot machines. And now, frustrated with his colleagues' inattention to the Merrill Lynch report, Cassibry had shared the report with Whitmore on November 2. That prompted Whitmore to speak with the AP reporter on November 6. Cassibry also had raised the stakes when he told the AP he had been informed that Harrah's had hired a law firm specializing in bankruptcies.

Colin Reed, Harrah's senior vice president, flew in from Memphis to try to contain the damage. Speaking in his clipped English accent, he told the casino board members on November 7 that Harrah's had not hired a bankruptcy firm, and he denounced Cassibry's claim as "irresponsible, malicious and unfounded." Reed downplayed the Merrill Lynch report and assured everyone that the permanent casino would open as planned. "This casino is going to be built, and Harrah's Entertainment is going to make sure it is built," Reed said.

The next day, however, Harrah's released more bad news: casino win in October was only $14.4 million. This didn't even match the July number of $14.8 million. For the six months the casino had been open, it was doing barely one-third of the expected business. New Orleans was now buzzing with speculation about the casino's fate. On November 12, Harrah's attempted to quell the rumors. The company published a full-page ad in The Times-Picayune, whose headline read: HARRAH'S NEW ORLEANS IS HERE TO STAY. BET ON IT. "To the recent irresponsible comments made that Harrah's New Orleans is in financial trouble and has engaged a law firm specializing in bankruptcy proceedings, I state, unequivocally and without qualification, that such comments are untrue and without foundation," wrote Ron Lenczycki, president of Harrah's New Orleans. "We are proud of the New Orleans casino project. We are proud of our employees. We are proud of this city and state. We have made a lot of friends here—thousands of employees, contractors and suppliers. We do not intend to let them down."

On November 13, Moody's Investors Service downgraded the Harrah's New Orleans junk bonds from B2 to B1. Harrah's Jazz the next day reported losses of $40 million in the July-through-September quarter. However, Joseph Boucree, who had replaced Whitmore as casino board president, provided Harrah's with favorable news on November 14 when he said he found no evidence that the casino was heading toward insolvency. Lenczycki once again offered reassuring words: "Our financing is secured, and the poor results at the temporary casino are having no impact on the progress of the permanent location. To judge us now would be like judging the [New Orleans] Saints in the preseason. You don't know exactly what will happen until the real games start."

On Monday, November 20, Max Chastain sent a confidential memo to his board colleagues. In it, he reported that members of Jazzville had just visited him and passed along several important developments. For months now, Jazzville and Harrah's had been feuding over Harrah's demand that Jazzville put up an additional $33 million in equity or risk having its ownership share of the casino be reduced. But Jazzville didn't readily have the money, and it accused Harrah's of strong-arm tactics. Two Jazzville partners—Wendell Gauthier and John Cummings, nationally known trial lawyers—in turn threatened to sue Harrah's, whose officials began privately calling Jazzville "the Bully Boys." In one development that Jazzville officials told to Chastain, Harrah's wanted to exercise its right to reduce its stake in the casino by 2.95 percent. This would effectively reduce Harrah's share to just below 50 percent, which would keep the company from having to carry the entire casino debt on its books, in case something went wrong. At this point, Chastain did not realize the potential significance of the change. In his memo, Chastain also reported that representatives for Harrah's, Jazzville, and Hemmeter were supposed to meet the next morning at 9:00 a.m. Chastain said he had asked them to brief board officials at 2:00 p.m. on their discussion.

Harrah's executives delayed the start of the next day's meeting with their two partners because they were engrossed in their own meetings. As the day wore on, Jazzville officials, in particular, became concerned that something was up, that the discussion with Harrah's would involve more than simply the latest fight over ownership share. Finally, at 4:00 p.m., Harrah's officials were ready to meet with Jazzville and representatives of developer Christopher Hemmeter. Michael Rose, Harrah's chief executive officer, had flown down on the company's jet from Memphis, and he had shocking news: Harrah's was planning to put the Harrah's Jazz casino into Chapter 11 bankruptcy.

Rose then detailed a series of developments over the past week that had prompted Harrah's decision. On Tuesday, the company had filed a 10Q report with the Securities and Exchange Commission showing a sharply lower forecast for the permanent casino. Where Harrah's had been projecting a casino win of $618 million a year, it was now estimating it to be as low as $406 million. Instead of the permanent casino in its first year earning $181 million in profits before interest payments, as previously projected, it could earn as little as $52 million, and then suffer a net loss of $38 million after factoring in the interest payments. Rose said that Bankers Trust, the lead bank, had responded the next day by asking Harrah's to provide additional financial information.

By now Harrah's Jazz had already spent some $450 million on the entire project and was about to tap into a $170 million loan from a group of banks led by Bankers Trust. When Harrah's provided the additional information on Friday, November 17, Bankers Trust sought an urgent meeting with Harrah's on Sunday in New York City. At that meeting, Rose explained to his partners from the Jazzville and Hemmeter groups, Bankers Trust officials said that a "material adverse change" had occurred in the casino project's status. In response, he said, Bankers Trust refused to provide the $170 million in loans needed to complete the permanent casino, unless Harrah's would guarantee the entire debt instead of its one-third share. Harrah's officials said that would expose the company to too much risk. So without the $170 million, Rose said, Harrah's had no choice but to declare bankruptcy for the New Orleans casino.

The Jazzville partners at the meeting took the news quietly, but insisted on passing it along immediately to the casino regulators. The group then went down one floor at Canal Place to brief Chastain and other casino board officials. It was now 5:30 p.m. on Tuesday, November 21, two days before Thanksgiving. Rose outlined the situation to Chastain, Cassibry, and several other board officials. He then added that they were trying to decide whether to shut down the temporary casino as well. At about 7:00 p.m., that meeting ended so the Harrah's Jazz partners could decide the casino's fate. They went back upstairs. Each of the three groups then huddled separately.

When they reconvened, Rose lowered the boom. He said Harrah's officials had decided to shut down the temporary casino and halt construction on the Rivergate casino. Jazzville officials immediately objected. "Shutting the casino down would put a lot of people out of work," said Wendell Gauthier, his voice rising. "You're not giving them any advance notice. Our reputations will be ruined. You don't live here, but we do."

Rose replied that the numbers left Harrah's with no choice. John Cummings of Jazzville then jumped in. "It wasn't Bankers Trust that pulled the money," Cummings shouted. "You told them to pull the money, and I'll prove it. You've orchestrated this whole thing." Rose tried to interrupt. "You don't impress me or anybody at this table," Cummings continued. "You shouldn't confuse us with people you can intimidate."

"We're going to shut it down with or without you guys," shouted Rose.

"Do whatever you're big enough to do," sneered Cummings.

Rose and his deputies then started to walk out. "Don't come back!" yelled Cummings.

But they did. Tempers cooled, and Rose then got the Harrah's Jazz board to approve the bankruptcy, the shutdown of the temporary casino, and an end to construction work on the permanent casino. Colin Reed of Harrah's then called Edwards to inform him of Harrah's decision. The governor was hunting in Texas, at the ranch of New Orleans Saints owner Tom Benson. Chastain had already called Edwards that evening with news of Harrah's plan to file for Chapter 11. Now when Reed told him that Harrah's would go further and shut down the entire casino project, Edwards was livid. His casino was going down the tubes.

"Why in the fuck did you have that big newspaper ad misrepresenting what you were going to do?" Edwards asked, referring to the full-page *Times-Picayune* advertisement two weeks earlier in which Harrah's vowed it would remain in New Orleans.

"Honestly, we thought when we wrote the ad that we were going to be able to do it, but it just didn't work out that way," Reed replied.

"OK," Edwards said, getting over his flash of anger to think ahead. "It's going to be a big, big black eye for the city and your organization, and for me and for the state. But what you need to do is immediately get started on the permanent casino and get it completed as soon as possible, because otherwise you're going to lose your license."

Reed was noncommittal.

Meanwhile, at the Municipal Auditorium, it was a typical Tuesday night. The crowd was modest, but the scene was noisy. Players were yelling out bets, and whooping it up when they won. Slot machine bells were ringing, and coins were clanging against hard metal surfaces. Gamblers at the craps tables were throwing dice, players at blackjack tables were slapping down cards, and the older men and women sitting on stools in front of the slot machines were feeding in one quarter after another. At 10:00 p.m., WWL-TV broadcast the shocking news: the casino was to shut down in a few hours. Word spread among workers in the casino. Few could believe it.

At 2:30 a.m., a craps player known as "Pops" was waiting his turn to roll the dice. His luck had been bad, and by now he was down to $100 and change. "He looked up at Chris the croupier and shook his head," reported *The Times-Picayune* in its account of the night's events. "'I hope they do close this place down,' he said. 'Then I won't have to come here anymore.'"

At 3:45 a.m., a muted voice came over loudspeakers throughout the casino: "Shut it down. Shut it down." Many gamblers initially didn't hear the announcement. Slot players, in particular, were absorbed in the timeless world of the clockless casino, where they pulled the slot handle every few seconds and sometimes were rewarded with the jangle of fresh coins. Then men in suits fanned throughout the casino to pass along the word. For players reluctant to leave, eternally convinced that they were about to score a big hit, the suits crowded close.

"Cash out, sir," a Harrah's official in a brown suit firmly told a man in blue coveralls. The man stared back, not comprehending the casino's fate. "Right now?" he asked. "They're shutting the building?" The Harrah's official confirmed the news and thanked the man for his patronage. The man now understood what was happening. "No, thank *you*," the man replied, tapping a plastic cup brimming with tokens. "Will I be able to get a cab?" It was 4:05 a.m., and the last players were leaving.

"Outside Harrah's main entrance a doorman in full regalia advised privacy-seekers to avoid the red-carpeted exit," *The Times-Picayune* reported. "'Y'all don't wanna be on the news tonight, make a left or a right turn,' he said, gesturing at the bank of television cameras set up dead ahead." Close to 5:00 a.m., Harrah's "workers began emerging for the last time, their colorful jester uniforms contrasting starkly with their long faces. Most clutched their walking papers, a letter from Lenczycki to 'Harrah's New Orleans Krewe members' titled simply 'Basin Street Closing.'"

At 6:30 a.m., shortly after construction workers arrived at the half-finished casino to begin the day's toil on the former Rivergate site, they were told the news. "We're all eating chicken for Thanksgiving," lamented Bryant McDonald, one of the workers. In all, 800 construction workers lost their jobs that day, in addition to the 2,500 employees at the temporary casino. A variety of creditors were owed $60 million. "We are looking at dire consequences," New Orleans mayor Marc Morial said grimly, at a press conference later in the day. "There are tough decisions that have to be made."

The closing blew a $23 million hole in the city's $425 million budget, as the mayor and the City Council had foolishly balanced their budget with projected casino revenue. Morial called on Harrah's executives to immediately reopen the temporary casino. Jazzville officials responded favorably. But Harrah's officials said they would reopen the casino and resume construction on the permanent casino only if the city and state granted tax concessions and if the bondholders deferred interest payments. Edwards, for one, said the state legislature had no desire to grant any relief.

Times-Picayune columnist James Gill captured the public mood when he wrote: "When fat cats screw up, they throw other people out of work, and when they screw up big-time they hand out pink slips on the eve of the holidays. The wrong people lost their jobs when the temporary casino turned out to be more temporary than advertised, and construction of the permanent casino was halted, leaving Harrah's with what looks more like a permanent disaster. The construction workers, and the 2,000 people who worked at the casino, are now paying the price for the breathtaking ineptitude of Harrah's, its consultants and all the city and state officials who sucked up copious amounts of snake oil. If there were any justice, a whole phalanx of number-crunchers, government planners and high-flying vice presidents would be looking for new positions this Thanksgiving."

On November 28, six days after shutting their doors, Harrah's senior executives made their first public comments when they appeared before the casino board. Once again it fell to Harrah's senior vice president, Colin Reed, to address the regulators. On November 7, he had been combative, almost pugnacious, when he appeared before the board to scold Whitmore, Cassibry, and other skeptics of the casino's future. "This casino is going to be built, and Harrah's Entertainment is going to make sure it is built," Reed had said then. Three weeks later, with the casino closed and in Chapter 11, Reed was subdued, apologetic. "There is no clear path here as we speak," he said haltingly. "We don't have a plan to lay out on the table for you today."

Michael Rose also addressed the board. When he was done, reporters descended on him, firing questions. Rose fielded a few and then, exasperated, yelled, "Get me out of here!" to his personal security detail. They hustled him onto an elevator. Rose obviously couldn't wait to leave New Orleans.

A *Miami Herald* reporter who visited the Rivergate site a few days later summed up the situation. "Here is what lies at the end of one rainbow: a huge, half-finished hulk of rusting I-beams and incomplete green copperplated domes, looming up like an abandoned Tower of Babel. Water is collecting in the basement. This city's golden dreams of gambling millions have burst like an iridescent bubble."

The Death of a Monarchy

O n October 16, 1993, Governor Edwin Edwards, trailed by an entourage of aides and political hangers-on, swept into the International Ballroom at the New Orleans Fairmont Hotel. The Cajun King was immediately engulfed by people wanting to shake his hand, say hello, ask a favor. Each of the 1,200 people in the crowd had paid $1,000 for the privilege of being there. The $1.2 million that Edwards would collect would help finance his reelection campaign, for Edwards told the crowd this evening that in 1995 he would seek an unprecedented fifth term as governor of Louisiana. He was getting an early start to discourage potential rivals and to lock up the early money.

Edwards had come a long way since his last campaign, in 1991. Then he had made a long-shot bid for governor facing Buddy Roemer, the incumbent who had beaten him four years earlier, as well as David Duke, the neo-Nazi apologist and former Ku Klux Klan grand wizard who had become a folk hero to hordes of politically frustrated white moderates and conservatives. Edwards's 1991 campaign was so broke that one day he frantically made phone calls to ensure that a $5,000 contribution from a Lake Charles supporter was deposited into the campaign's Baton Rouge bank account in time to cover several checks that had been written.

In the fall of 1993, as he began his reelection campaign two years in advance, Edwards's control of gambling alone would eliminate his fund-raising worries. Among those attending the Fairmont Hotel fund-raiser were Wendell Gauthier, John Cummings, and Carl Eberts of Jazz-ville; Colin Reed and Ron Lenczycki of Harrah's; Arthur Goldberg of Bally Manufacturing; and representatives of nearly all fifteen riverboat casinos.

In addition to the gambling projects, Edwards's administration was about to initiate a number of taxpayer-funded projects, and, in almost every case, Edwards would influence which companies got the contracts. These included a sports arena adjacent to the Louisiana Super-dome in New Orleans, an expansion of the New Orleans Convention Center, a volleyball facility in a suburban area of New Orleans known as the West Bank, and a minor league baseball stadium in the New Orleans suburb of Metairie. Edwards's longtime adviser Bob d'Hemecourt said it was a breeze raising money now compared to 1991. "When you're a sitting governor, you've appointed every board," said d'Hemecourt. "Everybody that does business with the state, or who could do business with the state, or who needs the political input from the governor or from people around the governor—they need to give money." D'Hemecourt then remarked that Warren Reuther, who owned a New Orleans riverboat cruise company as well as a share of the Hilton riverboat casino in New Orleans, had given him $2,000 that very day. "He was a big Roemer supporter, and Roemer appointed him to the convention center board. We removed him [after taking office in 1992]. I asked him to buy two tickets." D'Hemecourt then added, "You don't think the Edwards machine is going to let anything fall through the cracks."

Edwards was in good spirits on the night of the Fairmont fund-raiser. His young girlfriend, Candy Picou, was on his arm, and the event swelled his campaign treasury to $2.1 million. Although his approval rating was below 50 percent, he felt certain that gambling and the other construction projects would boost the state's economy—and his political fortunes—by election day in 1995. At age sixty-six, only poor health, it seemed, could keep Edwards from running again. "Every fiber in my body, every part of me, is committed to this course of action," he said that evening. "I feel, at the risk of offending some people, that this is my destiny, my role in life, my purpose in being, insofar as work is concerned. There was never a time in my adult life that I did not want to be governor."

While Edwards saw gambling as key to keeping the job he loved, his close ties to the gambling industry would soon begin to boomerang, due to a cascade of unmet promises, social and economic problems caused by gambling, and plain political corruption. All of this would cast doubt on his ability to win the Governor's Mansion one final time.

Only eight days after the fund-raiser, *The Times-Picayune*, Edwards's longstanding nemesis, published a damaging article. The newspaper reported that all four of Edwards's children either had contracts with riverboat companies or were seeking them. Stephen, the elder son and a Baton Rouge lawyer, was the most aggressive. Profane, balding, and with a profound sense of entitlement, Stephen had inherited his father's keen desire to make a buck, but lacked his finesse and cleverness. Stephen Edwards had established Riverboat Merchandising Incorporated, a Baton Rouge company that sold baseball caps, T-shirts, plastic cups, and other gift-shop items to riverboat casinos. The company had agreements to sell merchandise to two riverboat companies, the Star Casino and Players Lake Charles, and had approached two others, Hilton's *Queen of New Orleans* and *Caesars on the River*. The *Star* casino and the *Treasure Chest* riverboat also had retained Stephen.

Edwards's younger daughter, Victoria, had sent a proposal to riverboat operators telling them that she had relocated to Hollywood—she was an aspiring actress—and had founded a company called Punchline Promotions. Victoria's company would stage variety shows between riverboat cruises. She had secured a commitment from at least one riverboat, the *Star*.

Edwards's older daughter, Anna, was helping Victoria with Punchline Promotions. In a cover letter to the riverboat casinos, Victoria wrote that she would be in New York recruiting entertainers for her "existing boat contracts." She added: "While on my talent search, Anna will be holding down the fort in Baton Rouge. Please give her a call at

504 342-5855 to schedule an appointment for us to get together." As any political insider knew, that was the main phone number at the Governor's Mansion, where Anna was living. Anna had joined Edwards's younger son, David, in two more business ventures aimed at the riverboat industry. Anna and David had bought a controlling interest in a company called Juice Systems, and they offered its services—the company sold liquor and juice-dispensing equipment—to riverboat operators. Anna, in a letter to the riverboats, also left the mansion's phone number. In the same letter, Anna and David noted that a Minneapolis-based company, Apogee Enterprises, had retained them to sell electronic surveillance equipment to floating casinos.

On the morning that *The Times-Picayune* article appeared, Stephen Edwards stormed into the Governor's Mansion office to accuse Sid Moreland, the governor's executive assistant, of leaking the information to the newspaper. Moreland served as Edwards's gatekeeper, playing a key role in determining who got to see or speak with the governor. "I'm sure you're behind it," Stephen Edwards shouted at Moreland. "You try to undermine everything our family tries to do. You're a cocksucker. I'd like to kick your ass. I don't know why my daddy is stupid enough to have a sorry motherfucker like you around anyway."

Stephen Edwards's verbal assault infuriated Moreland, but he said only, "You'll need to take that up with your dad."

That afternoon, the Edwards children met at the law office of Lewis Unglesby, a frequent adviser to the family, to discuss the article and how to react. Edwards asked his executive counsel, Al Donovan, to attend the meeting. Victoria, Anna, and David told the gathering that they would quit the riverboat business if it caused political problems for their father. Stephen, however, said, "If y'all think I'm walking away from $1 million a year because my old man is governor, you're fucking crazy. I didn't tell the son of a bitch to run."

Donovan exploded. "My job is to protect the governor," he told Stephen. "If I have to run over your sorry ass, I'll do it." Donovan stalked out of the meeting.

The *Times-Picayune* article caused a public furor. Callers to talk-radio stations wanted to discuss nothing else, with virtually every person chastising Edwards and bringing up his 1991 campaign pledge to run a clean administration if elected. State representative David Vitter, a Republican from Metairie, filed an ethics complaint, noting that the contracts fell under the oversight of the State Police, which regulated riverboat gambling and which answered directly to Edwards. Doug Moreau, the district attorney for East Baton Rouge Parish, announced that a grand jury would examine the business dealings to see whether the four children had violated state law. Edwards initially dismissed the complaints, saying, "If I were concerned, I would have stopped it."

However, five days after *The Times-Picayune* broke the story, Edwards announced that his children would stop doing business with the riverboat companies. He said he remained convinced that they had done nothing wrong. Nevertheless, "I just don't want them to be the focal point of an ongoing controversy," he said. "It's damaging to them and damaging to the state. I don't want my children to be brutalized the way I have been brutalized," he added without irony, "in my opinion sometimes unfairly."

Edwards's announcement didn't stop the criticism. Jack Wardlaw, the longtime *Times-Picayune* capital bureau chief, recalled past controversies and wrote, "Edwards seems to be firmly convinced that as long as a course of action is at least technically legal, there's no reason not to go forward with it. . . . The problem is, here is a governor who will go down in history as the father of legalized gambling in Louisiana. To see him or his family rushing in to share in the profits just emits a bad odor, no matter what kind of mask is put on it. Edwards was right to put an end to the situation. But I doubt that the political damage has been undone."

Moreau eventually dropped the investigation. He could not gather enough evidence to issue indictments.

On February 8, 1994, *The Times-Picayune* hit Edwards again. A front-page article revealed that Edwards had been hosting a weekly poker game at the Governor's Mansion that included players with ties to gambling companies that were in business thanks to Edwards and his appointed boards. Pots at the games sometimes reached $10,000, the newspaper reported, and it wasn't uncommon for players to win or lose $10,000 to $20,000 in an evening. One of the players was Robert

Guidry, who had come from nowhere to get an operating license from Edwards's riverboat commission to operate the *Treasure Chest* on Lake Pontchartrain in Kenner. Guidry had told associates privately that he had made sure to lose heavily at the mansion poker games. Another player was Gus Mijalis, who with his nephew was involved with Capital Gaming, which would have a casino boat operating on the Mississippi River in New Orleans. A third player was Brent Honore, who owned a Baton Rouge construction company and was a consultant to a Baton Rouge riverboat.

Edwards dismissed questions about the poker games with his typical bravura. "If I was going to hustle these people," he said, "I'd use a more subtle form to do it. I wouldn't have them show up at the mansion for a poker game." He said he wouldn't end the poker games and added, "Matter of fact, I hope from the publicity I'll have some volunteers because some of these people are falling by the wayside." Responded *The Times-Picayune* in an editorial: "The appearance of impropriety eats away at whatever confidence citizens have left in elected officials. . . . It is hardly a consoling thought for Louisiana voters concerned that the state's foray into legalized gambling has been overtaken by regrettably familiar cronyism and other corruption."

As with its aggressive coverage of Christopher Hemmeter in 1992, the newspaper was playing a major role in shaping the gambling debate. Most of the Edwards exposés were written by Peter Nicholas, a thirty-one-year-old reporter based in the Baton Rouge bureau. A native of Long Island, Nicholas had an investigative reporter's zeal, and he cultivated sources who fed him a steady diet of scoops. Edwards hated Nicholas. At one press conference, Edwards rebuked him by saying the reporter wanted to catch him in a lie because "it would be as close to an orgasm as he has come." Edwards's put-downs didn't deter Nicholas.

On February 23, 1994, yet another Nicholas article hit Edwards. This one reported that while the four Edwards children had agreed to stop doing business with the riverboat casinos, Stephen Edwards was raking in big money representing the boats as a lawyer. Capital Gaming was paying Stephen $130,000 for a year, and three other boats—the

Star, the *Grand Palais,* and the *Treasure Chest*—had also hired him for undisclosed amounts.

Yet it wasn't only the Edwards children who were trying to cash in from gambling. The governor's cronies and political allies were joining in as well. Topping the list was Gus Mijalis, who, along with his nephew Sammy, stood to make $26 million from the riverboat *Capital Gaming* by trading on his political influence. Mijalis was a Shreveport business-man who frequently accompanied Edwards on his gambling junkets to Las Vegas and who raised big bucks for his political campaigns.

In July 1991, Louisiana's Oil Bust forced Mijalis into bankruptcy, leaving him owing $26 million. Among the creditors were Harrah's Lake Tahoe ($100,000) and the Dunes Hotel in Las Vegas ($80,000). But with Edwards's election in November 1991, Mijalis's luck sud-denly improved. Edwards appointed him to the state Board of Regents for higher education, and had Mijalis as an overnight guest at the Gov-ernor's Mansion. In April 1993, Mijalis's business fortunes began to improve when Capital Gaming signed up Republic Corporate Ser-vices, the firm operated by Mijalis and his nephew Sammy, as a river-boat partner, even though Republic didn't put up any cash initially. Mijalis's deal with Republic came two months after Edwards appointed Gia Kosmitis, a Shreveport lawyer close to Mijalis, to the riverboat com-mission. Kosmitis was one of the commission members who in June 1993 voted to give Capital Gaming a preliminary operating certificate, even though the company had little gambling experience and was undercapitalized. Afterward, in political and gambling circles, Capital Gaming was known as "Gus's boat."

On March 5, 1994, *The Times-Picayune* reported that Billy Broad-hurst, a longtime Edwards confidant, was getting a piece of the action. Broadhurst, who already was expected to score big by owning a share of the Harrah's Jazz land casino, also had his hand in riverboat gam-bling. According to the paper, he had a $350,000 contract as a consul-tant to Casino America, which owned half of the Isle of Capri casino riverboat in Bossier City.

In the coming months, a host of news reports would show that one public official after another had jumped aboard the gambling gravy train. State representative Ken Odinet, who voted in 1991 to legalize riverboat gambling, was providing engineering work for the riverboat casino that was slated for St. Bernard Parish, inside his suburban New Orleans legislative district. Sammy Nunez, the powerful president of the State Senate, sold insurance through his company, Nunez Insurance Agency, to a shipbuilder who was constructing six gambling boats. Jefferson Parish councilwoman Anne Marie Vandenweghe did $14,000 of legal work for one gambling boat. The brother of state senator Francis Heitmeier, who sponsored the 1991 law that legalized riverboat gambling, had a contract worth at least $2.4 million a year to provide crew members to another gambling boat. The brother, Robert Heitmeier, had no prior experience running a company.

Law enforcement officials in Louisiana were not to be outdone by the politicians. Harry Lee, the powerful sheriff of Jefferson Parish, formed a company that sold handrails to gambling boats. In Gretna, across the Mississippi River from New Orleans, Chief of Police Beauregard H. Miller Jr. and his deputy, Arthur Lawson, owned a video poker business and had machines in twenty-nine bars inside city limits. They insisted that no bar owner should feel compelled to buy from them. Getting in the video poker business was a natural for Miller. His father had been Gretna's chief of police during the 1940s, '50s, and '60s when gambling was wide-open and Carlos Marcello was the local crime boss. Media reports at the time said that Beauregard H. Miller Sr. got payoffs from the gambling owners to allow them to stay in business.

Bob Ragsdale, second in command to Sheriff Lee, also tried to get into video poker but was less successful. Ragsdale signed a contract to buy $2.3 million worth of machines, planning to put them in bars and lounges throughout Jefferson Parish. Ragsdale was supposed to buy the machines from Worldwide Gaming, but the deal fell through when he couldn't get financing. (Federal authorities later shut down Worldwide Gaming for being controlled by organized crime.) Not to be left out, the deputy New Orleans police chief, Antoine Saacks, had a secret deal with United Gaming, a Las Vegas–based video poker firm, that paid him $325,000. United Gaming in 1992 won the single most lucrative contract in New Orleans, to provide video poker machines to the city's racetrack and off-track betting parlors. But United Gaming officials afterward kept Saacks at a distance because they discovered that the deputy police chief, who was partial to $700 silk suits and diamond pinkie rings, had close ties to a twice-convicted felon and reputed mobster named Frank Caracci.

The politicians had promised that the benefits from gambling would be widespread when they legalized casinos and video poker in the early 1990s. They had not mentioned that they would be the prime beneficiaries.

Nor had they shown much concern for gambling's losers. But the downside soon surfaced in every corner of the state. In Vidalia, across the Mississippi River from Natchez, Betty Yakey played five-card draw as fast as her fingers could hit the poker machine's buttons in the back room at Robin's Café. A sixty-five-year-old widow with three children and four grandchildren, Yakey sat entranced before the machine for five or six hours at a stretch, playing two hands a minute, betting $2 a hand. After months of playing, her losses totaled $190,000. Yakey wiped out a college savings fund that she and her late husband had established for their fourteen-year-old grandson, Jeremy, with money from the sale of the family farm. "Normally, I'm a pretty sensible person," Yakey said later. "I don't drink, and I don't run around. But when I played that machine, I didn't worry about nothing. It was like being in a dream."

Rose Hosty said that when she played video poker, "I fell instantly in love with one machine. I didn't have to argue with it. Sitting at that machine was the only time I was happy. I didn't have to be a wife, a lover or a mommy. It was like I went into a trance." Hosty, a forty-year-old mother of eight, had never gambled until she tried a Cajun Fever video poker machine in a doughnut shop near her home in New Orleans. Once she started, she couldn't stop until she had gambled away all profits from her snow cone shop—and had pawned her jewelry and had stolen pocket change from her husband and children. One day, Hosty lay on her bathroom floor with a .38-caliber pistol pressed against her skull. She didn't pull the trigger, feeling in part that the state of Louisiana was responsible for her gambling addiction. "My problems are of no concern to the powers that be in this state," she said later.

Jerry Rabalais won big on his first night playing blackjack on one of Shreveport's riverboat casinos. Rabalais, a mathematician, cleared $12,000 and thought he could beat the odds. He couldn't. He began to lose and responded by increasing the amount he bet to try to cover his losses. "It was like being on crack cocaine," he said later. "The euphoria of gambling got my adrenaline going and put me on the high of all highs. Then I'd be on the downside, and I couldn't function." It got so bad for Rabalais that he would sleep in his car in the casino parking garage so he could return to the blackjack table as soon as possible. In time, Rabalais had gambled away his youngest daughter's college education fund and he had sold his prized '65 Corvair coupe, his golf clubs, his cameras, and some of his wife's jewelry. He lost his job and forced his wife into bankruptcy by taking huge cash advances on credit cards he had obtained in her name. In all, he lost more than $100,000 playing blackjack, as well as his marriage.

In Baton Rouge, overdue and uncollected rents from public-housing tenants remained rampant, even as the economy improved, because the tenants gambled away their meager incomes. Even areas like Grant Parish, which had no casinos, felt the effect. The number of worthless checks written in the parish doubled in the two years after an Indian casino opened in nearby Marksville. "I ask people everywhere I go, and without exception every local business person I talk to tells me they have seen a [negative] impact from casino gambling," said Ed Tarpley, Grant Parish's district attorney.

The social costs from gambling piled up in other ways. To feed her video poker habit, a woman from the New Orleans suburb of Slidell stole $3,019 from the Time Saver convenience store where she worked, according to authorities. The manager of a Kenny Rogers Roasters chicken restaurant near the New Orleans suburb of Covington stole $80,000 from the restaurant and lost it all gambling, authorities said. In another case, a man from the town of Bush stole $4,447 from the chemical company where he worked to feed his video poker addiction.

Beyond the social ramifications, the economic costs from gambling began to hurt businesses large and small, both in the public and private sectors. For example, after the *Boomtown Belle* riverboat casino opened across the Mississippi River from New Orleans, sales at Terry Camardelle's snack shop on the ground floor of the state office building in Harvey fell by 50 percent. At the Star Castle Dinner Theatre in Gretna, which catered to tour bus groups, business dropped 10 percent to 20 percent. "The casinos offer a free bus ride, $10 worth of chips, a $5 buffet, free drinks, entertainment," said Sandy Bravender, the Star Theatre's co-owner. "It's hard to compete."

The casinos also caused shortfalls for the Louisiana Lottery and charitable gambling. In 1991, for example, 140 charitable organizations raised money from bingo in Jefferson Parish. Four years later, only eighty did. One of the groups forced out of bingo was the Jefferson SPCA, which picked up stray animals.

As word of the downside spread, the gambling industry felt the heat. Casino and video poker owners responded by stepping up their political influence in Baton Rouge. A stunning display of this came one day in May 1994. It took place in the Senate chamber, which featured marble columns, a fifty-foot-high ceiling, plush carpeting, brass railings, and lobbyists arrayed along the walls. Senate president Sammy Nunez held sway in the chamber, overseeing the day's debate from a rostrum that towered above the other thirty-eight senators. Normally, when Nunez left the rostrum to visit with senators, he was handing out committee assignments or sounding out colleagues on an upcoming vote. On this day, Nunez was carrying a stack of envelopes full of checks. He stopped at the desk of each favored senator and handed over the goodie: a $2,500 campaign contribution from Louie Roussel III, a horse race owner who also owned a major stake in the *Star* riverboat casino on Lake Pontchartrain and who—as a member of the Jazzville group— owned a small share of the Harrah's Jazz casino in New Orleans.

On the other side of the Capitol, House Speaker John Alario performed a role similar to Nunez's, if not as brazenly. Alario asked lawmakers to visit his office off the House floor to collect their $1,000 checks from Roussel. In no time, the line spilled out of Alario's office into the marble corridor where Huey Long had been assassinated sixty-one years earlier.

Nunez and Alario had not violated any laws, but the audacity of handing out campaign checks where the legislators conducted their duties deeply concerned many people. To them, it provided further evidence that the gambling industry was changing how life was conducted in Louisiana, and not for the better.

During the 1991 gubernatorial campaign, a young, slender, blond woman with a sweet, small-town smile made the rounds regularly enough with Edwin Edwards that it became clear she was not just his latest conquest. Edwards and Candy Picou had met in 1990 at a downtown Baton Rouge restaurant called Maggio's, a place that featured red beans and rice on Mondays, fried chicken on Thursdays, and fried catfish on Fridays. By chance, one day Edwards and attorney friend Lewis Unglesby were seated next to Candy and a group of friends. A few days later, Edwards called her at the law office where she worked as a legal secretary to earn spending cash while finishing nursing school. "The receptionist said, 'You're not going to believe this—Edwin Edwards is on the phone for you.' And I said, 'What?'" Candy recalled later. Married at the time, she turned down the ex-governor. A few months later, Edwards learned that Candy's marriage had ended. He called again, and they agreed to meet at Maggio's. He romanced her with a poem that he wrote and slipped into her menu. In the coming days, he turned on his legendary charm. Edwards was sixty-three, Candy twenty-five.

As the relationship progressed, Candy's mother and close friends voiced concern about his reputation for womanizing. It was well founded. Edwards's extramarital flings first won widespread attention following publication in 1977 of *Just Takin' Orders,* a tell-all book by Clyde Vidrine, who had had a falling-out with Edwards over a business deal after being one of the governor's closest aides during his first term. According to Vidrine and others, Edwards's sexual appetite was insatiable, but he preferred quick encounters to longer dalliances.

BAD BET ON THE BAYOU

While tales of philandering would destroy most politicians, Edwards, through double entendres and humorous asides, defused much of the criticism. Asked once by reporters outside a federal courthouse if he thought his telephone was tapped, he answered no, but added, "Except by jealous husbands." On another occasion, he casually told a group of reporters that a respected state politician had a mistress.

"You're telling us," a reporter asked, "that he cheats on his wife?"

"He's not as good at it as I am," replied Edwards, "but he does."

Edwards's responses reflected his belief that he could use humor to deflect potential scandal. He also realized that most people were forgiving of those who admitted to human frailties, that hypocrisy was the more off-putting sin.

That philosophy was behind the advice he gave Bill Clinton when the Democratic presidential candidate landed at Baton Rouge Airport in 1992 while making a campaign stop in Louisiana. After the plane landed, Clinton's aides informed him that Gennifer Flowers had just been on national television, spilling the details of their relationship.

In a story that Edwards related a few years later, he and Clinton were driving away from the airport when Clinton told him, "She's telling the press we had a torrid twelve-year love affair. How in the hell am I going to handle that?"

"I'll tell you how I would do it. But I don't think you would," Edwards responded.

"How?" asked Clinton.

"I would simply say that nobody has a twelve-year torrid love affair: twelve days maybe, twelve weeks. But nobody has a twelve-year torrid love affair."

"Oh, I can't say that," Clinton replied.

"I didn't think you would. But that's exactly what I would say."

For reasons that Elaine Edwards never explained publicly, she put up with her husband's womanizing through his first two terms. But when he moved back into the Governor's Mansion for a third term after winning the 1983 election, Elaine did not accompany him. The antebellum home became a bachelor pad. The State Police troopers who guarded the back entrance came to expect a call nearly every night from the governor, saying that he was about to have a visitor and would they please allow her to take the elevator up to the second floor. An hour or two after she arrived, his female friend would descend in the elevator and disappear into the night. Edwards had a lot of female friends.

In a 1990 interview, he tried to explain his fascination with women. "Each one is different, each one is interesting," he said.

By then, he and Elaine had been divorced for a year, after four decades of marriage.

Candace Picou was from Gonzales, a small town about thirty miles east of Baton Rouge. At St. Amant High School, she was voted "cutest" and "best dressed" for the tenth, eleventh, and twelfth grades. In 1984, at the Jambalaya Festival in Gonzales, she was runner-up for the title of Miss Jambalaya. Ironically, Elaine Edwards was one of the judges.

Anyone who met Candy invariably came away describing her as sweet and friendly. "She doesn't have a malicious bone in her body," marveled Victoria Edwards, one of the governor's two daughters, in a 1991 interview. "What she's doing in a family full of barracudas is beyond me."

With his characteristic irreverence, Edwards joked about his new girlfriend. "A man is as old as the woman he feels," he told an uproarious group of supporters one night during the 1991 governor's race.

During the campaign against former Klansman David Duke, Edwards liked to say the two had one thing in common: "We're both wizards under the sheets."

When Edwards took office again in January 1992, Candy moved into the Governor's Mansion. A nursing student, she kept a low profile, although the decision to host her tenth high school reunion at the Governor's Mansion in 1992 did attract notice.

Outwardly, Edwards seemed to have settled down. However, he slipped away to play poker from time to time with a group of acquaintances at a private Baton Rouge residence, and used the game as a cover for trysts. The game would begin at 7:00 p.m., and after an hour or so, Edwards would excuse himself and tell the state trooper accompanying him that if Candy called, the trooper should say that Edwards was in the restroom. The trooper then should call him on a cellular phone so he could return her call.

Edwards would return to the private residence after an absence of sixty to ninety minutes. Before returning to the game, he would take care to eliminate any leftover fragrance by putting his shirt in the dryer for about twenty minutes. He would then borrow a cigarette and blow smoke up the unbuttoned sleeves to cover up any unwanted scents that remained.

Ironically, given his own activities, Edwards was extremely possessive of Candy, always wanting to know where she was going and whom she was seeing. At least once, he hired a private detective to tail her, for fear that she was having an affair.

Despite their problems, Edwards and Candy were deeply attached to each other. On May 26, 1994, with no fanfare and little notice, the two got married in a small private ceremony in the rose garden behind the Governor's Mansion. Edwards was sixty-six, while his bride was twenty-nine. Only family and two friends attended, along with a reporter and photographer from the Associated Press, who were invited to record the news. Chief Justice Pascal Calogero of the Louisiana Supreme Court performed the ceremony. The governor's brother Marion was the best man. Two of Edwards's four children—Stephen and Victoria, both of whom were older than Candy—witnessed the ceremony. "We wanted an unpublicized, private ceremony to avoid the appearance of politicizing this special moment," Edwards said afterward.

After a brief honeymoon in Colorado, Edwards made his next move. Naturally, this time it involved politics. On the night of June 6, he was scheduled to inaugurate a special session of the Louisiana legislature. That morning, his chief lawyer, Al Donovan, heard a startling rumor: Edwards, in his speech to legislators, was going to announce that he would retire from politics by not running for reelection in 1995. Donovan immediately called Sid Moreland, who operated out of an office next to Edwards's in the Governor's Mansion. Moreland told Donovan that he knew nothing about it. That afternoon, Donovan went to the mansion, where he found Moreland crying. The rumor was true. After dominating Louisiana politics like no one else since Huey P. Long, the original King-fish, Edwards would retire and not seek reelection the following year.

Very few people knew this, however, when Edwards went to the well of the House to address lawmakers. For nearly an hour, he spoke of his goals and desires for the special session. Then he dropped his bombshell. "There is one reason and one reason only," he explained to stunned lawmakers. "I want to do something else with the rest of my life." He did not disclose his plans. But he went on to say, his voice breaking with emotion, "I am content to allow history to judge the record of my administration. I made it work. I did it my way." He ticked off a list of what he considered his major accomplishments, starting with efforts that in 1973 produced Louisiana's modern constitution. Edwards said he was proud to call himself a politician. "History will confirm it was necessary for someone with my personality to serve you as governor. It takes a politician to get things done," he said.

Political obituaries flowed. "Edwards is an impossible act to follow," James Gill wrote in *The Times-Picayune*. "One thing we know about the next election is that the winner will seem dull and pedestrian by comparison. No question we need a new beginning, but there will always be a certain hankering for the days of the governor with great flaws but talents to match."

"He was the most effective, skilled, wily politician I ever knew," said former governor Buddy Roemer. "I'm not talking about his pro-grams, policies or purposes," which Roemer said he found appalling. "But in terms of pure politics, he was the best."

"He was devoid of principle," said David Duke, "but at least he was honest about it."

"We'll never see quite as colorful a character in this era of blow-dried politics," added John Maginnis, a Louisiana political pundit.

"It's the death of a monarchy," said Mark McKinnon, a political consultant. "I mean, you could imagine Edwards with rouged cheeks and purple cape passing out doubloons to the serfs. He was the king."

Only later would it be understood that gambling was causing a political backlash and that Edwin Edwards was its first casualty.

Web of Deceit

When Governor Edwin Edwards announced his upcoming retirement in 1994, many people assumed that would end the gambling scandals. Instead, the controversies only mounted. Where before they had mostly involved the New Orleans land casino, now the controversies also encompassed the floating casinos and video poker, both of which the legislature had authorized in 1991. And where the scandals with the land casino often involved outsiders like Christopher Hemmeter and Memphis-based Harrah's, the controversies with the riverboats and video poker involved mostly Louisianians.

The first floating casino in Louisiana did not begin operations until November 1993 when the *Star* on Lake Pontchartrain in New Orleans opened for business. As required under the law, the *Star* was a paddle wheeler meant to evoke images of nineteenth-century gambling on the Mississippi River. But the boat also featured late-twentieth-century engines and navigational equipment. Nevertheless, on November 8, 1993, on what was supposed to be the *Star's* maiden ninety-minute voyage, the vessel remained at its Lake Pontchartrain mooring. The captain said winds on the lake might reach 22 knots, 12 knots above the level that he said was safe for the boat. Three days later, despite blue skies and gentle breezes, the *Star* continued to remain at dock while customers gambled.

What was happening with the *Star* would all too often be the story with the three forms of gambling that the Bayou State legalized in the 1990s: Louisianians would get far more gambling than they had been promised. And the gambling would develop deeper tentacles into the community than had been expected.

Lawmakers had originally said that the riverboat casinos would take three-hour cruises and be tourist attractions. Before the *Star* opened, however, gambling officials persuaded the state board that regulated the boats to interpret the law to say that a three-hour cruise actually consisted of ninety minutes of sailing with forty-five minutes at dock before and forty-five minutes afterward—for the loading and unloading of passengers. In effect, the boats could remain at dock for at least ninety minutes at a stretch throughout the day—and longer if the boat didn't take its regularly scheduled cruises. The boat owners greatly favored the gambling board's interpretation for several reasons. One was that staying at dock reduced their fuel costs. More important, gamblers could come and go as they pleased when the boat was dockside. This meant more gambling by customers who would otherwise leave the boat before a cruise because they didn't like being on the open water. The boat could therefore capture gamblers who might otherwise be left at the dock during the ninety-minute cruise. In all, dockside gambling could inflate profits by as much as 25 percent.

By the summer of 1994, it had become clear that all casino boat owners—not just the *Star*'s—were exploiting a quirk in the floating-casino law to remain dockside for virtually the entire time. The quirk was this: the boat had to cruise unless weather or water conditions were deemed unsafe. Who made that determination? The boat captain, who was working for the casino owner.

So each boat came up with a fanciful excuse not to leave the dock. The *Star* initially remained dockside because gentle winds were held to threaten the boat's seaworthiness. *Star* owner Louie Roussel III then cited mysterious underwater obstructions. After steel I-beams were pulled up from the lake bottom, another excuse popped up—a fuel tank on the dock had to be moved in case the *Star* smashed into it while docking. Meanwhile, the *Treasure Chest,* dockside on Lake Pontchartrain in suburban Kenner, pointed to low-hanging power lines a few hundred yards offshore that would snag on the ship's superstructure. When the power lines were finally raised, the *Treasure Chest* stayed dockside; its owners blamed crab traps in the lake's waters. Owners of Hilton's *Queen of New Orleans* said fast currents in the Mississippi River made cruising too dangerous. This excuse strained credulity, however, because pleasure boats full of tourists went out nightly from an adjoining dock. Officials with the *Boomtown Belle* on the Harvey Canal in Gretna, a suburban New Orleans waterway popular with barges, came up with perhaps the most brazen excuses of all. At first, they blamed barge traffic for having to remain at dock. After facing criticism for that excuse, the boat began cruising during the day. When asked why the boat didn't cast away at night, *Boomtown Belle* officials cited darkness.

The boats' myriad excuses prompted *Times-Picayune* columnist James Gill to write scornfully: "The river, little more than a harmless rill when riverboat legislation was being debated, became a treacherous torrent once the boat was ready for business, and prudence requires that the Queen not venture out from port. If the *Queen of New Orleans* folks were shocked to find large boats on the Mississippi, the owners of the *Boomtown Belle* must have been close to cardiac arrest when they opened for business on that picturesque old southern waterway, the Harvey Canal. Surveying the scene, they could scarce believe their eyes, for there, right in the middle of the canal, were barges. Barges, it turned out, are not equipped with wheels and therefore tend to be attracted to canals. This was not exactly classified information, barges having plied the Harvey Canal for more than fifteen years, but you could have knocked Boomtown management down with a feather. Cruises, obviously, were out of the question. Over in Kenner the *Treasure Chest* was found to be too tall to pass under power lines and was also given permission to remain tied up. The power lines, of course, were there first, and, if you wanted to be picky about it, you might ask why the *Treasure Chest* owners should be allowed to flout the law just because they screwed up in designing the boat." Regulators mostly shrugged their shoulders at such criticism, saying they couldn't do anything. Governor Edwards didn't seem to mind.

The excuses, however, galvanized Doug Moreau, the district attorney for East Baton Rouge Parish. In the latter part of 1993 and early 1994, Moreau had already investigated, without bringing charges, the business dealings of Edwards's four children in the riverboat gambling industry. Moreau had been a star football player for Louisiana State University in the 1960s, and had gone on to play tight end for the Miami Dolphins. In 1970, after four operations in as many years, he flunked the Dolphins's physical exam, but passed his law-school admission test. With his playing days behind him, Moreau became an assistant district attorney and then a judge. In 1991, he was elected district attorney. A good-government Republican, he became a chief nemesis of Edwards's.

In September 1994, Moreau began seeking answers as to why the boats were not cruising. He summoned two captains for the *Queen of New Orleans* before the grand jury. "We figured since they aren't sailing, it won't be an impediment" for them to testify, Moreau explained. Shortly afterward, Moreau notified the captain of the *Belle of Baton Rouge* that he expected the riverboat casino to begin cruising regularly. The boat complied. Moreau then wrote other district attorneys with gambling boats in their parishes, suggesting that they ought to make the boats within their jurisdictions begin cruising, too. Harry Connick Sr., the district attorney for Orleans Parish, took the bait. Connick was a onetime record store owner whose son, Harry Jr., had become a superstar singer. The elder Connick had been elected district attorney for Orleans Parish in 1973 when he defeated Jim Garrison. (Garrison had lost favor in New Orleans after a laughably poor attempt to prove that a local man had been the supposed mastermind behind President Kennedy's assassination, a story loosely told in Oliver Stone's film *JFK*, which infuriated locals by lionizing Garrison.)

By 1994, Connick was looking for ways to hang on to his job as a white elected official in a high-crime city that was now 60 percent black. He calculated that the public was becoming increasingly disenchanted

with gambling and wanted the casino boats to follow the law and begin cruising. On November 19, Connick fired his first shot, sending letters to captains of the two New Orleans boats, the *Star* and the *Flamingo* (which had replaced the smaller *Queen*), with the warning that they must begin sailing or face possible prosecution. Two weeks later, the *Flamingo* began to comply. The *Star,* however, remained defiant. On December 5, the hammer came down on the *Star* when the State Police closed the vessel for not sailing. Two gambling-friendly judges allowed the boat to reopen the next day. Six weeks later, however, the *Star* shut down to avoid possible prosecution by Connick. Soon after, in early 1995, the *Star* was sold to a casino company, which moved the boat to Lake Charles, near the Texas border.

Owners of another gambling boat, the *Belle of Orleans,* then announced they would scrap plans to open on the Mississippi River in New Orleans and would instead take the *Star*'s spot on Lake Pontchartrain. Other boats engaged in a high-stakes game of musical chairs. The *Crown,* which had lost a yearlong battle to open in St. Charles Parish, up the Mississippi River from New Orleans, also moved to Lake Charles, which already had two boats that were attracting hordes of Texans crossing the border to gamble. In St. Bernard Parish, Circus Circus had been planning to open a floating casino in the Bayou Bienvenue. But various delays—and criticisms that the bayou was so narrow and shallow that the boat wouldn't be able to cruise—forced Circus Circus to abandon the project after spending $30 million and only partially building the boat.

By spring 1995, Christopher Hemmeter was back in the news with a riverboat project he called River City. Hemmeter had disappeared from public view after the state casino board in August 1993 had selected Harrah's Jazz, on a 5–4 vote, to operate the New Orleans land casino. Following the shotgun wedding brokered by Edwards, Hemmeter still owned one-third of the casino, but Harrah's, which had the capital, was in charge. Hemmeter hadn't given up on his grand visions for gambling in New Orleans, however. He still had a riverboat license, thanks

to Edwards's having intervened with the State Police in December 1993 at the behest of Billy Broadhurst, the governor's friend who was on the developer's payroll.

Throughout 1994, Hemmeter kept a low profile as he drew up plans to develop Louisiana's grandest and most lavish riverboat-casino project yet. After several false starts, he settled on the River City plan in conjunction with another company, Capital Gaming International, which had little gambling experience but had Gus Mijalis, another of Edwards's friends, to run political interference. The plan called for the two boats to be docked side by side at River City, a gambling complex that Hemmeter was creating on what had been a barren patch of land just up the Mississippi River from the New Orleans Convention Center and the Crescent City Connection Bridge. Hemmeter called his boat the *Grand Palais*—the same name he had proposed for his land casino—while Capital Gaming named its vessel the *Crescent City Queen*.

With two boats, Hemmeter figured, he would create a mini gambling mecca. To deal with the possibility that the boats would have to cruise, he arranged the schedule so that one vessel would always be at the dock. Hemmeter was confident that his grand vision for River City would appeal to tourists and locals alike. The interior of his 80,000-square-foot terminal was designed to re-create what he described as "the gracious charm of the 'Old South.'" It featured the façade of an antebellum mansion, two dozen fake oak trees—costing $75,000 apiece, or $1.8 million overall—and a fake nightscape complete with twinkling "stars" painted on the ceiling. There was a fake bayou, the simulated chirping of crickets, and the simulated croaking of frogs. "It promises to be an unforgettable experience for casino visitors," gushed Eugene Hu, River City's vice president of design. Hemmeter announced that star chefs Wolfgang Puck and Paul Prudhomme would open restaurants within the River City terminal. (They said, however, that they were only in negotiations to do so.) Outside, Hemmeter built a huge well-lit parking lot with a grand entrance created by a row of palm trees. "We suggest [Hemmeter] owns one of the best sites not only in the city, but in the state," Donaldson, Lufkin & Jenrette analyst Mark Manson said in a report.

Hemmeter's investment partner, Daniel Robinowitz, opposed River City's site. Echoing the concerns of others, Robinowitz said it was too remote from the main attractions to attract tourists and was too close to the crime-filled St. Thomas housing project to attract locals. Hemmeter shrugged off Robinowitz's concerns and moved forward with his plans.

There were other signs that Hemmeter might be facing trouble in River City. As Roland Jones, the state revenue agent, had cautioned the State Police in December 1993—a warning the agency's troops had ignored after getting a phone call from Governor Edwards—Hemmeter had little money. That hadn't bothered banks and investors, who saw casino investments as a sure bet and financed the project with more than $200 million in junk bonds. But when Hemmeter went over budget by $28 million—River City's cost rose from $195 million to $223 million—he was left with no cash in reserve. Despite the overspending, he completed only 40 percent of the complex. To finish it, Hemmeter would have to use profits from the boats' operation, a risky proposition.

What happened if the boats didn't perform as well as expected? The New Orleans Dock Board, which owned the Mississippi River wharves that Hemmeter and Capital Gaming were using for the riverboat project, took note of Hemmeter's financial plight. Normally, the Dock Board would have required River City to provide one year of rent payments as a security deposit before approving a lease. In this case, the Dock Board approved the lease, but with the proviso that it would not refund any of the $14 million it had collected from the boats' owners to finance improvements to the wharf area, in case River City defaulted in its rent payments. In case of a default, the Dock Board also would reclaim the wharves, including Hemmeter's improvements. Billy Broadhurst, representing the developer before the Dock Board, dismissed the naysayers, insisting that even in a worst-case scenario, the riverboat gambling complex would break even.

River City opened on March 29 with the promise that it would provide "the most fun since they invented New Orleans." However, rain that evening dampened the festivities, which included free champagne and hors d'oeuvres, plus hosts in black tie and hostesses in silken

gowns with petticoats. Hemmeter greeted guests with a smile and a handshake in the *Grand Palais*'s grand foyer. To Lambert Boissiere, the former New Orleans city councilman who had gone on the 1991 trip to Hawaii, Hemmeter looked nervous when he offered congratulations. "It looks good," Boissiere said.

"It's not quite ready," Hemmeter replied. "I didn't really want to open tonight."

Only 40 percent of the terminal was completed, and the Capital Gaming vessel, the *Crescent City Queen,* wasn't even ready to open that night. It hadn't passed the test of a "mock cruise" required by the State Police. (The boat would open a week later on April 4.)

When Ron Brinson arrived early for River City's opening night, he saw an ominous sign: workers were still stapling down the carpet and hanging paintings in the "antebellum mansion." Brinson, the chief executive officer of the Port of New Orleans, the Dock Board's policy-making arm, thought that Hemmeter looked drawn and tired. Brinson was also unimpressed with the décor. River City reminded him of a tacky cathouse he had seen in Vietnam. When Brinson left that evening, he turned to a friend and predicted that River City wouldn't last long. "Six months," he said. "Six months."

River City's two boats were supposed to take in $18 million a month, or $9 million apiece. Those were highly optimistic numbers. The New Orleans area's most successful riverboat, the *Treasure Chest* in Kenner, was averaging about $8.5 million a month. The *Flamingo,* located about fifteen blocks downriver from River City, was averaging about $7 million a month. In April 1995, River City's first month of operation, the *Grand Palais* and the *Crescent City Queen combined* took in only $7 million. That was equivalent to the *Flamingo* alone, and it was $11 million below the projected level for the two boats. Investment analysts were aghast. Junk bonds for the project, which had been trading at 100 when they were issued, plummeted to the mid-60s.

The news would only get worse. In May, the boats took in only $6 million combined. Daniel Robinowitz was right: River City was too isolated from tourists and too close to the housing project for locals. Besides, gamblers now had plenty of other options in the New Orleans

area. They could gamble aboard the *Treasure Chest,* the *Boomtown Belle,* or the *Flamingo.* And River City was now competing against the Harrah's Jazz casino, which had opened on May 1 in the Municipal Auditorium, about two miles from River City. The overspending that left no room for error was coming home to roost. In mid-May, Hemmeter and Capital Gaming laid off three hundred of the two thousand employees and jettisoned River City's president and chief executive officer. Capital Gaming's junk bonds dropped to 36. "Obviously, things can't get much worse," said Robert Lipps, a junk-bond analyst at BT Securities New York.

But they did. On June 1, the day after Lipps made his comment, Capital Gaming executives announced that they might file for bankruptcy protection from creditors. Without an infusion of cash, the company's executives said, they wouldn't make an $8.6 million payment to junk bondholders that was due on August 1. Capital Gaming's stock, which had once sold for $12 per share, now traded at less than $1.

The end also was near for Hemmeter. On June 6, at 3:15 p.m., a voice came over the loudspeaker on his boat: "The *Grand Palais* will be closing in approximately 45 minutes." Only one of the three floors on the boat was open at the time, and it contained only a handful of gamblers. A few managers sat in the grand foyer where Hemmeter had basked on opening night. As on that night, the managers were drinking champagne, but on this day it was out of paper cups. Now they were mournfully toasting the boat's demise, not its promised success. At 4:00 p.m., a craps dealer at one table called for the dice. "Ladies and gentlemen, the *Grand Palais* is history," he said with a flourish.

"This is a terrible day," Joann DiFlorio, a pit boss, told a reporter. "But write something good about us. This was a good bunch of people." DiFlorio was among 750 people who lost their jobs that day.

Roland Jones, the state Department of Revenue agent who had said Hemmeter wasn't financially fit to have a riverboat license, learned of the shutdown while watching the television news at home that night. Having been attacked by Hemmeter and Governor Edwards for his analysis in December 1993, Jones now sat back in a chair as he took in the news of Hemmeter's demise. He felt vindicated.

Time also quickly ran out on Capital Gaming to get the infusion of cash the company needed. On June 9 at 4:00 a.m., the *Crescent City Queen* shut down, sixty hours after the *Grand Palais* had done so. The *Grand Palais* had been open for only seventy days, while the Capital Gaming boat had lasted for only sixty-six days. Both riverboats left behind dozens of creditors and millions of dollars of debts.

Times-Picayune columnist James Gill weighed in. "Now that the two riverboats at River City have proved a huge and instant flop, we are reminded again that investment bankers and developers are often just snake-oil salesmen in expensive suits," Gill wrote. "When casino promoters descended on New Orleans, they and their stooges in government assured us that strangers would flock to the city, dropping dollars and saving our bacon. Instead, the populace is being thoroughly fleeced by a bunch of latter-day carpetbaggers. Since all the casinos are taking in most of their money from local suckers rather than the out-of-state variety, the market is much smaller than projected, and revenue figures so far augur a general collapse. . . . Christopher Hemmeter, having arrived here a couple of years ago to show us simpletons the road to full employment and prosperity, became the first casino operator to make a fool of himself when his Grand Palais riverboat gave up the ghost this week. Grand Palais' River City twin, Capital Gaming Inc.'s Queen [followed] suit. . . . The closure of River City will throw 2,000 people out of work, apparently without so much as a word of explanation from Hemmeter and his partners. This seems odd, given that nothing was dearer to their hearts than creating jobs for the natives, but perhaps they are just too choked up to express their sympathy."

On July 7, 1995, a month after River City's collapse, Christopher Hemmeter suffered his final indignity in New Orleans. He was evicted from his French Quarter office at 111 Iberville Street for failing to make the $14,663 monthly rent payments in June and July. At the lavishly decorated office, Hemmeter had charmed politicians and leading businessmen with his visions for New Orleans as a gambling mecca and him as the mastermind. But that was then. Now a judge's order gave the landlord possession of all equipment and the antiques inside the office. Hemmeter by then had skipped town. He also had left

behind a large bill for the suite he rented at the Westin Hotel, on Iberville Street, across from his office.

In November, Hemmeter Enterprises, which owned the *Grand Palais* riverboat, filed for bankruptcy. Bondholders took over the company, whose assets included two small Colorado casinos. A publicly traded real estate investment trust, Resort Income Investors, which Hemmeter headed and which invested most of its money in Hemmeter projects, also went down the tubes. He and his various enterprises owed the trust $36.6 million. In 1997, Hemmeter, now living in Los Angeles, suffered the coup de grâce when he filed for personal bankruptcy. It was quite a fall. In 1988, he had occupied a prized spot on the Forbes 400 list of the country's wealthiest Americans, with $225 million in assets. In 1997, he had $726,927 in assets and $86.7 million in liabilities, owed to eighty-nine individuals and companies. In interviews Hemmeter blamed his financial plight on being overly optimistic about New Orleans as a gambling market. "I'm trying to pretend that this era of my life is an era gone by," he told one reporter. Christopher Hemmeter vowed to steer clear of gambling in the future.

The demise of River City in June 1995 further tarnished the reputation of gambling in Louisiana. And more bad news was just around the corner. This time it would involve video poker, which the legislature had legalized in 1991. With that vote, lawmakers had allowed every bar and restaurant in Louisiana to have three video poker machines and had permitted highway truck stops to have up to fifty machines apiece. Unexpectedly, crafty businessmen had built truck stops throughout the state just so they could install the lucrative video poker machines.

At 1:24 p.m. on August 16, FBI agents arrived unannounced at the Baton Rouge office of lobbyist Joe Wood with a judge's order to search the premises. Nine minutes later, another group of agents with search warrants descended upon the suburban Baton Rouge home of state senator Larry Bankston, chairman of the State Senate committee through which all gambling legislation had to pass. That same day, federal agents also searched Bankston's law office and the offices of Fred Goodson, a businessman who owned a video poker truck stop in the New Orleans

suburb of Slidell, and Carl Cleveland, a New Orleans attorney who represented Goodson in his business dealings. For the past eight months, federal agents had been bugging the phones of Bankston and Goodson, in a case that had originally begun with the investigation of efforts by the Jena Choctaw tribe to open an Indian casino in central Louisiana.

Five days after the FBI searches, the investigation became public when prosecutors unsealed FBI affidavits seeking a judge's approval to carry them out. The affidavits alleged that Goodson had plotted with Wood and her husband, Lynn Berry, to influence a dozen state lawmakers, plus Bankston, in a desperate attempt to keep the legislature from killing the controversial video poker industry. News of the federal investigation packed a wallop. WEB OF DECEIT, read *The Times-Picayune*'s front-page headline.

The FBI affidavits showed that state lawmakers enjoyed a cozy relationship with the lobbyists. The federal transcripts revealed, for example, that the husband and wife team of Berry and Wood ran the "Green House," a private club where lobbyists wined and dined lawmakers during lunch in an unpretentious house a few blocks from the Capitol. Berry was heard on tape devising plans with Goodson and other video poker truck stop owners to buy memberships for Berry and Wood at the Sherwood Forest Country Club in Baton Rouge so they would have a place to entertain legislators. Berry also planned to give legislators illegal gifts, such as expensive golf bags. In addition, Goodson hatched plans for truck stop owners to funnel hundreds of thousands of dollars to lawmakers in the form of campaign contributions.

The goal of Goodson and his allies was to get legislators to kill an anti-gambling measure that would give voters in each parish the right to repeal video poker. While video poker was legal in every restaurant and bar that had a liquor license in Louisiana, the truck stop owners, who had the greatest profits at stake, were spearheading the defense against the anti-gambling legislators. The FBI affidavits, for example, showed that Goodson pocketed $1.3 million in profits from his O'Aces video poker truck stop in Slidell in 1994. In one taped conversation, Goodson said he planned to make $200,000 in campaign contributions, which he called "the cost of doing business."

Failed promises had cost video poker in the eyes of voters. Passage of the legislation had been touted in 1991 as a way to stamp out the illegal video poker machines in bars throughout Louisiana, and as a way to create jobs. By the summer of 1995, voters were realizing that video poker was failing on both counts. State Police reports showed that many bars still had the illegal machines. And since video poker catered to locals, the money that gamblers poured into the machines was money not spent at the grocery store or the mall. So video poker created few if any new jobs.

On top of that, video poker was highly addictive. A Las Vegas psychologist called it the "crack cocaine of gambling" because it hooked so many of his patients. Middle-aged women who did not work—like Betty Yakey in Vidalia—were especially vulnerable because the machines, in dimly lit bars or truck stops, could be a hypnotizing diversion. By factoring in the social problems—the bankruptcies, forged checks, and theft—many analysts thought video poker was a net negative. Polls showed that 60 percent to 70 percent of the public would vote to repeal video poker if given the chance. The polls also showed that 90 percent to 95 percent wanted the right to vote on video poker and the other forms of gambling—something that legislators had never given them.

Several anti–video poker bills were offered during the 1995 legislative session. Most significantly, the House passed a bill that would have allowed voters to close riverboat casinos and video poker operations. Bankston's committee buried it. The Senate did pass a bill giving voters in each parish the opportunity to kill video poker, but the measure permitted existing operations to remain in business. The House refused to accept the grandfather clause, and so the bill died. When the legislative session ended on June 19, the video poker operators were still in business. "I've never seen an issue like gambling," said Bernie Pinsonat, a Louisiana pollster. "Ninety-five percent of the electorate has said from Day One that they wanted a chance to vote locally on these issues. Yet the gambling lobby did something I've never seen before: They stopped 95 percent of the public." The video poker payoffs provided a good explanation why.

That the federal investigation became news in August 1995 was especially bad for lawmakers. The FBI affidavits were released only two months before election day, when all legislators and gubernatorial candidates would be on the primary ballot. The legislators mentioned in the affidavits suddenly were under suspicion. And not surprisingly, they were virtually a who's who of the men who ran the Louisiana legislature—Governor Edwards's staunch pro-gambling allies.

Topping the list of those under a cloud was Larry Bankston, who with his committee chairmanship held enormous sway over gambling measures. He was serving his second four-year term in the Louisiana Senate. It seemed that Bankston, forty-four, had been weaned for a political career. His father, Jesse, had been the longtime chairman of the Louisiana Democratic Party. Jesse Bankston also was remembered as the man whom Governor Earl Long had fired in 1959 as director of the state hospital board because he had refused to free the mentally unbalanced Long from a state mental institution. (Bankston's successor freed the governor.) Until the video poker scandal broke in August 1995, Larry Bankston, a Democrat, was a shoo-in for a third term. With his telegenic looks, easy charm, and political smarts, Bankston was even seen as a possible gubernatorial candidate down the road.

The FBI affidavits showed that Bankston had played the lead role with Goodson in plotting to kill anti–video poker bills during the 1995 legislative session. In a December 28, 1994, conversation taped by the FBI, Bankston told Goodson, "Let me tell you what I view my job is: that no piece of legislation gets passed, period. Nothing." On May 19, 1995, Bankston was captured telling lobbyist Joe Wood, "We are willing to take the blood oath to do whatever it takes either to have no local option or have the local option . . . that just has the words local option and [are] not meaningful." In addition, in a phone call the day after the session ended, an FBI agent summarized: "Goodson told Bankston he appreciated all of Bankston's efforts and that he had done an excellent job."

The FBI affidavits indicated that Bankston stood to get plenty in return. He was captured on tape agreeing to accept a hidden interest in Goodson's truck stop company and to accept $100,000 in stock from Goodson in a medical-waste company. Goodson was also described by prosecutors as paying a bribe to Bankston through a practice known as "travel-less renters." Records showed that Goodson had paid Bankston $1,555 to spend a week at Bankston's Alabama Gulf Coast condo in June 1995, but hadn't made the trip. Bankston and his wife had spent that week at the condo, records showed. Bankston didn't refund the money to Goodson until after the FBI searches. Bankston's wife, Lynn, had been caught on tape saying they needed to recruit "travel-less renters" to help pay for the condo's mortgage.

Also mentioned prominently in the FBI affidavits was state senator Benjamin Bura (Sixty) Rayburn, a living legend in Louisiana politics. A protégé of Earl Long's, he had first been elected to the Louisiana House of Representatives in 1948. In 1951, he was elected to the Louisiana State Senate and had won every election since then. In 1995, he was completing his forty-seventh year in the legislature. Rayburn, a Democrat, represented a rural area north of Lake Pontchartrain, living on a farm near the town of Bogalusa. Rayburn loved to tell stories about Earl Long. Once, the story went, Rayburn sought Long's support for a hospital in Bogalusa. Long was trying to get several tax increases through the legislature and asked Rayburn, "How you feel about my taxes?"

"I'm opposed to taxes," Rayburn replied.

"Well, I'm opposed to hospitals," Long shot back.

Long was reminded that he had promised during his election campaign to put a hospital in Bogalusa. Rayburn then asked Long how he should explain to his constituents what Long was now saying.

"Tell 'em I lied," Long said.

Rayburn had gotten his nickname because he was assigned seat 60 in seventh or eighth grade. He was a pipefitter when he got his start in politics, and his opponents said 60 actually referred to his IQ. But while Rayburn may not have been an intellectual giant, he had a Ph.D. in politics. Every governor of Louisiana—populist and anti-populist alike—had to contend with Rayburn, particularly on state budget matters. By 1995, Rayburn was seventy-eight and looked the part of a veteran rancher. He was tall and had a weather-tanned face. On the Senate floor, he favored cowboy boots and string ties.

But was he a crook, too? The FBI wiretaps captured Fred Goodson discussing how he had given a secret share in his video poker company to Rayburn's three children. Tommie Jean Rayburn, one of the senator's daughters, was "hyperventilating" over the windfall of $7,000 to $8,000 a month, according to an FBI agent's report. The wiretaps also showed that a video poker truck stop owner had covered $400 of Rayburn's expenses on a quail-hunting trip.

Other lawmakers mentioned in the FBI affidavits were:

- Representative Raymond (La La) Lalonde, a Democrat from Sunset, which proudly called itself "the cockfighting capital of the world." Lalonde, the director of a government-funded vocational-technical trade school, was a wily Cajun who knew how to get bills passed. He had sponsored the 1990 lottery bill and the 1992 New Orleans casino bill. One truck stop owner was heard telling another on tape that Lalonde wanted to avoid criticism for accepting campaign contributions from truck stop owners. Lalonde was said to have asked the owners to disguise their campaign contributions by giving the money in small amounts— $250 or $500—and in the names of their children or cousins.

- Senator Gerry Hinton, a Republican from Slidell. It was Hinton who sponsored the 1991 amendment that legalized video poker machines at truck stops. He had done so at the suggestion of Fred Goodson, a friend and constituent, or as Hinton at the time had called him, a "God-fearing Baptist." Now Goodson was said to be rewarding Hinton.

- Senator Don Kelly, a Democrat from Natchitoches. Kelly, a college football running back who carried himself on the Senate floor like John Wayne, was the single most powerful state lawmaker. He had co-sponsored the video poker bill in 1991 and the New Orleans casino bill in 1992. Goodson was caught on tape discussing payments to Kelly that were to be disguised as campaign contributions.

- Senator Marty Chabert (*Shaw-bare*), a Democrat from the bayou town of Chauvin. Chabert was elected to replace his father, a popular state senator who died of cancer while in office. Goodson was heard planning to make payments to Chabert, who owned a video poker truck stop.

- Senate president Sammy Nunez, a Democrat from the New Orleans suburb of Chalmette. Nunez, who had served in the State Senate since 1969, was still trying to recover politically from news reports in 1994 that he had handed out campaign contributions from a casino owner on the Senate floor. Goodson on tape also mentioned Nunez as a recipient of payments.

- Senator Armand Brinkhaus, a Democrat from Sunset. Brinkhaus was an unabashed supporter of gambling and chaired the Senate committee that invariably killed good-government legislation. Goodson mentioned him, too, as a recipient of payments.

- Senator Ron Landry, a chain-smoking Democrat from the New Orleans suburb of LaPlace. Landry typically kept gambling bills alive in Senate committees by voting for them, but voted against the measures on the Senate floor to make his conservative constituents think he was anti-gambling. Goodson also was heard wanting to send money to Landry.

Not surprisingly, all of the lawmakers denied having violated any laws. Those who admitted getting money from the truck stop owners said the payments were legitimate campaign contributions or—as Rayburn argued—were among the legal perks for legislators.

The video poker scandal broke at a time when the state legislature was already reeling from charges of misconduct and abuse of power. *The Times-Picayune,* after winning a court order, had published a list of students who in recent years had been awarded tuition waivers by lawmakers to study at Tulane University. Under an 1884 agreement, every state legislator was permitted to award a one-year scholarship to

Tulane every year. But only political insiders knew about the scholarship program. Deserving students from nonpolitical families were shut out. The list published by the newspaper showed that many lawmakers awarded the tuition waivers to children of relatives, judges, doctors, lawyers, and campaign contributors. For example, the children of Governor Edwards's close friend from Crowley, Edmund Reggie, got twenty-seven years' worth of scholarships to Tulane's undergraduate and graduate schools. The children of U.S. senators John Breaux and J. Bennett Johnston got scholarships, as did a son of former governor David Treen and the children of U.S. congressmen Jimmy Hayes and Bob Livingston. One state legislator, it was discovered, had even given himself the scholarship. In all, the Tulane scholarship revelations outraged the public and added to the uneasiness caused by the various gambling scandals.

In a survey done for a citizens' watchdog group shortly before the video poker scandal broke, pollster Frank Luntz found that voters in Louisiana were probably more dissatisfied than those in any other state.

A *Times-Picayune* computer analysis added more fuel to the fire. The September 17, 1995, report showed that the nascent gambling industry had already emerged as the most generous supporter of politicians, pumping more money into legislators' campaigns than the next four industries combined. In all, the newspaper found, various gambling interests combined accounted for about 20 percent of all contributions given to legislators in 1993 and 1994. This was three times as much money as the petrochemical industry, traditionally a dominant force in state politics, had given. The single biggest donor was Louie Roussel III, who owned the *Star* casino gambling boat and who had a small share of the Harrah's Jazz casino. Roussel gave more money— $147,000—than such Fortune 500 companies as Philip Morris and Texaco. It was Roussel's campaign checks that Senate president Sammy Nunez and House Speaker John Alario had personally given out to favored lawmakers. The second biggest donor in 1993 and 1994 was Christopher Hemmeter's Grand Palais casino, with $100,000 in contributions. Jim Beam, the longtime editor of the *Lake Charles American Press,* summed up the view of many when he wrote, four days after *The*

Times-Picayune's report, "Politicians in this state can't continue to serve two masters. It's either gambling interests or the rest of us."

By the fall of 1995, the political backlash was in full force. With Edwards out of the running for reelection, all of the gubernatorial candidates sought to distance themselves from gambling by swearing off campaign contributions from gambling interests. Former governor Buddy Roemer, the front-runner, came under fire for not having vetoed legislation that legalized video poker and riverboat gambling in 1991 during his final year in office. One gubernatorial candidate, state treasurer Mary Landrieu, called Roemer "the father of gambling in this state." Roemer, too, tried to separate himself from the gambling industries he had spawned by calling for the repeal of the video poker truck stops.

In the campaign's final weeks, gambling became the favorite whipping boy. "Right now, gambling is making political cronies rich at the expense of our children," declared Landrieu in a television ad. In a televised debate, another gubernatorial candidate, businessman Phil Preis, asserted that "the only growth industry we've got in Louisiana right now is the FBI."

The political casualties piled up even before election day: Senators Bankston, Kelly, Hinton, and Chabert decided not to run for reelection. Meanwhile, Edwards, in his final months in office, enjoyed only a 30 percent positive rating with voters.

The general elections were held on November 18, and after the votes had been counted, it was clear that an era had ended. Governor Edwards, of course, was on his way out, as were his four Senate allies who had also chosen not to run for reelection. Voters added to the turnover by defeating Senator Sixty Rayburn, Representative La La Lalonde, Senator Armand Brinkhaus, and Senate president Sammy Nunez. Senator Ron Landry barely survived.

Former governor Roemer faded in the stretch and would not reclaim his old job. The new governor would be a bald, overweight state senator who had served an undistinguished two terms in the Senate and who had barely registered in the polls four months earlier. His name was Murphy (Mike) Foster. Few political insiders had taken Foster seriously. To anyone who paid attention to him, it seemed that the main reason he was seeking the Governor's Mansion was that his grand-father, Murphy Foster, had served as governor from 1892 to 1900. How-ever, as voters grew dissatisfied during the 1995 campaign, Foster was well positioned to be an agent of change. He was plain-speaking and didn't look like a politician. His TV ads reinforced the point. In one, he was shown welding. In another, he sat atop a tractor mowing a field. Foster rose in the polls so quickly and so late that contradictions in his background and record got little attention. While he looked like a man used to working with his hands, he actually had inherited perhaps $30 million and lived in a plantation home, in the southwest Louisiana town of Franklin, that was larger than the Governor's Mansion.

Gambling opponents had high hopes for the new governor. Foster had spoken out harshly against gambling during the campaign, saying that the negatives were likely greater than the benefits. He also had supported giving voters the right to repeal gambling. Gambling oppo-nents drew further inspiration from the legacy of his grandfather, Gov-ernor Murphy Foster, who had earned a place in history by helping shut down the crooked Louisiana Lottery one hundred years earlier. Mike Foster could now play a similar role. But overlooked in the gambling opponents' optimism was that the incoming governor had been a reli-able Edwards voter on most issues in the Senate. In 1991 he had voted to legalize riverboat gambling, and in 1992 he had voted to legalize the New Orleans land casino.

Ironically, it was four days after Foster's November 1995 election that the Harrah's Jazz casino shut down at 3:45 a.m. With his anti-gambling campaign statements, Mike Foster now had the chance to keep the coffin closed on the land casino in New Orleans and earn a place in history, much like his grandfather had, for helping kill gam-bling in Louisiana.

After winning office for a fourth time, Edwin Edwards had returned to the Governor's Mansion in January 1992 backed by a never-before-seen coalition of business leaders and poor blacks who had joined together to defeat David Duke. But Edwards squandered a rare opportunity to try to modernize the state's tax structure, to dramatically improve the backward education system, and to bridge the state's huge racial divide. Instead, for two years he devoted much of his energy to gambling legislation, initially getting the legislature to legalize a land casino in New Orleans and then manipulating the licensing of riverboat and video poker applicants to ensure that his friends and political supporters got licensed. He allowed his children, particularly his elder son, Stephen, to cash in on the Edwards name to win big contracts from would-be riverboat operators.

In Edwards's last two years as governor, close friends and advisers noticed that he wasn't quite as sharp as before. While he continued to look ten years younger than his age, health problems and the stress of his job were taking their toll. Edwards had to be fitted with a hearing aid; he fell off a horse, fracturing a bone in his back; and he had heart bypass surgery. He lost his once all-consuming passion for the job. On weekday afternoons, he would try to head upstairs in the mansion to watch *Jeopardy* and take a nap. He also began taking long hunting trips. When he was back at the mansion, he limited the number of people he was willing to see or speak with. Two months before Edwards's term as governor expired, the Harrah's casino in New Orleans shut down. It was a personal failure because when he got the legislature to legalize the casino early in his term, he had assured the public and the lawmakers that it would revitalize New Orleans and Louisiana. During his final days in office, Edwards would take credit for Louisiana's improved economy and would remind audiences of his desire to help the poor. But the state's strengthened economy had more to do with national trends than anything Edwards did, and his wealthy friends did far better than did Louisiana's poor. In reality, he could boast of few legitimate accomplishments during his final term. When Edwards left office in January 1996, he seemed relieved to pass the baton of power to Mike Foster.

The Louisiana Way

On a warm spring afternoon in 1996, a man with a graying beard and thinning hair was heading east on Hollywood Boulevard, north of Miami, when his pager began vibrating. Casually dressed, he was on his way to play golf with two men he wanted to get to know better. They knew him as Geoffrey Sands, the salty part-owner of a ship-repair company. In reality, he was Geoffrey Santini, a New Orleans–based undercover FBI agent preparing to make one of the final busts of a long and successful career. In this scam, companies were paying kickbacks to procure contracts to repair ships used by the defense industry. Santini's golf partners could help him make the case.

Focused on the outing, Santini wanted no interruptions. But his pager displayed his boss's phone number, followed by the emergency number 911. So Santini pulled his luxury rental car over at the first pay phone he found and called Freddy Cleveland, who headed the FBI's public-corruption squad in New Orleans. As soon as Cleveland recognized Santini's voice, he said, "I need you back here immediately."

"What's going on?" asked Santini. "What do you need?"

"I can't talk to you on the phone," replied Cleveland. "It's too sensitive. You'll find out when you get back here."

Santini made arrangements to fly right away from Miami to New Orleans. The date was April 29, 1996.

The events that led to the phone conversation had begun to unfold ten days earlier at the Grand Casino in Gulfport, Mississippi. That day, an Assistant United States Attorney named Steve Irwin had been sitting on a couch outside a third-floor conference room in the hotel casino when a man in a blue pinstriped suit approached and asked to speak with him. Irwin had just given a speech at a gambling law seminar sponsored by the American Bar Association. His topic: the twenty-one guilty pleas and convictions he had helped secure in the past year in eliminating the remnants of the Carlos Marcello mob—which had joined forces with New York's Gambino mob to secretly own a video poker company in New Orleans that did business with Bally Gaming International. The man in the blue pinstriped suit congratulated Irwin on the case and introduced himself as Charlie Blau, an attorney from Dallas. He asked if he could pull up a chair to discuss an important matter, and Irwin said that was fine.

After a bit of small talk, Blau got down to business. Blau said he represented two clients from Houston who would surely be indicted for tax evasion. Irwin interrupted to say that he had no jurisdiction over Texas cases. Blau said he understood and noted that he had spent eleven years working as a United States prosecutor and top Department of Justice official in Washington, D.C., before becoming a criminal defense attorney. "I know how the system works," Blau assured Irwin. Leaning forward in his chair, he said, "I have a story I want to tell you. It's a story about political corruption in Louisiana. It's a story about payoffs, bribes, and kickbacks. And, most important, it's an ongoing story."

"What do you mean, it's an ongoing story?" Irwin asked.

"Some of the activities are ongoing today," Blau replied. "My clients have obtained a contract with a government agency in Louisiana. There is evidence of favors and kickbacks in obtaining the contract. They are also involved in other activities in Louisiana. On the surface, it appears to be quite proper. But when you peel away the onion, there are questions about the activities."

Blau then said he would like his clients to meet with Irwin and other federal authorities in New Orleans to discuss their illegal activities in Louisiana, in exchange for help with their tax problems in Texas and a guarantee that none of the information they provided about Louisiana would be used against them. In legal terms, this deal was known as a "proffer." Blau then spoke more specifically about his clients' crimes, saying that they involved the prison industry as well as the Louisiana sports authority. "The corruption involves the governor," he added casually, while closely watching for Irwin's reaction.

As he had hoped, Blau's final comment succeeded in piquing Irwin's interest. Mike Foster, Irwin thought to himself, had just become Louisiana's governor and was starting off with a reputation as an aboveboard guy. Could Blau have something on Foster? Or was Blau talking about the former governor, the notorious Edwin Edwards? Irwin chose not to ask, and Blau volunteered no additional details.

After nine years with the United States Attorney's office, Irwin, a forty-one-year-old former cop who reveled in prosecuting bad guys, was accustomed to defense lawyers trying to secure a break for their clients. Most of the time, he couldn't help them and the conversation went nowhere. But Blau had good credentials as a former federal prosecutor, and he had gotten Irwin's attention. "Why don't you come to Louisiana and make a proffer about what these guys are involved with?" Irwin said.

"I'd be delighted," responded Blau.

The meeting took place a few days later at the United States Attorney's office, on the second floor of the Hale Boggs Federal Building in downtown New Orleans. There to listen to Blau were Irwin and Freddy Cleveland. Blau began by getting an oral agreement from the federal officials that nothing he discussed in the meeting would be used later against his clients. Everyone also agreed that if the case went forward and his clients were helpful, Irwin would make this known to the courts in Texas in their pending tax case. With those matters resolved, Blau began to tell his clients' story. Reading from notes on a yellow legal pad, Blau for the first time revealed their identity. They were brothers named Michael and Patrick Graham, and he noted that they had quite a checkered history. Mike Graham had already been convicted of evading

$120,000 in taxes in 1989, and both brothers were under investigation for not paying $700,000 in taxes apiece for 1990. The brothers had such an unsavory reputation, Blau confessed, that when he had visited the FBI and the United States Attorney's office in Houston earlier that month to ask them to hear the Grahams' story, they practically threw him out of the office. However, Blau said he thought that Irwin and Cleveland would show more interest because his clients' information involved the corruption of top Louisiana politicians.

Blau paused to make sure that he had everyone's attention and then plunged ahead with his presentation. The Grahams, he said, were involved in a crooked deal to build a juvenile prison in the central Louisiana town of Jena. Blau then stood up, walked to a whiteboard, and began laying out the complicated transaction. The prison was to cost $35 million and be privately owned. But it could not be built and opened without approval from public officials. Since the Grahams and their partners had no money, state government—specifically the Louisiana Bond Commission—was supposed to finance the prison by approving the sale of public bonds. In addition, the Louisiana Department of Public Safety and Corrections had agreed to provide inmates for the prison and pay for their upkeep. To get these approvals, Blau said, his clients were making illegal payments to state officials. Blau paused once again and saw both federal officials listening closely.

He then described two other illegal schemes involving the Grahams. One involved a highly publicized but failed effort to move the Minnesota Timberwolves basketball team to New Orleans. The other involved an effort to get local governments to use a new form of waste disposal that would turn household garbage into simulated-wood products. Blau said the Grahams were making payoffs to Louisiana officials in these two deals as well.

He returned to the Jena prison project. In that deal, he said, the payoffs thus far were nearly $1 million. "And the money went to the most powerful politician in Louisiana," Blau said, "the former governor, Edwin Edwards."

Upon hearing that bombshell, Steve Irwin betrayed no trace of emotion, but his mind began racing. Edwin Edwards, after all, was widely believed to be corrupt, but authorities had never caught him—not for a lack of trying, though, given the two mid-1980s trials. Freddy Cleveland, however, sat up straight and leaned forward at the mention of Edwards. He, too, knew Edwards's background and knew that he would be a big catch, if the FBI could land him.

For the next several minutes, Irwin and Cleveland asked questions of Blau. Satisfied with his answers, Irwin then asked if Blau could return to New Orleans, this time accompanied by the Grahams. The attorney said he would be happy to do so.

After Irwin returned to his office, he clicked on the West Law computer site and began searching for newspaper articles on the Grahams. He quickly found a host of negative news stories in Houston featuring them. For three hours, Irwin read article after article. He learned that Mike was forty-six and the elder of the two. Pat was forty-five. They had been in business together for nearly their entire adult lives, and they had been in constant trouble. The brothers had started off by running separate men's clothing stores. Both stores failed, leaving suppliers and vendors out $50,000 and banks out $60,000. Undeterred, Mike Graham borrowed $250,000 with two other men in 1979 and opened a teen disco. It closed two years later, leaving investors holding the bag. Pat tried to open a doughnut shop, but it was sued twice before it even got off the ground. A subsequent venture, selling forklifts, involved both brothers and also ended in failure, leaving behind a slew of creditors. For a time, the brothers went their separate ways. By 1985, Mike was successfully selling luxury condos and limited partnerships. He and Pat then started an investment banking firm. It wasn't long before several investors discovered that hundreds of thousands of dollars had disappeared.

Steve Irwin would later describe the Graham brothers as "the most manipulative con men probably on the face of the world." That, simply put, explained why they could continually get investors to pony up money, even though the money would often vanish into the Grahams' pockets. Like the best flim-flam artists, the brothers dressed sharply, owned big homes, drove big cars, and threw big parties. Mike, full of bluster, was skilled at making promises—and then more promises—

that had enough truth to them to string along the hapless target. Pat was smoother, nicer, and more soothing. He could pull up to a ranch in a dusty pickup truck and, in faded blue jeans and scuffed cowboy boots, seem at ease standing in a pasture. A day later, he could seem equally at home in a $1,000 suit giving a presentation to high-powered businessmen in a Houston office tower. No matter the occasion, the brothers seemed to know what to say, especially Pat. Invariably over time these professional con artists grew friendly with Texas politicians. And they milked their political connections for all they were worth. Visitors to their office would remember meetings being interrupted by phone calls from former governor Mark White, Attorney General Jim Mattox, or Clayton Williams, a flamboyant oilman who lost narrowly to Ann Richards in the 1990 gubernatorial election.

In 1988, the Grahams developed a new scheme. With the assistance of White and Mattox, they would build six privately owned prisons in rural Texas counties and count on overflow from state prisons to make it a successful venture. In October 1989, they closed the deal to finance the prisons by selling $78 million of bonds. Mike Graham celebrated that day by buying a Rolls-Royce and driving it off the showroom floor. But only a fraction of the state inmates anticipated by the Grahams actually materialized, in part because the Grahams had contributed generously to Williams's losing campaign for governor, a fact apparently remembered by Governor Richards's administration. By 1991, the prison bonds were worthless and the Grahams found themselves in court once again. A jury found that the Grahams and their partners had engaged in fraud and securities violations, and a judge ordered them to pay $33 million in damages.

Amazingly enough, that did not shut down the two brothers. In 1993, they joined forces with a former mayor of Houston, Fred Hofheinz, in trying to get approval from Louisiana officials to build the privately owned juvenile prison in Jena. For a time, the Grahams also played a central role in helping Hofheinz try to buy the Timberwolves and move them to New Orleans. Pat Graham even appeared alongside Governor Edwards at a 1994 press conference where they announced the team had agreed to the move. The National Basketball Association, however, nixed the deal because Hofheinz, the Grahams, and their partners were financing it with a wink and a smile. The Grahams shrugged off the NBA's rebuff and refocused their efforts on winning approval to build the Jena juvenile prison.

Meanwhile, Pat started another scam. He posed as a high-ranking official with the Texas prison system who could arrange a jail break and new life for a convicted murderer in exchange for $750,000 from the convict's girlfriend. She tipped off authorities, and the con man got conned. Graham was arrested outside a Houston mall in January 1996, just after receiving a $150,000 down payment that was actually part of a government sting operation.

Charlie Blau had warned Irwin that the Grahams had a checkered past. But after reading the newspaper articles describing their misdeeds in full detail, Irwin was dismayed. How, he wondered, could they ever make a case against Edwin Edwards by relying on such disreputable characters? Nevertheless, Irwin decided to hold the meeting that he had scheduled with Blau and the Grahams. Because Blau was a former prosecutor, he had credibility, and Edwards was tempting bait.

The meeting took place just after lunch on April 30, 1996, on the twenty-second floor of the downtown New Orleans high-rise that housed the FBI. With both sides sitting at one end of a long conference table, Blau introduced his clients and made a few remarks. He then turned to Pat Graham, to his left, and asked him to begin his presentation. For the next two hours, Pat Graham did most of the talking. He had been more directly involved in the Graham brothers' activities in Louisiana. And just as important, his easygoing charm would play better with the FBI agents and Assistant United States Attorneys attending the meeting than would his brother Mike's rough and blustery demeanor.

Pat told the same story that Blau had sketched out just a few days before, but in far greater detail. He devoted most of his talk to the prison, standing at times before a whiteboard to diagram the deal and the players involved. Besides Edwards, the other key player was Cecil Brown, a cattle auctioneer in the southwest Louisiana town of Eunice and a long-standing friend of Edwards's. In September 1993, Graham told his audience, he had gone to the Governor's Mansion with Brown, who was helping him on the Jena project, carrying $245,000 in cash in a bag. Once inside, Graham said, he gave the bag to Brown, who then took it to the governor's first-floor office. When Graham entered the office a few minutes later to greet Edwards, he did not see the bag.

In December 1994, Graham continued, he had gone to the mansion again with Brown, this time with $600,000 in cash in a box. As before, Brown went in to see Edwards alone, carrying the box. When Graham entered the office a few minutes later, he said, the box was empty.

Pat Graham normally had a backslapping personality, but in the presence of the federal officials, he restrained himself and spoke in a matter-of-fact tone as he described payoffs to the man with the power to green-light or kill the prison project, Governor Edwards. Watching his performance, Freddy Cleveland, who headed the FBI's public-corruption squad, was impressed. He thought that Graham could well be telling the truth. If not, Cleveland reasoned to himself, they could soon find out by running him through a series of questions about times, dates, and places. Cleveland had had a lot of experience with con men and knew how to smoke them out.

Steve Irwin was more skeptical. "These guys are full of shit," he thought to himself. "This is contrary to everything I have heard about how Edwards does business. It's too blatant and open. It doesn't sound right. We're not going to go anywhere with this."

FBI agent Geoffrey Santini, who had returned from Miami that morning after Cleveland paged him the day before, also was doubtful. "If it's true, there's no fucking way we can prove this," he thought. "There's no way Edwards will put himself in a position so we can verify this information."

With Cleveland's permission, Santini wanted to return to his undercover case in Miami, not mess with Pat Graham. He was willing to stick around a few days to flush Graham out because the Texan had provided a lot of detail. But Santini did not want to waste much time discovering whether Graham was telling the truth.

Just then, Irwin spoke up. "You've got us interested," he told Blau. "But your guys have a lot of baggage. Unless they can produce something right away, there's not a lot we can do."

"My guys are ready, able and willing to do anything they can," Blau replied. "Let us know what you want them to do."

Cleveland asked if Pat Graham would record phone calls and wear a body wire to record conversations. Blau looked at his client. Graham nodded yes.

A practiced chameleon, he liked the intellectual challenge that came with being a government informant. Of course, he also hoped that helping the federal government might keep him out of prison on the tax charge. "Don't do this halfway," Blau told Graham after the meeting. "You're going to work for the government now."

"I understand," he responded.

On May 5, 1996, five days later, Pat Graham called Santini and told him that he had a previously scheduled meeting with Cecil Brown and Edwards on May 8 in Baton Rouge. Santini welcomed this news because it would provide an initial opportunity to determine if Graham was leveling with them. Step one for Santini was to determine if Graham even knew Cecil Brown. So Santini asked Graham to call Brown, with Santini listening in, and confirm that they were to meet in three days. Graham made the call; then he and Brown discussed the upcoming meeting.

With that first test passed, Santini wanted Graham to record the meeting with Brown and Edwards. The FBI required an agent to follow strict procedures before allowing an informant to do this, however. As would be required throughout the investigation, Santini wrote a memo to Cleveland and other higher-ups detailing what he thought the recorded conversation would yield. The word back from Cleveland was favorable. When Santini began to make plans for the recording, Graham explained that he normally drove from Houston and picked up Brown in Eunice, and the two of them then traveled together in Graham's car to Baton Rouge. Graham said he was willing to record the conversation during the two-hour drive between Eunice and Baton Rouge. "Fine," replied Santini. "This is what I want you to do. You drive to New Orleans first. We'll put a recording device in your car overnight. In the morning, you and I will drive to Eunice, but you'll drop me off before we get there. You then pick up Cecil and make the drive with him like normal to Baton Rouge." Graham agreed. Santini also told Graham to make sure that he let Brown do most of the talking and that he avoid interrupting his passenger.

Santini, forty-five, had grown up in Miami. As a teenager, influenced by a popular television show starring Efrem Zimbalist Jr. as a crusading FBI agent, he had decided he wanted to be an FBI agent himself. He started out as a support employee at eighteen and became a full-fledged agent at twenty-four in 1975. Over the next twenty-one years, he specialized in undercover operations. Santini became a master at assuming a fake identity, setting up a phony company, and then nailing the bad guys. This required nerves of steel, street smarts, and an ability to think quickly on your feet, especially when working undercover buying drugs. Santini once negotiated the purchase of sixty kilos of cocaine for $1.5 million. On another assignment, he engaged in a shootout with drug traffickers. He emerged unscathed, but another agent was wounded.

Santini liked the excitement of his work, and he liked hanging out with criminals, who were invariably more interesting than the typical straitlaced FBI agent. Not surprisingly, Santini had little regard for bureaucratic niceties, and he sometimes clashed with FBI higher-ups. Nonetheless, because of his success in handling complex investigations, he was Freddy Cleveland's choice to handle the Edwards case. Santini had worked a few public corruption cases. He was lead agent in the probe that led Congress to remove United States Judge Alcee Hastings of Florida from the bench in 1989. He also played a role in the 1995 video poker investigation that put under suspicion more than a dozen Louisiana lawmakers, caused several of them to lose their reelection bids, and led to the conviction of Louisiana state senator Larry Bankston. But Edwards would be new to Santini, who had spent most of the governor's final term working undercover cases outside of Louisiana.

Santini had little patience with con men like Pat Graham. In his book, you gave them absolutely no latitude. Besides, he wanted to return to his case in Miami, not spend time on an investigation that most likely wasn't going anywhere. So on the May 8 drive to Eunice, Santini told Graham point-blank: "If you get near the line, if you fuck with me, I'll bury you." He also made another demand. "I've written down seven things I want you to get on tape," Santini told Graham. Heading the list was getting Cecil Brown to acknowledge that he and Graham had given $245,000 on one occasion and $600,000 on another to Edwards at the Governor's Mansion. Santini also wanted to hear Brown lay out the details of the Jena prison deal. "If you don't get these things, pack your bag and head back to Houston," Santini told Graham. "I'm not going to waste a lot of time on this. If you can't get these things from Cecil Brown's mouth, we ain't got shit."

Just before arriving in Eunice, they pulled over. Santini exited Graham's car and got into an FBI vehicle that had been trailing them. Graham then drove on to Eunice and picked up Brown, and together they traveled to Baton Rouge. Unbeknownst to Graham, agents followed them in several cars, and the FBI even had a plane overhead monitoring the trip. Santini and his bosses wanted to keep a close eye on Graham to ensure that the day's events happened just as the Texan said they would.

The FBI didn't have the capability that day to overhear the conversation between Graham and Brown as it occurred. So it wasn't until after Graham had dropped Brown off back in Eunice and the FBI agents had parted ways with Graham that Santini began to listen to tapes of the conversation. By the time Santini had reached Baton Rouge on the way back to New Orleans, he had heard Brown confirm everything he had asked Graham for—and much more. As he drove, he exclaimed aloud, "Goddamn, that son of a bitch Graham is telling the truth." Santini was now convinced that Brown and Graham were involved in an illegal deal and that he had the evidence to prove this. Brown, of course, wasn't the ultimate target. Santini began thinking ahead, about how they needed to get direct evidence that Edwin Edwards also was participating in the crime.

Step one would be getting proof that Brown and Graham actually knew the former governor. Contrary to expectations, Edwards's brother

Marion had stood in for him at the May 8 meeting that Brown and Graham had attended in Baton Rouge. A crawfish boil in Eunice hosted by Brown three weeks later would provide the opportunity. With Graham wearing a body wire, he spent a few minutes chatting with Edwards. It was sufficient for the FBI to establish that the former governor definitely knew the con man.

Now federal authorities wanted approval to wiretap Brown's phones. As a first step, a federal judge on May 21 had approved placing a "pen register" on phones at Brown's home and office, Brown's Auction. The device registered the phone number Brown was calling and, in most cases, the number of anyone calling Brown. It wasn't long before the pen register on Brown's phones showed him calling and receiving calls from Edwards as well as Pat Graham. To bolster their case, Santini directed Graham to tell things to Brown that would prompt him to call Edwards. When Brown phoned Edwards after speaking with Graham, Santini had additional proof that Edwards and Brown were engaged in a criminal conspiracy.

Santini and Steve Irwin prepared the evidence to seek a judge's permission to wiretap Brown's phones. The evidence included not only the pen-register information, but also the phone and person-to-person conversations that Pat Graham had recorded. Santini and Irwin could not apply for the wiretap of Brown's phones without permission from the Department of Justice. Edwards's involvement in the case made their request extra sensitive, given his high profile and the previous failure to convict him. Getting approval for the wiretap turned out to be a major ordeal. Justice officials couldn't believe that Santini and Irwin had probable cause to show that recording Brown's calls would place him in a criminal conspiracy with Edwards. They didn't think that Edwards would ever say anything incriminating on the phone. Edwards was too sly and crafty, justice officials told Irwin.

In the meantime, however, Santini continued collecting more evidence, enough finally to get the Justice Department to approve the application. Irwin and Cleveland flew to Shreveport to present it to federal judge Don Walter. Walter reviewed the application carefully and then approved it. To maintain secrecy, the judge took the extraordinary step of withholding the document from the clerk of the court and instead secured it in his office safe. The wiretaps on Brown's home and office began on June 26, 1996, less than two months after the first FBI meeting with the Grahams.

Cecil Brown had known Edwards since he was first elected governor in 1971. Brown's role was not to provide political advice; Edwards had other friends for that. Brown was simply an entertaining guy to have around. A fun-loving cowboy, he was always laughing and joking, telling colorful stories about life in the country. At various times, Edwards owned ranches in Texas and Mississippi, so he and Brown would talk about cattle and horses. They also loved talking about women and gambling. Brown even accompanied Edwards on gambling junkets to Las Vegas, although he had no spare money to lose. Not surprisingly, Brown became fiercely loyal to his charismatic friend, who in turn trusted him with sensitive matters.

One day at lunch, while Edwards was governor, Brown introduced Pat Graham to Sid Moreland, Edwards's executive assistant. "I have heard such great things about you," Graham gushed to Moreland. "Cecil says you're the man who runs government." Moreland did have enormous influence, because he served as Edwards's gatekeeper, controlling who got to see and call the governor. However, Graham's immediate attempt to ingratiate himself put off Moreland. Having grown up in the northern Louisiana Bible Belt town of Homer, Moreland also was turned off by Graham's appearance: expensive suit, tasseled loafers, slicked-back black hair, glasses with small gold rims. The next morning, Edwards's executive counsel, Al Donovan, told Moreland that he, too, had met Graham and thought he "was as phony as a $3 bill." Donovan said he wanted to check Graham out. A few days later, he reported to Moreland that Graham was bad news. The two of them agreed that they would have to tell Edwards immediately.

They walked into Edwards's office and sat down in two chairs facing the governor's desk. He was reading the newspaper. "What y'all got?" Edwards asked, not looking up.

"Governor, I know you hate bad news and hate to hear anything bad about anybody," Moreland began. "But Al and I feel we would be

remiss in our jobs if we didn't tell you some information we have and action we've taken on your behalf."

Edwards looked up.

"You remember that guy who came over here with Cecil the other day, a guy by the name of Pat Graham? Well, he's in a lot of trouble in Texas."

Donovan then described Graham's legal troubles, including his indictment and the huge court judgment for the failed prison venture.

Moreland broke in to say, "I have told Cecil not to bring Pat Graham over anymore. Either he's wearing a wire to save his own ass or he is in some prison-building scam in Louisiana as he was in Texas."

"I agree with Sid," Donovan chimed in.

Edwards leaned forward, threw down the newspaper, and snatched off his reading glasses. "Obviously, I'm not giving you two enough work if all you have to do is sit around and spy on people," Edwards said. Referring to his 1985–1986 legal troubles in the hospital fraud case, he added, "I've been indicted. Does that make me a bad person? Get your asses out of here and go to work."

The next day, Cecil Brown brought Graham back to the Governor's Mansion for lunch.

By the fall of 1996, with the pressures of the governor's office behind him, Edwards was beginning to take it easy for the first time in his life. He was sixty-nine years old, still handsome, with gray hair and a pink, unlined face, and clearly enjoying semiretirement after four decades in public life. He and his thirty-one-year-old wife, Candy, had moved to a million-dollar home in the gated Country Club of Louisiana on the outskirts of Baton Rouge. He reopened a law practice with his son Stephen, but worked only part-time. He enjoyed free time at home, and trips with Candy and her parents, who were about Edwards's age. At restaurants or other public places in Louisiana, ordinary citizens would greet him and frequently say they wished he would run for governor again. Edwards would smile and answer with a quick quip.

Of course, he couldn't keep his hands out of politics. Longtime allies would regularly visit him at his law office, alongside Interstate 10 next

to Ruth's Chris Steak House, to ask his advice or to plot strategy. Edwards had helped numerous people throughout the state government bureaucracy whom he could now turn to for favors. So behind the scenes, he still exercised considerable political power. For example, in April 1996, Edwards called Governor Foster and asked him to authorize the State Police to allow the sale and transfer of the *Grand Palais* gambling boat, owned by developer Christopher Hemmeter in New Orleans until it went bankrupt in mid-1995, to a company that wanted to move the boat to Lake Charles. Foster had the State Police comply with Edwards's request. Foster, in fact, would call Edwards from time to time and ask for political advice himself.

In its office in the Mobil building in downtown New Orleans, the FBI had a special room where agents listened in on wiretapped conversations. An agent would sit at a table wearing headphones, with a large tape machine in front of him. When the tapped phone was picked up or called, the recorder would automatically switch on and the agent would hear everything through the headphones. If the conversation involved suspect business deals, the agent would stay on the line. Otherwise, the agent was required to shut off the recorder. The agent would check back every few seconds or every few minutes to see if the tapped conversation had returned to a suspect subject. If so, the agent would again switch on the recorder. The persons being recorded would not know that an agent was listening in. Indeed, the agent could talk with colleagues while recording a conversation. It was tedious work, though, having to sit at a table for long hours of eavesdropping, and agents generally didn't enjoy the job.

The initial FBI wiretaps of Brown's conversations with Edwards convinced Santini that Brown made money by introducing people to Edwards who needed the governor's backing for their projects. The wiretaps recorded Brown talking to Edwards about the Jena prison, the Evergreen waste-disposal deal, the Timberwolves' failed move, and several other dubious transactions. Edwards was guarded in his phone conversations with Brown, but now that he was out of office for good,

the former governor was not as circumspect as the Feds had expected. It became clear that he had used his position as governor to procure payoffs, so Santini began gathering the necessary evidence for the next step: a wiretap on the former governor's home phone. On September 10, 1996, Santini secured a judge's approval to put a pen register on Edwards's phone.

As a parallel step, Santini had wanted Pat Graham to pass government money into Edwards's hands. This would help make the case that Edwards was receiving illegal payoffs. On October 10, in the parking lot of Ruth's Chris Steak House in Baton Rouge, Graham delivered $100,000 to Brown in marked $100 bills. Brown later gave $25,000 of it to Edwards, the Feds came to believe.

On October 18, in a major escalation of the probe, federal judge John Parker gave the FBI permission to place a wiretap on Edwards's home phone. Never before had the FBI closed the circle on him this tight. When Edwards was on trial for taking payoffs in 1985 and 1986, the Feds didn't have him on tape, which had seriously hampered their case.

The wiretap paid immediate dividends. At 1:30 p.m. on October 18, in the sixth conversation recorded by the FBI, Edwards received a phone call from a relatively new friend. His name was Edward J. DeBartolo Jr., and he was calling about a subject previously unknown to Geoffrey Santini and the other FBI agents working the case. From the call, it was apparent that Edwards was helping DeBartolo's bid to open a riverboat casino in the Shreveport–Bossier City area.

Under Governor Foster, the legislature had replaced the separate land-casino and riverboat-casino boards with a single licensing and regulatory board. One of the new board's first responsibilities would be to award the last available riverboat license. Since Louisiana allowed only fifteen riverboats, it became known as the "fifteenth license." Circus Circus had relinquished this license when it abandoned plans to put a gambling ship in Chalmette, a downriver suburb of New Orleans. DeBartolo had formed DeBartolo Entertainment and paired with Hollywood Casino as one of five bidders for the license.

As soon as he got Edwards on the phone that October afternoon, DeBartolo asked whether they would win the fifteenth license.

Demonstrating his continued political influence, Edwards told DeBartolo that he was talking to members of the gambling board—who were not allowed to discuss business with any of the bidders' representatives—and was optimistic about their chances. "Will you stay in touch with this?" DeBartolo asked.

"Oh, sure," Edwards replied. "I'll be here, and I'm watchin' it, and I'll keep in touch with you."

DeBartolo ended the call by saying, "You know we'll do what we have to do."

"All right," responded Edwards.

Eddie DeBartolo was obsessed with getting Louisiana's fifteenth riverboat license. Born and bred in Youngstown, Ohio, he had been fabulously successful as owner of the San Francisco 49ers football team. When his father bought the team for him in 1977, the 49ers were one of the worst franchises in the National Football League. Over the next twenty years, under DeBartolo, the 49ers amassed the best record in the National Football League and won the Super Bowl a record five times without any defeats. DeBartolo had the foresight to hire Bill Walsh, who had been passed over by other teams, as his head coach. Walsh installed a precise, passing attack that became known as the "West Coast" offense and that revolutionized the game. To build a dynasty, DeBartolo paid his players the league's highest salaries, and he treated them like thoroughbred studs. In trend-setting moves, he built a state-of-the-art training facility, provided a wide-bodied charter jet so the team could stretch out, allowed players to have their own rooms on the road, and had a private chef accompany the team to serve fresh, high-quality food. "It was like arriving at Oz," marveled Matt Millen, a star linebacker who signed with the 49ers late in his career.

Unlike the typical imperious NFL team owner, the diminutive DeBartolo—he stood only five feet six inches—befriended his players, stars and scrubs alike, and it was not unusual for him to join them for a few drinks after practice. Impetuous and emotional, DeBartolo even invited players to visit him in Youngstown during the off-season, and they would find a present—a gift certificate from Neiman Marcus, a CD player, a Rolex watch—each night at their hotel. After the 1990

Super Bowl victory, he took the entire team to Hawaii as well as the players' wives or girlfriends. DeBartolo footed the entire bill—airfare, accommodations, food, rental cars. For entertainment, he flew over Huey Lewis and the News. *Sports Illustrated* named him "the best owner in pro sports."

Bill Walsh and others would express their fondness for DeBartolo. He didn't put on airs, despite his immense wealth. Married to his high school sweetheart who, like Edwin Edwards's wife, was named Candy, he seemed rooted in Youngstown, even after he and Candy moved to the San Francisco Bay Area in 1995.

But there would be occasional flashes of the spoiled rich kid. One evening in February 1992, DeBartolo enjoyed a night out with a group of Youngstown buddies, 49ers players, and young women. Afterward, the party moved to his nearby condo and a tipsy twenty-four-year-old waitress ended up in his bedroom. According to her police statement, DeBartolo said he wanted to have sex, and she turned him down. "Eddie did not say anything but struck her with the back of his hand, across the face, knocking her to the floor," the police report said. "She looked up at him saying, 'What are you doing? I can't believe you are doing this to me.'" He struck her a second time. She fell to the floor. She then fled downstairs and out the front door, screaming and crying. The waitress called the police a short time later. Police found that her panties and pantyhose had been ripped and that she had been bruised.

DeBartolo was not charged in the incident because the local prosecutor said he found "inconsistencies" in the young woman's statement. Three months later, DeBartolo was reported to have paid her several hundred thousand dollars in an out-of-court settlement.

Another disturbing incident occurred in January 1996. After the 49ers lost a playoff game to the Green Bay Packers, DeBartolo and an aide came to blows with taunting fans. They were charged with assault and battery. The charges were dismissed after DeBartolo agreed to pay $2,500 to a Wisconsin charity, according to *The Wall Street Journal*.

Paul Martha, a star player at the University of Pittsburgh in the 1960s, served as general counsel of the 49ers during DeBartolo's early years, and then headed the family's sports interests in Pittsburgh. He

affectionately called DeBartolo "the Prince." "When he got wound up, he could be aggressive," Martha said in a 1998 interview. "He pushed and shoved a couple of people. He had his scrapes."

One of Martha's responsibilities was to keep DeBartolo out of trouble. "You had to keep him under toe," Martha said. "I took care of Eddie to the extent I could. Sometimes he'd get so crazy, we couldn't slow him down."

What concerned Martha and Bill Walsh was that DeBartolo—big-hearted, wanting to please others—was vulnerable to friends and associates who sought to take advantage of him. "He's listened to the wrong people at times," Walsh said in a 1997 interview. "He's been pulled into high-risk business dealings that weren't in his best interest. I think he's suffering from trying to live up to his dad's reputation."

And that was a tall order. Starting with nothing, the elder DeBartolo had built the world's largest shopping-mall empire, working 15 hours a day and never vacationing. "Some people consider 40 hours a week working," he told an interviewer once. "That's not work."

It was through his father that Eddie DeBartolo Jr. met Edwards. The elder DeBartolo bought a horse racing track in Bossier City in the early 1970s, and later developed a shopping mall in New Orleans. From time to time, DeBartolo Sr. would seek Edwards's help. "He would fly in on his jet, his limo would take him to the mansion, I would meet him, he would state his business," Edwards recalled. "I would tell him what I could or could not do. He would say, 'Thank you,' and leave. He didn't want to impose on me, didn't want to take my time, and he was always very congenial and very pleasant." From these visits, they developed a deep trust.

On his visits to the Governor's Mansion, DeBartolo Sr. would occasionally fret about his son, who was consumed with the 49ers, and liked to stay out late at night, but was less interested in running the family business. "Eddie Jr.'s got to grow up someday," DeBartolo Sr. would tell Edwards. DeBartolo Sr. promised Edwards a job as a legal troubleshooter with the 49ers and his mall empire when Edwards finally retired from politics. However, in 1994, DeBartolo Sr. died at age eighty-five. In one of his final conversations with Eddie Jr., the old man told him that Edwards was one of the most honorable people he

had ever met and was one of the few people in public life who hadn't tried to hustle him.

With the old man gone, Edwards's job with the 49ers and the DeBartolo Corporation failed to materialize when he left the governor's office in January 1996. Still, Eddie DeBartolo felt he owed a debt to the former governor. Plus he believed that Edwards could play a key role in helping DeBartolo Entertainment win the fifteenth and final riverboat license. After his father's death, Eddie DeBartolo had decided to make a name for himself in the gambling industry. The Louisiana riverboat, if approved, would be his first venture. He badly wanted the state board's approval to launch it.

On October 21, 1996, the wiretap on Edwards's home phone yielded more dividends. The FBI learned of a new scheme, this one involving apparent payoffs to Edwards from a group of midwestern investors who had tried but failed to get two riverboat licenses in 1993 from the Edwards-appointed board. The go-between was Cecil Brown, who blabbed about the deal in phone calls to Edwards.

On November 19, via wiretap, the Feds learned of yet another scheme. This one involved Bobby Guidry, who in June 1993 had come from nowhere to win one of the final seven preliminary certificates from the governor's riverboat-casino board. Guidry, a tugboat owner, won the license for the upriver New Orleans suburb of Kenner, beating out Popeye's Fried Chicken founder Al Copeland, who thought the license would be his. What was Guidry's advantage? A friendship with Edwards and a seat at the table during the weekly Thursday night poker games at the Governor's Mansion. At the time, Guidry boasted privately that he had made sure to lose large sums to Edwards. Now, three years later, the telephone taps were picking up discussions of additional payoffs, with Andrew Martin, the governor's executive assistant during the final term, acting as the go-between. Martin had grown up with Guidry on a bayou in Lafourche Parish and had brought him into Edwards's inner circle.

When Geoffrey Santini heard the Guidry scheme on tape, he reacted with characteristic irreverence. "Holy shit! There's a lot of stuff

going on here," he told a colleague. Assistant United States Attorney Steve Irwin had a subtler analysis. Irwin, who had just prosecuted members of New York and New Orleans mob families in the video poker case, compared Edwards to a Mafia chieftain. "Edwin *is* the boss," he thought. "He has lieutenants who carry out his orders. This is an organized-crime prosecution without Italians. He has absolute influence over almost any political decision that is made."

Justice Department officials, after reviewing the mounting evidence gathered by Santini and Irwin, approved the next step in the investigation: a request for judicial permission to place microphones in the law offices of Stephen and Edwin Edwards and to place a video camera in Edwin Edwards's office. On December 6, Judge Parker approved the request. A clandestine FBI team then went to Baton Rouge to carry out the task. The team first spent several nights outside the office getting a feel for its rhythms: when the last person left for the day, whether janitorial crews showed up at night, and if the police ever passed by. On the chosen night, the secret FBI team was ready to enter the building. Other agents were deployed throughout Baton Rouge to keep an eye on law office employees, to make sure they didn't unexpectedly return to work.

A hitch developed: someone stayed on in the building for hours. "Who the hell is in there?" wondered FBI agent Freddy Cleveland, who was supervising the job. Finally, the office lights switched off, and a young man and a young woman, apparently law students, emerged from the building. Cleveland checked his watch. It was 3:00 a.m. There wasn't time to carry out the mission that night.

When the FBI team returned the next night, the young law students were again working late. This time they left around midnight. The agents then broke in and installed a video camera and microphone above Edwards's desk and a microphone above Stephen's desk. The net drawn around the former governor had grown even tighter.

This Is Trouble

fter the FBI placed a microphone and a video camera in the ceiling of Edwin Edwards's law office, Geoffrey Santini was struck by how differently the former governor conducted business face-to-face, compared with over the phone. Edwards was guarded as he discussed his shady deals in telephone conversations. As Santini, the lead FBI agent, listened to Edwards talk over matters with his son Stephen, his former executive assistant Andrew Martin, his friend Cecil Brown, and others in the law office, he noted that Edwards spoke much more openly. Edwards obviously assumed that the Feds would never install recording equipment into his private workspace.

The bug in Edwards's office soon uncovered yet another scheme. This one involved apparent payoffs from the Players casino in Lake Charles to Edwards and Stephen. The boat had gotten its preliminary certificate in 1993 from Edwards's riverboat board. The go-between in this deal was Ricky Shetler, the owner of a Lake Charles pizzeria and Stephen's closest friend.

In a conversation with his father on January 9, 1997, Stephen Edwards made a passing reference to payments from his friend in Lake

Charles. "I gotta get with Shetler," Stephen said, "because he still owes you the big check for November, all of December, which should be six, seven, eight, nine thousand dollars."

"All right," responded Edwards.

Another conversation on January 9, between Edwards and Andrew Martin, would become one of the most important recorded by the federal government. Stocky and with a thick head of wavy black hair—looking like he could be cast as an Irish cop in the movies—the fun-loving Martin had had few duties during Edwards's fourth term. He accompanied the governor practically every time he left the Governor's Mansion. He also organized the Thursday night high-stakes poker games and kept track of the running ledger.

During the 1997 conversation, Martin began by expressing concern that Bobby Guidry, who owned the *Treasure Chest* floating casino in Kenner, would renege on a deal they had. "We had an understanding, Bobby and I, that after [the Edwards administration's term ended] he was gonna give me a contract to go to work for him," Martin complained.

Edwards responded that he and Guidry had been hunting the previous weekend and that Guidry had asked Edwards to reassure Martin that he would hold up his end. Edwards's comment reminded Martin of a conversation he had had with Edwards several years earlier, at a time when Guidry needed the governor's help to get his riverboat license. According to Martin, he told Guidry, "I went to the governor. I said I want all my green stamps from all the times I helped you [Edwards] in the past. . . . That's my retirement plan." To Santini, this meant that Martin told Edwards back then that he wanted the governor's help in arranging an illegal slice of the *Treasure Chest,* as his "retirement plan."

Returning to the hunting trip, Edwards said he reminded Guidry that the riverboat owner had agreed to make payments to Edwards, his son Stephen, and Martin as well. Edwards said that Guidry replied by telling him that he had given Martin an additional 2 percent interest in the boat.

"Which I haven't collected a nickel," Martin interrupted.

"I understand that," Edwards replied, and then returned to his hunting trip conversation with Guidry. "I said, 'Bobby, y'all oughta get all that straightened out because I don't like to see any disagreement in the family.' He [Guidry] said, 'I'm gonna keep my word to you. I'm gonna keep my word to Andrew. I'm gonna keep my word to Stephen.'"

Martin speculated that Guidry's lawyers might be keeping the casino boat owner from making the promised payments.

Edwards then counseled his former executive assistant, "Let me just say this to you. There ain't nothing we can make him do. Not a fuckin' thing we can make him do. . . . What the fuck can you do if he don't wanna do it? You can't make him do it. You can't sue him." Edwards then advised Martin to tell Guidry, "We had an agreement. I trust you."

Moments later, Edwards added, "I don't wanna give him any excuses to say, 'I'm backing out of the whole deal' because there ain't a fuckin' thing you can do about it if he does."

"Well, that's true," responded Martin. "Nothing we can do about it."

"You were the one that brought him to me," Edwards reminded Martin a few minutes later. "I didn't even know Bobby Guidry."

"We are close," agreed Martin. "We are close."

"Y'all go back a long, long way."

"We are close," Martin repeated. "We were only born two blocks away from the house. We were raised together. We are close. But I don't know. He's so goddamn uptight. . . . It's just his lawyers. It's bullshit now."

Six weeks later, on February 25, 1997, Martin was still complaining that Guidry hadn't paid him yet. Guidry apparently was still concerned about how he could get money into the hands of Edwin Edwards, Stephen Edwards, and Martin without leaving a paper trail. After lunch that day, Martin sat in Edwards's office and told the former governor that he was losing faith in Guidry. "That was supposed to be my retirement deal," he lamented. Martin then suggested a scheme to move an oil rig and have Guidry pay them for that. "Maybe if we bought a boat he could rent it from us and jack up the rental," Edwards countered.

Martin liked that idea. "My intention is to go ahead and get back into the [tug]boat business. What I thought about is maybe we could get a little company together, have one boat, us three together, and we would bill him. . . . If y'all are interested in doing that, then we can sit down and say [to Guidry], 'Hey, this is what we can do.'"

"The answer is absolutely because we gotta find some way to work that out with Bobby," responded Edwards.

"I don't know what else to do," said Martin.

Edwards said they could carry out the boat scheme very easily "because instead of paying us $2,400 a day for a boat, he could pay us $3,000 something, $3,300. A boat is a boat is a boat. I mean, just pay us in rent."

Martin warmed to the idea. "I don't see where this thing [the oil industry] is gonna go bad till six, seven, eight years down the road," he said. "And if you're making that type of money, the boat there can be paid off very easily within a couple two or three years."

"It's a natural for Bobby," offered Edwards, "because he's been in the boat business for years."

"I've been in the boat business, too," noted Martin.

A few minutes later, Martin began discussing a deal in which Guidry was supposed to pay him, Edwards, and Stephen a total of $100,000 a month. "I'll tell you what, if something happens to Bobby, we're in trouble," Martin said.

Edwards laughed. "Not only that," he said, "I'm worried about him every month taking that out of some bank or someplace. If ever he gets checked, he's gonna have a hard time explaining what happened to all that."

"The thing is right now, chief," Martin said a short time later, "and listen to this: You get 30/30/30, so that's 90, when actually we should be getting 180." They were figuring that an extra $90,000 a month from Guidry would supposedly finance the tugboat purchase. "That's a no-lose situation for us," Martin said.

"And then you're better off because at the end of the deal, you got the boats paid for, an asset," said Stephen Edwards, who by now had walked into his father's office and joined the conversation.

"Then you've got some showable income," agreed Edwin Edwards. "That's another thing. This other stuff, you got to hide it."

Santini and his FBI colleagues were working under extremely tight security, with orders not to discuss the investigation. But on three occasions, the secret investigation came perilously close to being detected. The first time occurred in late January 1997 when the FBI's microphone and video camera in Edwards's law office suddenly went dead. It took agents a few minutes to determine what had happened. A separate FBI video camera that scanned the front of the building's entrance—as well as the parking lot—showed a phone company truck parked outside the building. The agents quickly surmised that a phone technician doing maintenance work that day had unknowingly cut the two lines that enabled agents to film and record the former governor. This revelation sent shivers through the FBI investigative team. They were sure that the technician would trace the source of the extra two phone lines—to find out why Edwards wasn't paying for them—and then discover the microphone and video camera hidden in the ceiling above Edwards's desk. The agents called Santini immediately. Expecting the technician to uncover the FBI equipment and alert Edwards to the eavesdropping, Santini and his supervisors mobilized a squad of agents that would raid the office and seize potential evidence inside before it could be destroyed. Sending in the agents would obviously blow the lid on the investigation prematurely, but Santini and his bosses concluded that if Edwards learned he was being recorded and filmed, they had no other choice.

Santini sat anxiously by the phone at the FBI's New Orleans office as the agents in Baton Rouge closely monitored the technician's movements. After a while, the phone technician exited the office, climbed into his truck, and drove off. He had cut the cables that provided sound and video from Edwards's office to the FBI. Had he also discovered that the FBI had installed the cables and notified Edwards of this? Santini and the other agents weren't sure. They kept an around-the-clock watch on the building over the next few days to see if Edwards began retrieving sensitive documents. He never made such a move. Santini and his bosses heaved a huge sigh of relief. The investigation was still alive and undetected. The FBI spook team returned and surreptitiously restored the microphone and video camera.

The second close call came on February 25, the same day that Edwards and Andrew Martin plotted how to disguise payoffs from Bobby Guidry as tugboat rent. On that day, Edwards, Stephen, Martin, and Cecil Brown met Pat Graham for lunch at Ruth's Chris Steak House in Baton Rouge. The Texan by now had become less important to Santini and his colleagues. While they could not have begun the investigation without Graham, the FBI wiretaps of Brown and Edwards were yielding so much information that Santini and Steve Irwin, the lead Assistant United States Attorney on the case, believed they had enough evidence to arrest and indict the former governor—at the proper time. In the meantime, they wanted to strengthen their case by getting government cash directly into Edwards's hands. This is where Graham continued to play a role. He still owed $1.3 million to Brown and Edwards from the Jena prison deal. So Santini and Irwin were planning to have Graham make a final payoff to Edwards. The FBI would then arrest the former governor, who would be caught red-handed with the government's cash.

While Santini and Irwin were still getting the necessary approvals from their bosses to arrange the final payoff, Graham ate lunch with Edwards and the others at the steakhouse. During the meal, Edwards seemed suspicious of Graham. At one point, Edwards began quizzing him about his legal problems in Texas. Graham replied that the problems were ongoing but would eventually be dismissed. His answers, however, didn't satisfy Edwards. The former governor told Graham that he was going to the rest room and wanted to meet him there in a few minutes. Graham immediately sensed trouble. After Edwards disappeared, Graham excused himself from the table, exited the restaurant, and dashed to his car. He jumped inside, yanked off the wire recorder that wrapped around his waist and ran down his leg, and stuffed the equipment under the seat. Graham returned to the restaurant, smoothed his appearance, and headed into the rest room. Edwards was waiting for him there. The former governor asked Graham more questions about his legal troubles in Houston, while running his hand up and down Graham's chest, back, sides, feeling for recording wires. It took just a few seconds. When he was done, Edwards looked Graham square in the eye for a moment, then, without a word, turned on his heel and walked out of the bathroom. Graham smiled and congratulated himself on ditching the wire just moments before.

After they returned to the table. Edwards mentioned that he was leaving the next day for his condo in Vail, Colorado. Graham said that he was planning to be in Colorado a few days later to pick up a private airplane. Edwards asked if Graham could take him back to Baton Rouge. Graham replied that he would be delighted to do so.

That afternoon, Graham told Santini about the conversation. The FBI agent saw the trip as a golden opportunity. For one thing, Graham still owed the $1.3 million to Edwards and Cecil Brown for the Jena deal. If Graham could fly the former governor in what appeared to be Graham's plane, Edwards and Brown would be more likely to think that he still had the financial juice to make the remaining payoff. Equally important, Santini wanted to use the plane trip to record Graham's conversation with Edwards. They would have plenty of time to talk, since the flight would last at least a couple of hours. Santini told Graham that he wanted to equip the airplane with a recording device, but that he did not want to use Graham's plane. Instead, he wanted to use an FBI plane flown by undercover FBI pilots.

On March 5, an FBI plane picked up Graham in Houston and flew him to Vail to collect Edwards for the flight to Baton Rouge. Beforehand, Santini warned his informant that the former governor was now likely to be extra careful with him, so Graham must not try to get Edwards to discuss any of their illegal deals openly. If Edwards wanted to talk, let him talk, counseled Santini. Just don't start the conversation yourself, he advised.

The flight turned out to be uneventful. With Graham acting cautiously, Edwards said nothing of substance. The plane landed at Baton Rouge Airport in midafternoon and taxied to the small aircraft terminal. Edwards got off, thanked Graham for the ride, climbed into a waiting vehicle, and drove off. He had an important engagement that evening.

Unbeknownst to Edwards, the FBI investigation was on the verge of being compromised a third time. It just so happened that the United

States Customs Service, doing a routine computer check of the plane's tail number, had flagged it as possibly belonging to a drug trafficker. Indeed, the FBI had used the same plane two weeks earlier in an undercover drug bust in which cocaine had been aboard. Greg Koon, a Customs agent responsible for Baton Rouge Airport, got the tip shortly before the plane landed. By the time he and three Baton Rouge police officers got to the airport, the plane had already landed and the pilots were beginning to refuel the aircraft. As the four law enforcement officials walked toward the plane, a member of the ground crew asked them, "You looking at that plane?"

"Yes," they acknowledged.

"Governor Edwards just got off that plane."

Koon and the three Baton Rouge police officers paused to look at each other and then headed over to the plane. Koon pulled one of the pilots to the side and asked him if they could search it. Without identifying himself, the undercover FBI pilot nervously gave Koon the go-ahead. Baton Rouge police officer Randy Scrantz then boarded the plane with a specially trained dog, a Belgian Malinois named Anoeska. Scrantz spent a couple of minutes aboard before Anoeska began frantically scratching at two different spots behind the cockpit. To Scrantz, that meant Anoeska had detected the odor of drugs. What's more, in her scratching, Anoeska had bumped up against an open carry-on bag, and a pistol had fallen out.

Scrantz calmly got off the plane, took Koon aside, and told him what Anoeska had found. Koon walked over to the pilot he had already spoken with and asked him to identify the bag's owner. The two climbed into the plane, and the pilot identified the bag as his. "Can I see some ID?" Koon asked.

"It's in the bag," the pilot replied and began to reach for it.

"Don't do that," Koon commanded.

The pilot kept reaching, until Koon, a heavyweight at six feet five inches, 230 pounds, grabbed him by the back of the neck and pulled him back. "I asked you not to reach for the bag," Koon said firmly.

He could see that the pilot was visibly shaking.

"I'm not supposed to tell you this," the pilot said and stopped.

"Tell me what?" demanded Koon.

"I'm an FBI agent," the pilot admitted.

"Where's your ID?" asked a skeptical Koon.

"It's in the bag."

Koon pulled out an FBI ID and a badge that was the size of a pin. To the Customs agent, it looked as if the badge had come from a gumball machine.

Incredulous, Koon told the pilot that he needed to give him the name of a supervisor to verify his employer. The two then disembarked from the plane.

Koon walked back to Scrantz. "What's the deal, Koon?" Scrantz asked.

"The guy is claiming to be an FBI agent," Koon replied. "He gave me a fake FBI badge."

Koon walked into the terminal and telephoned the person the pilot had asked him to call: special agent Geoffrey Santini in New Orleans. When Koon told him the situation, Santini was dumbfounded. "Oh, shit!" he said to himself. Quickly regaining his composure, he confirmed that the pilots were fellow FBI agents working on an undercover operation. Fearful that the attempted drug bust had blown the Edwards investigation, Santini asked Koon, "Did Edwards see you?"

"No," the Customs agent replied.

Santini paused to give thanks for a moment and then asked Koon to free the pilots. Koon refused, telling Santini that he couldn't be sure if Santini was on the level. A call from Koon's boss in New Orleans a few minutes later settled the matter.

Koon told the pilot that he and his FBI undercover colleague could depart, no hard feelings. Koon then explained to his three colleagues that they had stumbled upon an FBI investigation of Edwards. "But this can't be talked about," Koon warned them. "We were never here. And this never happened." The three policemen nodded gravely.

It was another close call.

Edwards had hurried to leave the airport that afternoon because he was expecting an important call from Eddie DeBartolo. Since the football owner had first contacted him in the summer of 1996 for help in winning the fifteenth and final riverboat license, the relationship between the two had deepened. DeBartolo invited Edwards to his wife's fiftieth birthday party in Las Vegas that summer, and in November Candy DeBartolo asked Edwards to act as the decoy for Eddie's surprise fiftieth birthday party in New Orleans. While the party guests secretly assembled, Edwards ferried DeBartolo in a limousine to various riverboat casinos in the New Orleans metro area. The final site they visited was the River City terminal on the Mississippi River that developer Christopher Hemmeter had built, and that was still vacant two years after two riverboat casinos, one owned by Hemmeter, had gone bankrupt. It was there that the guests—including the retired 49ers superstar quarterback Joe Montana—had gathered for DeBartolo's surprise party.

Throughout the latter part of 1996 and the early part of 1997, DeBartolo became increasingly impressed with Edwards's political influence, even though Edwards was out of office. For one thing, as Edwards told DeBartolo in one of their many conversations taped by the FBI, one of the state gambling board's members—in violation of the board's rules—was giving him insight into the board's deliberations. Edwards also displayed his influence in late February 1997 when DeBartolo called to ask if he could get a copy of the board's "executive summary." This document, prepared by the Louisiana State Police, outlined the pros and cons for each of the five bidders and was confidential. Only board members were supposed to have it. Yet a day after DeBartolo's call, Edwards FedExed a copy to him.

On that day that Pat Graham—actually the FBI—had flown Edwards home to Baton Rouge, DeBartolo called the former governor shortly before 6:00 p.m. DeBartolo was flying to Baton Rouge that evening because DeBartolo Entertainment and its partner, Hollywood Casino, were scheduled the following day to make a presentation before the gambling board in their joint bid for the fifteenth riverboat license. They were proposing to spend $194 million to build a 170-acre casino, resort, and shopping center on the banks of the Red River in Bossier City. The other four bidders also were scheduled to make their presentations that day, with the board selecting the winner in eight days.

"How's your time schedule?" DeBartolo asked Edwards during the phone call. Edwards replied that he would like to meet DeBartolo that evening at the Baton Rouge Radisson Hotel, where the owner of the 49ers would be staying.

"I'll go by the Radisson between 9:00 and 9:30," Edwards said.

Edwards found DeBartolo sitting in the hotel's Patio Grille and Lounge with several men from the DeBartolo Entertainment/Hollywood Casino team. Edwards was introduced around the table and then tugged on DeBartolo's elbow. The would-be casino owner excused himself and suggested that the others eat dinner next door at Ruth's Chris Steak House. As the others left, Edwards guided the 49ers' owner to a secluded table. DeBartolo ordered a drink. Edwards, a teetotaler, asked for iced tea. The two men talked for a few minutes about their chances of getting the riverboat license. Edwards expressed optimism, which DeBartolo found heartening. The former governor then said he wanted a 1 percent share of the casino's profits for his help with the licensing process. In the meantime, he expected a nice down payment. Edwards reached into his pocket and slid a piece of paper to DeBartolo. On it was written a single figure: $400,000. "This has to be taken care of by next week or there is going to be a serious problem with your license application," Edwards said.

"I'll take care of it," DeBartolo replied.

Later that evening, when Ed Muransky, president of DeBartolo Entertainment, returned to the hotel from dinner at Ruth's Chris, he noted that DeBartolo was upset. Muransky, a hulking former defensive lineman for the Oakland Raiders, saw one of his roles as protecting DeBartolo from unsavory characters. Like former 49ers head coach Bill Walsh, Muransky had discovered that DeBartolo didn't always choose his associates wisely. Muransky had been suspicious of Edwin Edwards ever since Edwards's condolence call to Eddie after DeBartolo Sr. died in 1994. Edwards had paid his respects and then mentioned to Eddie that the old man had promised Edwards a job after he left politics. When Eddie related the story to Muransky, he expressed gratitude that Edwards, then governor, had taken the time to call. Muransky had a different reaction, thinking it inappropriate for Edwards to mention the job promise while DeBartolo was grieving.

Since then, Muransky noted, the former governor had tried to get his son Stephen a $50,000-per-month consulting contract with DeBartolo Entertainment and had even asked DeBartolo for a share of the riverboat casino's profits without having to invest any cash in the project. Each time, Muransky had persuaded DeBartolo to reject Edwards's request. Jack Pratt, chairman of Hollywood Casino, also had warned DeBartolo against doing business with Edwards, saying the former governor's involvement, if it became known publicly, would taint their bid.

After returning to the Radisson from dinner, Muransky asked DeBartolo why he was upset. DeBartolo told him about the exchange with Edwards. Muransky blew up. For several minutes, he raged against Edwards, saying that DeBartolo Entertainment and Hollywood Casino were on the verge of getting the fifteenth license. DeBartolo said he was afraid that Edwards would use his influence to sink their bid if he wasn't paid the $400,000. Muransky emphasized again that they had the best bid and shouldn't make the payment to Edwards. DeBartolo ended up saying he agreed with Muransky and assured him that he wouldn't pay Edwards anything.

On March 8, three days later, Edwards called Ralph Perlman, who had served as budget chief while Edwards was governor and who was now one of the six members of the state's casino licensing board. When Edwards told DeBartolo over the previous few weeks that he had held conversations with a board member, he had been referring to Perlman. Now, five days before the board would vote, Edwards wanted to get a final assurance on where the DeBartolo Entertainment/Hollywood Casino bid stood. The FBI's wiretap on Edwards's home phone captured the conversation. "Without violating any confidences, should we be encouraged?" asked Edwards.

"Yes," replied Perlman. "Yes, you should be encouraged, but it's not gonna be easy."

On March 11, DeBartolo told Muransky that Edwards was flying from Vail to San Francisco the following day to meet the owner of the 49ers for lunch. DeBartolo told his chief adviser that he would be making a $400,000 payment to Edwards. Muransky once again raged, telling DeBartolo that they shouldn't pay Edwards anything. DeBartolo dismissed Muransky's complaints, saying that the payment had nothing to do with the fifteenth riverboat license. Muransky questioned this statement, but DeBartolo told him to mind his own business. Muransky gave up and walked off, still fuming.

On March 12, DeBartolo picked up Edwards at San Francisco International Airport and drove him to Max's Opera Café, five minutes away. In preparation for their meeting, DeBartolo had his secretary at the 49ers office convert $400,000 of checks into $100 bills and then put the cash into a leather briefcase. During their lunch, DeBartolo told Edwards that he had the cash in the briefcase in the trunk. But he questioned whether Edwards could pass through the airport X-ray machine undetected when he returned to Vail that day. "How do you plan on moving this money through the airport?" DeBartolo asked. "It's in a briefcase. That's a red flag."

"That's not a problem," Edwards responded. Already dressed in bulky clothes, Edwards opened his thick plaid shirt and showed DeBartolo a chest-high, double-layered money vest. The former governor would hide the cash there.

During lunch, they talked mostly about the gambling board's vote the following day. Edwards said he thought that the vote would be 3–3 or possibly 4–2 in their favor, but added that he would make last-minute calls to help their cause.

When they walked back to DeBartolo's car after lunch, DeBartolo opened the trunk, retrieved the briefcase, and placed it behind Edwards's seat. He drove to the airport. When they got there, Edwards pulled out the briefcase, they said goodbye to each other, and then the former governor disappeared into the airport terminal with the $400,000 still in the briefcase.

The gambling board met the following day in an oak-paneled conference room at the State Capitol to award the fifteenth license. Representatives of the five casino companies were there, as was Stephen Edwards. Jenifer Schaye, the board's attorney, noted his presence with concern, not knowing he had been involved with any of the five bidders.

She reflected that it was a big day for the new gambling board because it would be its first major decision. Governor Mike Foster had promised that his gambling board would be free of the taint associated with Edwards's two casino boards. So when Schaye informed the new board's chairman, Hillary Crain, that Stephen Edwards was in the audience, Crain expressed dismay and made a point of announcing prior to the vote, "We want the word to go forth to this industry that you do business straight up in this state. Connections make absolutely no difference."

DeBartolo was having his hair cut when Edwards called a few minutes later with news of the board's decision. It was 6–0 in favor of DeBartolo Entertainment/Hollywood Casino. The 49ers owner cried tears of joy. With this gambling venture, Eddie DeBartolo Jr. could now step out of his father's shadow and prove to the world that he was a success in his own right.

Of course, connections still mattered, even with Governor Foster's gambling board. Edwards had a direct line into Ralph Perlman, his former budget director. He also had a line into board member Ecotry Fuller through state senator Greg Tarver, a longtime Edwards ally who had gotten Foster to appoint Fuller to his position. The FBI wiretaps disclosed that Edwards in late February 1997 had turned to Tarver to get a copy of the executive summary requested by DeBartolo. Edwards believed that he had a line into a third board member, Sherian Cadoria, through Cleo Fields, one of Louisiana's most powerful black politicians.

Fields, a Democrat from Baton Rouge, was first elected to the State Senate in 1988. A passionate advocate of liberal causes, Fields's choirboy looks—he appeared barely old enough to vote—belied a crafty political mind. In 1992, he was elected to Congress. In 1995, he ran for governor. In the primary, he finished ahead of state treasurer Mary Landrieu and former governor Buddy Roemer to make the runoff against then–state senator Mike Foster. In a racially divided state, where blacks made up only about 30 percent of the electorate, Fields had little chance against Foster, losing 64 percent to 36 percent in the runoff.

In that 1995 governor's race, Fields had spoken out against gambling and refused to take campaign contributions from the gambling industry. But like most Louisiana politicians, he was two-faced. On several occasions, Fields had played a behind-the-scenes role in helping friends involved with gambling. In 1992, he had Edwards appoint a family friend, Sallie Page, to the board that would select the New Orleans casino operator. At the time a lowly clerk working for the city of Alexandria, Page had been out of her league on the board and barely spoke at meetings. However, she had been willing to do Fields's bidding when the then-congressman met secretly with her in August 1993, on the night before the board selected the casino operator. Acting at the behest of friends in the Jazzville group, Fields had gotten Page to support the Harrah's Jazz partnership. Her support had proved pivotal. Harrah's Jazz had prevailed on a 5–4 vote.

At Fields's urging, Edwards had also appointed an elderly Baton Rouge doctor, Louis James, to the now-defunct board that in 1993 awarded the state's fifteen riverboat preliminary certificates. James had been clearly out of his league as well because he, too, had rarely contributed to the board's activities. But like Page, he had been susceptible to political influence. In June 1993, the day before the riverboat board had awarded the final seven certificates, Edwards had called James to the Governor's Mansion, handed him a list of the six boats he favored, and asked him to support them. With James's help, all of Edwards's preferred boats had won licenses the following day.

In 1996, just months after losing the governor's race, Fields suffered another defeat. A federal court ruled that his district had been unconstitutionally gerrymandered to elect a black candidate. Fields chose not to run for reelection that November in a white-majority district. By March 1997, Fields no longer held elected office, but he was about to be appointed to a top position in the Clinton administration overseeing the inner-city empowerment-zone program. In the meantime, he had been secretly working with Edwards to help DeBartolo Entertainment/Hollywood Casino get the fifteenth riverboat license.

On March 24, 1997, Fields and Edwards met at the latter's law office at about 11:15 a.m. The FBI wiretap and video camera captured what transpired next. Almost as soon as Fields sat down in the leather chair facing Edwards's desk, the former governor handed the former congressman a thick wad of $100 bills, totaling $20,000. Fields stuffed the cash into his front left pants pocket.

"Those people that I've been talkin' to are kinda playin' games with me," Edwards said, adding that DeBartolo and his people hadn't paid him everything he was owed. "So they wanna wait until after the election."

Edwards went on to say that "this man is claiming credit for that lady"—that is, Senator Tarver was claiming credit for Sherian Cadoria's vote in favor of the DeBartolo Entertainment/Hollywood Casino project. Fields laughed. He had been telling Edwards that *he* was responsible for Cadoria's vote. Edwards then told Fields that Tarver was under investigation by the federal government (for supplier contracts his family had gotten from Shreveport–Bossier City riverboats). "You need to make sure that everybody involved is careful about how that [money] is passed out," Edwards said, "because, as you know, that other guy is under very serious, serious, serious investigation." Geoffrey Santini, Steve Irwin, and Freddy Cleveland, who headed the FBI's public-corruption squad, would later conclude that Fields was supposed to give a portion of the $20,000 to Tarver for influencing his friend on the board, Ecotry Fuller. They concluded that Edwards did not want to give the money directly to Tarver because of the scrutiny Tarver was under.

Fields and Edwards talked a few more minutes. The former congressman then asked, "Have you got an envelope [or] a plain white piece of paper?" Edwards handed over a piece of paper. Fields pulled the stack of money out of his pocket and wrapped it in the paper. After glancing about the room, he put the hastily wrapped money back into his pocket. He and Edwards talked politics for a few minutes before Fields said goodbye and left with the cash.

By the beginning of April 1997, the Feds were nearing the end of their investigation. Santini, Irwin, Cleveland, and the others involved in the case thought that they had more than enough evidence to indict

Edwin Edwards, Stephen Edwards, Cecil Brown, Andrew Martin, Bobby Guidry, Ricky Shetler, Eddie DeBartolo, Cleo Fields, Greg Tarver, and several others on payoffs involving riverboat licensing. To be certain of their case, the Feds wanted to gather at least another month's worth of evidence. On April 7, however, the FBI investigation was once again on the verge of being compromised.

It turned out that one of the three Baton Rouge police officers who had inadvertently found out about the investigation on March 5—as Edwards and Pat Graham flew into Baton Rouge Airport—had not kept his mouth shut. On the evening of March 6, officer Brandon Hyde went drinking with several other policemen. Drinking beer chased by shots of tequila, Hyde told the owner of the Country Tavern about what had happened the day before, adding that he wanted to get word to Edwards. A day later, the bar's owner called Gil Dozier, who had spent four years in prison for exacting kickbacks from dairy processors while serving as Louisiana's elected agriculture commissioner during Edwards's second term. The bar owner relayed to Dozier what Hyde had told him. Dozier, who played poker with Edwards and who had gotten him to restore his citizenship rights during the third term, promised to pass the information on to the former governor.

After getting Hyde to verify the story a few days later, Dozier showed up at Edwards's office on April 7 and laid out the story: The FBI had gotten the United States Customs Service to walk away from his plane on March 5 by telling Hyde and the other officers that FBI pilots were flying the plane and that Edwards was the target of an undercover investigation. Edwards listened to Dozier and then told him that he had it wrong. They're after Pat Graham, not me, he responded. Edwards added that Graham couldn't have been trying to ensnare him, since it was he who had asked Graham for the plane ride, not the other way around. Dozier left, having failed to convince Edwards that he was under investigation.

Still, Edwards's suspicions were aroused enough that two days later he warned Cecil Brown in a phone call to be careful with Graham because he believed that Graham was under FBI investigation. Nervous about Dozier's visit, which had been picked up on the FBI surveillance gear, Santini, Irwin, and Cleveland decided it was now too risky to have Graham give Edwards the planned $1.3 million payoff. Instead, they began making plans to end the investigation. They chose May 13 for the day they would execute search warrants and go public with the case.

On April 24, an Assistant United States Attorney named Sal Perricone was sitting in his downtown New Orleans office when he got a phone call. On the line was Bill Elder, a veteran anchor and news reporter for WWL-TV, the highest-rated New Orleans station. Perricone and Elder had known each other for years. Elder told Perricone he had received word that the Feds were about to execute a search warrant on Edwin Edwards's Baton Rouge home in the gated Country Club of Louisiana. Elder also told Perricone that he would keep this information quiet if the Feds would give him an exclusive to film the raid as it occurred. "I cannot confirm or deny any federal investigation," Perricone said, giving a stock answer.

But Elder's comment shook him up. Aside from a small circle of federal officials, no one was supposed to know anything about the projected raids. Elder next told Perricone that the information came from a reliable source, and then he asked for the exact date they would raid Edwards's home. "If you don't give me this information, Sal, I'm going to park a satellite truck outside of the Country Club of Louisiana until you show up."

"Bill, do what you have to do," replied Perricone, trying to make sure that his voice did not betray any emotions. After they hung up, Perricone thought to himself, "We definitely have a leak."

Steve Irwin, who from the beginning had quarterbacked the investigation for the United States Attorney's office in New Orleans, was giving a speech on the Mississippi Gulf Coast when he got a 911 page a few minutes later. He hurried through his presentation, phoned his office, and learned about the Elder call. Irwin jumped into his car and raced back to New Orleans.

Meanwhile, Jim DeSarno, who headed the FBI's New Orleans office, had decided how to respond to Elder's demand. "No news person is holding me hostage," DeSarno told Santini. "We're shutting this thing down." To avoid taking a chance that word would leak from Elder or anyone else to Edwards, the Feds would execute the search warrants as soon as possible, instead of waiting until May 13 as originally planned. DeSarno briefed FBI director Louis Freeh, who gave the go-ahead.

First, the Feds had to prepare the search warrants, and since there would be eleven of them, that was no simple task. Irwin began writing the search warrants several hours after Elder's call, and he worked late into the night. Geoffrey Santini, who had led the investigation for the FBI, joined him early the next morning, a Friday. They worked through another night and were done by noon on Saturday. Now they needed Judges Parker and Walter to review and sign the warrants. That presented a problem. Parker was attending a granddaughter's dance recital in Manhattan, while Walter was visiting relatives in the southwest Louisiana town of Jennings.

With the search warrants in hand, Santini and Irwin arranged to meet Judge Parker in New York City. Dead tired after thirty hours without sleep, they dozed on the plane. Upon arrival, they failed to connect with the FBI agent who was supposed to take them to Parker's hotel, a block from Central Park. Irwin bumped into a friend, who gave them a lift into Manhattan. By the time they arrived at the hotel, however, Parker had left for the dance recital. Irwin and Santini walked to Central Park, sat down on a bench, and took catnaps until the judge was available. He returned to the hotel late in the afternoon, carefully reviewed the search warrants, and signed them. Irwin and Santini caught a plane back to New Orleans, arriving at 2:00 a.m.

Each man drove home, took a shower, and put on a fresh set of clothes. They then set out together by car for Jennings, to meet with Judge Walter. On the way, they encountered more misfortune, this time in the form of a torrential rainstorm that made driving difficult for the exhausted men. After about a three-hour drive, they arrived at the Piggly Wiggly supermarket in Jennings. Walter had told them to call him from there. When Irwin got the judge on the phone, Walter tried to explain how to get to his relatives' house. The directions were so complicated that he gave up and said he would meet them in the Piggly Wiggly parking lot, where, dressed in a T-shirt and shorts, Walter took a couple of hours to review the documents before signing them. Santini and Irwin thanked the judge and then drove back to New Orleans. In the meantime, Jim DeSarno and Freddy Cleveland had arranged to have several dozen agents from other FBI offices come to New Orleans. By now, it was late Sunday afternoon. In less than twenty-four hours, the FBI would go public with the most sweeping criminal raid in the modern history of Louisiana politics.

The FBI would serve the search warrants on Monday morning at 9:00 a.m. at eleven different locations: the home and office of Edwards, the home of Stephen Edwards, the office of Bobby Guidry, the office of Ricky Shetler in Lake Charles, the home and office of Cecil Brown in Eunice, the office of Brown's lawyer in Eunice, the office of the Evergreen waste-disposal company in Texas, the office of former Houston mayor Fred Hofheinz, and the office of the Louisiana prison system in Baton Rouge.

Cleveland chose a low-key agent of twenty-five years named John Fleming to serve the subpoena on Edwin Edwards, along with another veteran agent, Bob Nelson. Edwards and Candy had gone to their condo in the Alabama Gulf Coast town of Orange Beach. Cleveland gave one instruction to Fleming: "Try to interview him. Maybe he'll say something."

"Right," replied Fleming sarcastically. He then predicted, "He's gonna slam the door in our face."

Fleming and Nelson drove to Orange Beach that evening. Upon arriving, they made a reconnaissance trip to find the Edwardses' condo, which was located on the fourteenth floor of the Phoenix complex, overlooking the gulf. The two agents were surprised to find that they could get to the former governor's condo without having to pass through any locked doors. Before leaving the area, they took note of Edwards's vehicle, with the EWE000 vanity plate.

Monday morning, April 28, 1997, was a typical sultry day on the Gulf Coast, with a light breeze off the water. At about 8:40 a.m., Fleming and Nelson, wearing suits and ties, left their beach motel and made the short drive to the Edwardses' condo. It was 9:00 a.m. sharp when they knocked on the door. Edwards answered. Casually dressed, he had just shaved and showered, and his hair was mussed up. "Mr. Edwards, FBI," Fleming said. "We have some papers to serve on you." To Fleming's surprise, Edwards invited them inside to take a seat at the dining room table. Edwards then excused himself briefly to tell Candy that they were there. When he returned, he sat down and reviewed a subpoena for him to appear before a federal grand jury. Again surprising Fleming, Edwards didn't express much concern. "What's this about?" he asked casually.

"Governor," Fleming said, "at this moment your office and your home in Baton Rouge are being searched, pursuant to a federal search warrant. They're going to want to get into the safe in your home. To make it easier for everyone, could you please furnish me with the combo or call someone who can open it? If necessary, they'll crack open the safe."

Edwards immediately pulled out his cellular phone and called his brother Marion. It turned out that Marion was at the Baton Rouge law office and was agitated because it was crawling with FBI agents. During a brief conversation, Edwards told his brother that FBI agents were at the condo, too, and that Marion needed to head over to his home immediately and open the safe; Edwards gave him the combo number. Fleming then read Edwards his rights. "Would you mind answering a few questions?" Fleming asked next. Edwards said he didn't mind, so for the next ten minutes he sat patiently answering Fleming's questions as the veteran agent took notes.

Fleming told Edwards that he also had a subpoena to serve on Stephen and asked the former governor if he would notify his son. Stephen, as it happened, was staying at another condo about a mile away. Edwards telephoned his son and asked him to come over immediately. While they were waiting, Fleming mentioned that he had relatives in Acadia Parish who had been long-standing Edwards supporters. When he mentioned their names, Edwards's face brightened, and he asked Fleming to send his regards to them. Edwards's friendliness and composure astounded the veteran FBI agent.

When Stephen arrived, he sat down at the table with his father, Fleming, and Agent Nelson. Fleming explained their purpose. Stephen

Edwards began swearing, and when Fleming asked if he would answer any questions, Stephen emphatically said no, then departed.

As Fleming and Nelson stood up to leave, Edwards said, "You know, I'm used to having the FBI knock on my door." Edwards then listed how many times FBI agents had interviewed him over the years, and how many times he had appeared before grand juries. He went on to say, "I've learned that when one FBI agent knocks on your door, that's one thing. But when two knock on your door, that's trouble."

"Governor," Fleming responded, "this is trouble."

He and Nelson shook hands with Edwards and left. A half hour later, they spotted Edwards and Candy racing back to Baton Rouge.

A Minimum Amount of High Respect

icture the typical politician facing a criminal indictment that could ruin his career. He's hunkered down in his office, hiding out from the press, worry lines etched in his face.

In February 1998, ten months after the FBI had raided his home and office and revealed that agents had been recording many of his conversations, Edwin Edwards was sitting in his lawyer's office in Baton Rouge. Casually dressed in a brown sport jacket and a brown checked shirt and slacks, he was not alone, and he didn't seem worried. In fact, he was swapping jokes with reporters about President Clinton's sexual indiscretion with Monica Lewinsky. "Did you hear about the poll they took in Washington?" he asked the reporters. "A thousand women. They were asked in view of all the recent revelations whether they would consider having sex with Clinton. Eighty-two percent said not again."

The reporters laughed. Edwards smiled and, the traces of his Cajun accent suddenly a little more marked, told another joke. "Do you know why Clinton wears fur-lined shorts? To keep his ankles warm."

A day later, Edwards was tossing off one-liners about the recent disclosure that he and his wife, Candy, hoped to have a baby. Seizing the moment, the Louisiana Oystermen's Association had talked him into doing a promo that played off the oyster's reputation as an aphrodisiac. "I don't want to eat too many of these things, I'd end up with triplets," Edwards said, eyeing a plate of them on the half shell.

Later that same week, he invited a reporter to join Candy and him for lunch at Ruth's Chris Steak House in Baton Rouge, much favored by politicians and lobbyists. Heads turned and people murmured as Edwards walked to his table with Candy, who with her blond hair and candy-red lipstick was a magnet for appreciative stares even without the famous ex-governor at her side. After they sat down, a judge, a public-service commissioner, lawyers, and others came by to shake Edwards's hand and wish him luck in his battle with the federal government.

Over lunch, Edwards was eager to discuss the case and his impending indictment on gambling-centered extortion and racketeering charges. He said that he had had no inkling of the investigation when the two FBI agents visited his Gulf Coast condo in April 1997 to deliver a subpoena to appear before a grand jury. "I never dreamed they were in the process of raiding my house and my office," Edwards recalled, spearing a piece of asparagus with his fork. "I was certainly not aware that my phones were tapped and my house was bugged and my office was bugged. I had no idea." When the agents handed him the subpoena, he said, he flashed back to Gil Dozier telling him about the Customs Service searching for drugs on the plane the FBI had used to pilot him and Pat Graham to Baton Rouge. Edwards said he thought Graham, the Texas con man, had convinced the FBI that they were dealing drugs together. It was only after seeing the names on the subpoena, which required the former governor to furnish documents for any dealings he had had with 178 people—and later reading the news leaks about the Feds' areas of interest—that Edwards realized the investigation centered on casino licensing.

At one point during lunch, a waitress handed him a note on folded brown paper. It told him that "Ernie" would win a bet and pay him $10,000 if he would come over to Ernie's table and acknowledge knowing everyone there but a prominent attorney named Bob Wright, whom Edwards did know. A few minutes later, Edwards ambled over. Leaning on Wright's chair, he began chatting amiably with everyone at the table but Wright. He finally turned to Wright and asked him who he was. Wright's jaw dropped. "Where are you from?" Edwards asked, adding insult to injury. The other three men at the table burst out laughing. Ernie told Wright about the note and told him he had lost their bet. "You don't have to pay me $10,000," Edwards told Ernie. "I'll settle for 10 percent." The table broke out in laughter once again. "I'll send it to you in cash," Ernie responded, provoking more laughter.

As he was about to leave the table, Edwards couldn't resist another Clinton joke. "You know what the new game in Washington is? Swallow the leader."

While Edwards kept up his public image as a wisecracking smoothie, the investigation deeply concerned him—not only because of what the Feds had on him, but because of the evidence they had gathered against his son Stephen. Even before either was indicted, Edwards authorized his attorney, Mike Fawer, to begin plea negotiations with the United States Attorney, Eddie Jordan Jr.

Jordan had grown up in New Orleans, where his father worked as a sculptor and art professor. During Edwards's 1985–1986 trials, Jordan had served as an Assistant United States Attorney, prosecuting drug dealers and postal thieves. He had been working for a small corporate law firm when President Clinton appointed him to his powerful position in 1994, at the behest of Congressman Bill Jefferson, who had been a partner in the firm. Then forty-one, Jordan was the first African American to serve as a United States Attorney in Louisiana.

Always bookish, Jordan acted cautiously and had a conservative manner. A *Times-Picayune* profile described him as "mild-mannered, soft-spoken and reserved to the point of woodenness. Even in a relaxed social setting, Jordan speaks in a deliberate monotone, as if reading from a script. His receding hairline, wire-frame glasses and conservative suits match his bookish personality. Only his oversized mustache makes him stand out in a crowd."

On November 20, 1997, Edwards and Fawer secretly met with Jordan and several other federal law enforcement officials at New Orleans's

Hotel Inter-Continental. During the meeting, Fawer offered to have Edwards plead guilty to a single offense—extorting $400,000 from DeBartolo in 1997—and receive a sentence of eighteen months. In return, Edwards would not have to testify against anyone else or admit to committing any crimes during his final term in office. In addition, Stephen would not be charged.

After the meeting, Jordan told his assistants that he wanted to accept the deal. It would achieve what he thought was the most important goal: putting Edwards in prison, if only for a short period of time. After all, no one could guarantee that a jury would convict the charismatic former governor. But Steve Irwin, the lead prosecutor on the case, forcefully opposed the deal. Given the volume of tapes and other evidence amassed by the FBI, he was convinced they had more than enough to convict Edwards. "This is bullshit!" he told Jordan in a heated conversation in the United States Attorney's office.

Freddy Cleveland and Geoffrey Santini, the two lead FBI agents on the case, also strongly opposed a deal. With intimate knowledge of their evidence, they argued that Jordan was proposing to let the former governor off too easily. Charles Mathews III, who headed the FBI's New Orleans office, agreed with his agents. Within a day of the Hotel Inter-Continental meeting, Mathews took the unusual step of spelling out the Bureau's concerns in a letter to Jordan, with copies to senior FBI and Department of Justice officials in Washington. The letter packed a punch. Rarely did the FBI put in writing its differences with a United States Attorney. Confronted with Mathews's objections, Jordan backed off, and the plea negotiations with Edwards ended. Afterward, Jordan showed no hesitation in pressing forward with the prosecution of Edwards.

During this same period, Jordan was putting himself at odds with his law enforcement associates on another highly sensitive matter: whether to indict Cleo Fields, who had lost the 1995 governor's race to Mike Foster while in Congress and was now back in the Louisiana State Senate. Along with Congressman Jefferson of New Orleans, Fields was considered by political observers to be one of Louisiana's two most powerful black politicians. Most of the federal officials working the Edwards case considered Fields to be corrupt.

On March 24, 1997, the video camera above the desk in Edwards's law office had captured Fields stuffing into his pocket a thick wad of $100 bills—totaling $20,000—that the former governor had just handed him. Freddy Cleveland, Geoffrey Santini, Steve Irwin, and the other Feds thought that Edwards had given Fields the cash to pay off a member of the gambling board to help secure the fifteenth and final riverboat license for DeBartolo Entertainment/Hollywood Casino. This videotape was enough to prompt the Clinton administration to withdraw a top White House job that Fields had accepted. Santini, Cleveland, Irwin, and others involved in the Edwards case wanted to see Fields indicted.

With a lawyer at his side, Fields met with two FBI agents in an attempt to head them off, but clammed up after only a few minutes of questioning. He and his lawyer then went straight to Jordan, who was more receptive. After the meeting, Jordan told his assistant prosecutors that he didn't think they had grounds to indict Fields. Practically all of them disagreed. When Fields appeared before a federal grand jury, he took the Fifth Amendment, bolstering their case.

In a later meeting, Freddy Cleveland repeatedly pressed Jordan to change his mind, arguing that if they didn't indict Fields, they wouldn't convince a jury to convict state senator Greg Tarver of Shreveport, who was also under investigation for helping Edwards improperly influence the gambling board. Because the case against Tarver hinged on the argument that Edwards had passed money to him through Fields, not indicting Fields would leave a missing link. "Cleo's the guy on tape who got the money," Cleveland told Jordan. Besides, he added, "if we don't indict this guy now, we'll be working him for the next twenty years." Less diplomatic, Steve Irwin blew a gasket in a separate meeting, screaming at his boss that they had to indict Fields. Jordan was unmoved, but he did remove Irwin from the case within three weeks.

Jim DeSarno, who preceded Mathews as head of the FBI office during the Edwards investigation, would later say of the decision not to indict Fields, "I think Eddie Jordan let him off the hook."

Privately, Irwin assumed that Cleo Fields had a political patron who kept Jordan from indicting him. Later, after Fields's brush with indictment became public, critics would say that Jordan was protecting Fields's political career. Jordan would reply simply that he was not sure why Edwards had paid Fields the cash.

On October 6, 1998, Jordan fortified the prosecution's case when Eddie DeBartolo Jr. pleaded guilty to failing to report that Edwards had extorted money from him in exchange for his helping to secure the fifteenth riverboat license. For his guilty plea and willingness to cooperate with authorities, DeBartolo got a light sentence: two years of probation and a $250,000 fine. But his involvement with Edwards had been costly, forcing him out of the planned riverboat deal and killing his dream of someday becoming a gambling magnate. He also had to relinquish control of his beloved 49ers to his only sibling, Denise DeBartolo York, his sister, who was already estranged from DeBartolo over his illegal activities in Louisiana.

On October 9, three days after DeBartolo caved, Ricky Shetler, Stephen Edwards's best friend, became the second major player to plead guilty. Shetler, the owner of a Lake Charles pizzeria, had parlayed his friendship with Stephen into a high-paying consultant's job with the Players floating casino in Lake Charles. Shetler admitted to paying $550,000 in cash and goods to Stephen and Edwin Edwards in return for their help in securing a license for Players and thwarting potential competitors after the boat had opened. Shetler's attorney predicted that his client would receive a reduced sentence of two and a half to three years in prison in exchange for his testimony.

On October 16, it was Bobby Guidry's turn. Guidry had finessed his friendship with Edwards's executive assistant, Andrew Martin, into a license to operate the *Treasure Chest* casino in Kenner. Until a week before, Edwards and his associates had not expected Guidry to cut a deal with federal prosecutors. "Bobby Guidry ain't gonna break," Edwards's close friend Bob d'Hemecourt had predicted in early 1998. But through the wiretaps, the Feds had too much incriminating evidence on Guidry, enough to threaten to indict his children and confiscate the $80 million he had earned by selling the *Treasure Chest*. Guidry admitted to cutting a deal with Edwards during his final term: Guidry would make payoffs to him, Martin, and Stephen Edwards in return for their help in securing Guidry a license. Beginning in February 1996, one month after Edwards stepped down, Guidry began delivering $100,000 per month to Martin, who split the cash with the Edwardses. In return for his plea, Guidry agreed to pay $3.5 million in fines, forfeitures, and restitution, and he faced up to five years in prison, depending on how useful he proved to the prosecution of Edwards. Afterward, outside the courthouse, Guidry told reporters, "We're not gonna answer no questions. I apologize to my family and friends that I let myself get into a situation where I got involved in a crime."

With the guilty pleas and promises of testimony from three of Edwards's former associates, prosecutors were finally ready to move against the former governor. On November 6, 1998, more than eighteen months after the FBI had raided his home and office, a federal grand jury indicted Edwin Edwards on twenty-eight counts of engaging in an organized conspiracy to extort $3 million from riverboat-casino companies both during and after his final term as governor. If convicted on all counts, Edwards would face 350 years in prison and more than $10 million in fines and forfeitures. Wearing a conservative dark-blue suit, Edwards appeared at the Baton Rouge federal courthouse, where he conducted a series of rambling interviews that began even before the conclusion of a brief hearing finalizing the indictments. "I can truthfully say if my sentence is 350 years, I don't intend to serve," Edwards joked. The impromptu press conference ended up spilling into the street, blocking downtown midday traffic. The ex-governor turned serious when discussing DeBartolo, Shetler, and Guidry and their decision to testify against him. "I have a minimum amount of high respect for them," Edwards said. "They got scared. The guys that plead guilty are the guys who made the money. These people couldn't take the pressure." At the trial, Edwards vowed, he would prove that payments from casino owners were for legitimate legal or lobbying services.

In his comments to reporters, Eddie Jordan made it clear that he saw Edwards's indictment as taking dead aim at the Louisiana Way, the ingrained practice of using public office for private gain. "We do this in hopes that one day, Louisiana will be an open, attractive and free market to those people and companies who seek to do business in an environment free of extortion and fraud," said Jordan, sporting an elegant Homburg for the occasion. "The indictment represents a landmark in not only our initiative committed to the eradication of public corruption in Louisiana, but also serves as a landmark in this state's history."

C. B. Forgotston, who had been the lead lobbyist opposing the New Orleans land casino and who had become Louisiana's most outspoken gambling foe, proclaimed: "This is showing that gambling has brought terminal political corruption to Louisiana. And these indictments are an indication that the corruption is way beyond the magnitude that anybody expected."

Also indicted on the same day as Edwards were five others:

- Stephen Edwards, forty-four, the former governor's elder son and a Baton Rouge lawyer. Stephen had cashed in after his father took office for a fourth term in January 1992, earning at least $683,000 over the next five years as an attorney and consultant for five riverboat casinos, all with ties to his father. In some cases, Stephen could provide no documentation that he had actually done any work for the money. When news of his lucrative legal contracts broke in 1994, he had told a group of people privately, "If y'all think I'm walking away from $1 million a year because my old man is governor, you're fucking crazy. I didn't tell the son of a bitch to run." At one point in 1994, the state ethics board had ruled that Stephen could not continue to represent the boats, since they were regulated by entities overseen by his father. But thanks to a favorable advisory opinion by a State Police attorney friendly to Edwards, Stephen was allowed to continue his legal work for the boats. He stood to make millions of dollars in additional legal payments until news of the FBI investigation became public, and he lost his contracts.

- Andrew Martin, sixty-two, Edwards's executive assistant during the final term. Raised alongside a bayou in Lafourche Parish, Martin struck it rich during the oil boom of the 1960s and 1970s, acquiring offshore-drilling rigs, a seafood plant, and a restaurant. Martin also played politics, contributing generously to Edwards's 1971 race for governor. Edwards rewarded him with a plum patronage job as chairman of the state mineral board, which leased drilling rights on state land to oil companies. Martin was flying so high he even became a part-owner of the New Orleans Jazz, an NBA franchise that eventually moved to Utah. Martin was overextended when the Oil Bust hit in the mid-1980s. Like many other Louisianians, his fortune disappeared, and he dropped from public view. So he was more than happy to sign on for Edwards's fourth term, beginning in 1992.

- Cecil Brown, an old friend of Edwards's. A onetime professional rodeo cowboy, Brown, fifty-five, sold cattle out of the Acadian town of Eunice, in southwest Louisiana. A natural storyteller, he often accompanied Edwards on gambling junkets to Las Vegas, although his role was to provide entertainment, since he didn't like to gamble. Lanky and with a rakish mustache, Brown would wear cowboy boots and blue jeans to the trial each day.

- Bobby Johnson, another friend of Edwards's. A seventh-grade dropout, Johnson, fifty-four, could neither read nor write. But he earned a small fortune in the construction business in Baton Rouge. The burly Johnson had health problems and would undergo open-heart surgery during the trial.

- State senator Greg Tarver, fifty-three, a Democrat from Shreveport. Arrested fourteen times during the civil rights movement, Tarver and two others in 1978 became the first African Americans elected to the Caddo Parish governing board, known as a police jury. Five years later, he was elected to the State Senate and ran unopposed in succeeding elections. To an unsophisticated observer of Louisiana politics, Tarver appeared to be an ineffective lawmaker because he rarely filed any bills. But he exercised considerable power behind the scenes and was particularly adept at adding a few key words to change the substance of a bill or secure a pork barrel project for his district. A man of slippery ethics who was shot and nearly killed by his second wife, Tarver nearly always walked in step with Edwards. "Without Edwin Edwards, blacks in this state would still be sweeping floors and waiting tables," Tarver said in a 1985 interview. By trade, Tarver was an undertaker, but his family had done quite well thanks to the riverboat casinos in the Shreveport–Bossier City area. In the previous four years, Tarver's third wife, Velma Jean Kinsey-Tarver, had sold $599,000 worth of office supplies to three riverboat casinos. A sister of Tarver's was among the owners of a food distribution company that made at least $1 million in 1995 from contracts with the boats. His brother Leon earned $136,000 as a board member and minority hiring coordinator for the *Casino Rouge* riverboat in Baton Rouge. "If you don't help your friends, who are you going to help, your enemies?" Tarver once asked. He added, "If I did not help to make black people money, who would? Am I foolish enough to think whites would do that?"

- Ecotry Fuller, sixty-two, a retired school principal from Shreveport who served on the board that awarded the fifteenth and final riverboat license, would be indicted later, making a total of seven defendants. The obese Fuller rarely spoke, but he made the motion to award the license to DeBartolo Entertainment/Hollywood Casino. Fuller owed his appointment to Tarver, who had prevailed upon Governor Mike Foster to appoint his friend.

Prosecutors divided their case into five separate "schemes." Edwards was the common link.

- *Scheme 1:* The Feds alleged that Edwards used his influence to ensure that the *Treasure Chest* got one of the coveted fifteen riverboat licenses, over the objections of Louisiana State Police officials, who were planning to veto boat owner Bobby Guidry because of his ties to New Orleans mobster Frank Caracci, his partner in a video poker company. According to the Feds, in exchange for Edwards's help, Guidry agreed to pay $100,000 per month to be divided among Edwards, his son Stephen, and Martin, after Edwards's term ended in January 1996. Guidry also agreed to give Martin a 2 percent ownership of the boat, according to the Feds. As part of his plea bargain, Guidry would testify against the three.

- *Scheme 2:* The Feds alleged that Cecil Brown, the Eunice cattle auctioneer and Edwards's friend, had extorted $350,000 from a group of midwestern businessmen seeking riverboat licenses to operate in Lake Charles and New Orleans. Brown, the Feds said, passed a portion of the money to Edwards. They also said Brown won the confidence of the businessmen by introducing them to Edwards at a crawfish boil and at a Super Bowl party at the Governor's Mansion. At the latter event, the governor told the casino hopefuls, "Cecil speaks for me." The Feds issued an indictment for this scheme even though the businessmen didn't get a license, on the grounds that Brown and Edwards had nonetheless carried out the extortion.

- *Scheme 3:* The Feds alleged that Ricky Shetler and Edwin and Stephen Edwards extorted $550,000 from operators of the Players floating casino in Lake Charles in exchange for helping secure the boat a license and for later keeping an Indian casino from opening early. Shetler would testify against Edwards and his onetime best friend, Stephen Edwards.

- *Scheme 4:* The Feds alleged that Bobby Johnson, a Baton Rouge contractor who was close to Edwards, had attempted to extort money from Mark Bradley, who was seeking a riverboat license in Baton Rouge for Jazz Enterprises. According to the Feds, Johnson planned to funnel a portion of the money to Edwards and Cecil Brown. But Bradley refused to play along, and Jazz Enterprises got a license anyway. It was the only boat to get a license that didn't have ties to a close Edwards associate. Of the five schemes, this was the only one not developed through wiretapping Brown and the Edwardses. Bradley had approached the FBI in Baton Rouge during the licensing process in 1994 with complaints that Johnson was trying to extort him. He ended up recording numerous conversations with Johnson and would testify during the trial.

- *Scheme 5:* The Feds alleged that Edwards extorted $400,000 from Eddie DeBartolo Jr. in March 1997, getting the payoff on the day before the gambling board awarded the fifteenth riverboat license to DeBartolo Entertainment/Hollywood Casino. As part of this scheme, the prosecutors alleged that in February 1997, Edwards got Senator Tarver to call in a favor from Ecotry Fuller and give him a copy of the confidential "executive summary" sought by DeBartolo. The summary, written by the board staff, assessed the strengths and weaknesses of each riverboat bidder. Tarver, the prosecutors said, passed along the summary to Edwards, who FedExed it to DeBartolo. The former 49ers owner would testify against Edwards and the others.

Not included in the indictment was the deal to get the state's permission to open the juvenile prison in the central Louisiana town of Jena, which had been the Feds' original target when they began their investigation of the former governor in April 1996. Indicting Edwards for Jena would have required federal prosecutors to rely on Patrick and Michael Graham as witnesses. The Feds preferred to keep the two con men out of the case. Besides, the Grahams, especially Patrick, had served their purpose already by giving prosecutors one final chance to catch the elusive Edwards.

The indictments were cumulative, the five schemes in many respects were interrelated, and the evidence in support of them, much of it on tape, was overwhelming. And yet, as the trial date approached, few outside observers expressed confidence that federal prosecutors would prevail against the conniving and charismatic Edwin Edwards.

The $64,000 Question

Would Edwin Edwards cut a deal and plead guilty? The question lingered in people's minds in the weeks leading up to the trial. Buddy Roemer, who had known Edwards since working for his campaign during the 1971 governor's race, handicapped his prospects this way: "There's nobody better at assessing his chances. He knows the difference between his intent and what they have. He will weigh the odds coldly and clearly. If they're stacked against him, he'll try to cut a deal. If they're within the margin of error—50/50 or 60/40—he'll take his chances with the people. He's got a good head with numbers."

In fact, Edwards would be taking his chances with a jury. He had not sought a plea deal since the secret negotiations with federal prosecutors had collapsed in late 1997.

"The guy on the street doesn't think Edwards can ever be convicted," offered Roemer. "And nothing has ever stuck on Edwards before. But I think something will stick here. I have a feeling that this time he's in trouble. There's the son's involvement, the cameras and the eavesdropping. There are the tapes playing over and over again, and the partners turning state's evidence."

But Roemer's was a minority view. "I wouldn't predict the outcome, especially when Edwin Edwards is on trial," said John Volz, the United States Attorney who tried but failed to convict Edwards in the 1985–1986 trials. "He is a unique individual. He has a constituency in this state that wouldn't convict him no matter what the government proves."

Indeed, in the days before the trial got under way, Edwards expressed great confidence that once again he would triumph over the Feds. "Everything we have learned and discovered since they raided our office has been neutral or positive for us," Edwards said in one interview, wearing blue jeans and a blue sweatshirt and sitting comfortably on his living room couch. "I had some concerns for a while until I knew what other people had said. I'm very, very buoyant and feel comfortable. There's nothing on the tapes that is very damaging or that can't be explained."

Exactly how confident was he? Edwards smiled and said, "If you get a chance to bet on the outcome of the case, let me know, and I'll put up the money. Bet that there will be no conviction."

Daniel Small became Edwards's lawyer three months before the trial began, and soon gained an appreciation for the former governor's continuing magic with the public. Small, a former federal prosecutor, had a mustache and wore his shaggy black hair parted in the middle. He practiced law in Boston and knew of Edwards's powerful hold on voters only by reputation when one day, shortly before the trial began, he joined Edwards for lunch at Picadilly's Cafeteria, a buffet-style restaurant in Baton Rouge. As soon as they sat down, Small was amazed to see people coming over from all directions to pay homage to his client. "Governor, we love you," said one person. "We're with you," said a second. "You'll beat it," said a third. On and on it went. The intensity of support impressed Small, who also noted that those greeting Edwards were young, old, black, white, male, female. As Edwards's lawyer, he thought the cross-section of support boded well come jury selection.

While it buoyed Dan Small, this popular support concerned Jim Letten, who served as Eddie Jordan's top assistant and was the lead prosecutor in the case. Letten, a forty-six-year-old New Orleans native, had been an altar boy, but became contemptuous of authority at his Catholic high school. At the University of New Orleans, he majored in journalism, played drums in a rock band, and wore shoulder-length hair. While at Tulane Law School, Letten enjoyed New Orleans night life so much that he graduated second from last in his class. He quickly settled down as a lawyer, working as an assistant prosecutor for Orleans Parish District Attorney Harry Connick Sr. In 1986, he was hired by the United States Attorney's office, where he specialized in organized-crime prosecutions. In 1994, Jordan made Letten his first assistant.

Letten had always been fascinated by the military, having grown up with his father's stories as a Seabee in World War II. In 1985, Letten had been commissioned into the Naval Reserve as an intelligence officer. He ended up specializing in foreign counterintelligence and rose to the rank of lieutenant commander. Letten wore his blond hair short, had a thick brush mustache, and carried himself with an erect military bearing. In his spare time, he liked to construct plastic German PT boats and U-boats.

Letten feared that despite the prosecution's best efforts, one or two dyed-in-the-wool Edwards supporters would successfully hide their allegiance and land a spot on the jury. Letten and Jordan thought that if they could get an open-minded panel, one that would consider the full weight of their evidence, they could convict the former governor. As they assessed the possible outcomes, Letten and Jordan could not foresee the jury's acquitting Edwards. They thought the worst-case scenario would be a hung jury. Small, while confident, was not quite as optimistic. Notwithstanding the former governor's jaunty remarks, he sensed that conviction was possible.

Federal prosecutors had three advantages over the team that had failed to convict Edwards in 1985 and 1986. First and foremost was the existence of so much evidence on tape. Another was that prosecutors had won their fight to hold the trial in Baton Rouge rather than New Orleans, the site of the earlier trials. Baton Rouge was more conservative, less freewheeling, and not an Edwards stronghold. New Orleans, of course, was the Big Easy and had always backed Edwards. Because

Baton Rouge had a proportionally whiter population, the jury pool would have fewer African Americans. Both the prosecution and the defense recognized that African Americans were overwhelmingly loyal to Edwards, the first governor to openly seek their votes and to bring them into state government, and the man who had vanquished former Ku Klux Klan grand wizard David Duke in the 1991 governor's race.

The third prosecution advantage was that United States District Judge Frank Polozola had been randomly assigned to preside over the case. The forceful judge was widely perceived to be friendly to the prosecution. A catcher on Louisiana State University's 1961 Southeastern Conference championship baseball team, Polozola cemented his pro-prosecution reputation when he rejected a request for leniency from onetime football star Billy Cannon, LSU's only Heisman Trophy winner, after Cannon was convicted of counterfeiting in 1983. Polozola, fifty-seven, had been appointed to the bench by President Jimmy Carter in 1980, but eight years later changed his registration to Republican. A devout Catholic, he mostly avoided the social circuit in Baton Rouge, preferring to devote himself to work, family, and church.

With a stern demeanor and a quick temper, the stocky Polozola was a stickler for insisting that court proceedings follow his rules. His no-nonsense, near-dictatorial manner prompted lawyers to privately dub him "the Ayatollah Polozola." Polozola already had imposed a gag order on the prosecution and the defendants that was keeping Edwards muzzled outside of the courtroom—to the dismay not only of Edwards but of reporters, who missed the juicy sound bites he could be expected to toss off every day. Polozola would command silence in the courtroom. Under his instructions, bailiffs would quickly threaten to oust anyone who maintained a whispered conversation for more than a few seconds.

The trial would take place in a third-floor courtroom in the Russell B. Long Federal Building and United States Courthouse, in downtown Baton Rouge, less than a mile from the State Capitol and the Governor's Mansion, where Edwards had made his mark during sixteen years in office. Eight towering live-oak trees shaded the entrance to the three-story building. Just in front of the courthouse steps, the media had built a two-tiered wooden stand that television cameramen and still photographers would use to capture Edwards's comings and goings each day. A podium in front of the media stand was available when Edwards wanted to make a statement. He would use it infrequently, however, for fear of violating Polozola's strict gag order.

The judge's courtroom had a vaulted ceiling, walnut paneling, eight chandeliers, and red carpeting. At the rear of the courtroom were five rows of wooden benches, divided by a center aisle, for spectators. The first two rows of benches on the left side facing the judge were for the friends, family members, or associates of the prosecution, while the first two rows on the right side were for the defense. The third row on each side was reserved for the press. The fourth and fifth rows were for the public. A hip-high wooden barrier separated the audience from the jury, the attorneys, the defendants, and the judge. The jury box occupied the left side of the courtroom and faced three rectangular tables. The prosecution had the table closest to the jury while the seven defendants and their attorneys occupied the other two. Edwards would typically sit at the middle table, giving him a clear view of the jurors, as they had of him.

The trial of Edwin Washington Edwards began on January 10, 2000. Suffering from a bad case of the flu, Edwards, seventy-two, looked terrible as the trial was gaveled to order. Polozola empaneled a pool of 125 jurors and told them that those selected for the trial would remain anonymous to prevent any potential tampering. Identifying them by number, Polozola began the tedious but crucial task of interviewing the would-be jurors about their opinions on legalized gambling, wiretaps, and Edwards, to weed out those with potential biases. One after another, the jurors revealed their connections, however glancing, to the former governor.

On the trial's second day, Edwards sat through most of the court proceedings with his head in one hand and his eyes closed. Late in the afternoon, pale and gasping for breath he left the courthouse, leaning on Candy and co-defendant Andrew Martin for support. He headed to the hospital, where he was admitted for dehydration, fever, and shortness of breath. Polozola halted the trial. "I don't think we should continue with jury selection without Mr. Edwards present," he said.

A week later, Edwards had recovered well enough for jury selection to resume. He coughed occasionally and complained about feeling weak, but displayed a whimsical glimmer in his eyes when Candy felt his forehead and said, "You're hot."

"Put that in the news," Edwards joked to a group of reporters accompanying him in a courthouse elevator.

When his wife looked puzzled, Edwards looked at her and said, "Oh, you're talking about temperature? I thought you were talking about something else."

Four days later, on January 24, Polozola seated a jury of twelve with six alternates. Among the twelve jurors were eight men and four women. Nine were white, two were black, and one was of mixed race. They included a fifth-grade teacher, a laboratory technician, a salesman, a bank worker, a general manager of a computer business, a laborer, an electrician, a machinist, a cashier, a retired equipment mechanic, and two homemakers. Both sides pronounced themselves happy with the jury's makeup.

Polozola told the jurors that he would not sequester them because the trial could last at least three months. But while at home, he warned them, they must avoid reading, listening to, or watching news reports on the trial. "You, ladies and gentlemen, will be the judges of the facts of this case," he said gravely. "It will be your responsibility to determine what the facts are. Not a newspaper reporter, not a radio reporter, not a television announcer."

On the following day, January 25, each side finally presented opening statements. Speaking first, lead prosecutor Jim Letten painted an unflattering portrait of Edwards, describing the former governor as the mastermind of "a corrupt, illegal enterprise."

Edwards "exercised his power, his notoriety, his fame and his influence" in a multi-million-dollar extortion scheme that corrupted Louisiana's riverboat licensing process to enrich himself, his family, and his friends, Letten added. "This case, ladies and gentlemen, is about corruption. Corruption in the gaming industry, corruption in the Governor's Mansion, corruption in the gaming commission."

Edwards's attorney, Dan Small, also used the Governor's Mansion as a backdrop, but he described it as the place where Edwards carried out good works: "Under Edwin Edwards, the mansion was a public building . . . he tried to help people. Friends? Yes. Strangers? Yes. He tried to help people, because to him, that was his job. Edwin Edwards is no racketeer. He is, the evidence will show, a loving husband, a generous father and a devoted grandfather."

Edwards sat, imperturbable, from his vantage point in the middle of the courtroom during most of the six hours of opening statements from prosecutors, Small, and attorneys for his six co-defendants. Reclining slightly in his chair, he closely watched each attorney, stealing glances occasionally at the jury for its reaction.

On January 28, the prosecution called its first star witness to the stand: Bobby Guidry. Short and wiry, with a toupee that one bailiff likened to a black cat sleeping on a fence post, Guidry climbed into the witness box to the judge's right, sat down, raised his right hand, and promised "to tell the truth, the whole truth and nothing but the truth, so help me God."

Under the questioning of prosecutor Fred Harper, Guidry recounted how the Riverboat Gaming Commission in June 1993 had awarded him a preliminary certificate to operate the *Treasure Chest* in Kenner. That turned out to be only the first step, however. Guidry still needed a State Police license—and that appeared to be an insurmountable hurdle after Captain Mark Oxley, who headed the State Police's gaming division, revoked Guidry's video poker license in December 1993. Oxley made the move after discovering that Guidry's partner in A.-Ace Video Gaming Company was Frank Caracci, a convicted mobster. It was a potentially disastrous decision for Guidry, not only because of the video poker income he would lose, but more so because it prompted Oxley to postpone a riverboat-casino hearing that was a requirement for licensing. By then, Guidry had invested at least $9 million of his own money in the riverboat and had borrowed $20 million more to file the application, pay attorneys, and get the boat built. He stood to lose millions and millions of dollars.

Guidry's reaction to Oxley's decision showed what was at stake. "It was probably the most devastating day of my life, except when my mother and father died," he testified to the court. That night, Guidry recalled, he had complained about Oxley's decision to Edwards during their regular Thursday night poker game at the Governor's Mansion.

Guidry also turned to the judicial system for help, going to court to block the State Police video poker ruling. As an additional step, he sought the assistance of Andrew Martin, his longtime friend and executive assistant to Edwards. Martin agreed to help him, but indicated "it would cost me," Guidry testified.

"He took his fingers together and did this," Guidry said, turning to the jury and rubbing his forefingers and thumbs together.

Martin also said he would "cash in his green stamps" to help him, Guidry testified.

The deal coalesced, Guidry said, at another meeting shortly thereafter at a Chili's restaurant in Baton Rouge. Martin said he wanted 3 percent of the boat's gross—or about $120,000—to be divided equally among Edwin and Stephen Edwards and Martin.

"I said, 'A year?'" Guidry testified. "He said, 'No, a month.'"

Guidry said he talked Martin down to $100,000 a month, with payments to start after Edwards left office in January 1996 to appease Martin's concerns about arousing suspicions. Guidry said his only condition was that he wanted to finalize the deal face-to-face with Edwards.

Guidry recalled that he and Edwards met later in an empty meeting room at the Baton Rouge Hilton Hotel in late April or early May 1994. Guidry testified that with Martin guarding the door, "Edwin said, 'I understand you and Andrew have an understanding.' I said, 'Yes.' He said, 'You have all your financing together?' I said, 'Yes.' He said, 'Fine, I'm going to see about getting you a hearing.'"

A short time earlier, Edwards had attempted to persuade the State Police to reverse its decision on Guidry. In January 1994, the governor had acted as if he were Guidry's lawyer and pressured Oxley and several

State Police colleagues to reinstate Guidry's video poker license and schedule a riverboat licensing hearing. They had refused to do so.

But shortly after Guidry met with Edwards at the Hilton, the long-stalled riverboat casino licensing process suddenly kicked into gear, Guidry remembered. By then Edwards had had State Police superintendent Paul Fontenot transfer Captain Oxley—and Lieutenant Riley Blackwelder, who also had opposed Guidry—out of the gaming division. With Oxley and Blackwelder out of the way, the State Police scheduled a hearing for May 17, 1994, and awarded Guidry a license the next day.

Guidry testified that he never told anyone—not his wife or Boyd Gaming, his operating partner in the boat—about the $100,000 monthly payments. He said he also had denied three times under oath that he had made any payoffs.

"Why didn't you ever tell anyone about the agreement when you were under oath?" asked prosecutor Harper.

"I knew it was illegal," Guidry answered.

After a long weekend break, the trial resumed on February 1, and Guidry took the stand again. Prosecutors played the first tapes, from early 1997, in which Edwards and Martin plotted to disguise payments from Guidry. Asked to explain what transpired, Guidry testified that he gave the Edwardses and Martin $1.5 million in cash between March 1996 and April 1997 in return for their help in arranging the 1994 State Police hearing that cleared the way for *Treasure Chest* to receive its operating license. He told the court that he left bundles of $100 bills for Martin to pick up in a doctors' office garbage container, a restaurant ash bin, and a maintenance trailer behind the headquarters of Guidry's tugboat business. Once, Guidry recalled, he even threw a paper sack stuffed with $65,000 in cash from his car into the open window of Stephen Edwards's van.

Guidry said he left the money in Dumpsters to express his displeasure with Martin's attempts to extort more graft in the form of a $40,000-a-month position with the *Treasure Chest*. The blunt multimillionaire said he had plenty of available cash to make the payments because he often kept $1 million or more at his apartment above the offices of his tugboat company, Harvey Gulf International Marine. In fact, he liked to stash some $400,000 in cash wrapped in aluminum foil in his freezer. "I shoved it under some ducks and deers I had in there," Guidry said. He added that he kept the abundant cash to feed his enormous gambling habit—the casino owner, it turned out, was a gambling addict himself—and to buy presents and to pay for cruises and family vacations to Disney World and New York.

On the following day, the defense began trying to blast holes in Guidry's story. Stephen Edwards's attorney, Jim Cole, got Guidry to admit that he made a number of payments to Stephen for legal fees. Cole then suggested that the $100,000-a-month payments to the Edwardses and Martin, which Guidry had been calling an illegal payoff, might actually have been for legal work. Guidry refused to back down. "Sir, all I can tell you is I was paying for the [riverboat] hearing," he responded.

A day later, Cole tried a new defense strategy, questioning whether Guidry had access to enough cash to make $1.5 million in payoffs. Using a courtroom projector to sketch a rough balance sheet for Guidry, Cole showed jurors a calendar in which Guidry recorded nearly $1.1 million in losses at casinos, at horse racing tracks, and in private card games. In one month alone—September 1996—Guidry lost $263,000 at casinos. The gambling losses occurred in the same fifteen-month period in 1996 and 1997 when Guidry had said he was making cash payoffs to the Edwardses and Martin in return for their help in arranging the State Police hearing.

Cole argued that Guidry's gambling losses and the alleged payoffs to Edwards totaled nearly $500,000 more than the amount of cash Guidry had on hand before the payoffs started, and the amount he withdrew from banks during the same period.

"There isn't enough money here," Cole told Guidry. He seemed to have undercut the *Treasure Chest* owner's testimony. Guidry countered Cole's assertion without hesitation, saying the attorney had not accounted for the money he had made before 1996—$3 million to $5 million a year for twelve years—and he also had plenty of cash.

"What do you know about 1990, '91, '92, '93, '94, '95?" Guidry asked Cole. "How do you know I didn't get the cash then? . . . In one of my safes, I guess the majority of that money is 1960s and 1970s bills. I've been having money for a long, long time." With his answers, Guidry seemed to have restored much of his credibility.

Cole finished his questions. Now Dan Small, Edwin Edwards's attorney, would try to rattle Guidry. Small took a different approach. The former governor had not extorted money from Guidry, Small argued; they were good friends. As evidence, he displayed nearly a dozen photos of the casino owner hunting, fishing, and partying with Edwards. In one instance, Small said, Guidry delivered a toast at a 1996 New Year's Eve party in which he called Edwards "the next most important man in my life" after his brother, Dick Guidry.

Guidry responded that it was all a façade: the Edwardses wanted his money, and he wanted to keep them from using the government to interfere with the *Treasure Chest*.

"They pretended to be my friends, and I pretended to be their friends," Guidry testified.

On Guidry's sixth and final day in the witness chair, Polozola began by calling attorneys into his conference room to notify them of a major development: he was removing Juror 453 from the trial. During the previous week, Polozola noted, the juror was obviously sleeping during testimony, his head propped up with his hands. The judge's decision disappointed the defense. Juror 453 fit the profile of someone favorable to Edwards. He was an African-American laborer from Baton Rouge who, during juror questioning, had said he tended to vote Democratic and sometimes visited casinos. He "strongly disagreed" that Edwards was responsible for past or current problems with gambling in Louisiana.

To make matters worse for the defense, Juror 453 was replaced with the first alternate juror, Juror 235, whose profile suggested he would be less favorable to Edwards. A white forty-nine-year-old research technician, Juror 235 said during juror questioning that he agreed "somewhat" that there was corruption in the casino licensing process and agreed that wiretaps and informers were acceptable investigative techniques.

The Edwards camp reacted bitterly to Polozola's move. "This judge is so against us," co-defendant Andrew Martin complained privately to a reporter.

"He wants to get all the blacks off the jury," added state senator Greg Tarver, another co-defendant. (Later, Polozola would remove a white man for hardship reasons and a white woman would take his place. The move did not spark protest.)

At dinner, over a plate of sushi, lead prosecutor Jim Letten mulled the impact of Bobby Guidry's testimony and concluded that he had been a strong witness. Prone to think in military terms, Letten thought the prosecution had drawn first blood with Guidry and had weakened the defense's morale. "We wanted to make an impression on the jury," he said.

Defense attorneys, however, did not share Letten's view, believing that they had raised doubts during cross-examination about whether Guidry had the money with which he claimed to pay off the Edwardses. Guidry had left the witness stand with his credibility in question, they believed. Observers lent credence to the defense's view, noting that the Feds had not tied any payments directly from Guidry to Edwards.

Prosecutors and the defense frequently sniped at each other in court, but were usually able to keep their anger under wraps to avoid provoking Judge Polozola. However, hostility between Edwards and the prosecution flared the day after Guidry finished testifying. It was prompted by a newspaper report that a judge in Texas had ordered Letten to give a deposition in Houston immediately after the Edwards trial on whether the prosecution had improperly given immunity to the Graham brothers for their Louisiana crimes. During the first court break, reporters crowded around Letten just outside the courtroom to ask about the potentially damaging news. As Edwards walked by, he smirked and told Letten in a voice loud enough for reporters to hear, "I would like very much to attend your deposition."

"Don't hold your breath," Letten shot back.

"Well, maybe then you'll tell the truth for a change," retorted Edwards.

When court resumed, Letten complained to Polozola that Edwards was acting unprofessionally. Small leaped to his client's defense and pinned the blame on the prosecutor. The back-and-forth went on for several minutes before Polozola growled that he didn't want to hear any more squabbling. A few minutes later, when defendants openly laughed at a prosecutor's mistake, the judge boiled over. "There are times when I have to bite my tongue in front of the jury," Polozola told the surprised courtroom audience. "I just want to slam somebody. I don't mean hit somebody . . . just dress them down in front of the jury."

During another break that day, Anna Edwards discussed her father with a reporter. Anna, the eldest of Edwards's four children, was attending court every day. "Daddy would have been a great televangelist," she said.

"You mean like Jimmy Swaggart?" the reporter asked, referring to the disgraced Baton Rouge–based minister.

"Daddy wouldn't have gotten caught," she replied. "And he wouldn't have been with a prostitute. Certainly not one that ugly."

After Guidry's testimony, the prosecution took up Scheme 2, the allegation that the Edwardses and Cecil Brown had extorted $350,000 from a group of midwestern businessmen who had unsuccessfully sought two riverboat licenses. Prosecutors thought that it was the weakest of their five schemes, and their evidence certainly didn't impress observers or the defense.

In the coming days, the court settled into a fairly normal routine. Each day's session usually began at 8:30 a.m. and ended at 5:30 p.m., with twenty-minute midmorning and midafternoon breaks and an hour to seventy-five minutes for lunch. The prosecutors, who were staying at a local Corporate Suites hotel, met each morning and lunch to discuss strategy at an office across the street from the courthouse.

The defendants were more freewheeling. They devoted the midmorning break to animated discussions of the day's luncheon menu, to be served at the home of their paralegal, two blocks away. One of the co-defendants' wives typically was responsible for the food. "You tried the bread pudding?" Bobby Johnson, the Baton Rouge contractor and a co-defendant, asked someone one day at lunch.

"Did you try the coconut cake?" he asked someone else a couple of minutes later.

"Man, these girls are going to put twenty pounds on me," he then said aloud to no one in particular, patting his stomach with both hands.

On February 18, the prosecution introduced Scheme 3, which involved the Players floating casino in Lake Charles. Two executives from Players began by testifying that after the Riverboat Gaming Commission had awarded them a preliminary certificate in March 1993, Stephen Edwards and Ricky Shetler pointed out that they still needed an operating license from the State Police. Patrick Madamba, a Players attorney, testified that as he left a meeting with State Police officials in April 1993, Stephen drove up in a van and motioned for him and another Players executive to climb in. After they sat down, Madamba said Stephen asked him: "What are you doing with those fucking assholes in there? Stick with us. We'll show you how business is done in Louisiana."

According to Madamba, Stephen went on to say: "All the other riverboats are buying merchandise from us. It would be good for you to buy from us, too." Players got the message and shortly afterward began buying souvenirs and trinkets from a company co-owned by Stephen, the first step toward an eventual $200,000 of such purchases from that company.

Players executive John Brotherton testified that within thirty minutes of his first meeting with Shetler, the Lake Charles pizza parlor owner told him that "Players needed to hire him at a high rate of pay, that it was in Players' best interests." Brotherton said Shetler emphasized his close ties to the Edwards family.

Brotherton took heed and advised the Players brass to hire Shetler because "these guys could hurt you." Shetler subsequently demanded big bonuses from Players, telling Brotherton that if Players didn't pay, "harm would come to us," Brotherton testified. In June 1993, Shetler began a $5,000-a-month consulting deal for a minimum 10 hours per week. In November 1993, Players paid Shetler two bonuses of $50,000 each. In December 1994, Shetler signed a more lucrative contract that would pay him $126,000 a year for seven years, for at least 20 hours of work a week.

On February 23, it was Ricky Shetler's turn to take the witness stand. Shetler would be the government's second star witness, but prosecutors weren't sure if he could withstand the blistering cross-examination expected from the defense. Before agreeing to become a government witness, Shetler had cried twice in the presence of federal officials, one time while curled up in a fetal position on the floor. Shetler had had drug, alcohol, and marital problems that added to his emotional instability. And to top it off, he would be betraying his best friend, Stephen Edwards, and a man he had held in awe, Edwin Edwards. Would he wilt under the pressure?

Prosecutor Peter Strasser began by having Shetler recount his friendship with Stephen, which dated back to the late 1960s, when they were in high school in Crowley. Stephen became a lawyer and Shetler opened two pizza parlors, and the friendship deepened when Stephen helped Ricky through his alcohol and drug addiction in 1981. "There's no doubt, Stephen has been a wonderful friend to me . . . very supportive," said Shetler, a graying forty-six-year-old who sat hunched forward and spoke in a slow, halting drawl.

The complicated extortion allegations described by Strasser clearly confused Shetler. The pizzeria owner frequently responded to Strasser's questions by saying he didn't always understand the details because Stephen Edwards developed most of the strategies for dealing with Players executives—after "he talked with his daddy"—and coached him on what to say. "I made pizzas," Shetler testified. "I was in the restaurant business. I didn't know about gambling."

Shetler said Stephen told him to warn Players executives that if they didn't pay him $300,000 a year, they would have trouble getting an operating license. "If y'all don't, you could get hurt. You know Stephen's daddy is governor," Shetler said he told Players, at Stephen's behest.

With a packed audience listening intently, Strasser played a 1993 phone conversation between Shetler and Stephen Edwards that Shetler had recorded and that highlighted his testimony. One snippet on tape was particularly damning. Referring to Players executives, Stephen told Shetler, "They know if they keep you happy, then you will keep me from fucking with them."

Throughout the testimony, Stephen Edwards sat rigidly at the defense table and stared straight ahead. He avoided eye contact with his erstwhile friend when Shetler entered and later left the courtroom through a small, swinging door no more than five feet away. During Shetler's testimony, Stephen's wife, Leslie, and his elder sister, Anna, frequently sobbed in the front row of the spectators' area.

Shetler returned for a second day of gut-wrenching testimony on February 24. He told the court how for two years he had split payments from Players with Stephen Edwards because Stephen had prevailed on his father to ensure that Players got a state operating license. After the State Police allowed Players to purchase and move the *Star* riverboat casino from New Orleans to Lake Charles in 1995, Stephen restructured the arrangement. Shetler himself had been getting 25 cents from each person who boarded either the *Star* or the *Players,* and Stephen now wanted a cut to go to his father, Shetler testified.

The new arrangement began in September 1995, he said. Because of the more complicated transactions, Shetler created a ledger of his payments to the Edwardses—a ledger that FBI agents had found when they searched his pizzeria in April 1997. Shetler testified that in his ledger, Edwin Edwards was shown as "2E"; Stephen Edwards, as "1S"; and Shetler himself as "3R." Shetler said he needed the ledger because "it got very confusing with all the money coming in." Prosecutor Strasser displayed Shetler's handwritten ledger on courtroom video monitors as he led the witness through the payments made to the Edwardses.

Instead of simply funneling cash from Players to the Edwardses, Shetler bought them a dizzying array of goods and services. For Stephen, the purchases included a $738 lamp, a $2,000 margarita-mixing machine, $30,000 of landscaping, a $38,000 Ford van, a trip to Disney World, and the lease of two Lincoln Mark VIII towncars. For the former governor, the purchases included $8,500 of kitchen appliances and a $24,000 Chevrolet Suburban.

Bolstering Shetler's testimony, Strasser showed receipts for the purchases, as well as canceled checks. The prosecutor also played tapes, and they were damning. In a January 9, 1997, conversation in Edwin Edwards's office, Stephen said to his father: "I gotta get with Shetler because he still owes you the big check for November and all of December, which should be six, seven, eight, nine thousand dollars."

In a February 25, 1997, conversation, also in Edwards's office, Stephen told his father, "Shetler's been calling me. I think I should just stay in and meet with him. He's coming in with your money."

"I'd rather you do that," responded the former governor, apparently wanting to keep his distance from the money transfer.

Shortly after the April 1997 FBI raid, Shetler said Stephen made the first of several attempts to develop a cover story. "We took a ride. He stopped, leaned up against the glass and said, 'You may never speak to me again, but I never gave that money to my daddy,'" Shetler testified. "Then, he winked."

Months later, Shetler said, he bumped into Stephen at the FBI office in New Orleans. Shetler said Stephen pulled him aside and suggested he tell prosecutors that he was repaying Edwin Edwards for money he had lent to Shetler to open a pizzeria in Shreveport. The "S" in his ledger coding system, Stephen said, could refer to the Shreveport pizzeria. And, Stephen added, couldn't the "E" in the ledger stand for "Edwards"? Shetler told the court that he could not follow Stephen's suggestion. "I was guilty," he explained.

For the second day in a row, a hushed courtroom watched closely as the witness, clearly pained, told his story. At times Shetler was on the verge of tears as he testified against his best friend of thirty years.

Stephen Edwards continued to avoid eye contact as Shetler walked in and out of the courtroom. Edwin Edwards, who had been remarkably unfazed during the six-week-long trial, now started to show his unease, sitting for long stretches during the testimony with his fingers pressed against his closed eyes.

By the end of Ricky Shetler's second day of testimony, practically everyone involved in the case knew that the dynamics had changed, that Shetler had proved to be a very damaging prosecution witness.

Stephen would not easily rebut his testimony. Edwin Edwards also was potentially vulnerable now because Shetler linked the payments to the former governor through Stephen.

John Maginnis, a veteran commentator on Louisiana politics, was attending the trial and digesting his observations in a weekly four-page publication faxed around the state to reporters, politicians, and political junkies. Following Shetler's second day on the stand, Maginnis asked his readers, "Is Ricky Shetler credible? In an odd way, he could be, for the jury may conclude that the slow-talking pizza store owner was too dim to extort Players on his own, as the defense asserts."

Jim Cole and Dan Small, the lawyers for Stephen and Edwin Edwards, respectively, were quite confident that they could crack the emotional witness. From the Edwardses, they knew that Shetler was a weak reed. And during the direct examination, Shetler had already laid bare his tangled feelings.

On Shetler's third day of testimony, the defense undertook its cross-examination. Cole wasted little time before challenging Shetler with aggressive, rapid-fire questions. He was attempting to show that Shetler was the extortionist, not Stephen and Edwin Edwards. "You used the name of the Edwardses when you didn't have their permission?" Cole asked with a sneer.

"No. No," Shetler protested, raising his voice to meet Cole's. "I said I used their name when I was told what to say."

"So you made a deal with the government to get out of trouble, didn't you, Mr. Shetler?" Cole asked several minutes later.

"I made a deal with the government because I was guilty," Shetler quickly replied.

After more questions, the showdown neared its climax. "Isn't what's happening here, Mr. Shetler, is that you got yourself in trouble and you decided to betray your friend to get out of trouble? Isn't that what happened?" Cole said in a loud voice.

"No. That is not it at all. That's totally wrong," Shetler shot back, red-faced with anger.

Cole said he had no further questions and returned to the defense table. Small smiled and patted him on the back. But Cole's aggressive tactics had backfired. Rather than crumbling, Shetler had gotten stronger and more forceful. In a word, he was believable.

John Hill, the long-standing capital bureau chief for the *Shreveport Times*, had been on the outs with Edwards when he was governor, but had grown close to him during the investigation and trial. Hill's take on Shetler's testimony was succinct. "By noon Thursday [during Shetler's second day on the stand], we knew Stephen was dead," Hill said in an interview. "You could feel the air getting heavy in the courtroom. It was like no one was moving, no one was rocking in his chair. Everyone was just watching Peter Strasser perform brilliantly. I haven't been able to talk to Stephen or Edwin since. I don't want to have to tell them what I think. I haven't run into anyone who thinks differently. This boosts [Bobby] Guidry by making him look more credible. Everyone thought they were starting out with the strongest witness in Guidry. It doesn't look that way now. It's possible they're going to convict them. The whole mood of things has changed."

Hill added that Edwards seemed to age before his eyes. "Good God, I'm looking at an old man," Hill recalled thinking to himself during Shetler's testimony. The natty former governor had even appeared disheveled that morning. "Normally, he is fastidious about his appearance," Hill noted.

But a few days later, Edwards had bounced back, amiably sharing a bag of popcorn outside the courthouse with prosecutor Strasser. "If Edwin Edwards is feeling the strain, he betrays few signs of it," marveled *Times-Picayune* columnist James Gill. "He strolls around during recesses with that familiar air of confidence, the quick wit undiminished as he notes holes in the government's case. . . ."

Stephen Edwards was less tactful. Gill encountered him in the courthouse men's room, surveying paper towels strewn on the floor. Stephen observed that there were "some pigs" around.

Gill couldn't resist asking, "So who do you suppose those pigs are?"

"Feds," replied Stephen.

On Saturday, March 4, 2000, Baton Rouge held its major parade of the Carnival season. True to tradition, the Mardi Gras floats struck satirical themes on the events of the day. "The trial got its share of spoofing," John Hill wrote in the *Shreveport Times*.

> One float was titled Unindicted Co-conspirators and featured three bags of cash—one for Edwin, one for Stephen and one for Ricky Shetler. Another float's theme was Jury Rigging. Pasted with dollar bills, the float included a Wheel of Fortune on the side. But instead of dollar amounts, each segment of the wheel had the names of Louisiana casinos, including those that figured in the trial: *Treasure Chest, Players* and *Jazz*.
>
> Finally, picking up on the Edwards defense lawyer's question to FBI search agents if they searched Candy Edwards' underwear drawer, there was, appropriately enough, a float called Edwin's Candy. It was covered with, what else, women's underwear, some of them looking like they were purchased on Bourbon Street.
>
> Another float had an altered Louisiana state seal. Louisiana: State of Confession it was named. There was no other explanation.

Back in the courtroom, the prosecution turned to Scheme 4, and on March 8, Mark Bradley, the star witness of this trial segment, took the stand. Bradley had been the point man and part-owner of Jazz Enterprises, which had won a preliminary certificate from the Riverboat Gaming Commission in 1993 to operate on the Mississippi River in Baton Rouge. As other riverboat operators had discovered, however, Jazz Enterprises still had to get the necessary State Police license before beginning operations. In 1994, while trying to get a State Police hearing on the matter, Bradley said an illiterate but street-smart Baton Rouge contractor named Bobby Johnson contacted him with a simple and unsubtle message: If Bradley didn't give Johnson a 12½ percent share of the riverboat, then Johnson would use his influence with Governor Edwards to deny Jazz Enterprises the State Police hearing. "Y'all ain't got nobody in your defense and y'all fixin' to end up in the street," Johnson told Bradley, in a recorded conversation played in court.

Bradley testified that Johnson bragged repeatedly of his friendship with Edwards, whom the millionaire contractor called the "little man" or the "old man." During a visit to the Governor's Mansion, Bradley testified, Johnson seemed to back up his boasts. After Johnson met privately with the governor in his hideaway office, the two walked out to Bradley. Edwards put his arm around Johnson's shoulder and declared, "Bobby's a good man," Bradley testified.

"See, I'm family here. I'm home here," Bradley recalled Johnson remarking as they left the mansion.

Bradley was duly impressed. "It without question convinced me that Bobby Johnson had the ability to fulfill every threat he had made to me at that point," he testified.

In one taped conversation played for the jury, Johnson told Bradley that he would split his 12½ percent share three ways. "I'm not keeping it all anyway, Mark, I mean it's none of your business where it's goin'. . . . It's gonna move around," Johnson was heard to say. To Bradley, this meant that the money would be divided among Johnson, Edwards, and the man Johnson described as his partner, co-defendant Cecil Brown, the cattle auctioneer.

Bradley testified that he felt vulnerable to Johnson's threats because, of the fifteen boats given preliminary certificates by the Riverboat Gaming Commission but all still needing a State Police license, only Jazz Enterprises lacked an Edwards friend or associate on its roster. But Bradley refused to bow to Johnson's demands. Instead, he went to the FBI, which enlisted him as an informant. Bradley began recording his meetings and phone calls with Johnson, and strung Johnson along in his demands that Bradley cut him in on the deal. Nonetheless, Johnson persisted. "Everybody's down to the wire and everybody's callin' all their friends and hollerin' and screamin' like a pig under a gate," Johnson told Bradley in a recorded April 6, 1994, conversation that the prosecution played in court. "I've got to get my answer to the old man 'cause he ain't gonna hold off much longer." Bradley was rewarded for calling Johnson's bluff. After an independent analyst gave the Jazz Enterprises proposal high marks, the State Police awarded his boat a hearing and then a license.

Johnson's extortionate demands, played on tape after tape in court, were so brazen that his attorney, Pat Fanning, had a difficult time devising a defense. Fanning brought out several outlandish claims made by Johnson, including his statement that he ran the state while Edwards was on trial in 1985–1986. In trying to show that his client's statements on tape about the riverboat were not to be believed, Fanning even called Johnson "a buffoon."

James Gill wrote that "the threats on the tapes are so unvarnished, the demands so hoggish, that it is hard to see how Johnson can beat this rap." Whether Mark Bradley's testimony would help convict Edwards remained an open question, however. The casino official had surprised the courtroom audience when he testified during his third day on the stand that he never thought Johnson planned to give any of the money to Edwards. "I don't believe it was for the governor's personal gain," Bradley said. Edwards's attorney, Dan Small, gasped audibly at the admission, while Edwards, who had sat impassively through more than three hours of testimony, raised his eyebrows and smiled slightly.

Once again, Edwards had benefited by being one person removed from any payoff. "I'm more pleased with the condition of the trial than I thought I would be," he said in an interview after Bradley had testified. "There's no evidence I'm connected with the scheme. I'm buoyant by the cloak of innocence."

At this point, a political science professor at Louisiana State University named Wayne Parent was giving the governor even odds. "This could go either way. . . . I'd say it's 50-50 that he'll be convicted."

Commentator John Maginnis also saw hope for the ex-governor. "Bradley's testimony was more damaging to Johnson than to Edwards, just as Ricky Shetler's was to Stephen Edwards and Robert Guidry's was to Andrew Martin," Maginnis wrote in a political column. Noting that former San Francisco 49ers owner Eddie DeBartolo would testify next, he continued: "The government's strategy is to build a compelling case against the alleged co-conspirators and front men, with the hope that DeBartolo, who did give Edwards money, will tie the whole plot back to the main target."

The trial, which had begun on January 10, was now nearing its conclusion as the prosecution took up the fifth and final scheme. As in the beginning, the $64,000 question remained unanswered: Did the Feds have enough evidence and testimony finally to nail Edwards? Many courtroom observers thought that Edwards's fate would hinge on DeBartolo's testimony. So on March 27, nearly everyone in the courtroom watched the diminutive businessman as he walked to the witness box.

Prosecutors had decided to limit DeBartolo's testimony. Assistant United States Attorney Mike Magner had him on the witness stand for only two hours. Sounding hoarse from an early-spring cold, DeBartolo described how he had gone to Edwards in 1996 seeking his help in obtaining the fifteenth riverboat license for the Shreveport–Bossier City area. According to DeBartolo, he felt that Edwards was putting the squeeze on him and that if he didn't comply with the former governor's demands, his hopes for getting the license would disappear. "I wasn't about to get Edwin Edwards upset or unhappy about anything," DeBartolo testified. "What it boils down to is the power, the relationships and what this man could do. I was always told by people smarter than me, 'Keep your friends close and your enemies closer.'"

Prosecutor Magner had DeBartolo focus on two events, both of which occurred within days of when the casino board would award the fifteenth license. One event occurred on March 5, 1997, during a meeting with Edwards at the Baton Rouge Radisson. Edwards wrote "$400,000" on a piece of paper and passed it to him, DeBartolo testified. "He said this has to be taken care of by next week or there's going to be a serious problem with your license application," DeBartolo told the court. So he told Edwards, "I'll take care of it."

"Did you believe you had no choice but to pay?" Magner asked DeBartolo.

"I had no choice," he replied.

The other event that Magner focused on occurred on March 12, the day before the casino board awarded the fifteenth license. DeBartolo described how he picked up Edwards at the San Francisco International Airport and drove him to a nearby restaurant, Max's Opera Café, for lunch. "He was dressed very woodsy," DeBartolo testified. "He looked like he was going hunting. He had jeans and heavy boots, a plaid shirt with a vest." Responding to Edwards's demand of a week earlier, DeBartolo testified that he had stowed four thousand $100 bills in a briefcase in his car.

At Max's, DeBartolo said he told Edwards that he feared the airport's X-ray machines would detect the cash inside the briefcase. "He said that's not a problem," DeBartolo testified. "He opened up his shirt. He showed me a money vest, where he intended to put the money."

After lunch, satisfied with Edwards's plan, DeBartolo told the court that they walked to his car. He took the briefcase out of the trunk, slipped it behind the passenger seat, and drove the former governor to the airport. When they arrived, DeBartolo said, Edwards opened the door, grabbed the briefcase, and disappeared inside the terminal with the $400,000.

Throughout most of his testimony, DeBartolo appeared somber, speaking without emotion and often limiting his answers to short statements. But his story during two hours of testimony held the courtroom rapt. DeBartolo was the only witness who had testified to putting money directly into Edwards's hands.

It now fell to Dan Small, Edwards's attorney, to damage DeBartolo's credibility during cross-examination. With his questions, Small suggested that Edwards's requests for money represented legitimate business dealings. As he responded, DeBartolo's tone grew sharper—much as Ricky Shetler's had under Jim Cole's cross-examination six weeks earlier. DeBartolo repeatedly dismissed Small's suggestions. "I am a victim," he snapped at one point. "I was a victim, and you can put it, phrase it any way you like."

Small pointed out that DeBartolo and Edwards sounded quite friendly during the taped phone conversations played in court, even after DeBartolo paid him the $400,000. Small asked DeBartolo if he could point to a single passage in the taped phone conversations that showed Edwards trying to extort money or issuing threats. The only overt threats, DeBartolo responded, occurred during their meeting at the Baton Rouge Radisson, which was not recorded. But DeBartolo said Edwards issued more subtle threats "between the lines."

"I know what's there, and I know what's lurking," DeBartolo added. "This guy still has his power, he still has his friends, he still has legislators he knows. . . . That's telling me he's got all his hands and all his tentacles wherever he needs them."

The cross-examination reached an emotional peak with Small's insinuation that DeBartolo, not Edwards, had insisted that the $400,000 payment be made in cash. Small suggested that the money was a legitimate consulting fee and asked whether DeBartolo was trying to hide the payment from his partners in Hollywood Casino. "That's ridiculous," DeBartolo snapped, his voice rising in anger. "Edwin Edwards did not want a check; he wanted cash. He wanted $400,000 in $100 bills, and that's what he got." DeBartolo added that of all the lobbyists and consultants he hired in Louisiana and other states, Edwards alone insisted on being paid in cash.

The following day, Small continued to press the 49ers owner. After one particularly pointed question, an angry DeBartolo leaned into the microphone and gave the most emphatic testimonial of his day-and-a-half court appearance. "I can sit here and you can harass me," he told Small. "You can try to make me change my mind. But what happened on March 5 and what happened on March 12 is done and that's why I'm here and that's why I had to plead guilty."

After six hours of questions by defense lawyers, Small was through. Prosecutor Magner asked a few final questions on redirect. He sought again to portray DeBartolo as the victim. Pleading guilty for failing to report Edwards's extortion attempt, DeBartolo said, had exacted "a very significant" toll, beginning with his sister, Denise DeBartolo York, who had opposed his Louisiana gambling foray. "It caused me to be totally estranged from the only blood relative, my sister, with whom I reached a property settlement agreement last week," DeBartolo told the court. "It cost me physically and mentally, as I'm sure it has everyone." He added that he could no longer vote or carry a firearm and now had to disclose to lenders on his Florida real estate ventures that he was a convicted felon.

During most of DeBartolo's testimony, Edwards rocked back and forth in his chair, his hands pressed together over his mouth, his chin resting on his thumbs. Occasionally, he closed his eyes.

Defense attorneys had questioned whether the four thousand $100 bills could fit in a briefcase, as DeBartolo had testified. So on March 30, prosecutors had FBI financial analyst Josephine Beninatti bring four thousand $1 bills into court and place them in a briefcase. The cash fit snugly. As Beninatti held the cash-laden briefcase open to the jury, she noted that $1 bills are the same size as $100 bills.

Beninatti was the sixty-sixth and final prosecution witness. After she stepped down from the stand, lead prosecutor Jim Letten stood up and announced, "The government rests."

Now it would be the defense's turn.

A Chinese Saying

iven what by then was an obsessive interest in Edwin Edwards's fate all across Louisiana, the trial's long-awaited climax arrived unexpectedly. With several low-level defense witnesses expected to testify, the courtroom was far from full on April 11 when Dan Small, Edwards's attorney, announced that his client would be the next witness. The former governor strolled to the stand as if he had not a care in the world. Seated as ever in the front row, his thirty-five-year-old wife, Candy, and fifty-year-old daughter Anna were not so cool. They looked on anxiously. Edwards may not have shown it, but his career, indeed how he would spend the remainder of his life, hung in the balance.

As he sat down in the witness box, Edwards was buoyed that he would finally have the opportunity to look the jurors right in the eye and make his case. He had said for months that he had a simple and convincing explanation to rebut each of the prosecution's contentions. But silenced by Polozola's gag order, he had said he would have to wait to tell his story directly to the jury.

No one over the past thirty years understood how to appeal to the average Louisianian better than did Edwards. And for the past three months, he had sat in the courtroom looking at the jury, taking their measure each and every day. Could twelve Louisianians turn their backs on the only man elected governor of the Bayou State four times? Could they vote to send him to prison?

As word spread that Edwards had taken the witness stand, the galleries filled and then spilled over into an adjoining courtroom served by a closed-circuit television feed. Those in the courthouse saw Small begin by having Edwards recount his impoverished upbringing as the son of uneducated parents, his father a sharecropper, his mother a midwife. Edwards particularly relished talking about his mother, "who loved people and helped deliver babies for people who couldn't pay her." Edwards described the family's farm near Marksville, in central Louisiana, noting that it did not have running water or electricity until his teen years. He explained that the family got electricity when Edwards, at the age of sixteen, read a book that taught him how to connect a wire from their house to an outside utility line. That he had just admitted to breaking the law, albeit nearly sixty years earlier, was taken in stride.

Small led Edwards forward in time, to his political rise as the populist heir to Huey and Earl Long, with a record four terms as governor of Louisiana. Edwards spoke proudly about how he oversaw the writing of the state's modern constitution in 1973 and pushed for a change in how Louisiana taxed oil and gas companies, a change that produced millions of dollars in extra revenue to state coffers. "I'm one of the best examples of what's great about America," he said. "I'm a poor boy who rose to be governor. . . . While I dealt with presidents and captains of industry, there was always a place for the voiceless, for poor people. I thought they deserved access to their government. . . . Why would I want to demean my office by doing something like this?"

Small turned to the specific allegations contained in the five schemes. "Tell the jury, are these charges in the indictment true, Governor?" Edwards swiveled his chair toward the jury. "Absolutely not," he said slowly in a strong, clear voice. He repeated that phrase several times in asserting his innocence.

Edwards emphasized that he had stayed clear of the riverboat licensing process. So many of his friends wanted licenses, he said, he was bound to disappoint more than he could satisfy had he intervened. "I had nothing to gain from that politically," Edwards maintained. While answering his attorney's questions for six hours, he frequently rocked back and forth in his chair. At times, asserting the falseness of the prosecution's claims, he leaned into the microphone or poked the front of the witness stand with his index finger.

Addressing the specific allegations, Edwards said DeBartolo had given him the $400,000 for consulting. He added that it was DeBartolo who wanted to pay him in cash, to keep his involvement hidden from Hollywood Casino executives. Ricky Shetler also lied, Edwards said, when he testified that he had made payoffs to him and his son Stephen. Yes, Shetler had paid them money, Edwards admitted, but it was to repay cash loans that Edwards had made to Shetler and his son as they launched an unsuccessful Shreveport pizza franchise.

The government's third marquee witness, Bobby Guidry, also lied, Edwards testified. He then told a story. Guidry phoned him on October 8, 1998, and asked to meet him at the Tanger Outlet Mall in Gonzales, Edwards said. "With tears in his eyes, he put his arms around me and apologized for what he was about to do," Edwards said. "He told me, 'I can't take the pressure anymore. I'm going to make a deal,'" Edwards testified. Guidry told him prosecutors were threatening to indict him and his sons for fraud in their tugboat business. "He told me it was worth $300 million, and he couldn't afford to lose it," Edwards said.

"I said, 'Tell them anything as long as it's the truth.' He said the government wanted him to say something bad.

"I said, 'Bobby, life is too short and eternity too long to do that. Stick with the truth.'"

Edwards added, "He left me with the distinct impression he was gonna have to, for want of a better word, fabricate a story in order to make a plea. That's what, in fact, happened."

In the midafternoon, after nearly six hours of putting questions to his client, Small asked one final question. "Tell the jury: Are these charges in the indictment true, Governor?"

Edwards swiveled his chair toward the jury. "Absolutely not," he replied, in a strong, clear voice.

Small had barely returned to his seat when Jim Letten, the lead prosecutor, strode to the podium and brusquely goaded Edwards: "You just lied, didn't you, sir? Lied to the jury, didn't you, sir?"

"They'll have to determine that," Edwards coolly replied, with a nod toward the jury.

Letten persisted.

"I did not lie," Edwards maintained.

Letten had long since concluded that cross-examining Edwards could make or break the prosecution's case. A member of the Naval Reserve, Letten liked the combat of a trial and favored aggressive tactics. But having spent hours preparing for this cross-examination, he realized he would have to be careful not to go overboard. Letten knew that during the 1985 trial, Edwards had taken the stand and demolished his hapless interrogator, United States Attorney John Volz. A fateful moment came when Volz said he was trying to find a certain passage in a prior transcript as he fumbled through a mass of pages. "It's on page 170," Edwards called out, and to the astonishment of everyone in the courtroom, he was correct.

Volz also had proven no match for Edwards's quips and quick asides, looking lead-footed next to the nimble governor. Letten was determined not to play the straight man for Edwards this time. He had resolved not to argue with the former governor or trade quips. Indeed, he was prepared to seek Judge Polozola's intervention anytime he thought that Edwards was playing to the jury. Underpinning this strategy was a decision to air the damning tapes over and over again, forcing Edwards repeatedly to give what the prosecutor believed to be implausible answers.

Letten and the former governor jousted for two hours on the afternoon of their first encounter. The battle intensified the following day. Edwards accused Letten of helping to invent Bobby Guidry's testimony that the riverboat owner made $1.5 million in payoffs to the former governor, his son Stephen, and Andrew Martin in return for getting the State Police to award a license to his *Treasure Chest* riverboat casino. "That only exists in your mind and in the story you and Mr. Guidry confected to make this plea bargain," Edwards said. "It has no relation to reality. I can look at you and this jury and my maker, who knows my heart. I never demanded anything from Bobby Guidry in my life."

Letten replied sharply that he had not taken part in Guidry's plea negotiations, and he accused Edwards of trying to embarrass him.

"Mr. Letten, I really don't think I have the capacity to embarrass you," Edwards retorted.

Letten pressed Edwards, accusing him of trying to be funny to win over jurors. "Funny?" Edwards said. "I'm on trial for my life, nothing funny about it at all."

Nonplussed, Letten recounted the most sensational elements of Guidry's testimony, including the riverboat-casino owner's account that he left sacks filled with $100,000 in $100 bills in Dumpsters for Martin to collect and distribute to the Edwardses. The former governor reacted disdainfully. "Mr. Letten, the Dumpster might have gotten it, but I didn't," Edwards said. "Not that time or any other time—in Dumpsters or trash cans or vans or otherwise—did Bobby Guidry transfer any money to me or Stephen."

The rapid-fire exchanges between Edwards and Letten produced enough heat to prompt two warnings from Polozola. And the enmity between the two men grew so intense in the early afternoon that the judge called for an early break.

Returning to the fray, Letten focused on a February 25, 1997, conversation between Edwards and Martin at the former governor's law office, a tape that prosecutors had played two months earlier with Guidry on the stand. Jurors again heard Martin propose that they buy a tugboat, lease it to Guidry, and "jack up the rental" rate to account for money they got from the *Treasure Chest* owner. The scheme, Edwards told them, would provide "showable income" so they could stop "stacking up money and looking for places to throw it away." Edwards also was heard saying that he was worried about Guidry's taking cash out of the bank every month. "If he ever gets checked, he's going to have a hard time explaining what happened to all that," Edwards said.

Letten then asked the former governor to explain what the prosecutor called a "sham" deal to hide Guidry's $100,000-a-month payoffs. Edwards replied that they discussed the plan as a way for Guidry to pay them for legitimate legal and consulting work without telling his attorneys, who were jealous of the Edwardses. Edwards told the court that "after sober reflection," he scrapped this plan. Letten probed further, wondering how often he "cooks up fraudulent schemes and doesn't carry them out."

"Every time I don't," Edwards replied.

He hastened to add that he wasn't saying that he never thought of doing anything illegal. The key issue, he said, was that he did not implement the plan. "It was all thoughts, no action at all. . . . I hate to have my whole life hang on a couple of words," Edwards said.

When Letten inquired if the former governor knew that the scheme would have violated federal law, Edwards shot back, "Well, so is shooting at the President, but what does that have to do with anything?"

At one point, Edwards countered the testimony of Gretna mayor Ronnie Harris, who had told the court in February that he tried to get Edwards's support for the *Gretna Belle* riverboat in his town, across the Mississippi River from New Orleans. Harris testified that at a crawfish boil at the Governor's Mansion in 1993, he approached Edwards to discuss the proposed boat and Edwards asked, "Who are you?"

Edwards told the courtroom audience that Harris was mistaken because had he truly not known who Harris was, he would have asked someone for the mayor's name and then spoken to him as though he had known him for years. "I'm a politician, Mr. Letten," Edwards said unashamedly as the spectators laughed. The jurors, however, remained stone-faced.

When the defendant returned to the witness stand for a third day, on Thursday, April 13, Letten deliberately lowered the temperature by cordially walking a relaxed and conciliatory Edwards through dozens of cash transactions from 1988 to 1996. Letten was bolstering a central prosecution theme: that Edwards took huge cash payoffs from would-be casino operators to cover his gambling losses and to purchase big-ticket items. At one point, Edwards acknowledged buying $243,000 worth of casino chips in 1990 that he used to gamble. Letten noted that Edwards had testified the day before that he did little gambling that year because he was planning to run for governor in 1991 and did not want to draw attention to his favorite sport. "Is $243,000 a little?" Letten asked.

"I would call that little by my standards," Edwards said with a smile.

The highlight of the day came when Letten resurrected some of the legendary anecdotes about Edwards's gambling habits that had become public during the 1985 corruption trial. Asked about the aliases he used at Las Vegas casinos, Edwards acknowledged then that he had gambled under the names "Ed Neff," "T. Wong" and "Muffuletta." Turning around Letten's questions now, Edwards added that he was "probably the only person in America" who could obtain a cash advance from a casino using an assumed name. "That's how honorable I am and how good my reputation is," Edwards commented. The courtroom audience laughed at these and other quips. The jurors, again, barely broke a smile.

The former governor returned to the witness stand for a fourth and final time on April 14. Letten had completed his often blistering cross-examination, and now Edwards's attorney, Dan Small, wanted his client to end on a high note. "I'm seventy-two years old. I've already lived my biblically allotted time," remarked a reflective-sounding Edwards. "Statistically, I have about five or six years. If I'm lucky, maybe eight or nine."

Not wanting to give Edwards the smallest advantage, Letten jumped out of his chair with an objection that cut off the former governor's self-serving comment in midsentence. Edwards's statements, Letten complained, were irrelevant testimony. Polozola sustained the objection, blocking Edwards's poignant close. So Small simply asked the former governor whether he had headed a conspiracy to extort payoffs from Louisiana riverboat-casino applicants.

"The charges are not true," Edwards said firmly. "Not at all."

Moments later, Edwards stepped down from the witness stand and strode back to his seat at the defense table, confident that he had emerged triumphant in the battle with Letten.

Lawyers for each of the other six defendants then walked to the podium in the center of the courtroom and one by one stated that their clients did not wish to take the witness stand. At 2:40 p.m., the defense rested its case.

The testimony completed, *Times-Picayune* columnist James Gill offered this take on how things stood:

> After all the tape-recordings of sleazy conversations and testimony from erstwhile alleged accomplices recast as extortion victims, it seems certain that some of the defendants are heading up the river. Those who have followed the trial daily, however, are not yet convinced that Edwards will be among them. In the course of an epic and frequently acrimonious tussle with prosecutor Jim Letten, Edwards was nimble enough to put a benign gloss on much of the evidence against him. It is not inconceivable that he could have sowed reasonable doubt in the mind of at least one of those inscrutable jurors.
>
> Still, this is clearly the best chance the Feds ever had to nail Edwards, and Letten came loaded for crucifixion. Some of the evidence was so devastating that the best Edwards could do was to admit felonious plans but claim he didn't go through with them.

Added John Volz, who had failed to convict Edwards in the 1985–1986 trials: "The government has used every tool at its disposal, including videotapes, wiretaps and co-defendants who pleaded guilty and testified. If they don't get him this time with everything they have, they should give him a certificate of immunity for the future because he's too slick."

On April 18, the team of prosecutors working for United States Attorney Eddie Jordan Jr. spent six hours giving final arguments. They mercilessly attacked Edwards, spelling out the details of their evidence in each of the five schemes. "We have unveiled for you and unmasked a terribly corrupt governor," said Letten, arguing that Edwards had dragged his son Stephen and their five co-defendants into the criminal activities that he masterminded.

The prosecution's case was summed up in a few sentences of imagery offered by Assistant United States Attorney Mike Magner. "Think about the smartest kid ever to come from Avoyelles Parish with his hand in the cookie jar up to his elbows and a smile on his face," Magner said. "He's able to talk his way out of trouble so many times that it becomes a habit."

Manuel Roig-Franzia, who covered the trial for *The Times-Picayune*, paraphrased the remainder of Magner's analysis: "The charming, precocious boy from Avoyelles Parish morphed into a scheming adult, Magner suggested, because of an unhealthy desire to rise from the very poverty that Edwards highlighted when he took the witness stand in his own defense last week. 'You grow up with an insatiable greed for things, material things. The key word here is insatiable, it's never satisfied,' Magner said. Nowhere was that greed more apparent, Magner and his fellow prosecutors said, than in Edwards' involvement with riverboat casinos during the last of his four terms as governor and after his 1996 retirement."

The following day, it was the defense's turn to close. Dan Small, who was from Boston, told the jurors that they reminded him of a band of Revolutionary War patriots who had repelled eight hundred British soldiers at Lexington, Massachusetts, 225 years ago that week. "Stand your ground for these principles that make us free," Small said. "We don't convict people in this country based on gossip, innuendo and lies. We ask you to end this nightmare and find Edwin Edwards not guilty on all charges." He added, "It is, as I've said many times, a corruption case without corruption."

Said Pat Fanning, contractor Bobby Johnson's lawyer: "We're here because this is the culmination of the government's thirty-year hunt for Edwin Edwards. . . . The government is after Edwin Edwards in the worst way."

During two hours of remarks the next day, Jim Cole, Stephen Edwards's attorney, emphasized the "unlimited resources" of the FBI that led to the bugging of Stephen's office and the home and law office of his father. Cole asked the jurors to hold the federal government in check. "You stand between the power of that large government and citizens," he pleaded.

In a final rebuttal by the government, prosecutor Fred Harper exhorted jurors to have the "courage" to confront Louisiana's only four-term governor. "Look him straight in the eye and tell him he's guilty," Harper demanded.

Each side having had their final say, Judge Polozola dismissed the jurors for a three-day Easter weekend. They would begin deliberations on Monday, April 24, exactly sixteen weeks after the trial had begun. Over the weekend, analysts speculated on how long the jury might take to reach a verdict. They noted that in Edwards's 1985 corruption trial, jurors deliberated for twelve days before the judge declared a mistrial because one or two jurors—depending on which count—held out for an acquittal. After the retrial the following year, the jury deliberated for only twelve hours over the course of two days before they agreed to acquit Edwards of all charges.

On Monday morning, Polozola took center stage as he read ninety-six pages of instructions for the thirty-three-count indictment—ninety-one individual charges—to the seven men and five women on the jury. The judge emphasized that all jury decisions had to be unanimous and that they had to vote on each defendant and on each count. In all, that would mean 169 different votes. Polozola had decided to allow jurors to go home every night, but he cautioned them to avoid news accounts or discussions with anyone. Polozola's instructions included a legal definition of "reasonable doubt." To find the defendants guilty, the evidence had to be "of such a convincing character that you would be willing to rely and act upon it without hesitation in the most important of your own affairs."

Finally, after taking three breaks to rest his voice, Polozola announced, "Ladies and Gentlemen, you may now begin your deliberations. The jury is excused. Good luck to you." Following protocol, everyone stood as the jurors filed out of the courtroom on their way to decide the fate of Edwin Edwards and his six co-defendants.

At 5:00 p.m., after nearly four hours of deliberations, the jurors returned to the courtroom with the news that they would quit for the night. But they had accomplished one major task by selecting Juror 64 as their foreman. He was a forty-year-old white man who said during jury selection that he worked as a machinist, was married, and had three children. He did not gamble, and while he had favored the legalization of gambling at one time, he no longer did. He also said that prior to becoming a juror, he had paid little attention to the case, despite the extensive news coverage following the FBI raid of Edwards's home and office in April 1997. Always impeccably dressed, he sat in the front row of the jury box during the trial, and he took numerous notes.

The next news of the jury's deliberations came two days later, and it bore favorable tidings for the defense. In a handwritten note, jurors informed the judge that they were deadlocked on at least one of the thirty-three counts. "We are not able to reach an agreement on any of what we are working on. . . . At what point do we give up and go on to another charge?" the jurors asked.

"You don't need to follow the jury verdict [form] I gave you," Polozola told them in open court. "You can go in any order you want. However you feel is the best way to discuss all of these charges is OK with the court."

"I'm on pins and needles," Candy Edwards said that evening. "I feel good about it, but you never know."

"It's looking all right," echoed her husband, "but you never know."

On the following day, April 27, 2000, jury deliberations stalled after only an hour because of a dramatic development that would remain hidden from the public for a week. One of the jurors—Juror 68— had become all but paralyzed by the moral burden he bore. A forty-year-old white man from East Baton Rouge Parish, married, and with a child, Juror 68 had not given a job description during jury selection. He had said that he was not opposed to gambling and that he believed Edwards was "somewhat responsible" for corruption in Louisiana's gambling industry. "I am very intimidated because of how I may feel," Juror 68 now wrote to Polozola, underscoring the word "very" three times. "There is such an awesome responsibility with the lives of people in our and my hands that I am trying to erase some doubts but can't seem to forget them in my mind." Concerned that his agonized feelings were disrupting deliberations, he asked Polozola to remove him from the case, a step the judge was reluctant to take.

The foreman handed his own note to a United States marshal that day. "Due to the stress of the day, we ask that we wait until tomorrow to start back," the note said. Polozola read it and then told the jurors, "Just be patient with yourselves and each other. . . . I don't want any of y'all to feel like you're being pushed to do anything. Don't feel pressured that somebody is waiting for you to do something."

Polozola's words apparently comforted the twelve jurors because the next day, a Friday, seemed to go well. The panel did not seek the judge's assistance, and when they filed into the courtroom at the end of the afternoon to be dismissed for the weekend, several of them were smiling. This day, April 28, 2000, marked the third anniversary of the FBI raid on the home and office of Edwards.

On Tuesday, May 2, however, the uncertainty over Juror 68 returned. A juror sent a note to the judge, saying that his colleague was biased, had refused repeated requests to participate in deliberations, and had asked one of the jurors not to speak to him. Polozola responded by taking the extraordinary step of closing the courtroom at 9:30 a.m. to everyone but the attorneys and the defendants. Over the next ten hours, the judge interviewed the jurors one by one. He reopened the doors at 7:30 p.m., but he did not explain to the public and press what he was doing.

On Wednesday Polozola halted deliberations for the second straight day. The judge was trying to understand exactly what was happening inside the jury room. As part of this process, he even interviewed Number 68's Pentecostal pastor and associate pastor. Polozola was proceeding carefully because he had entered a legal minefield. The juror was required to deliberate, and Polozola could remove him if he wasn't doing so. However, if the judge erred in removing the juror, he would create grounds for an appeal.

By now the uncertainty caused by Juror 68 had become public. "Everybody is on millimeter-thin ice with this one. There's a very fine line for the judge to walk and avoid a mistrial," said Harry Rosenberg, Eddie Jordan's predecessor as the United States Attorney in New Orleans, now in private practice.

Given the doubts that Juror 68 expressed about the case, lawyers for both sides viewed him as favorable to Edwards and his six co-defendants. As a result, prosecutors sought his ouster, arguing that Juror 68 was biased in favor of Edwards and was violating rules by not deliberating with his colleagues. Defense lawyers countered that he ought to remain on the panel, arguing that he was deliberating properly. Ironically, about midway through the trial, someone had reported to the court that Juror 68 had vowed to vote for Edwards's conviction. An investigation by the United States marshals found no grounds to support the allegation. But until the recent incident, the prosecution had viewed Number 68 favorably, while the defense had seen him as a problem.

On Thursday Polozola kept the courthouse doors closed until 1:50 p.m. After the press and the spectators had reassembled, he brought in the jury—minus Juror 68. The judge had removed him. "We will now proceed with eleven jurors," Polozola told the courtroom audience. The deliberations could continue without Juror 68 because both sides had agreed before the trial began that the jury would continue its work one shy of the normal dozen, rather than start the deliberations over again after adding an alternate.

Polozola told the remaining jurors that they should not let the events of the past several days affect their work. "The fact that Number 68 is no longer on the jury should not enter into your deliberations," the judge said. He said his decision to remove the juror "doesn't mean I sided with him or anyone who agreed with him." He went on to say, "I think each of you should show respect to each other. Give everyone the opportunity to speak."

Once Polozola made his decision, the legal arguments over Juror 68 continued. The defense contended that the juror's removal should prompt a mistrial. Jim Cole, Stephen Edwards's attorney, said the dismissal "gives a clear signal that Number 68 was wrong" and that "whoever was in conflict" with the juror "had won." Cole added that the court's inquiry on this matter had done "irreparable damage" to the case.

Sonny Garcia, Andrew Martin's attorney, said, "There are no changes that can fix the problems." He added that he believed the jury was "tainted" and "unable to be fair."

Speaking for prosecutors, Assistant United States Attorney Todd Greenberg vigorously objected to these arguments. "There was no signal by the court that those who sided with Juror Number 68 were wrong," Greenberg said.

As on repeated occasions throughout the trial, Polozola sided with the prosecution. The jury's deliberations would continue, he ruled. None of the defendants responded visibly. But Edwards's daughter Anna and Stephen Edwards's wife, Leslie, dabbed tears from their eyes. Edwin Edwards's other daughter, Victoria, buried her face in her hands.

Mindful of Polozola's strict gag order, Edwards only shrugged when reporters outside the court asked for his reaction to the judge's dismissal of Juror 68. "Is this a low blow?" one asked. Edwards leaned forward and looked down at his crotch. "We'll take that as a yes," wrote commentator John Maginnis.

Freed from the distractions of Juror 68, the eleven-member jury deliberated without incident the next day, a Friday. After taking the weekend off, the jury remained behind closed doors on Monday for almost nine hours, making only brief appearances in the courtroom in the morning and early evening to be greeted and dismissed by Polozola.

By now, it was clear that a verdict could come at any time. Polozola had said that once the jury entered the courtroom after finishing its deliberations, the marshals would lock the doors and not allow anyone to leave until all ninety-one verdicts on the seven defendants had been read, beginning with Edwards and ending with gambling board member Ecotry Fuller. Anyone watching the results by closed-circuit television in the adjoining overflow courtroom, however, could leave before all the verdicts were in. Louisiana television stations, which normally had two or three people apiece at the trial, responded to these rules by beefing up their forces and making elaborate plans to air the news live immediately. Radio and TV stations planned to have reporters—or runners—view the verdict in the adjoining courtroom and then sprint outside to feed colleagues with the news.

Waiting for the jury, reporters and camera crews lounged on park benches and on the steps outside the courthouse entrance. Also lounging in the area was a black cat adopted by the media. One of the reporters had named him Bullpen, because he liked to hang around the two-tiered wooden stand—known as the media bullpen—that the television cameramen and still photographers used to record the day's events. "We think it's the ghost of a corrupt politician," one television reporter quipped. Of course, the tranquil scene would disappear in an instant when word passed that the jury had reached a verdict. When that happened, Polozola said everyone would have thirty minutes to assemble in the courtroom.

May 9, 2000, marked the twenty-eighth anniversary of Edwin Edwards's first inauguration as governor. The weather on this Tuesday was pleasant as Baton Rouge enjoyed yet another rainless day of unseasonably mild temperatures. In Pittsburgh, Arizona senator John McCain was meeting with Texas governor George W. Bush to tell him he had no interest in being on the Republican ticket as Bush's vice president in the upcoming presidential election. In Washington, D.C., former Presidents Gerald Ford and Jimmy Carter were endorsing President Bill Clinton's plan to give permanent trade status to China. Closer to home, in Baton Rouge, the Louisiana legislature was continuing to stumble in its efforts to balance the coming year's budget, with one lawmaker calling the impasse "a Mexican standoff."

The big news in Louisiana this day would take place downtown, less than a mile away from the Capitol, in the Russell B. Long Federal Building and United States Courthouse. At about 1:15 p.m., Judge Polozola's clerk began making phone calls. One went to the defense team, and another went to the prosecution's office. The message was short, not entirely clear, but urgent: The jury had given a note to the judge that required everyone to get to the courthouse immediately. What did the note say? The clerk did not offer an answer.

Geoffrey Santini, who had been the lead FBI agent during the investigation and had spent more than two weeks testifying during the trial, was finishing lunch at Ruby Tuesday's when he got word. Jim Letten, the lead prosecutor, had just eaten lunch with two colleagues and had stopped at a hobby shop to buy a wind-up glider for his son.

Most of the defendants and their lawyers were gathered at their normal lunch spot, the home of paralegal Mary Jane Marcantel, which served as their headquarters, only two blocks from the courthouse. They had just polished off a batch of baby back ribs from Tony's Seafood restaurant. Former governor Edwin Edwards, dressed in a dark blue suit, was on his way home from getting a haircut when he was called on his cell phone. His wife, Candy, wearing a pink pantsuit, was having lunch at the Silver Spoon restaurant. She made a U-turn across four lanes of traffic to race to the courthouse.

After everyone had reassembled in the courtroom, Polozola read the jury's note. It was succinct: "We have finished our deliberations. We now need the final verdict forms. So that we can turn them over to the court." Eighteen weeks and one day after the trial had begun, the panel had finally reached a verdict. The tension was excruciating. At 3:23 p.m., the jury entered the courtroom. The foreman gave the eleven-page verdict form to Polozola. As the judge flipped through it, Edwards's younger son, David, sat with his eyes closed in the second row, using one hand to clasp the hand of his wife, Laura, and the other to cradle the neck of his twelve-year-old nephew, Christopher, who had walked into court in soccer shorts. As the atmosphere intensified, Edwin Edwards craned his neck from his seat at the defense table. Polozola cut the tension, however, by looking up and announcing that the jury had not completed the form properly. "I hate to send you back," the judge said as he did so nonetheless. Stephen Edwards sighed audibly, then turned and winked at his wife, Leslie, in the front row. Less than a minute later, the jury walked back into the room and again turned over the verdict form. Ever confident, Edwin Edwards smiled and winked at Candy in the front row.

At long last, Polozola began to read the verdicts. From the very first count, it was clear that Edwards had found little favor in jurors' eyes. He was guilty on the charge of engaging in a criminal enterprise, known as the RICO statute (Racketeer Influenced Corrupt Organizations Act).

He was guilty of extorting the Players casino through Ricky Shetler. He was guilty of extorting Eddie DeBartolo Jr. He was guilty of money laundering in hiding payoffs made by Bobby Guidry, owner of the *Treasure Chest* casino. For thirty years, Edwin Edwards had stayed one step ahead of the law. Now the Feds had caught him. He was a convicted crook.

In all, Edwards was found guilty on seventeen of twenty-six counts. The seventy-two-year-old former governor was facing more than two hundred years in prison along with more than $1 million in forfeitures. Poker-faced as always, Edwards marked the results on a verdict form as Polozola proceeded count by count. Candy Edwards, however, could not contain her emotions. She doubled over and began sobbing.

The news was equally bad for Stephen Edwards. The jury found him guilty of extorting Guidry, DeBartolo, and Players. In all, he was convicted on eighteen of twenty-three counts. Leslie Edwards collapsed into her mother's arms, crying. Anna Edwards, whose brother and father had just been found guilty, also sobbed audibly.

Cecil Brown, the Eunice cattle auctioneer, whose friendship with Houston con man Patrick Graham had been crucial in initiating the FBI investigation four years earlier, was guilty on all four counts of extorting Jazz Enterprises, the Baton Rouge riverboat. Andrew Martin, Edwards's former aide and Bobby Guidry's pal, was guilty on all six counts of extorting Guidry. Bobby Johnson, the illiterate Baton Rouge contractor who was accused of extorting Jazz Enterprises, was guilty on all nine counts.

Two of the seven defendants got good news. State senator Greg Tarver, charged with helping Edwards extort money from DeBartolo and furnish a confidential gambling board summary to the 49ers owner, was acquitted on all eleven counts. "Way to go," mouthed Edwards to Tarver, sitting behind him at an adjoining defense table. Ecotry Fuller, who was indicted on the same charges as his friend Tarver, was acquitted on all twelve counts. As FBI agent Freddy Cleveland had predicted two years earlier when Eddie Jordan refused to indict state senator Cleo Fields, without Fields the jury could not connect payoffs to Tarver and Fuller from DeBartolo through Edwards.

Polozola needed fifteen minutes to read the verdicts. When he had finished, he and the jury exited through opposite doors. Everyone stood as the judge and jurors filed out—everyone, that is, but Candy, Leslie, Anna, and Victoria Edwards, who remained seated in protest. Edwin Edwards turned to shake hands with his attorneys. He then walked over to Candy and embraced her. They headed out of the courtroom, arm in arm. Just before exiting, Edwards hugged his older brother, Marion, who had been best man at their wedding six years earlier. "Brother, I want you to take care of the family," Edwards said. "You're in charge now."

Mary Jane Marcantel, the defense team's paralegal, kept the pack of reporters and curious spectators out of the courthouse elevator as the former governor and several family members stepped inside. As the doors shut, Candy Edwards collapsed into the arms of her husband, who was leaning against the corner of the elevator with a somber look on his face. By the time the elevator had descended two floors, however, the Edwardses had composed themselves.

Holding hands, they walked through the open glass double doors and out of the courthouse. Their hands disengaged, and Candy paused momentarily as Edwards strode ahead to a phalanx of microphones on the courthouse steps. Candy caught up and took her place to his left, her arm looped through his. Stephen, Anna, and David Edwards stood behind them. Elaine Edwards, their mother and Edwards's first wife, joined them, nearly anonymous behind her dark sunglasses. They all looked distraught.

Edwards paused briefly, then said, "We're still under a gag order so I'm restricted in what I can say." He then thanked his family and supporters. "I regret that it has ended this way," he said, "but that is the system. I lived seventy-two years of my life within the system. I'll spend the rest of my life within the system. Whatever consequences flow from this, I'm prepared to face."

He said he would file an appeal and was hopeful that it would be successful. "In due course, whatever comes, comes," he added.

Then he said, "The Chinese have a saying that if you sit by the river long enough, the dead body of your enemy will come floating down the river." He cocked his head slightly to the right. "I suppose the Feds sat by the river long enough, so here comes my body."

Edwards briefly answered five questions, turned to his left, and began walking away. As he did, he gave two taps to a courthouse hand railing with the jury verdict form.

Reporters pressed around the now convicted former governor, asking him more questions. As the pack surrounding Edwards crossed Main Street, rush-hour traffic halted. Several cars honked their horns. A woman in the passenger seat of one car leaned out the window and urged Edwards to stay the course. "You go, Governor," she said. Amid the tumult, he did not hear her and continued to walk away from the courthouse. Visible about ten blocks in the distance stood the Louisiana State Capitol, the towering house that Huey Long had built and that his political and ethical heir had dominated for the past thirty years, perhaps until this very moment.

Epilogue

bout an hour after a jury of ordinary citizens had pronounced Edwin Edwards guilty on corruption charges, a verdict that seemed likely to send him to prison for the remainder of his life, Bob d'Hemecourt called his close friend, unsure of what to say. Edwards got on the phone and immediately asked, "Aren't you glad I don't smoke?"

"What?" replied a puzzled d'Hemecourt.

"Aren't you glad I don't smoke?" Edwards repeated.

"Yeah, I'm glad," d'Hemecourt responded, hesitantly. "But why?"

Edwards paused. "Now you don't have to sneak cigarettes into the prison when you see me," he said.

Two weeks later, d'Hemecourt was still shaking his head at Edwards's comments. "He calmed me down," d'Hemecourt said. "He made me feel better."

How many people under such terrible circumstances could have come up with such a clever and disarming comment? And therein lies the tragedy of Edwin Edwards. His incredible gifts made him the only man to be elected governor of Louisiana four times. He could charm a society matron one moment and an oil-rig worker the next; he could fashion a compromise that would bring peace to two warring camps; he could throw off prying reporters with a well-timed quip; he could divine the solution to a political mess when others saw only confusion. Like too many politicians in Louisiana, however, he believed it was right to use his public office for private gain, for himself and for his closest friends and political allies. The son of a sharecropper, raised in a home without electricity or running water, he reveled in being a high-stakes gambler, having a long line of mistresses, and accumulating a seven-figure bank account. In sum, he used only a fraction of his awesome talents to better the lives of Louisiana's 4.5 million residents.

Consider where the Bayou State stood in relation to Georgia, South Carolina, North Carolina, Alabama, Mississippi, and Arkansas when Edwards first took office in 1972. And consider how much those other states have advanced since then, while Louisiana has seemed frozen in time. Today, Louisiana is last or next to last in virtually every social and economic index. The state is down to one Fortune 500 company—Entergy—that nearly moved to Florida in 2000. Some New Orleans public schools still don't have air conditioning.

What makes the state's laggard pace even more striking is that if one state has had an advantage over the past thirty years, it is Louisiana, because it has had one political leader—Edwards—during most of that period. But Louisiana has proceeded on its wayward path. In 2000, three of the eight people elected to statewide office in 1991—Edwards, insurance commissioner Jim Brown, and elections commissioner Jerry Fowler—were convicted of crimes.

And, thanks largely to Edwards's actions, gambling interests have once again sunk their tentacles deep into the political, social, and economic flesh of Louisiana. One measure of gambling's power has been the behavior of Governor Mike Foster, who campaigned to succeed Edwards on an anti-gambling platform in 1995. Once in office, however, Foster repeatedly did the bidding of the casino and video poker interests. He kept the legislature from banning video poker in 1996.

He had no interest in investigating allegations of corruption in how
Harrah's Jazz had won the casino license in 1993 or in answering questions surrounding the actions of Harrah's and Bankers Trust in the
casino shutdown just before Thanksgiving in 1995.

Had the millionaire governor been bought off? Not likely. Foster's
performance highlighted a sadder truth: without significant economic
development in any other sector of the Louisiana landscape, gambling,
Foster apparently concluded, did not merit the active opposition of
even an "anti-gambling" governor.

It was on Foster's watch that the Harrah's casino reopened in New
Orleans on October 28, 1999, in the Canal Street building erected on
the site of the Rivergate. The casino would have remained closed if Foster hadn't gotten a state law changed at Harrah's behest. (Harrah's once
again misjudged the market, however, and the casino performed poorly.)

Another measure of gambling's long reach: as a state senator in
1992, Marc Morial had opposed the proposal to create the New
Orleans casino. But as New Orleans's mayor, he fervently supported
Harrah's. Like Foster, Morial headed a government that was addicted
to gambling revenue. (It shouldn't be discounted that friends of Morial's also snagged a few choice casino contracts.)

Even David Treen—Edwards's long-standing political rival, the
state's first Republican governor since Reconstruction, and a paragon
of good government—was not immune from gambling's sway. Three
years after denouncing gambling's influence during an aborted 1995
gubernatorial campaign, Treen was shilling for casino interests. "I'm so
mad about that that I can't think straight," fumed Treen's friend, Billy
Nungesser, who had repeatedly challenged Harrah's as a member of
the casino commission.

Louisiana's history has been marked by the intermittent flowering
and repression of gambling. In the years following the Civil War, the
outrages of the Louisiana Lottery led to its abolition. The casinos operated by mobsters Frank Costello and Carlos Marcello through the
middle decades of the twentieth century were eventually shut down
amid scandal.

In its latest resurrection, legalized gambling has needed less than a decade to supplant the petrochemical industry as the state's most powerful interest group. Gambling's easy access to cash and its proclivity for buying favor has meshed all too perfectly with a state full of purchasable lawyers, lobbyists, and politicians.

On January 8, 2001, United States District Judge Frank Polozola sentenced Edwin Edwards to a ten-year prison sentence for his role in the riverboat gambling corruption case. Edwards remained characteristically undaunted. "This is not over with," he said on the courthouse steps after the sentencing. "As they say in the opera, the fat lady has not yet sung." Indeed, surprising just about everyone but Edwards, the Fifth United States Circuit Court of Appeals announced three weeks later that the seventy-three-year-old former governor could remain free, pending appeal, along with his son Stephen Edwards, former aide Andrew Martin, and cattle auctioneer Cecil Brown.

Regardless of Edwards's fate, it was clear that his era was over. In the aftermath, one overarching question loomed: Did Edwards's demise attest to gambling's now unrelenting grip on the state, or was it gambling's last gasp, the harbinger of a political backlash that might reverse gambling's gains? Naturally, only the citizens of Louisiana can answer that question. But in a state with a culture of corruption since its founding after the Louisiana Purchase nearly two hundred years ago, change that could reverse gambling's harmful gains in the Bayou State will not come easily. To begin with, federal officials—agents from the FBI and prosecutors from the United States Attorney's office—and the state's newspapers will have to continue to play a key watchdog role.

But Louisiana will have to go much further so that there will be economic alternatives to gambling. The public and the politicians will have to take such basic steps as improving education (higher teacher salaries, up-to-date classrooms, and a demand for better performance), reforming the state's tax system (which today relies too heavily on sales taxes), and ending its reliance on quick fixes to solve economic problems. Replacing oil and gas revenue with gambling taxes has proven disastrous. Ultimately, the state will have to shed its affinity for practicing the Louisiana Way.

A Note on Sources

I covered many of the events depicted in this book while writing about the legalization of gambling and its aftermath—from March 1992 to February 1996—as a reporter for *The Times-Picayune*. To augment my initial reporting and to get details on the stories I didn't cover, I collected—and then reviewed—legal depositions, court transcripts, legislative bills, official meeting transcripts, FBI affidavits, official letters, architectural renderings, financial documents, more than a thousand *Times-Picayune* news articles, and a much smaller number of articles from other newspapers and magazines. (*The Times-Picayune* did a terrific job of essentially serving as the newspaper of record as Louisiana entered a new, perilous era.) I returned to Louisiana repeatedly to interview more than one hundred people involved in the key gambling developments, and I did numerous follow-up phone calls from Florida. I interviewed about twenty-five people more than a dozen times.

Interviews for the book were different than those for my earlier newspaper articles. For the newspaper, I wanted to know what happened, and I wanted good quotes so I could capture a snapshot event. For the book, I wanted my sources to recall what they and others said, and what they were thinking and feeling at the time of the events in question. As an author, I wanted to establish a narrative in which I reproduced scenes and dialogue. That can be a tricky proposition, so I am using quotes for the book from direct participants. In most cases, to double-check accuracy, I called sources to read back sections where I was planning to quote them.

Of course, memories are fallible, and some people recall events with a more positive spin for themselves than they deserve. To counter that, I interviewed as many people as possible with direct knowledge of the key events. In some cases, accounts differed. For example, on August 18, 1993, the day it appeared that Christopher Hemmeter would not come to terms with Harrah's Jazz for the New Orleans land casino, two people remembered Governor Edwin Edwards as dramatically noting the time of the breakdown as 7:15 p.m. But more people there recalled the time as 5:15 p.m. What clinched 5:15 p.m. for me: two of Edwards's aides told me that the development was carried on the 6:00 p.m. news in Baton Rouge, and that Edwards would have concluded the negotiations in time so he could eat supper as usual at 6:00 p.m.

In cases where two people had different memories of an event, I relied on the more credible account. In some cases, where I couldn't decide which account was more accurate, I simply omitted the conflicting detail. This happened with the account of the December 14, 1993, private meeting to decide whether the Louisiana State Police would license Hemmeter for his riverboat. Roland Jones described a startling detail during the meeting that I wanted to include in the book. But none of the others there did. I wasn't sure what to do: Jones and the rest had all been reliable sources. In the end, to be safe, I kept out the detail.

Notes

INTRODUCTION

3 *Liebling called Louisiana:* A. J. Liebling, *The Earl of Louisiana* (New York: The New Yorker Magazine Inc., 1960), p. 18.

3 *Earl Long once offered:* Michael L. Kurtz and Morgan D. Peoples, *Earl K. Long* (Baton Rouge: Louisiana State University Press, 1990), p. xiii.

3 *Huey Long, in one of his: Los Angeles Times,* August 14, 1985.

4 "Yat" comes from the popular phrase "Where are you at?" In "Yat-speak," it's "Where y'at?"

4 *As Richard Leche:* John Maginnis, *The Last Hayride* (Baton Rouge: Gris Gris, 1984), p. 26.

5 *One native summed it up:* Telephone interview with James Carville, February 4, 2000.

5 *the number of states:* Telephone interview with Naomi Greer of the American Gaming Association; *International Gaming & Wagering Business,* August 2000.

7 England controlled a small portion of Louisiana north of Lake Pontchartrain from 1763 to 1783.

7 *In an 1820 letter:* Albert A. Fossier, *New Orleans: The Glamour Period, 1800–1840* (New Orleans: Pelican Publishing Company), p. 383.

7 *"we should compel": Times Picayune,* January 7, 1986.

7 *When his father died:* Edward Larocque Tinker, *The Palingenesis of Craps* (New York: The Press of the Woolly Whale, 1933). Most of the material on Marigny that follows is from this short publication.

7 *According to one account:* Ibid.

8 *"poque": Times-Picayune,* September 22, 1957.

9 *One of the era's noted gamblers:* American Mercury, August 1936.
9 *"A finer-mounted troop":* Ibid.
9 *"When we were ordered":* Ibid.
10 *The amount offered:* Louisiana Historical Quarterly, October 1944, p. 974.
10 *reportedly spending $250,000:* Henry Chafetz, Play the Devil (New York: Bonanza Books, 1960), p. 301.
11 *"The Lottery Company":* Louisiana Historical Quarterly, July 1948, p. 764.
11 *Determined to bankrupt:* Louisiana Historical Quarterly, October 1944, p. 1002.
11 *"New Orleans became":* Collier's, January 20, 1951.
12 The estimated 1890 lottery figures are from Timothy L. O'Brien, *Bad Bet: The Inside Story of the Glamour, Glitz, and Danger of America's Gambling Industry* (New York: Times Books, 1998), p. 107.
12 *As one magazine:* The Forum, January 1892.
13 *A senator who:* Century, February 1892.
13 *"At no time":* Joy J. Jackson, New Orleans in the Gilded Age (Baton Rouge: Louisiana State University Press, 1969), p. 127.
13 *in the summer of 1890:* Louisiana Historical Quarterly, October 1944.
15 *A woman who arrived:* Literary Digest, March 24, 1917.
15 *a typical handbook:* Louis Vyhnanek, Unorganized Crime: New Orleans in the 1920s (Lafayette, La.: The Center for Louisiana Studies, 1998), p. 95.
16 *In May he announced:* Literary Digest, June 15, 1935.
16 *Long didn't disclose:* Kurtz and Peoples, p. 102; Saturday Evening Post, April 28, 1951.
16 *In one account:* Michael L. Kurtz, "Longism and Organized Crime" in Huey at 100: Centennial Essays on Huey P. Long (Ruston, La.: Louisiana Tech University, 1995), p. 111.
18 *The FBI afterward:* Kurtz and Peoples, p. 88.
18 *"Outside of politics":* Ibid., pp. 28–29.
18 *"Earl, according to":* Ibid., p. 88.
19 *"The condition I let":* The Item, September 14, 1952.
19 *In one of the first:* The Item, January 14, 1947.
19 *In another article:* The Item, January 15, 1947.
19 *The newspapermen reported:* The Item, January 27, 1947.
20 *Each time:* The Item, January 25, 1951; Times-Picayune, January 26, 1951.
21 *On the second day:* Times-Picayune, January 27, 1951.
21 *Sheriff Rowley was:* The Item, January 28, 1951.
21 *Kefauver asked him:* Ibid.
22 *At Club Forest:* The Item, January 31, 1951.
22 *On his fifth day:* Louisiana Trooper, Summer 1990.
22 *The day after:* Ibid.
23 *"Heil Hitler!":* Ibid.
23 *Grevemberg took this mission:* Ibid; Collier's, April 1, 1955.
24 *When that approach:* Louisiana Trooper, Summer 1990.

24 *Most police officers:* Edward F. Haas, *DeLesseps S. Morrison and the Image of Reform* (Baton Rouge: Louisiana State University Press, 1974), pp. 98–118.

25 *he was offered: Saturday Evening Post,* February 29, 1964.

25 *When* Life *magazine came: Life,* September 1, 1967.

26 *"He's the strongest":* John H. Davis, *Mafia Kingfish: Carlos Marcello and the Assassination of John F. Kennedy* (New York: Signet, 1989), p. 14.

CHAPTER 1

27 *The large crowd: Times-Picayune,* January 5, 1992. The New Year's Eve account is from this article.

29 Background on Edwards: Interview with Edwards, Baton Rouge, February 3, 1998, and June 10, 1999; John Maginnis, *The Last Hayride* (Baton Rouge: Gris Gris, 1984), pp. 10–16.

30 *"I remember when": New Orleans,* May 1991.

31 *"This must be":* Interview, June 10, 1999.

31 *a man named Warren (Puggy) Moity:* Interview, February 3, 1998.

32 *would dub this: Times-Picayune,* November 8, 1998.

32 *In some instances:* Maginnis, pp. 17–18; *People,* February 13, 1984.

32 *For example, when asked: Times-Picayune,* March 9, 1980.

32 *Responding to a book's claims: Philadelphia Inquirer,* June 1, 1991.

33 *"I think people": Times-Picayune,* March 9, 1980.

33 *Stanley Bardwell Jr.: Los Angeles Times,* August 14, 1985.

33 *Treen, he said: Los Angeles Times,* October 13, 1991.

34 *Edwards also cracked: People,* February 13, 1984.

34 *Edwards was so: Philadelphia Inquirer,* June 1, 1991.

34 *Sighed a befuddled Treen: Time,* March 11, 1985.

34 *"The debt": Times-Picayune,* October 9, 1995.

34 *Edwards won $15,000:* Maginnis, p. 339.

34 *Walker Percy put it:* Associated Press, March 29, 1985.

35 *Prosecutors charged that Edwards: Times-Picayune,* November 7, 1985.

35 *Edwards denied the charges: Los Angeles Times,* August 14, 1985.

35 *"I do not collect stamps": Times-Picayune,* July 7, 1991.

35 *In time, the Las Vegas casinos: Times-Picayune,* August 2, 1992.

36 *In sensational testimony: Times-Picayune,* December 3, 1985.

36 *A Caesars executive: Times-Picayune,* November 8, 1985.

36 *Edwards attempted to hide:* Ibid.

36 *When he took: Times-Picayune,* December 3, 1985.

36 *"It's indicative":* United Press International, October 26, 1985.

36 *On other days:* Ibid.

37 *a reporter shouted: New Republic,* January 27, 1986.

37 *"Edwin Edwards will return": Los Angeles Times,* May 11, 1986.

37 *"Everybody laughs":* Associated Press, March 29, 1987.

37 *Edwards outlined his plan:* Times-Picayune, January 7, 1986.

38 *or as one legislator put it:* Associated Press, March 29, 1987.

38 *"Nosey feds are":* Ibid.

39 *"I want a governor":* Los Angeles Times, October 13, 1991.

40 *"I guess the big jury":* Times-Picayune, October 26, 1987.

40 *"He was blessed":* Ibid.

40 *"If Buddy Roemer":* Times-Picayune, October 27, 1987.

41 *"We are losing":* Times-Picayune, March 28, 1991.

43 *If the legislature:* Times-Picayune, June 6, 1990.

44 Background on Peppi Bruneau: Interview with Bruneau, New Orleans, July 31, 1998.

44 *Emile Bruneau also:* Davis, pp. 142, 160.

44 *"These machines are":* Times-Picayune, May 23, 1991.

44 *In a letter to the editor:* Times-Picayune, June 12, 1991.

45 *"I've got a friend":* Interview with Bruneau.

46 *"We don't want":* Ibid.

46 *"Mr. Scogin, if you":* Ibid.

46 *Two days after:* Baton Rouge Morning Advocate, July 10, 1991.

47 *"This follows what":* Times-Picayune, July 19, 1991.

47 *Aware of his concerns:* Interview with Bruneau; interview with Don Kelly, Natchitoches, La., July 27, 1998; telephone interview with Roemer, August 4, 1998.

48 Background on David Duke: Tyler Bridges, *The Rise of David Duke* (Jackson: University Press of Mississippi, 1995).

48 *also was a high roller:* Times-Picayune, July 7, 1991.

49 *Two bumper stickers:* Bridges, p. 232.

49 *even though exit polls:* Ibid., p. 236.

CHAPTER 2

50 Account of the meeting with the Brennans and background on Forgotston: Interview with Forgotston, New Orleans, October 27, 1996; Forgotston, undated memo to himself written shortly after the meeting.

52 *When a* Times-Picayune *reporter:* Times-Picayune, January 5, 1992.

52 *But James Gill:* Times-Picayune, January 8, 1992.

53 *But Edwards stepped:* Times-Picayune, February 15, 1992.

53 Background on Lalonde: Interview with Lalonde, Sunset, La., September 1, 1996.

54 *He was still insisting:* Times-Picayune, April 1, 1992.

54 Background on Copelin: Times-Picayune, September 16, 1990; the author also has researched Copelin as well as Senator Kelly and Billy Broadhurst.

56 *In 1979, Broadhurst's law firm:* Times-Picayune, May 5, 1987.

57 *Raymond Strother, a Louisiana:* Telephone interview with Strother, April 14, 1993.

57 *Broadhurst's bubble: Miami Herald,* May 3, 1987.
57 *"I asked around":* Interview with Robinowitz, Dallas, September 7, 1996.
58 *Lalonde particularly blamed: Times-Picayune,* May 7, 1992.
58 *On May 12, Edwards convened: Times-Picayune,* May 13, 1992.
58 *Edwards met with: Times-Picayune,* May 22, 1992.
59 *With these deft: Times-Picayune,* May 14, 1992.
59 *sharply disagreed: Times-Picayune,* May 17, 1992.
60 *"Gambling is no longer": Times-Picayune,* May 21, 1992.
60 *Nevertheless, Speaker John Alario: Times-Picayune,* May 22, 1992.
61 *"This thing smells": Times-Picayune,* June 5, 1992.
61 *Another opponent:* Ibid.
61 *Countered Representative Lalonde:* Ibid.
61 *He added: Baton Rouge Morning Advocate,* June 5, 1992.
62 Account of how casino bill failed: Telephone interview with Stine, November 20, 1996; others interviewed about that day were Barthelemy adviser Ron Nabonne, New Orleans, August 31, 1996; Edwards counsel Al Donovan, Metairie, La., September 6, 1996; Representative Quentin Dastugue, telephone interview, October 30, 1996; Representative Charles Lancaster, telephone interview, November 1, 1996; Barthelemy aide Wayne Collier, New Orleans, October 31, 1996; anti-casino lobbyist Tom Spradley, Baton Rouge, November 1, 1996; anti-casino lobbyist C. B. Forgotston, New Orleans, October 27, 1996; Speaker John Alario, Westwego, La., December 3, 1997; Representative Chuck McMains, Baton Rouge, December 6, 1997; pro-casino lobbyist Billy Broadhurst, New Orleans, July 31, 1998; Representative Peppi Bruneau, New Orleans, July 31, 1998.
63 *The next day, Alario: Times-Picayune,* June 6, 1992.
63 *Added Edwards:* Ibid.
63 *The day after:* Interview with Alario.
64 *Keeping his cards:* Ibid.
65 Account of how casino bill passed: *Times-Picayune,* June 9, 1992; interviews: pro-casino lobbyist and Edwards friend Bob d'Hemecourt, New Orleans, July 30, 1993; Dastugue, New Orleans, June 24, 1992, and October 30, 1996; Lalonde; Nabonne; New Orleans city councilman Lambert Boissiere, New Orleans, September 2, 1996; pro-casino lobbyist Hank Braden, New Orleans, September 4, 1996; Donovan; House clerk Butch Speer, Baton Rouge, September 6, 1996; Alario; Senator Kelly aide Dee Dee Fulmer, Baton Rouge, October 30, 1996; Lancaster; Forgotston; Spradley; Stine; Representative Don Higginbotham, telephone interview, November 24, 1996; McMains; lobbyist George Brown, Baton Rouge, June 8, 1998; Representative Steve Windhorst, telephone interview, June 8, 1998; Representative Danny Mitchell, telephone interview, June 8, 1998; Representative Jimmy Dimos, telephone interview, June 8, 1998; Broadhurst; Bruneau; Edwards aide Sid Moreland, Baton Rouge, May 27, 2000.
69 *The next day: Times-Picayune,* June 12, 1992.
69 *Edwards offered: Times-Picayune,* June 19, 1992.

CHAPTER 3

70 *"The city is"*: New York Times, July 7, 1992.

71 *"We're like a 60-year-old"*: Ibid.

71 *"Daniel Robinowitz: A success"*: Dallas Morning News, December 19, 1965.

71 Account of how Robinowitz envisioned the casino, carried out his plans with Barthelemy and Wynn, and hooked up with Hemmeter: Interview with Robinowitz, Dallas, September 7, 1996; also telephone interview, October 9, 1996; interview with New Orleans city councilman Lambert Boissiere, New Orleans, September 2, 1996; interview with Barthelemy aide Wayne Collier, New Orleans, October 31, 1996; Times-Picayune, August 8, 1993.

76 Background on Hemmeter: Interview with Hemmeter, New Orleans, April 13, 1992; New Orleans, January 1993.

76 *"flat broke"*: Rocky Mountain News, July 5, 1992.

76 *Hemmeter exaggerated:* Mountain View High School yearbooks, 1954–1957.

76 *Charlie Cooke, who coached:* Telephone interview with Cooke, February 18, 1994.

77 *This was echoed:* Telephone interview with Steve Flynn, February 18, 1994.

77 *Hemmeter described his rise:* Interview with Hemmeter; New Orleans, January 1993.

77 *To build it:* Hawaii Business, July 1, 1985; Los Angeles Times, June 21, 1987; Business Week, March 30, 1987; Continental Profiles, September 1988; In Paradise, February 1990.

78 *"The men who"*: People, October 19, 1987.

78 Forbes *estimated:* Forbes, October 24, 1988.

78 *"We're not in"*: New York Times, September 16, 1987.

79 *The mega-resort age:* Times-Picayune, May 16, 1992, and February 10, 1993.

80 *When Rittvo got off:* Interview with Steve Rittvo, New Orleans, October 31, 1996.

80 *Robinowitz and Hemmeter:* Times-Picayune, April 16, 1992; interview with Hemmeter, New Orleans, April 15, 1992. For full account of Hawaii trip: interviews with Robinowitz, Boissiere, and Collier. For description of home: Sotheby's International Realty brochure; Honolulu Star-Bulletin, September 28, 1990.

82 *Hemmeter would construct:* Interviews with Steve Rittvo, New Orleans, October 1, 1996, and May 24, 1997; Steven Bingler, New Orleans, September 3, 1996.

82 *Bingler was incredulous:* Ibid.

83 *headlined a story:* New Orleans City Business, February 24, 1992.

84 *Hemmeter also secretly flew:* Times-Picayune, April 16, 1992.

84 *Edwards thought that Hemmeter:* Interview with Edwards, Baton Rouge, February 3, 1998.

84 *showered gifts on lawmakers:* Times-Picayune, January 5, 1994, and January 6, 1994.

85 *After introductions:* Interview with Wilson, New Orleans, April 14, 1992.

85 *"I've never been treated"*: Interview with Boissiere, New Orleans, September 2, 1996.
85 *Hemmeter cursed*: Interview with Robinowitz, Dallas, September 7, 1996.
87 *the newspaper disclosed*: Times-Picayune, April 16, 1992.
87 *"Chris is an absolute"*: Times-Picayune, May 16, 1992.
87 *he unveiled it*: Times-Picayune, April 29, 1992.
89 *"It looks like"*: Interview with Boissiere.
89 Background on Gauthier: Interview with Gauthier, Metairie, La., July 7, 1992; Peter Pringle, *Cornered: Big Tobacco at the Bar of Justice* (New York: Henry Holt, 1998), pp. 36–38.
90 *As he read*: Interview with Gauthier.
91 *The group met*: Interviews with John Cummings, New Orleans, August 30, 1996; Louie Roussel III, Metairie, La., October 27, 1996; Pete Rhodes, New Orleans, October 31, 1996; George Solomon, Harahan, La., December 4, 1997; Calvin Fayard, Denham Springs, La., November 30, 1999.
91 *He announced that he had*: Times-Picayune, June 25, 1992.
92 *"That's it"*: Telephone interview, July 1, 1992.
92 *had made an "absolute guarantee"*: Gambit, May 11, 1992.
92 *"To have a Las Vegas"*: Interview with Hemmeter, New Orleans, May 7, 1992.
92 *The newspaper, in an editorial*: Times-Picayune, June 26, 1992.
92 *It reported*: Times-Picayune, June 27, 1992.
94 *weighed in*: Times-Picayune, October 25, 1992.
95 *Barthelemy began by saying*: Times-Picayune, November 6, 1992.
95 *In Baton Rouge*: Interview with Donovan, Metairie, La., September 6, 1996.

CHAPTER 4

97 *Hemmeter now proposed*: Times-Picayune, January 17, 1993.
97 *"Fountains, choreographed to music"*: Celebration Park Site Plan, January 1993.
98 *"It's his immorality"*: National Public Radio, February 25, 1993.
98 *nine neighborhood groups*: Times-Picayune, February 25, 1993.
98 *While others asked*: Times-Picayune, February 27, 1993.
98 *Governor Edwards . . . told Barthelemy*: Interview with Edwards, Baton Rouge, July 30, 1998.
99 *slammed the project*: Forbes, March 1, 1993.
99 *Edwards dismissed*: Times-Picayune, February 19, 1993 (note that the Forbes article became public in mid-February).
99 *To do so*: Times-Picayune, February 17, 1993.
99 *took aim*: 60 Minutes video, March 21, 1993; Times-Picayune, March 22, 1993.
100 *"These folks knew"*: Times-Picayune, August 6, 1993.
100 *"I've dealt with him"*: Times-Picayune, August 8, 1993.
100 *He struck out*: Interview with Edwards, Baton Rouge, February 3, 1998.
100 *The company's founder*: Harrah's People, Spring 1995.
101 *Pushed by an ambitious lawyer*: Forbes, December 7, 1992.

101 *With a reputation: Times-Picayune,* April 23, 1995.

102 *"Harrah's is": Times-Picayune,* August 22, 1993.

102 *"Why don't you":* Interview with Edwards.

102 *But he dashed:* Telephone interview with Gauthier, August 5, 1993; Solomon interview; telephone interview with Morgan, September 19, 2000.

103 *"Business and professional": Times-Picayune,* June 11, 1992.

104 *A day later: Times-Picayune,* June 13, 1992.

104 *Wary of the governor's:* Interview with Nungesser, New Orleans, December 3, 1997.

104 *Edwards trumpeted: Times-Picayune,* June 20, 1992.

104 *Three months later: Times-Picayune,* September 3, 1992.

105 *"I'm very happy": Times-Picayune,* September 11, 1992.

105 *disclosed that Hanna: Times-Picayune,* October 6, 1992.

105 *Ten days later: Times-Picayune,* October 16, 1992.

105 *followed a week later: Times-Picayune,* October 24, 1992.

106 *Edwards defended: Times-Picayune,* December 6, 1992.

106 *"The casino board": Times-Picayune,* December 9, 1992.

106 *"I'm going to":* Interview with Chastain, Diamondhead, Miss., July 26, 1998.

107 *Frank, for example: Times-Picayune,* April 30, 1993.

107 *"We have spent":* Ibid.

107 *"The blatant disregard":* May 1, 1993.

108 Description of the two bids: *Times-Picayune,* June 5, 1993.

109 *"The crucial difference": Times-Picayune,* August 6, 1993.

109 *Wendell Gauthier of Harrah's Jazz: Times-Picayune,* August 12, 1993.

109 *Hemmeter retorted:* Ibid.

109 *had secretly given: Times-Picayune,* July 14, 1993.

109 *"Why were we": Times-Picayune,* July 15, 1993.

109 *"It remains to be": Times-Picayune,* July 22, 1993.

110 *Daniel Robinowitz asked:* Interview with Robinowitz, September 7, 1996; interview with Cummings, August 30, 1996; interview with Solomon, December 4, 1997; interview with Broadhurst, New Orleans, July 31, 1998.

110 *on its front page: Times-Picayune,* August 11, 1993.

111 Account of the Sallie Page meeting: Interviews with Cummings; Broadhurst, New Orleans, September 10, 1996; Solomon; Edwards, February 3, 1998.

112 *When Louie Roussel:* Interview with Roussel, October 27, 1996.

112 *When Bob d'Hemecourt:* Interview with d'Hemecourt, Metairie, La., August 31, 1996.

113 *"There's gonna be":* Interview with Frank Donze, New Orleans, June 24, 1998.

113 Account of the vote: Interview with Max Chastain; WWL-TV New Orleans news video, August 11, 1993; *Times-Picayune,* August 12, 1993; *Baton Rouge Advocate,* August 12, 1993; interview with Bert Rowley, Chalmette, La., December 1, 1997; interview with Billy Nungesser, December 3, 1997; interview with Joan Heisser, New Orleans, May 23, 1997; interview with John Cummings, New Orleans, October 28, 1996; interview with Pete Rhodes, October 31, 1996; inter-

view with Solomon; interview with Hemmeter attorney Basile Uddo, New
Orleans, January 26, 1997; interview with casino board attorney Tom Barbera,
December 5, 1997; interview with Caesars representative George Nattin, Bossier
City, La., July 28, 1998; interview with Gerard Thomas, Natchitoches, La., July
28, 1998; interviews with Broadhurst and Robinowitz.

114 *After a while:* Interview with Robinowitz.

115 *Edwards got word:* Interview with Edwards, July 30, 1998; interview with Moreland, Baton Rouge, May 27, 2000.

115 Account of Barthelemy getting the news: Interview with Nabonne, New Orleans,
August 31, 1996; interview with Braden, New Orleans, September 4, 1996.

116 *Meanwhile, Hemmeter that night:* Interviews with Robinowitz and Uddo.

116 *Sallie Page did tell: Times-Picayune,* August 12, 1993.

116 *When he ran:* Federal election campaign finance reports, 1994, housed at the
Louisiana secretary of state's office, Baton Rouge.

117 *"more practical": Baton Rouge Advocate,* August 12, 1993.

117 *He told reporters:* Ibid.

117 *For his part, Edwards:* Interview with Edwards, February 3, 1998.

117 *he told aides privately:* Interview with Al Donovan, September 6, 1996; interview
with Moreland.

118 *Meeting alone:* Interview with Edwards.

118 *Robinowitz left open:* Telephone interview with Robinowitz, September 13, 1998;
interviews with Uddo and Solomon.

119 Account of meeting at Governor's Mansion: *Times-Picayune,* August 19, 1993;
Baton Rouge Advocate, August 19, 1993; interviews with Donovan, Roussel, Solomon, and Edwards.

119 *he brought the two sides: Times-Picayune,* August 18, 1993.

121 *In a court filing: Baton Rouge Advocate,* August 21, 1993.

121 *Harrah's Jazz fired back: Times-Picayune,* August 24, 1993.

121 Account of discussion at football game: Interview with John Alario, Westwego,
La., December 3, 1997; interviews with Solomon, Donovan, and Edwards.

122 Account of deal coming together: Interview with Wendell Gauthier, Baton
Rouge, August 25, 1993; interview with Tom Morgan, Baton Rouge, August 25,
1993; Solomon.

122 *The agreement, he proclaimed: Baton Rouge Advocate,* August 26, 1993.

122 *"Everybody involved": Times-Picayune,* August 26, 1993.

CHAPTER 5

124 Account of meeting at Governor's Mansion: *Times-Picayune,* May 20, 1992;
interview with riverboat applicant Gordon Stevens, New Orleans, June 9, 1998;
telephone interview with riverboat applicant Bill Dow, June 9, 1998; interview
with riverboat attorney Jim Smith Jr., New Orleans, June 11, 1998; interview with
riverboat lobbyist George Brown, Baton Rouge, June 24, 1998.

125 *On March 12: Times-Picayune,* March 13, 1993.

126 *Two weeks later: Times-Picayune,* March 27, 1993.

127 *Of the first four boats: Times-Picayune,* December 4, 1994, and December 5, 1994.

129 *"People said":* Interview with Ken Pickering, New Orleans, June 11, 1998.

130 *"Nobody in Gretna":* Interview with Ronnie Harris, Gretna, La., June 23, 1998.

130 *Instead, Edwards told him:* Ibid.

131 *"Look, you have": Times-Picayune,* December 5, 1994.

131 *Landry then added:* Interview with Bernie Klein, Mandeville, La., June 4, 1998.

132 *Harris reminded Alario:* Interview with Harris.

132 *When they were done:* Interview with Klein.

132 *Meanwhile, Bill Dow was:* Interview with Dow.

133 *Gaughan also had:* Telephone interview with Gaughan, September 14, 1998.

133 *Gaughan pulled out:* Interview with Dow.

133 *Later he would say:* Telephone interview with Gaughan, April 22, 1994.

135 *As he developed:* Interview with Copeland adviser Wiley McCormick, New Orleans, June 27, 1998.

135 *After one riverboat commission:* Interview with Bill Biossat, executive director of Louisiana Riverboat Gaming Commission, Baton Rouge, June 23, 1998.

135 *The unpublicized poker games: Times-Picayune,* February 8, 1994; interview with Sid Moreland, May 27, 2000.

136 *About a week before:* Interviews with Pickering, Biossat, and Edwards.

137 *After some chitchat:* Interviews with Pickering and Klein.

137 *But because of Mayor Harris's doubts:* Interview with Klein.

138 *he called Ronnie Harris:* Interviews with Harris and Klein.

139 *When Klein arrived:* Interviews with Pickering and Klein.

139 *On the morning of the vote: Times-Picayune,* June 18, 1993.

140 *"Mijalis rolls the dice": People,* February 13, 1984.

140 *Caught overextended: Shreveport Times,* July 16, 1991.

141 Account of the riverboat commission meeting: *Times-Picayune,* June 19, 1993; *Baton Rouge Advocate,* June 19, 1993; transcript of meeting; interview with Pat Fahey, New Orleans, June 4, 1998, and June 22, 1998; interviews with Klein, Brown, Dow, Stevens, Harris, Pickering, Biossat, Smith, McCormick and Edwards; interview with Bob d'Hemecourt, Metairie, La., June 9, 1998; interview with Darryl Berger, New Orleans, June 10, 1998; interview with C. J. Blache, New Orleans, June 11, 1998; telephone interview with riverboat analyst Larry Pearson, June 22, 1998; interview with *Times-Picayune* reporter Frank Donze, New Orleans, June 24, 1998; interview with Aaron Broussard, Harahan, La., July 29, 1998.

143 *Nevertheless, James went: Times-Picayune,* December 5, 1994.

143 *At the mansion:* Interview with Moreland.

147 *Barely able to contain:* Interviews with Pickering and Edwards.

147 *Still in disbelief:* Interview with Klein.

147 *Gilliam lamented:* Ibid.

149 *didn't have a college degree:* Times-Picayune, December 6, 1994.

150 *The troopers assigned:* Interview with Major Mark Oxley, Baton Rouge, July 23, 1998; interview with Lieutenant Riley Blackwelder, Baton Rouge, July 27, 1998; interview with Major Joey Booth, Baton Rouge, July 27, 1998.

151 *"It was overwhelming":* Interview with Blackwelder.

151 *He responded by:* Baton Rouge Advocate, October 2, 1992; interviews with Blackwelder, Oxley, and Edwards.

152 *Edwards continued to insist:* Interviews with Blackwelder and Oxley.

153 *decided to deny:* Times-Picayune, December 4, 1994; interviews with Blackwelder and Oxley.

153 *had just admitted:* Lake Charles American Press, July 28, 1992.

154 *"token of appreciation":* Ibid.

154 *On September 14, 1992:* Interview with Oxley.

154 *To Oxley's dismay:* Ibid.

155 *Two weeks later:* Ibid.

155 *Terrell had been convicted:* Times-Picayune, December 4, 1994.

155 *On July 14, 1992:* Interview with Oxley.

156 *Six years later:* Times-Picayune, January 7, 1999.

157 *FBI documents:* Times-Picayune, April 7, 1994.

157 *Caracci was convicted:* Ibid.

157 *The New Orleans police:* Times-Picayune, November 30, 1993.

157 *In 1990, he traveled:* Times-Picayune, November 23, 1993.

157 *Because of his organized-crime ties:* Interview with video poker lobbyist George Brown, Baton Rouge, June 24, 1998.

157 *In fact, Caracci signed:* Times-Picayune, December 3, 1993.

158 *the State Police revoked:* Times-Picayune, December 17, 1993; interviews with Blackwelder and Oxley.

158 *On the following day:* Times-Picayune, April 7, 1994; interviews with Blackwelder and Oxley; Oxley private memo of meeting, written January 10, 1994.

159 *"I would have":* Times-Picayune, April 1, 1994.

160 *In September of that year:* Interview with Oxley; interview with Lieutenant Colonel Kenny Norris, Baton Rouge, June 23, 1998.

161 *Jones had no firsthand knowledge:* Interview with Jones, New Orleans, June 12, 1998.

162 *What caught his attention:* Ibid.

163 *Robinowitz thought that:* Interview with Robinowitz, September 7, 1996.

163 *To make matters worse:* Interview with Jones.

164 Account of licensing hearing: Hearing transcript; Times-Picayune, January 15, 1994; Times-Picayune, December 4, 1994; interviews with Oxley, Jones, Booth, and Norris; interviews with Billy Broadhurst, June 12, 1998, and July 31, 1998; interview with Wiley McCormick, June 27, 1998; telephone interview with Daniel Robinowitz, September 13, 1998; interview with Brian Etland, Metairie, La., December 2, 1999.

CHAPTER 7

170 *One summer day:* Times-Picayune, October 29, 1995; transcript of Christopher Tanfield testimony in federal trial, *United States of America v. Sebastian Salvatore, et al.*, New Orleans, October 11, 1995; *Atlantic City Press*, October 3, 1993; telephone interview with Steve Bolson, May 30, 2000.

171 *A day or two later:* Ibid.

171 *Tanfield and Gilpin were:* Tanfield testimony; interview with FBI agent Rick McHenry, Lafayette, La., December 1, 1999.

171 *In 1990, the FBI:* New York Times, February 18, 1990.

172 *John Gammarano, a soldier:* Transcript of FBI agent George Gabriel testimony in federal trial, October 11, 1995; interview with McHenry.

172 *Tanfield pitched:* Tanfield testimony.

172 *Accompanying them:* Ibid.

172 *an acting capo:* Gabriel testimony; interview with McHenry.

172 Background on Marcello: John H. Davis, *Mafia Kingfish: Carlos Marcello and the Assassination of John F. Kennedy* (New York: Signet, 1989), pp. 19–21 and 30–61; *Times-Picayune*, February 14, 1982.

173 *It took mob leaders:* Davis, pp. 354–356.

173 *Control of New Orleans's mob:* Interview with McHenry; McHenry testimony in federal trial, October 16, 1995.

174 *At the suggestion:* Tanfield testimony; interview with McHenry.

174 *In 1967, while chairman:* Times-Picayune, September 22, 1967; interview with Aaron Mintz, New Orleans, February 5, 2000.

175 *Mintz's name also:* Times-Picayune, January 26, 1984.

175 *On October 31:* Tanfield testimony; interviews with McHenry and Mintz.

176 *Bally Gaming was born:* Times-Picayune, March 30, 1995; deposition of Bally executive Gary Simpson in the matter of bankruptcy of Louisiana Route Operators and Worldwide Gaming Inc., bankruptcy court, New Orleans, April 11, 1994.

176 *Bally had been indicted:* Times-Picayune, December 2, 1971.

177 *The executive:* Tom Niemann memo, February 6, 1992.

178 *Recording his thoughts:* Mike Wright memo, February 13, 1992.

178 Account of Cleo Fields fund-raiser: Wright memo; interview with FBI agent Rick Richard, New Orleans, November 29, 1999; interview with State Police agent Walter Wolfe, Baton Rouge, November 30, 1999; interviews with McHenry and Mintz; *Times-Picayune*, December 7, 1994.

179 *reported in early March:* Village Voice, March 10, 1992; interview with Bolson.

179 *prompted Tanfield to huddle with:* Tanfield testimony.

180 *A company executive:* Deposition of Bart Jacka in the matter of bankruptcy of LRO and Worldwide, April 13, 1994.

180 *Bally officials would later:* Times-Picayune, December 7, 1994.

180 *Morabito visited:* Morabito testimony in federal trial, October 12, 1995.

181 *Mintz, for example, billed Worldwide:* Examiner's report in the matter of bankruptcy of Worldwide Gaming Inc. and Louisiana Route Operators (undated, but was probably filed in late 1993).

181 *also embezzled about $40,000:* Murton Schlesinger letter to Bolson, August 30, 1993; in a reply by Bolson's attorney, Jack Martzell, September 7, 1993, Martzell said that Bolson thought the cost was $11,000 to $15,000, while noting that Bolson had repaid $5,000. Simpson deposition, April 12, 1994, and Jacka deposition, April 13, 1994, also discuss Bolson's embezzlement.

181 *Later, he billed Worldwide:* Examiner's report.

181 *They misled Bally:* Tanfield testimony; Bolson letter to Bally President Alan Maiss, March 12, 1992.

182 *"I sat Chris down":* Transcript of FBI wiretap at Frank's Deli, New Orleans, September 24, 1992.

182 *"My impression is":* FBI wiretap, July 23, 1992.

183 *McHenry had been transferred:* Interview with McHenry.

183 *By March 1992:* McHenry testimony.

184 *It didn't take long:* Interview with McHenry.

184 *"We got to pay":* FBI wiretap, September 10, 1992.

185 *A week later:* FBI wiretap, September 17, 1992.

185 *"Chris is a great":* FBI wiretap, September 23, 1992.

185 *"We shouldn't get out":* FBI wiretap, September 24, 1992.

186 *This prompted the FBI:* Interviews with McHenry and Richard.

186 *Before taking over:* Interview with Richard.

187 *Goldberg also was:* Telephone interview with Richard, September 22, 2000.

187 *Goldberg's name was mentioned:* Ibid.

187 *Adding it all up:* Richard affidavit filed in federal court, New Orleans, in support of resuming a wiretap of Worldwide's phone, January 26, 1993.

187 *Richard was undercut:* March 22, 1995, letter from Assistant United States Attorney Jim Letten to defense attorneys in Worldwide case.

187 *Still, Paul Coffey:* April 19, 1995, letter from Paul Coffey, head of Organized Crime and Racketeering Section of the Justice Department's Criminal Division, to Michael Chertoff, attorney for Arthur Goldberg.

187 *several former FBI agents: New York Times,* March 14, 1995.

188 *Bally corporate records:* Fax from Jacka to Maiss, September 28, 1992; memo from Jacka to Bally executive John Garner, September 29, 1992; Integrated Gaming Specialists memos to Worldwide Gaming, September 24, 1992 (one is labeled memo "A" and the other is memo "B"). The memos' author, Tom Ward, sent them to John Garner and Gary Simpson on September 24, 1992.

188 *to undertake background checks:* Fax from Jacka to private investigator Del Hahn, October 12, 1992.

188 *In November 1992:* Hahn memo to Jacka, October 27, 1992; Jacka deposition. Jacka spelled out the findings to Maiss in a confidential memo, November 5, 1992.

188 *On the evening of November 17:* Testimony of Tanfield and McHenry.

188 *A short time later:* Richard affidavit in support of resuming wiretap of Worldwide's phone, January 26, 1993. The conversation between Bolson and Simpson occurred on November 20, 1992, according to the affidavit.

189 *Instead, Maiss asked:* Deposition of Jerry Flynn in bankruptcy, April 12, 1994.

189 *When Flynn called:* Ibid.

189 *He reported his findings:* Memo from Flynn to Maiss, November 25, 1992; Flynn deposition on April 12, 1994, and April 22, 1994.

189 *In one meeting:* Flynn memo to himself, January 7, 1993; *Times-Picayune,* December 7, 1994.

190 *Afterward, at the New Orleans International Airport:* Flynn memo to himself, January 8, 1993.

190 *"I was afraid":* Flynn deposition, April 12, 1994.

190 *still cursing a crooked business:* FBI wiretap, January 8, 1993.

191 *"OK, here it starts":* *Times-Picayune,* March 14, 1993.

191 *In September, the Louisiana:* *Times-Picayune,* September 10, 1993.

191 *the FBI arrested:* *Times-Picayune,* June 1, 1994.

192 *Christopher Tanfield's Pensacola-based:* Telephone interview with Santurri, November 11, 1999.

192 *pleaded guilty to lesser charges:* *Times-Picayune,* September 10, 1993, and September 13, 1993.

193 *"I consider this":* U.S. Department of Justice press release, October 23, 1995.

193 *were among those who thought:* Interview with Joe Whitmore, Baton Rouge, November 30, 1999; interview with Wolfe.

193 *The federal probe did net:* *Times-Picayune,* April 4, 1996, and May 2, 1996.

CHAPTER 8

197 *But in the summer of 1993:* Interview with Robinowitz, Dallas, September 7, 1996.

198 *The proposed site:* Interview with Gregory Meredith, New York City, December 16, 1996.

198 *For the temporary building:* *Times-Picayune,* September 22, 1993, and October 2, 1993; interview with Ron Lenczycki, New Orleans, September 26, 1998.

198 *"It seems to me":* *Times-Picayune,* September 9, 1993.

199 *"They can pack":* *Times-Picayune,* September 10, 1993.

199 *warned that construction:* *Times-Picayune,* September 24, 1993.

199 *So on October 13:* *Times-Picayune,* October 14, 1993.

200 *Now he wanted to save:* Interview with Tommy Tucker, New Orleans, December 5, 1997.

201 *he told his appointee:* Ibid.

201 *"Thomas Tucker and":* *Times-Picayune,* March 4, 1993.

202 *kept Harrah's from:* Interviews with Robinowitz, Meredith, and Lenczycki.

202 *"Tucker could be":* *Times-Picayune,* November 13, 1993.

203 *His chief legal counsel:* Telephone interview with Jenifer Schaye, December 6, 1997.

203 *In a final meeting:* Telephone interview with Raymond Strother, September 6, 1996.

204 *Ieyoub announced:* Times-Picayune, April 23, 1994.

204 *"Wall Street is":* Ibid.

204 *Publicly, he questioned:* Ibid.

204 *"The governor was":* Times-Picayune, April 27, 1994.

205 *This strange twist:* Times-Picayune, May 14, 1994.

205 *reported optimistically:* Times-Picayune, June 10, 1994.

206 *"Now we'll find":* Times-Picayune, July 13, 1994.

206 *"Such municipal single-mindedness":* Ibid.

206 *"then there will be no casino":* Times-Picayune, July 14, 1994.

207 *"down the drain":* Ibid.

207 *was inclined to yank the plug:* Interview with Lenczycki; interview with George Solomon, Harahan, La., December 5, 1997.

207 *"It was a day":* Times-Picayune, July 17, 1994.

208 *Despite the handicaps:* Interview with Dixie Boyles, Slidell, La., December 4, 1997.

209 *Its attitude was summed up:* Telephone interview with Schaye, October 28, 1996; interview with Bert Rowley, Chalmette, La., December 1, 1997.

209 *Six of the casino board members:* Times-Picayune, July 15, 1994.

209 *Minutes after the vote:* Interview with Max Chastain, Diamondhead, Miss., July 26, 1998; interview with Billy Nungesser, New Orleans, November 3, 1997.

210 *Nonetheless, Nungesser kept:* Interview with Nungesser.

210 *As Boyles investigated:* Interview with Boyles.

211 *So when she and Boyles:* Interview with Schaye.

211 *"You shame them":* Telephone interview with Schaye, December 6, 1997.

211 *"Yes, I think we have to":* Interview with Boyles.

211 *Boyles got to work:* Ibid; interviews with Schaye and Nungesser.

211 *The documents showed:* Los Angeles Times, December 2, 1996; Forbes, October 21, 1996; Jazzville partners Louie Roussel III and George Solomon also discussed the relationship in interviews.

211 *The documents obtained:* Memo from Boyles and attorney general's staff to Louisiana Economic Development and Gaming Corporation, October 11, 1994; interviews with Boyles and Schaye; interview with Basile Uddo, New Orleans, January 26, 1997; interview with Billy Broadhurst, New Orleans, July 31, 1998; interview with Robinowitz.

211 *Donald (Chick) Foret:* Memo from Boyles.

212 *A law partner of Foret's:* Ibid.

212 *When Boyles and another investigator:* Interview with Boyles.

212 *"Should I go":* Telephone interview with Schaye, November 1, 1996; interview with Boyles.

213 *he called Whitmore:* Interview with Wilmore Whitmore, New Orleans, December 2, 1997.

213 *He added that he:* Ibid.
213 *Chastain was incensed:* Interview with Chastain.
213 *During the board meeting:* Interviews with Schaye, Boyles, and Whitmore.
214 *Attorney General Richard Ieyoub: Times-Picayune,* October 13, 1994.
214 *Chastain issued:* Louisiana Economic Development and Gaming Corporation press release, October 12, 1994.
214 *"It raises more": Times-Picayune,* October 14, 1994.

CHAPTER 9

215 *company officials announced: Times-Picayune,* November 17, 1994.
215 *"The Guinness Book": Times-Picayune,* November 19, 1994.
216 *Donovan grew exasperated:* Interview with Donovan, Metairie, La., September 6, 1996.
216 *He called his friend:* Ibid.
216 *Edwards ended up concluding:* Interview with Edwards, Baton Rouge, February 3, 1998.
216 *He met with an attorney: Times-Picayune,* January 25, 1995.
216 *He recommended to Harrah's officials: Times-Picayune,* February 18, 1995.
216 *In a transgression: Times-Picayune,* April 25, 1995.
217 *Newspapers reported that: Baton Rouge Advocate,* October 28, 1994; *Times-Picayune,* October 29, 1994.
217 *Vilas's mother: Times-Picayune,* November 17, 1994.
217 *A second board member: Baton Rouge Advocate,* October 28, 1994; *Times-Picayune,* October 29, 1994.
217 *A third board member:* Ibid.
217 *The living arrangements:* Letters to the three board members, January 24, 1995 (to Vilas) and January 26, 1995 (to Page and Thomas).
217 *Whitmore, in his report: Times-Picayune,* January 11, 1995.
218 *Acting at Harrah's behest: Times-Picayune,* January 25, 1995.
218 *the board overruled: Times-Picayune,* February 2, 1995.
218 *The board's decision: Times-Picayune,* February 3, 1995.
218 *wrote sarcastically: Times-Picayune,* February 12, 1995.
218 *Five days later: Times-Picayune,* February 17, 1995.
219 *the remarks were kept: Times-Picayune,* May 2, 1995; *Baton Rouge Advocate,* May 2, 1995.
220 *"It's wonderful to see": Times-Picayune,* May 2, 1995.
220 *"The poor people":* Ibid.
221 *"The location at": Times-Picayune,* June 13, 1995.
221 *"some serious questions":* Ibid.
221 *In his analysis:* Letter from Tommy Tucker to Louisiana Economic Development and Gaming Corporation, April 26, 1994.
221 *"I do not have":* Letter from Tommy Tucker to Louisiana Economic Development and Gaming Corporation, April 28, 1994.

NOTES

222 *Nap Overton, a gambling analyst:* Times-Picayune, June 18, 1995.
222 *But another analyst:* Ibid.
222 *"I look at":* Times-Picayune, July 12, 1995.
222 *"can absorb":* Ibid.
222 *Dave Wolfe, an analyst:* Times-Picayune, August 10, 1995.
222 *"We felt pretty good":* Ibid.
223 *"Every city has":* Associated Press, June 14, 1995.
223 *"Labor Day was":* Times-Picayune, September 9, 1995.
223 *was ready to render:* Times-Picayune, September 10, 1995.
224 *called the numbers:* Times-Picayune, October 7, 1995.
224 *"It's got to be":* Ibid.
224 *Whitmore called on the board:* Times-Picayune, November 7, 1995.
224 *Whitmore was basing:* Times-Picayune, November 8, 1995.
225 *he told the casino board:* Ibid.
226 *The company published:* Times-Picayune, November 12, 1995.
226 *However, Joseph Boucree:* Times-Picayune, November 15, 1995.
226 *"Our financing is secured":* New Orleans City Business, November 20, 1995.
226 *a confidential memo:* Memo from Max Chastain to Louisiana Economic Development and Gaming Corporation board members, November 20, 1995.
226 Account of developments that led to casino shutdown: *Times-Picayune*, November 22, 1995; interview with Solomon; interview with casino board attorney Tom Barbera, New Orleans, December 5, 1997; interview with John Cummings, New Orleans, December 6, 1997; interview with Cummings, New Orleans, November 29, 1998; telephone interview with Jenifer Schaye, December 6, 1997; interview with Chastain; interview with Edwards; interview with Edwards, Baton Rouge, July 30, 1998; interview with Wilmore Whitmore, New Orleans, December 2, 1997; interview with Lenczycki; deposition of Harrah's executive Bill McCalmont in Harrah's casino bankruptcy, April 17, 1995; deposition of Harrah's executive Phil Satre in bankruptcy, April 16, 1995; deposition of Harrah's chairman Michael Rose in bankruptcy, May 7, 1996; deposition of Harrah's chief financial officer Charles Ledsinger in bankruptcy, May 8, 1996.
229 Description of casino shutdown: *Times-Picayune*, November 23, 1995.
231 *"We're all eating":* Ibid.
231 *"We are looking":* Ibid.
231 *captured the public mood:* Times-Picayune, November 24, 1995.
232 *Three weeks later:* Times-Picayune, November 29, 1995.
232 *"Get me out":* Ibid.
232 *"Here is what lies":* Miami Herald, December 6, 1995.

CHAPTER 10

233 *Edwards told the crowd:* Times-Picayune, October 17, 1993.
234 *it was a breeze:* Telephone interview with Bob d'Hemecourt, October 15, 1993.
235 *"Every fiber in my body":* Author's notes, New Orleans, October 16, 1993.

⋆ **395** ⋆

235 *The newspaper reported:* Times-Picayune, October 24, 1993.

235 *"While on my talent":* Ibid.

236 *"I'm sure you're":* Interview with Sid Moreland, Baton Rouge, May 27, 2000.

236 *"If y'all think":* Interview with Al Donovan, Metairie, La., September 6, 1996.

237 *Edwards initially dismissed:* Times-Picayune, October 26, 1993.

237 *"I just don't":* Times-Picayune, October 30, 1993.

237 *"Edwards seems to be":* Times-Picayune, October 31, 1993.

237 *hit Edwards again:* Times-Picayune, February 8, 1994.

238 *"If I was going to":* Ibid.

238 *"Matter of fact":* Times-Picayune, February 12, 1994.

238 *"The appearance of":* Ibid.

238 *At one press conference:* Telephone interview with Peter Nicholas, February 9, 1999.

238 *This one reported:* Times-Picayune, February 23, 1994.

239 *getting a piece of the action:* Times-Picayune, March 5, 1994.

240 *State representative Ken Odinet:* Times-Picayune, March 10, 1994.

240 *sold insurance:* Times-Picayune, April 22, 1994.

240 *$14,000 of legal work:* Times-Picayune, April 27, 1995.

240 *had a contract worth:* Times-Picayune, November 18, 1993.

240 *formed a company:* Times-Picayune, July 19, 1994.

240 *In Gretna, across the Mississippi:* Times-Picayune, January 9, 1994.

240 *Ragsdale signed a contract:* Ibid.

240 *Not to be left out:* Times-Picayune, November 23, 1993.

241 *After months of playing:* Washington Post, March 4, 1996.

241 *"I fell instantly":* Ibid.

242 *"It was like":* Shreveport Times, January 7, 1996.

242 *"I ask people":* Associated Press, December 11, 1995.

243 *"The casinos offer":* Times-Picayune, June 18, 1995.

243 *He stopped at the desk:* Times-Picayune, May 27, 1994.

243 *Alario asked lawmakers:* Times-Picayune, June 4, 1994.

244 *"The receptionist said":* Times-Picayune, December 26, 1999.

245 *Asked once by reporters:* John Maginnis, The Last Hayride (Baton Rouge: Gris Gris, 1984), p. 28.

245 *On another occasion:* Maginnis, p. 27.

245 *In a story:* Interview with Edwards, Baton Rouge, February 3, 1998.

246 *he tried to explain:* Interview with Edwards, Baton Rouge, May 25, 1990.

246 *"She doesn't have":* Times-Picayune, December 22, 1991.

246 *"A man is as old":* Author's notes, New Orleans, August 2, 1991.

247 *"We wanted an unpublicized":* Times-Picayune, May 27, 1994.

247 *Donovan immediately called:* Interview with Donovan, Metairie, La., June 22, 1998; interview with Moreland.

248 *"There is one reason":* Times-Picayune, June 7, 1994.

248 *"History will confirm":* Washington Post, June 8, 1994.

248 *"Edwards is an impossible act":* Ibid.

248 *"He was the most effective"*: *Washington Post*, March 4, 1996.

248 *"He was devoid"*: Ibid.

248 *"We'll never see"*: Ibid.

248 *"It's the death"*: Ibid.

CHAPTER 11

250 Star *owner Louie Roussel*: *Times-Picayune*, January 20, 1994.

251 *The boats' myriad excuses*: *Times-Picayune*, November 18, 1994.

252 *"We figured since"*: *Times-Picayune*, September 8, 1994.

253 *Connick fired his first shot*: *Times-Picayune*, November 20, 1994.

254 *"the gracious charm"*: *Times-Picayune* (advertisement), March 29, 1995.

254 *"It promises to be"*: River City press release, March 29, 1995.

254 *"We suggest [Hemmeter]"*: *Times-Picayune*, March 26, 1995.

255 *Hemmeter's investment partner*: Telephone interview with Daniel Robinowitz, September 13, 1998.

255 *Billy Broadhurst, representing the developer*: *Times-Picayune*, February 1, 1995.

255 *with the promise*: River City press release, March 29, 1995.

256 *Hemmeter looked nervous*: Interview with Lambert Boissiere, New Orleans, September 2, 1996.

256 *River City reminded him*: Interview with Ron Brinson, New Orleans, June 11, 1998.

257 *"Obviously, things can't get"*: *Times-Picayune*, June 1, 1995.

257 *a voice came over*: *Times-Picayune*, June 7, 1995.

257 *"This is a terrible"*: Interview with Joann DiFlorio, New Orleans, June 6, 1995.

257 *learned of the shutdown*: Interview with Roland Jones, New Orleans, June 22, 1998.

258 *"Now that the two riverboats"*: *Times-Picayune*, June 9, 1995.

258 *Now a judge's order*: *Times-Picayune*, July 8, 1995.

259 *$726,927 in assets*: *Times-Picayune*, September 28, 1997; Hemmeter's Chapter 7 bankruptcy, Los Angeles, September 26, 1997.

259 *"I'm trying to pretend"*: *Los Angeles Times*, December 2, 1996.

260 *News of the federal investigation*: *Times-Picayune*, August 23, 1995.

260 *The FBI affidavits*: Application and Affidavit for Search Warrant, United States District Court, New Orleans, August 15, 1995, to search 607 St. Charles Ave., New Orleans, and 1662 Gause Blvd., Slidell, La.; Search Warrant, United States District Court, Baton Rouge, August 15, 1995, to search 965 Monterrey Blvd., Baton Rouge; 9585 Airline Highway, Baton Rouge; and 25412 Renee Ct., Jackson, La. *Times-Picayune*, August 22, 1995, and August 23, 1995.

260 *"the cost of doing"*: *Baton Rouge Advocate*, May 16, 1997.

261 *"I've never seen"*: *Times-Picayune*, September 3, 1995.

262 *"Let me tell you"*: *Times-Picayune*, May 21, 1997.

262 *"We are willing"*: *Baton Rouge Advocate*, May 30, 1997.

262 *"Goodson told Bankston"*: *Times-Picayune*, August 23, 1995.

263 *"travel-less renters":* Ibid.

263 *Records showed that Goodson: Times-Picayune,* July 27, 1996.

263 *Long was trying: Times-Picayune,* July 13, 1980.

264 *was "hyperventilating": Washington Post,* August 29, 1995.

264 *The wiretaps also: Times-Picayune,* May 14, 1997.

264 *One truck stop owner: Times-Picayune,* August 22, 1995.

264 *Senator Gerry Hinton:* Ibid.

264 *Senator Don Kelly:* Ibid.

265 *Senator Marty Chabert:* Ibid.

265 *Senate president Sammy Nunez:* Ibid.

265 *Senator Armand Brinkhaus:* Ibid.

265 *Senator Ron Landry:* Ibid.

265 *a list of students: Times-Picayune,* July 23, 1995, and October 15, 1995.

266 *In a survey: Washington Post,* August 29, 1995.

266 *nascent gambling industry: Times-Picayune,* September 17, 1995.

267 *"Politicians in this state": Lake Charles American Press,* September 21, 1995.

267 *One gubernatorial candidate: Times-Picayune,* August 25, 1995.

267 *"Right now, gambling": Wall Street Journal,* September 11, 1995.

267 *In a televised debate: New York Times,* September 26, 1995.

CHAPTER 12

270 *Focused on the outing:* Interview with Geoffrey Santini, New Orleans, May 22, 2000. Follow-up telephone interviews on May 30–31, 2000, June 8, 2000, and September 16, 2000.

270 *As soon as Cleveland:* Interview with Santini, May 22, 2000; interview with Freddy Cleveland, Picayune, Miss., May 21, 2000.

271 Account of meeting at Grand Casino: Telephone interview with Steve Irwin, May 15, 2000; interview with Irwin, Gulfport, Miss., May 24, 2000; telephone interviews with Charlie Blau, May 23, 2000, and June 8, 2000.

272 *Blau began by getting:* Interviews with Irwin, Cleveland, and Blau.

274 *He quickly found: Houston Press,* March 28, 1996, and April 4, 1996.

274 *Steve Irwin would later:* Court proceeding in bankruptcy proceeding, *Rosalind Graham v. Hofheinz Foundation,* Houston, Tex., September 16, 1996.

275 *With the assistance: Houston Press,* March 28, 1996.

275 *A jury found:* Ibid.

276 *He posed as a high-ranking official: Houston Chronicle,* April 30, 1997.

276 *The meeting took place:* Interviews with Blau, Cleveland, Santini, and Irwin.

278 *Pat Graham called Santini:* Interviews with Santini, New Orleans, May 22–23, 2000; telephone interview with Santini, June 8, 2000; telephone interview with FBI agent Rick McHenry, June 2, 2000.

281 *It wasn't long:* Interview with Santini, May 22, 2000; interview with Irwin, May 24, 2000.

281 *Justice officials couldn't believe:* Ibid.

282 *Cecil Brown had known:* Telephone interview with Bob d'Hemecourt, May 26, 2000; telephone interview with Edwards, August 29, 2000.

282 *One day at lunch:* Interview with Sid Moreland, Baton Rouge, May 27, 2000.

284 *Edwards called Governor Foster: Shreveport Times,* November 21, 1997.

284 *The wiretaps recorded Brown:* Interview with Santini.

285 *Santini had wanted:* Interview with Santini; telephone interview with Freddy Cleveland, June 13, 2000.

285 *As soon as he got:* Transcript of FBI wiretap on Edwards's home phone, Baton Rouge, October 18, 1996.

286 *"It was like arriving": St. Louis Post-Dispatch,* January 28, 1990.

286 *Unlike the typical:* Telephone interview with former 49er Jack Reynolds, February 10, 1998; telephone interview with former 49er Jeff Fuller, February 10, 1998; telephone interview with former 49er Ronnie Lott, February 12, 1998; telephone interview with former 49er Jamie Williams, February 12, 1998; telephone interview with former 49er Roger Craig, February 26, 1998.

287 *"the best owner": Sports Illustrated,* September 10, 1990.

287 *According to her police statement:* Menlo Park Police Department Police Report, statement by Gina Baross, February 19, 1992.

287 *DeBartolo was not:* Associated Press, March 12, 1992.

287 *Three months later:* Associated Press, June 2, 1992.

287 *The charges were dismissed: Wall Street Journal,* February 19, 1998.

287 *He affectionately called DeBartolo:* Telephone interview with Paul Martha, February 12, 1998.

288 *"He's listened to":* Interview with Bill Walsh, Palo Alto, Calif., December 30, 1997.

288 *"Some people consider": Beacon Journal,* November 27, 1983.

288 *"He would fly in":* Interview with Edwin Edwards, Baton Rouge, February 3, 1998.

288 *On his visits:* Ibid.

288 *In one of his final conversations:* Ibid.

289 *yielded more dividends:* Transcript of FBI wiretap on Edwards's home phone, October 21, 1996.

289 *the Feds learned of:* Transcript of FBI wiretap on Edwards's home phone, November 19, 1996.

289 *he reacted:* Interview with Santini.

290 *Irwin, who had just:* Interview with Irwin.

290 *A clandestine FBI team:* Interviews with Santini and Irwin; telephone interview with Cleveland; telephone interview with Jim DeSarno, then special agent in charge of FBI's New Orleans office, May 31, 2000.

CHAPTER 13

291 *As Santini, the lead FBI agent:* Interview with Geoffrey Santini, New Orleans, May 22, 2000.

291 *In a conversation:* Transcript of FBI wiretap of Edwards's office, January 9, 1997.

292 *Another conversation on January 9:* Ibid.

293 *Six weeks later:* Transcript of FBI wiretap of Edwards's office, February 25, 1997.

295 *The first time occurred:* Interview with Santini, May 22, 2000; telephone interviews with Santini, June 8, 2000, and June 14, 2000.

296 *The second close call:* Interviews with Santini, May 22–23, 2000.

297 Account of what happened after plane landed: Interview with Freddy Cleveland, Picayune, Miss., May 21, 2000; interview with Santini, May 23, 2000; Factual Basis in plea of Brandon Hyde, United States District Court, Baton Rouge, July 10, 1997; telephone interviews with Randy Scrantz, June 27, 2000, and September 25, 2000; telephone interview with Greg Koon, September 25, 2000; *Times-Picayune,* July 16, 1997; *Baton Rouge Advocate,* July 16, 1997.

300 *Candy DeBartolo asked Edwards:* Interview with Edwin Edwards, Baton Rouge, February 3, 1998.

300 *as Edwards told DeBartolo:* Transcripts of FBI wiretap of Edwards's home phone, October 18, 1996, and November 6, 1996.

300 *Edwards also displayed:* Transcript of FBI wiretap of Edwards's office, February 25, 1997; *San Jose Mercury,* October 6, 1998; *Shreveport Times,* March 28, 2000.

301 *"How's your time":* Transcript of FBI wiretap of Edwards's home, March 5, 1997.

301 Account of what happened at the Radisson and the Muransky/DeBartolo conversation afterward: *Times-Picayune,* March 25, 2000; *Baton Rouge Advocate,* March 25, 2000; *Lake Charles American Press,* March 25, 2000; *Times-Picayune,* March 28, 2000; *Baton Rouge Advocate,* March 28, 2000; *Chicago Tribune,* March 28, 2000; *Dallas Morning News,* March 28, 2000.

302 *Edwards called Ralph Perlman:* Transcript of FBI wiretap of Edwards's home phone, March 8, 1997.

302 *DeBartolo told Muransky:* Times-Picayune, March 25, 2000.

303 Account of what happened on March 12: *Times-Picayune,* March 25, 2000, and March 28, 2000; *Shreveport Times,* March 28, 2000; Associated Press, March 25, 2000; Associated Press, March 28, 2000; *San Francisco Examiner,* March 27, 2000; telephone interview with Edwards, April 4, 1998; telephone interview with Geoffrey Santini, June 14, 2000; telephone interview with DeBartolo attorney Aubrey Harwell, June 26, 2000.

304 *She reflected that:* Telephone interview with Jenifer Schaye, June 27, 2000.

304 *"We want the word":* Baton Rouge Advocate, October 8, 1998.

304 *The 49ers owner:* Times-Picayune, March 25, 2000, and March 28, 2000.

304 *The FBI wiretaps:* Transcript of FBI wiretap on Edwards's home phone, February 24, 1997.

306 *Almost as soon:* Transcript of FBI wiretap of Edwards's office, February 24, 1997.

306 *thought that they had:* Interviews with Santini, Cleveland, and Irwin.

307 *told the owner:* Factual Basis in plea of Brandon Hyde.

307 *A day later:* Times-Picayune, September 4, 1999.

307 *After getting Hyde:* Interviews with Santini, Cleveland, and Irwin.

307 *Still, Edwards's suspicions:* Interview with Santini; *Baton Rouge Advocate,* August 26, 1997.

308 *Elder told Perricone:* Telephone interview with Sal Perricone, May 24, 2000; interviews with Santini and Cleveland.

308 *"No news person":* Interview with Santini; telephone interview with Jim DeSarno, March 31, 2000.

309 Account of writing search warrants and getting judicial approval to execute them: Interviews with Santini, Cleveland, and Irwin.

310 *Cleveland gave one instruction:* Telephone interview with John Fleming, May 26, 2000.

310 Account of FBI agents serving search warrant on Edwards: Telephone interviews with John Fleming, May 26, 2000, July 31, 2000, and August 10, 2000; interview with Edwards, Baton Rouge, February 11, 1998; telephone interview with Edwards, August 29, 2000.

CHAPTER 14

313 *"Did you hear":* George, July 1998.

313 *told another joke:* Author's notes, Baton Rouge, February 4, 1998.

313 *A day later:* Author's notes.

314 *Later that same week:* Author's notes, Baton Rouge, February 3, 1998.

315 *described him as: Times-Picayune,* March 29, 1998.

315 Account of Edwards's plea negotiations: Interview with Freddy Cleveland, Picayune, Miss., May 21, 2000, and telephone interviews, June 13, 2000, and June 20, 2000; interview with Geoffrey Santini, New Orleans, May 23, 2000, and telephone interview, May 30, 2000; telephone interview with Steve Irwin, June 20, 2000.

317 *thought that Edwards had given:* Interviews with Cleveland, Irwin, and Santini.

317 *would later say of the decision:* Telephone interview with DeSarno, May 31, 2000.

318 *pleaded guilty to bribing: Times-Picayune,* October 7, 1998.

318 *On October 9: Times-Picayune,* October 10, 1998; *Lake Charles American Press,* October 10, 1998.

318 *On October 16: Times-Picayune,* October 17, 1998; *Shreveport Times,* October 17, 1998; *Baton Rouge Advocate,* October 17, 1998.

319 *On November 6: Times-Picayune,* November 7, 1998; *Baton Rouge Advocate,* November 7, 1998; *Los Angeles Times,* November 7, 1998.

320 *"We do this in": Times-Picayune,* November 7, 1998.

320 *"This is showing":* Ibid.

321 *Martin struck it rich: Times-Picayune,* October 17, 1998.

321 *Arrested fourteen times: Monroe News-Star,* November 2, 1998; telephone interview with Tarver, September 25, 2000.

322 *"Without Edwin Edwards": Los Angeles Times,* August 14, 1985.

322 *Tarver's third wife*: Times-Picayune, November 10, 1998.

322 *"If you don't help"*: Telephone interview with Tarver.

322 *Ecotry Fuller, sixty-two*: Times-Picayune, August 5, 1999.

322 Description of schemes: *Times-Picayune*, November 7, 1998; indictment for violations of the Racketeer Influenced Corrupt Organizations Act, extortion, mail fraud, wire fraud, money laundering, interstate travel and communications in aid of racketeering, false statements, illegal wiretapping, and conspiracy, United States District Court, Baton Rouge, November 6, 1998.

CHAPTER 15

326 *"There's nobody better"*: Interview with Buddy Roemer, Baton Rouge, November 30, 1999.

327 *"I wouldn't predict"*: Associated Press, January 8, 2000.

327 *"Everything we have learned"*: Interview with Edwin Edwards, Baton Rouge, December 1, 1999.

327 *Small was amazed*: Telephone interview with Daniel Small, June 21, 2000.

328 *Letten feared that*: Interview with Jim Letten, Baton Rouge, February 6, 2000; interview with Letten, New Orleans, May 25, 2000.

331 *"I don't think we"*: Associated Press, January 12, 2000.

331 *"You're hot"*: Times-Picayune, January 19, 2000.

331 *Polozola told the jurors*: Baton Rouge Advocate, January 25, 2000.

331 *Speaking first, lead prosecutor*: Baton Rouge Advocate, January 26, 2000.

331 *"exercised his power"*: Times-Picayune, January 26, 2000.

332 *but he described it*: Ibid.

333 *"It was probably"*: Times-Picayune, January 29, 2000.

333 *"it would cost me"*: Ibid.

333 *The deal coalesced*: Ibid.

333 *Guidry testified that with Martin*: Ibid.

334 *he never told anyone*: Shreveport Times, January 29, 2000.

334 *Asked to explain*: Times-Picayune, February 2, 2000.

335 *"I shoved it under"*: Ibid.

335 *"Sir, all I can tell you"*: Times-Picayune, February 3, 2000.

335 *Using a courtroom*: Times-Picayune, February 4, 2000.

335 *"There isn't enough money"*: Ibid.

335 *"What do you know"*: Ibid.

336 *In one instance*: Ibid.

336 *"They pretended to be"*: Ibid.

336 *He was an African-American*: Shreveport Times, February 8, 2000.

336 *A white forty-nine-year old*: Ibid.

336 *"This judge is so"*: Comments made to author, Baton Rouge, February 7, 2000.

337 *"He wants to get"*: Ibid.

337 *mulled the impact*: Interview with Jim Letten, Baton Rouge, February 6, 2000.

337 *did not share*: Telephone interview with Small; telephone interview with Tarver attorney Mary Olive Pierson, June 15, 2000.

337 *As Edwards walked by*: Author's notes, Baton Rouge, February 8, 2000.

338 *"There are times"*: Author's notes.

338 *Anna Edwards discussed*: Author's notes.

338 *"You tried the bread pudding?"*: Author's notes.

339 *"What are you doing"*: Times-Picayune, February 19, 2000.

339 *"All the other riverboats"*: Ibid.

339 *"Players needed to hire"*: Shreveport Times, February 23, 2000.

339 *"these guys could hurt you"*: Ibid.

339 *"harm would come to us"*: Ibid.

340 *had cried twice*: Interview with Geoffrey Santini, New Orleans, May 22, 2000; interview with Steve Irwin, Gulfport, Miss., May 24, 2000.

340 *"There's no doubt"*: Times-Picayune, February 24, 2000.

340 *"I made pizzas"*: Ibid.

340 *"you could get hurt"*: Shreveport Times, February 24, 2000.

341 *"They know if they"*: Ibid.

341 *Shetler himself had*: Baton Rouge Advocate, February 25, 2000.

341 *"it got very confusing"*: Times-Picayune, February 25, 2000.

341 *Instead of simply*: Ibid; Shreveport Times, February 25, 2000.

342 *"I gotta get with"*: Shreveport Times, February 25, 2000.

342 *"We took a ride"*: Times-Picayune, February 25, 2000.

342 *"I was guilty"*: Ibid.

343 *"Is Ricky Shetler"*: Louisiana Political Fax Weekly, February 25, 2000.

343 *"You used the name"*: Shreveport Times, February 26, 2000.

343 *"So you made"*: Ibid.

343 *"Isn't what's happening"*: Ibid.

344 *"By noon Thursday"*: Telephone interview with John Hill, February 28, 2000.

344 *"If Edwin Edwards"*: Times-Picayune, March 5, 2000.

345 *"The trial got its share"*: Shreveport Times, March 6, 2000.

345 *"Y'all ain't got"*: Shreveport Times, March 9, 2000.

346 *Edwards put his arm*: Times-Picayune, March 9, 2000.

346 *"It without question"*: Ibid.

346 *"I'm not keeping"*: Shreveport Times, March 9, 2000.

346 *he felt vulnerable*: Ibid.

346 *"Everybody's down to the wire"*: Times-Picayune, March 9, 2000.

347 *In trying to show*: Times-Picayune, March 11, 2000.

347 *"the threats on the tapes"*: Times-Picayune, March 12, 2000.

347 *"I don't believe"*: Times-Picayune, March 11, 2000.

347 *"I'm more pleased"*: Telephone interview with Edwards, March 12, 2000.

347 *"This could go"*: Philadelphia Inquirer, March 11, 2000.

347 *"Bradley's testimony"*: Gambit, March 13, 2000.

348 *"I wasn't about to"*: Times-Picayune, February 28, 2000.

348 *"He said this has"*: Ibid.
348 *"Did you believe you had"*: Baton Rouge Advocate, March 28, 2000.
349 *"He was dressed very woodsy"*: Times-Picayune, March 28, 2000.
349 *"He said that's not a problem"*: Ibid.
349 *"I am a victim"*: Ibid.
350 *"That's ridiculous"*: Ibid.
350 *"I can sit here"*: Times-Picayune, March 29, 2000.
350 *"a very significant"*: Shreveport Times, March 29, 2000.
350 *"It caused me to be"*: Ibid.
351 prosecutors had FBI: Times-Picayune, March 31, 2000.

CHAPTER 16

353 by having Edwards recount: Times-Picayune, April 12, 2000.
353 *"who loved people"*: Ibid.
353 *"I'm one of the best"*: Washington Post, April 18, 2000.
353 *"Tell the jury"*: Baton Rouge Advocate, April 12, 2000.
354 *"I had nothing to gain"*: Times-Picayune, April 12, 2000.
354 Addressing the specific: Ibid.
354 *"With tears in his eyes"*: Baton Rouge Advocate, April 12, 2000.
354 *"Tell the jury"*: Ibid.
355 *"You just lied"*: Chicago Tribune, April 12, 2000.
355 Letten had long since: Interview with Jim Letten, Baton Rouge, February 6, 2000; interview with Letten, New Orleans, May 25, 2000.
355 *"That only exists"*: Times-Picayune, April 13, 2000.
356 *"I really don't think"*: Ibid.
356 *"Funny?" Edwards said*: Ibid.
356 *"Mr. Letten, the Dumpster might have"*: Ibid.
357 *"after sober reflection"*: Lake Charles American Press, April 13, 2000.
357 *"cooks up fraudulent"*: Ibid.
357 *"It was all thoughts"*: Times-Picayune, April 13, 2000.
357 *"Well, so is shooting at"*: Lake Charles American Press, April 13, 2000.
357 *"I'm a politician"*: Baton Rouge Advocate, April 16, 2000.
357 When the defendant: Times-Picayune, April 14, 2000.
358 *"Is $243,000 a little?"*: Ibid.
358 Asked about the aliases: Ibid.
358 *"probably the only person"*: Ibid.
358 *"I'm seventy-two"*: Times-Picayune, April 15, 2000.
358 Not wanting to: Ibid.
358 *"The charges are not"*: Ibid.
359 *"After all the tape-recordings"*: Times-Picayune, April 16, 2000.
359 *"The government has used"*: Shreveport Times, April 17, 2000.
359 *"We have unveiled"*: Times-Picayune, April 19, 2000.
360 *"Think about the smartest"*: Ibid.

360 *paraphrased the remainder:* Ibid.

360 *"We don't convict people":* Baton Rouge Advocate, April 20, 2000.

360 *"It is, as I've said":* Times-Picayune, April 20, 2000.

360 *"We're here because":* Ibid.

360 *"unlimited resources":* Times-Picayune, April 21, 2000.

361 *"You stand between":* Ibid.

361 *"Look him straight":* Ibid.

361 *"Ladies and Gentlemen":* Shreveport Times, April 25, 2000.

362 *He was a forty-year-old:* Times-Picayune, April 25, 2000.

362 *"We are not able":* Times-Picayune, April 27, 2000.

362 *"You don't need to":* Ibid.

362 *"I'm on pins and needles":* Telephone interview with Candy Edwards, April 27, 2000.

362 *"It's looking all right":* Telephone interview with Edwin Edwards, April 27, 2000.

362 *"I am very intimidated":* Times-Picayune, May 7, 2000.

363 *"Due to the stress":* Times-Picayune, April 28, 2000.

363 *"Everybody is on":* Times-Picayune, May 4, 2000.

364 *"We will now proceed":* Shreveport Times, May 5, 2000.

364 *"The fact that":* Ibid.

364 *"I think each of you":* Associated Press, May 5, 2000.

364 *said the dismissal:* Lake Charles American Press, May 5, 2000.

365 *Sonny Garcia:* Ibid.

365 *"There was no signal":* Shreveport Times, May 5, 2000.

365 *"Is this a low blow?":* Louisiana Political Fax Weekly, May 5, 2000.

366 *"We think it's the ghost":* Comment by Paul Murphy, Baton Rouge, February 7, 2000.

366 *"a Mexican standoff":* Times-Picayune, May 10, 2000.

367 *As the judge flipped:* Ibid.

367 *"I hate to send you back":* Ibid.

368 *"Way to go":* Ibid.

369 *"Brother, I want you to":* Ibid.

369 *Holding hands:* WWL-TV New Orleans news video, May 9, 2000; *Baton Rouge Advocate* published a transcript of Edwards's remarks, May 10, 2000.

370 *A woman in the passenger seat:* Times-Picayune, May 10, 2000.

371 *About an hour:* Interview with Bob d'Hemecourt, Metairie, La., May 26, 2000.

373 *"I'm so mad":* Telephone interview with Billy Nungesser, February 2, 1998.

374 *"This is not over":* Times-Picayune, January 9, 2001.

Acknowledgments

Many people helped make this book a reality, and I would like to thank them. I must begin with Jim Amoss and Peter Kovacs, my editors at *The Times-Picayune,* who, following the political demise of David Duke, reassigned me in 1992 to cover the effort to legalize the New Orleans land casino. They had the good sense to see it first and foremost as a political story.

After I left *The Times-Picayune* in early 1996 and started working in earnest on the book at *The Miami Herald,* Jim and Peter made the newspaper's casino archives available to me, which was invaluable. It fell to Nancy Burris and Danny Gamble, the newspaper's top two librarians, actually to collect the documents. They accomplished this task—and then answered countless follow-up requests—with professionalism and humor. Jill Arnold, the *Baton Rouge Advocate*'s chief librarian, also helped me repeatedly.

I interviewed more than a hundred people for the book. I will list their names, feeling a pang of guilt that it is too complicated to single out those who agreed to long, face-to-face interviews (some lasted six hours) and then answered numerous follow-up phone calls. They have my utmost thanks. (You know who you are.)

Those I interviewed for the sections on the New Orleans land casino: John Alario, Tom Barbera, Steven Bingler, Lambert Boissiere, Dixie Boyles, Hank Braden IV, Earl Bridges, Max Chastain, Wayne Collier, John Cummings III, Quentin Dastugue, Frank Donze, Calvin Fayard, C. B. Forgotston, Dee Dee Fulmer, Joan Heisser, Don Higginbotham, Raymond (La La) Lalonde, Charles Lancaster, Ron Lenczycki, Chuck McMains, Gregory Meredith, Ron Nabonne, Billy Nungesser, Chris Pickren, Duplain (Pete) Rhodes III, Steve Rittvo, Bert Rowley, George Solomon, Alfred (Butch) Speer, Tom Spradley, Tim Stine, Raymond Strother, Gerard Thomas, Tommy Tucker, Basile Uddo, Wil Whitmore, Peggy Wilson, and Steve Windhorst.

For the sections on riverboat gambling: Darryl Berger, Bill Biossat, Ron Brinson, Bill Dow, Jimmy Dimos, Brian Etland, Pat Fahey, Michael Gaughan, Ronnie Harris, Bob Harvey, Francis Heitmeier, Roland Jones, Bernie Klein, H. Baylor Lansden, Patrick Martin, Wiley McCormick, Doug Moreau, Kenny Norris, Larry Pearson, Ken Pickering, and Jim Smith Jr.

For the sections on video poker: John Georges and Ronnie Jones.

Some people helped me in more than one area. For the sections on the New Orleans land-casino and riverboat gambling: Daniel Robinowitz, Billy Broadhurst, Aaron Broussard, Jenifer Schaye, Louie Roussel III, C. J. Blache, and George Nattin Jr.

For the sections on riverboat gambling and video poker: Riley Blackwelder, Joey Booth, Mark Oxley, Billy Rimes, and Buddy Roemer.

For the sections on the New Orleans casino, video poker, and riverboat gambling: George Brown, Charles Emile (Peppi) Bruneau Jr., and Don Kelly.

For the chapter on Bally Gaming/Worldwide: Steve Bolson, Pauline Hardin, Herb Larson, Buddy Lemann, Rick McHenry, Aaron Mintz, Ed Newman, Sal Perricone, Rick Richard, Tom Santurri, Katherine Wheeler, Joe Whitmore, and Walter Wolfe. (Thanks to Karen Dixon for the trial transcripts.)

For understanding Edwin Edwards and gambling developments during his final administration: Bob d'Hemecourt, Al Donovan, and Sidney Moreland.

For understanding Eddie DeBartolo Jr.: Robert Adley, Roger Craig, Glenn Dickey, Jeff Fuller, Bryan Krantz, Ronnie Lott, Mike Mackey, Paul Martha, Ira Middleberg, Jack Reynolds, Bill Walsh, Bubba Webb, and Jamie Williams.

For the chapters on the investigation of Edwards and the subsequent trial: Charlie Blau, Freddy Cleveland, James DeSarno, John M. Fleming, Aubrey Harwell, Steve Irwin, Eddie Jordan Jr., Greg Koon, Jim Letten, Jack Martzell, Mary Olive Pierson, Geoffrey Santini, Randy Scrantz, Dan Small, and Greg Tarver.

For the section on the history of gambling in Louisiana: Sherrie S. Pugh, the archivist at the Louisiana Office of the Adjutant General, Jackson Barracks Military Library, provided background on Huey Long. Judith Bethea did terrific work researching gambling history for me at the New Orleans Public Library. Francis Grevemberg shared memories of his tenure as superintendent of the Louisiana State Police during the 1950s, in a lengthy phone interview. Michael L. Kurtz and Edward F. Haas, two fine Louisiana historians, helped ensure that I accurately told the story of the state's long involvement with gambling.

For videotapes of news broadcasts from WWL-TV, New Orleans, that helped me re-create key gambling developments: Bill Elder and Sandy Breeland.

For help in securing photographs: Doug Parker of *The Times-Picayune,* Mike Hults of the *Baton Rouge Advocate,* Robert Mann, and Ronnie Jones.

For those who read parts of the manuscript and offered needed suggestions: Gady Epstein, Burt Hoffman, Jed Horne, Mike Hughlett, Kevin Kearney, Peter Nicholas, Manuel Roig-Franzia, Bob Sanchez, Kevin Shelly, and Glenn Sorensen Jr. (Jed and Glenn deserve extra thanks and the promise of free sushi for life.)

Special thanks to: Walter Abbott, Shelly Bell, C. B. Forgotston, John Hill, John Maginnis, and Curtis Wilkie.

John Glusman, my editor at Farrar, Straus and Giroux, was supportive, enthusiastic, and insightful—all the things that a writer could want. His assistant, Aodaoin O'Floinn, oversaw all the details needed to transform a manuscript into a book.

Flip Brophy, my agent, encouraged me to believe that my manuscript would see the light of day in book form, and helped make it happen. She is a writer's dream agent.

Last, I want to thank Edwin Edwards. He was reluctant to speak with me when I first approached him in 1998, remembering how we had tangled during his final term as governor. But after one of his friends intervened on my behalf, he agreed to have lunch with me. Over the next two years, he graciously consented to several more face-to-face interviews and answered questions during more than a dozen additional phone calls. His wife, Candy, always treated me kindly.

I doubt that I will ever cover another politician as interesting, and beguiling, as Edwin Edwards.

Index

Louisiana Highway Safety Commission, 127

Louisiana House of Representatives, 13, 57, 84, 121, 130, 263; Appropriations Committee, 51; Copelin elected to, 55–56; Duke elected to, 48; gambling-interest campaign contributions to members of, 243, 266; gambling legislation in, 41, 43–46, 53–54, 56, 57, 60–69, 261; Guzzardo forced to resign from, 193

Louisiana Office of Financial Institutions, 136

Louisiana Oystermen's Association, 313–14

Louisiana Purchase, 7, 88, 374

Louisiana Riverboat Gaming Commission, 123, 129, 140, 150, 151, 156, 158, 161, 332, 345

Louisiana Route Operators (LRO), 177, 179, 180, 184–91, 193

Louisiana Senate, 13, 24, 73, 85, 105, 121, 124, 131, 138, 142, 144, 240, 262–65, 268, 316; African Americans in, 86, 206, 321; and casino board appointments, 106, 108; Duke defeated in run for, 48; Edwards in, 31; gambling-interest campaign contributions to members of, 243, 266; gambling legislation in, 43–47, 56–60, 69, 259, 261; reelection defeats of Edwards's allies in, 267

Louisiana State Lottery Company, 10–14

Louisiana State Police, 149–50, 193, 300; and Grevemberg's crackdown on illegal gambling, 22–24, 149; riverboat casinos licensed by, 150–52, 159–61, 164–69, 237, 253–56, 284, 320, 323, 332–35, 339, 341, 345, 347, 355; video poker licensed by, 44, 47, 151, 169, 150–56, 159, 174, 177, 179, 180, 191, 334

Louisiana State University, 3, 30, 42, 252, 329, 347

Louisiana Supreme Court, 13, 60, 220, 247

Luke and Terry's casino, 22

Luntz, Frank, 266

Maestri, Robert, 17

Mafia, 18, 20, 39, 171

Maginnis, John, 38, 248, 343, 347, 365

Magner, Mike, 348–50, 360

Maiss, Alan, 189–93, 217

Manson, Mark, 254

Marcantel, Mary Jane, 367, 369

Marcello, Carlos, 17–18, 20, 25–26, 39, 43, 44, 129, 157, 172–73, 175, 182, 240, 373

Marcello, Joseph, Jr., 173, 175, 185, 188, 192

Marcello, Vincent, 17

Marcello crime family, 176, 182, 186, 188, 191, 193, 217, 271

Marigny de Mandeville, Bernard Xavier Philippe de, 7–8

Martha, Paul, 287–88

Martin, Andrew, 135, 156, 289, 291–94, 296, 307, 318–19, 321, 323, 331, 333, 335, 336, 347, 355, 356, 365, 368

Mathews, Charles, III, 316, 317

Mattox, Jim, 275

McCain, John, 366

McCall, Harry, 202

McCall, Henry, 202

McCormick, Wiley, 167

McDonald, Bryant, 231

McHenry, Rick, 183, 184, 186

McKeithen, John, 25–26, 173, 175

McKinnon, Mark, 248

Medicaid, 56

Melton, Leroy, 106, 107, 110, 113, 209

Meredith, Gregory, 198

Merrill Lynch, 224–25

Metairie Racing Club, 11

Methodists, 30

Metropolitan Crime Commission, 43

Metz, Tom, 183

MGM, 205

MGM Grand Hotel fire (Las Vegas, 1980), 90

Miami Dolphins football team, 252

Miami Herald, 57, 232

Mijalis, Gus, 105, 127, 136, 138, 140–41, 143–46, 177, 238, 239, 254

Mijalis, Sammy, 140, 141, 239

Millen, Matt, 286

Miller, Beauregard H., Jr., 240

Miller, Beauregard H., Sr., 19–21, 25, 130, 240

Millet, Earl, 162

Mills, John, 94

Minnesota Timberwolves basketball team, 273, 275–76, 284

Mintz, Aaron, 174–75, 178–82, 191, 192

Mirage Casino, 73–74, 80, 88, 93–95, 101, 102, 205

Miranda, Carmen, 17